Political Ideologies

D1407092

Now in its fourth edition, *Political Ideologies: An introduction* continues to be the best introductory textbook for students of political ideologies. Completely revised and updated throughout, this edition features:

- A comprehensive introduction to all of the most important ideologies
- Brand new chapters on multiculturalism, anarchism, and the growing influence of religion on politics
- More contemporary examples of twenty-first-century iterations of liberalism, socialism, conservatism, fascism, green political theory, nationalism, and feminism
- Enhanced discussion of the end-of-ideology debates and emerging theories of ideological formation
- Six new contributors.

Accessible and packed with both historical and contemporary examples, this is the most useful textbook for scholars and students of political ideologies.

Vincent Geoghegan is Professor of Political Theory at Queen's University Belfast, UK.

Rick Wilford is Professor of Politics at Queen's University Belfast, UK.

The contributors to this volume have all taught or carried out research at the School of Politics, International Studies and Philosophy at Queen's University Belfast, or have close research connections with the School.

Political Ideologies

An introduction

Fourth edition

**Edited by Vincent Geoghegan
and Rick Wilford**

Routledge
Taylor & Francis Group

LONDON AND NEW YORK

First edition published in 1984
by Unwin Hyman

Third edition published in 2003 by Routledge
Fourth edition published in 2014

By Routledge
2 Park Square, Milton Park, Abingdon, Oxon
OX14 4RN

and by Routledge
711 Third Avenue, New York, NY 10017

*Routledge is an imprint of the Taylor & Francis
Group, an informa business*

British Library Cataloguing in Publication Data

A catalogue record for this book is available from
the British Library

Library of Congress Cataloging in
Publication Data
Political ideologies : an introduction /
edited by Vincent Geoghegan and Rick
Wilford.—4th ed.
          pages cm
Includes bibliographical references
and index.
1. Political science.   2. Ideology.
I. Geoghegan, Vincent, editor of
compilation.   II. Wilford, Rick, 1947–,
editor of compilation.
JA74.P63 2014
320.5—dc23
                                      2013034484

ISBN: 978-0-415-61816-8 (hbk)
ISBN: 978-0-415-61817-5 (pbk)
ISBN: 978-1-315-81438-4 (ebk)

Typeset in Century Old Style
by Keystroke, Station Road, Codsall,
Wolverhampton

MIX
Paper from
responsible sources
FSC® C013604

Printed and bound by CPI Group (UK) Ltd, Croydon, CR0 4YY

Table of Contents

CONTENTS

CONTENTS

The meaning of ideology

Iain MacKenzie

The 2010 UK general election witnessed the return of ideology to the centre stage of British political debate. It returned, however, in a curious way: curious, at least, for students of political ideologies. While, for the majority of the twentieth century, UK politics was ideologically driven, such that it was relatively uncontroversial to map socialist, conservative and liberal ideologies on to the major political parties, since the 1990s British politics has seen a gradual shift away from this simple correlation. Most notably with the arrival of New Labour, British political debate began to replace its distinctive ideological flavours with populist political programmes that claimed to appeal to everyone's tastes. While traditional party political divisions remained strong, these were no longer motivated by deep ideological disputes. Yet, in the wake of the 2008 financial crisis, we began to hear of ideology again but with a significantly different meaning.

During the 2010 election campaign, in particular, each of the major parties accused the others of proposing ideological solutions to the problems engendered by the crisis. While in the past it was expected that each party should have an ideological position, to have an ideological solution to this crisis was to be accused of failing the British public; ideology became a term of abuse. Consider this example from Alistair Darling, the Chancellor of the Exchequer of the then Labour government, speaking just before they were ousted: 'The Tories did not look at the facts or the dangers. They were driven by ideology' (speech delivered 28/04/2010). And this example from Nick Clegg, leader of the Liberal Democrats at the time: 'good economics has been crowded out by political dogma' (speech delivered 16/03/2010). The ground of the debate had shifted: it was not about which political ideology would provide the best solution; rather it was about which solutions were ideological and which were not. Those that were thought to be ideological were said to serve the interests of only a section of society, and those that were not were said to serve the interests of 'the whole British public'. It is a theme that has continued since the general election of 2010. David Cameron put it plainly when he stated: 'I'm not interested in ideological arguments about intervention versus laissez faire. I want an industrial strategy that works' (speech delivered 21/11/2011). As we will see, using the term 'ideology' in this way, to mean a body of ideas that must be false and dangerous because they express the interests of only a section of society, has an almost Marxist ring to it. Out of the ruins of ideological political debate, therefore, there has returned an idea of ideology that many had thought had been left firmly behind. Something curious has indeed happened. To understand this, and related phenomena, it is necessary to chart developments within and between political ideologies, but it is also necessary to understand the ways in which the term 'ideology' has changed its meaning.

While the aim of this book is to map the ideological landscape by drawing out the contours of the major ideologies that continue to shape our social and political environment, it is the aim of this introduction to expose the geological shifts and tensions of the ground that political ideologies rest upon by examining the meaning of ideology itself. As we dig through the topsoil of political ideologies, the first thing we discover is that they all rest upon three interlocking strata that give them shape at any particular moment: these are the *empirical*, *normative* and *practical* dimensions of all political ideologies. The empirical layer is the description of the realities of social and political life that we find within each political ideology. The normative layer is an account of how that reality could be bettered: that is, of the rules and standards that we ought to employ in government, given the perceived political realities. We find the practical layer when we come across the strategies and policies that relate to the transformation of political realities in accordance with the normative ideals each political ideology articulates. It is worth saying a little more about each of these layers before delving any further into the changing and contested meanings of the term 'ideology'.

The empirical dimension of political ideologies helps us to make sense of the complex social world in which we live. Each political ideology provides a description of society – an intellectual map – which enables us to locate ourselves in the social landscape. Liberals, for example, tend to treat the social and political world as made of individuals who, even if they act together, remain first and foremost defined by their individuality. Political life, on this account, is best understood as a series of individual choices and decisions about how we should get along together. Socialists, particularly those of a more radical or Marxist persuasion, often view social and political life in terms of class conflict. Accordingly, it is not the actions of individuals but the ways in which social classes are brought into conflict by economic imperatives beyond the control of any one individual that define politics. Every ideology, we can say, embodies an account of the basic elements and core dynamic that constitutes and propels political life.

While providing a description of social reality, ideologies also embody a set of political ideals aimed at detailing the best possible form of social organisation. Along with a map of reality comes a set of norms about how we *should* behave politically: a map that is at its most striking when these norms cohere into a full-blown picture of an ideal society. Nationalists, for instance, view the nation as the form of political organisation ideally suited to the recognition of the deep-seated connections between people who share a sense of place, a common history and certain forms of social and cultural expression. Many ecologists, however, see the nation as a barrier to the kind of global perspective that informs their vision of a democratic and sustainable society that affords respect to the idea that humans are first and foremost an intimate part of the natural world. In general, then, every ideology provides both an account of existing social and political relations and a description of how these relations ought to be organised for the betterment of all.

Each political ideology also contains within it a set of strategies and policies about how to move the current political situation in the direction of its vision of the good, or even ideal, society. This practical dimension links the descriptive and the normative in ways that often cause tensions within and between political ideologies. Certain feminists may share with socialists a broadly egalitarian agenda but argue that this will not be realised unless women can first organise in consciousness-raising groups that allow them to determine their own vocabulary without interference from male-dominated discourse. Conservatives may share a distrust of strongly utopian politics and they may agree on the importance of national political traditions, yet they may disagree about whether or not the appeal to tradition is sufficient to ward off what they perceive to be the dangerous outcomes of more radical political ideologies. Whilst we can accept that all ideologies have their own particularities, what they commonly share is that their empirical, normative and practical dimensions are intimately interlocking elements that can be difficult to distinguish: difficult, but not impossible, as the following chapters make clear.

Beyond these initial shared features, the concept of ideology can be difficult to get to grips with, not the least because the meaning of ideology is hard to disentangle from the philosophical traditions that have shaped the modern world. A good place to start, on that basis, is a brief history of the term, thereby enabling us to lend substance to what otherwise may seem to be a rather intangible concept. Following this brief history the discussion will turn to Michael Freeden's *Ideologies and Political Theory* (1996), arguably the most significant development in ideology theory in recent years. In response to a series of key questions about the nature of ideology, the penultimate section will bring into view some of the conceptual tensions that underlie the study of ideology. The conclusion will dwell upon how these geological explorations help us make sense of the return of ideology to the centre stage of the national (and, indeed, global) political landscape.

From ideology to ideologies

The emergence of the idea of ideology is indissociable from the complex and multifaceted processes that created the modern Western world. From the last days of the Roman Empire to the sixteenth century, a period of roughly 1,000 years, a mix of Aristotelian philosophy and Christian theology dominated the social, political and intellectual climate of the Western world. Moreover, this combination of classical philosophy and 'other-worldly' theology was deeply entwined with political hierarchies that served the interests of powerful church leaders, feudal lords and 'divine' monarchs. These mutually sustaining forces created a world wherein superstitions and prejudices were deeply rooted in people's minds. In his magnum opus, *Novum Organon*, Francis Bacon, an English polymath of the late sixteenth and early seventeenth century, referred to these 'false notions' as 'idols' and 'phantoms'. Only proper scientific method, he concluded, could disentangle truth from error. The onset of modernity in the West, therefore, is the period of intense transformation during which these interlocking forces and the distorted beliefs they bolstered began to wane as scientific method replaced old sources of knowledge. In all areas of life, the established order of things was no longer taken for granted; the West witnessed the rise of new industries, new philosophical ideas and new forms of political organisation.

These processes of modernisation, including industrialisation, rationalism and secularisation, together with growing dissent from traditional sources of authority and knowledge, came to a climax in the great upheaval of the eighteenth century: the French revolution. It was in the midst of this attempt to overthrow the *ancien régime* and replace it with a new rational system of government based on the universal principles of liberty, equality and fraternity that the term 'ideology' emerged. Antoine Destutt de Tracy (1754–1836), in whose writings it first appears, had been a key player in the revolution, only to find himself imprisoned with the onset of the Terror in 1793–94. It was in his cell that he began to formulate an approach to the rational study of ideas that he called ideology (from idea/ology). As Eagleton has put it, 'the notion of ideology was thus brought to birth in thoroughly ideological conditions' (1991: 66).

For de Tracy the aim of ideology was to establish a solid and unquestionable method to distinguish true from false ideas. The overall aim of this project was to foster the use of reason in the governance of human affairs for the betterment of society as a whole. In other words, the father of ideology shared the ultimate goal of the Enlightenment movement, namely to shed light on the dark corners of thought and life for the good of all. True to this revolutionary spirit, his grand science of ideas was thus conceived as the final and only real measure of human intellectual capacity. If Isaac Newton had discovered the laws of gravity, thought de Tracy, why would it not be possible to discover the laws that govern human thought? What was required was a 'Newton of the science of thought', a role he saw himself as fulfilling. Upon his release from prison he pursued this grand project as a member of the *Institut National*, attempting to create a liberal system of national education that would put into practice his science of ideas.

However, as Napoleon came to power and a new nobility emerged in France, the overt rationalism of de Tracy's science of ideas did not find favour with the increasingly autocratic regime. Napoleon saw a threat to his authority in the thought of de Tracy, and of those who sympathised with him in the *Institut National*. Their liberal and republican political ideas were to become for Napoleon the source of 'all the misfortunes that have befallen our beloved France', and he dismissively labelled these thinkers 'the ideologues'. Thus, at the very birth of the term, we find that ideology assumed two contrasting meanings: ideology as a scientific method for the discovery of true ideas (de Tracy) and ideology as a set of false, even subversive, ideas (Napoleon). As will become apparent, this dichotomy has dogged the idea of ideology ever since.

While ideology was brought to life in the ferment of the French revolution, it matured under different revolutionary conditions. As technological developments in the productive process increased dramatically and the new factories drew ever more people into the burgeoning cities, the hitherto disjointed progress of economic modernisation escalated into a full-blown industrial revolution. At the head of this revolution was the new breed of capitalists who owned the means of production and the economists and philosophers who justified their headlong rush towards ever-increasing profit. It was the well-documented hardships that capitalism wrought on its workforce that provided the impetus and context for a new attempt at demarcating the ideological realm found, famously, in the writings of Karl Marx and Friedrich Engels.

The first truly collaborative work of Marx and Engels was *The German Ideology*, most of which was written in 1845–46, although it was published only posthumously in 1932, after their failure to find a publisher and their subsequent decision to leave the manuscript to 'the gnawing criticism of the mice'. The full text of this work contains long and detailed criticisms of Marx and Engels's contemporaries in German philosophy: in particular, Ludwig Feuerbach, Bruno Bauer and Max Stirner. The aim of the critique was to expose the false premises upon which these thinkers and others of the German tradition had built their philosophical edifices:

> Hitherto men have constantly made up for themselves false conceptions about themselves, about what they are and what they ought to be. They have arranged their relationships according to their ideas of God, of normal man, etc. The phantoms of their brains have got out of their hands. They, the creators, have bowed down before their creations. Let us liberate them from the chimeras, the ideas, dogmas, imaginary beings under their yoke of which they are pining away. Let us revolt against the rule of thoughts . . . the present publication has the aim of uncloaking these sheep, who take themselves and are taken for wolves; of showing how their bleating merely imitates in a philosophic form the conceptions of the German middle class; how the boasting of these philosophic commentators only mirrors the wretchedness of the real conditions in Germany.
>
> (1974: 37)

Amidst this stinging critique it is possible to discern the various features of ideology already discussed. First, there is a reiteration, although probably unwittingly, of the Baconian notion of 'phantoms', of illusions deeply rooted in the human mind. Second, the radical spirit of Enlightenment, the pursuit of truth in the face of error, shines through their condemnation of existing German philosophy. Third, Marx and Engels conduct their critique with all the vitriol of Napoleon's attack on the 'ideologues' and are similarly concerned that erroneous ideas spell disaster for national and political culture. Yet within *The German Ideology* there is also a new position on the idea of ideology, namely that false ideas are false precisely because they reflect class interests, in this case the interests of the German middle class, rather than the interests of all. For Marx and Engels, therefore, the only way to remove the ideological frameworks of society is to overcome the contradictions created by conflicting class interests inherent in the economic and social realms. As the Marxist critic Istvan Meszaros puts it, ideology is 'insurmountable in class societies' and therefore theoretical reason alone, *contra* de Tracy, will not in itself enable us to overcome false ideas about the nature of society (1989: 10–11). For Marx and Engels, theoretical reason must be allied with revolutionary practice aimed at dissolving class conflict. The contradictions of class-based societies must be overcome in practice if the reign of false ideas is to be destroyed once and for all.

If we combine this new account of how erroneous ideas emerge with the claim made by Marx and Engels in *The Communist Manifesto* (1848) that 'the history of all hitherto existing society is the history of class struggle' (2000: 246), then we can discern a theory of how it is that any particular society at any particular time comes to have the ideas about itself that it does. Ideology, in this sense, is no longer simply a science for the generation of true ideas, or simply a set of false and dangerous ideas, but a general theory of how ideas emerge from the material base of social and economic conditions. It is, therefore, an account of how the dominant ideas of our age have come to be so dominant by virtue of their relationship to developments in the economic sphere. It is in this sense that Marx and Engels, particularly in their later writings, view liberalism: as an ideology that blinds the populace to the excesses of capitalist exploitation while also maintaining that liberalism itself is sustained by the economic forces at work within the capitalist mode of production. The intimate link between liberalism and capitalism maintains the dominance of both, making it virtually impossible for the vast majority of people to imagine a world without either. Such is the force of this ideology, according to many of today's 'anti-globalisation' and 'anti-capitalist' protesters, that it seems easier to imagine global ecological disaster than to imagine changing the economic, social and political structures that, arguably, are drawing us ever closer to the collapse of our biosphere. Mark Fisher, a British writer and lecturer, calls this 'capitalist realism', by which he means 'the widespread sense that not only is capitalism the only viable political and economic system, but also that it is now impossible to imagine a coherent alternative to it' (2009: 2). It is, Fisher argues, a failure of the imagination that must be challenged if humanity is to have a future at all.

After Marx and Engels, but within the tradition of twentieth-century Marxism, the idea of ideology began to take a different shape. Emphasis on the all-encompassing nature of ideology led some Marxists to downplay the notion that ideologies are conglomerations of false ideas supported by class divisions. Instead, many Marxists stressed a view of ideology that conceptualised it as the basis of all social and political action. We can see this in Lenin's analysis of the revolutionary struggle facing Russians at the beginning of the twentieth century. In *What Is to Be Done?* (1902) he talks of *socialism* as 'the ideology of struggle of the proletarian class'. For Lenin, breaking from the classical conception of Marx and Engels, ideology no longer simply represents the ideas of the ruling class. The crucial factor is the extent to which ideology is an effective weapon in the class war. As Boudon puts it, the novelty of Lenin's approach is that regardless of whether ideologies are true or false, they are 'useful' (1989: 18). This addition to the classical Marxist conception opens the way for an understanding of ideology that portrays all forms of action as, in some sense, ideological.

It was a theme picked up in the writings of many subsequent Marxists (for example, Gramsci, Benjamin and Adorno), but it is especially clear in the work of the French neo-Marxist philosopher Louis Althusser. According to Althusser, ideology is the 'cement' that binds human societies together. In this sense, 'ideology is . . . an organic part . . . of every social totality' and 'human societies secrete ideology as the very element and atmosphere indispensable to their historical respiration and life' (1969: 232). Furthermore, social and political life is made up of a number of institutions that create an ideological circulatory system: schools, churches, trade unions and the family all constitute what Althusser calls 'Ideological State Apparatuses'. Schools, for example, are not the seedbed from which free and rational individuals flower but rather one medium, among many, through which we are socialised into deference towards our 'superiors', and in which we are taught to compete against each other and ultimately moulded into the compliant 'good citizens' required by a liberal capitalist society.

The usefulness of Althusser's understanding of ideology is twofold. First, it helps us understand the ways in which the institutions of social life are relatively self-sufficient, each working in its own distinctive way, while they are nonetheless ultimately bound together by economic imperatives derived from capitalist productive processes. Second, as Althusser argues, all societies need institutions such as these to function properly and, as such, every social formation will 'secrete ideology'. For him, this means that ideology would not disappear in a post-capitalist society: 'it is clear that ideology (as a system of mass representation) is indispensable in any society if men are to be formed, transformed and equipped to respond to the demands of their conditions of existence' (1969: 235). The ideology of the school, for example, would still exist but in a form that sustained the bonds of post-capitalist society. In this sense, Althusser echoed the Leninist view that socialism is itself an ideology.

That said, Althusser continued to insist upon the strict separation of ideology and science, in a manner reminiscent of the way classical conceptions of ideology derived their force from the Enlightenment desire to rid social and political life of false ideas. Yet Althusser's rendering of the division between ideology and science remained distinctly Marxist in outlook. The problem he faced was this: if ideology binds social life together and is, therefore, an irreducible element of our political existence, was Marxism itself not just another ideology and, therefore, with no persuasive claim to being a true account of the way the social and political world operates? His initial solution to this problem is the one that he is most known for, although he altered his views on it throughout his career. For the early Althusser, Marx's analyses of the workings of capitalism could be understood as scientific, that is, as not ideological, if they were grounded on the basic premises of Marxist philosophy rather than on a non-Marxist philosophy of science. Marxist philosophy, in other words, is the guarantor of the scientific status of Marxist political economy. Later, this led Althusser to the claim that Marxism is both a philosophy of science and a science itself: a claim not without a certain paradoxical character, as subsequent commentary has revealed (Callinicos, 1976; Assiter, 1990).

Whether this approach manages to marry the classical idea of ideology as a set of false ideas with the idea that all activity within social and political life is ideological is open to question. Nonetheless, it provides a glimpse of the deep layers of philosophical inquiry that have had to be unearthed in order for those within Marxism to make sense of the idea of ideology. Recent work, loosely under the banner of post-Marxism, has pursued even deeper geological excavations of the basic strata of ideology, such that one is often confronted with the kind of theoretical complexity that leaves one gasping for air. Nonetheless, it is the work of post-Marxists like Ernesto Laclau and Slavoj Zizek that has done much to revitalise the idea of ideology in an era dominated by talk of the end of ideology. As the final chapter in this volume makes clear, contemporary work on the nature of ideology serves to remind us that the legacy of Marx and Engels continues to exert a powerful influence over cutting-edge research in political ideologies.

It would be a mistake, though, to assume that all the interesting work on the idea of ideology has emerged from a (more or less) Marxist perspective. Throughout the first half of the twentieth century the concept of ideology quickly spread across theoretical schools and academic disciplines. Even if scholars were not persuaded by the basic economic determinism underpinning the classical Marxist appropriation of ideology, the idea that the vast majority of the population held beliefs about social and political life that dominated, in some sense, everyday social and political interaction continued to have resonance and currency within intellectual circles. Within mainstream Anglo-American social science, for example, political ideology came to denote tightly interwoven constellations of belief. For example, liberal ideology is understood as a set of interlocking ideas about liberty, equality, justice and the like, while conservative ideology is understood as a different set of beliefs about the meanings and priorities embodied by these key terms and the relationships between them. In this sense, ideologies are said to offer contrasting interpretations of *essentially contested concepts*, where an essentially contested concept is one which does not, and could not, have an agreed meaning (Gallie, 1955/6; Connolly, 1983).

We are familiar with the debates around the concept of freedom, for example, between conservatives and socialists: freedom from the state in a market framework versus freedom to fulfil one's creative capacities in a collective setting. This is a staple of British party politics. Are taxes, for instance, an infringement of personal liberty in that they remove the right of individuals to spend their money in the way they see fit? Or are they a key instrument of redistribution that enables people to fulfil their potential as free and equal human beings? Within the Marxist tradition of ideological critique, the focus is on the underlying realities of such party political debate. The Anglo-American approach, however, has always been more concerned with the nitty-gritty of conceptual contestation, looking for the nuances of meaning and understanding that separate and/or link, for example, different ideas of liberty and equality.

As Freeden notes, within the Anglo-American tradition of the study of ideology there is a shift away from the idea of ideology to the study of ideolog*ies*:

> No longer is ideology regarded as an aberration of perception or of understanding; instead, a positivist empiricism is harnessed to identify and investigate a widespread social phenomenon: the existence of organized, articulated, and consciously held systems of political ideas incorporating beliefs, attitudes and opinions, though latent beliefs are also included.
>
> (1996: 15)

Furthermore, this emphasis on ideologies within Anglo-American political science also brings with it a certain historical approach that dwells on how and why beliefs about concepts have mutated within and between ideologies. Of course, this is not the Marxist sense of history, where history is governed by the laws of political economy, but a rather more idealist history that focuses on the contributions of great thinkers and politicians within various ideological traditions.

For example, where a Marxist might look to understand David Cameron's 'Big Society' by reference to *the ideology* at work in this new doctrine, political theorists of a more Anglo-American bent would tend to examine the 'Big Society' in terms of the *various ideological strands* that are blended together by its proponents. It may seem like a subtle distinction, but the rift between Marxist and non-Marxist approaches to ideology has deep significance for how we understand contemporary social and political formations. Are the various ideologies that make up our ideological landscape resting on one idea of ideology that can, in principle at least, be unearthed with a view to explaining and possibly removing ideological conflict, as a Marxist might hold? Or, does ideological contestability go 'all the way down', such that we cannot really talk of one single meaning of the term 'ideology' itself? Without hoping to resolve this deeply troublesome issue, it is worth turning our attention to the most systematic account of ideologies within the non-Marxist tradition of recent times, that offered by Michael Freeden in his book *Ideologies and Political Theory* (1996).

The morphology of ideologies

From the outset, Freeden distances himself from Marxist approaches to ideology and places himself firmly within the purview of Anglo-American studies: '[t]he thinking encapsulated in ideologies deserves examination in its own right, not merely for what it masks' (1996: 1). Leaving such Marxist approaches behind, however, Freeden focuses his critical gaze on another form of political theorising that fails to accord ideologies their full due, namely the Anglo-American tendency to reduce them to the abstract claims of moral and political philosophy. For Freeden, scholars tend to miss crucial dimensions of political life if their sole concern is to clarify the logical connections between distilled ideas. In particular, contemporary liberal political philosophy has become overly concerned with delimiting the precise nature of justice, rights, freedom, equality, and so on, to the detriment of 'our comprehension of political thought as a phenomenon reflecting cultural as well as logical constraints' (1996: 2). Without an appreciation of the cultural life of ideas, he argues, political thought remains a rarefied activity with little hope of understanding either the impact of political ideas on political action or, equally important, the impact of political activity on the formation and shaping of political ideas. One cannot simply map out the logical coherence of a solution to a moral dilemma and either expect the populace to fall into line behind the logic of the argument or use philosophical rigour as justification for calling to account those who do not see the logic of the argument.

The political realm, for Freeden, is much more complex and demanding than this traditional Anglo-American approach suggests, and in order to understand this complexity it is necessary to examine the realm of ideologies on its own terms. Freeden, in short, wishes to approach the nature of ideologies without subordinating their contribution to political life under either the banner of Marxist political economy or that of analytical moral and political philosophy. In the terms outlined at the beginning of this chapter, Freeden's approach to political ideologies emphasises their practical unity rather than focusing on either their empirical (true/false) or their normative (moral philosophical) dimensions.

According to Freeden, ideologies are 'those systems of political thinking, loose or rigid, deliberate or unintended, through which individuals and groups construct an understanding of the political world they, or those who preoccupy their thoughts, inhabit, and then act on that understanding' (1996: 3). In this encompassing definition, packed with the kind of vagueness so abhorrent to those of a strongly analytical bent, Freeden manages to convey the nature of ideologies from the perspective of those who make them what they are: ordinary people engaged in social and political life. As such, Freeden respects his opening intuition that ideologies must be placed firmly in the cultural and not just the logical realm. But how do students of ideology study the cultural life of ideas? What image of scholarly practice is produced as a result of this deliberately open definition?

Freeden acknowledges that scholars of ideologies within the Anglo-American tradition have dwelt rightly on both the temporal and the spatial aspects of ideology: that is, how ideologies change over time (say, the ways in which British liberalism has mutated throughout British history) and how they manifest themselves within different cultures (say, the different emphases found within British and French liberalism). But according to Freeden this is not the whole story. To fully appreciate the role of ideologies within political life, one must also look at the morphology of ideologies. Morphology refers to the study of form and structure, and it is Freeden's contention that the study of ideologies must address the ways in which ideologies are structured by the linkages between the concepts that make up any particular ideology. He proposes that ideologies can be thought of as assemblages of concepts, some of which will be concepts that form the core of the ideology, while other concepts will be either adjacent to the core or at the periphery of the ideology.

> Central to any analysis of ideologies is the proposition that they are characterised by a morphology that displays core, adjacent, and peripheral concepts. For instance, an examination of observed liberalisms might establish that liberty is situated within their core, that human rights, democracy and quality are adjacent to liberty, and that nationalism is to be found on their periphery.
>
> (1996: 77)

Alongside the temporal and the spatial study of ideologies, Freeden emphasises that concepts change and gain meaning not only through time or cultural setting but also through the ways in which they are related to each other within ideologies. Interestingly, this amounts to an extrapolation of the idea of essentially contested concepts, mentioned above. Where it was traditionally thought that the essential contestability of the concepts that make up ideologies was a product of the intrinsic complexity and value-ladenness of the concepts themselves, Freeden stresses that contestability at this level is a product of a deeper contestability to be found in the structure of relationships between concepts that make up an ideology's morphology. The essential contestability of concepts, in other words, is not simply the result of our inability to agree on the meaning of key concepts. Rather, it is derived from the fact that the meaning of concepts changes, depending on the relationships concepts are thought to have with each other. From this perspective, we cannot agree on the meaning of liberty because we cannot agree on its relationships with other concepts such as equality, democracy, rights, justice, and so on. Indeed, the study of ideologies is, in large measure, the study of the various ways these and other concepts have been related to each other within the political domain.

Having established the centrality of morphology in the study of ideology, Freeden is quick to point out that this does not mean that any particular ideology – liberalism, say – has a fixed set of core, adjacent and peripheral concepts. On the contrary, he maintains that the study of morphology brings the various changes within ideologies all the more clearly into focus, a claim he makes good in the chapters of the book which deal with liberalism, conservativism, socialism, feminism and ecologism. Moreover, the student of ideology should not fall prey to the idea that morphological analyses are somehow divorced from the historical and cultural construction of ideologies. In summing up his argument at the end of the book, Freeden cautions that the relationship between the history, culture and morphology of ideologies must be examined 'without slavishly following any single viewpoint' (1996: 552). And here again we are reminded that Freeden wishes to demarcate the realm of ideologies from both the Marxist tendency to reduce ideology to matters of political economy and the Anglo-American tendency to treat ideologies as forms of lazy thinking that need to be corrected through the intervention of logical constraints. Ideologies are, in contrast, that particular form of thinking about politics that can be truly said to be political – that is, the changeable and practically oriented thinking of citizens in the social and political world.

The big questions

The Marxist and the non-Marxist accounts of ideology reveal a deep rift in thinking about the nature of ideologies. This apparently rigid dichotomy often leaves the student of ideology perplexed and unable to judge the claims of various ideologies. Nonetheless, there are a series of key questions that can be formulated which can help to sharpen one's critical focus when faced with the troubling question 'What are ideologies?' The following questions help to bring out the 'big issues' in the debates about the nature of ideologies and can be used both to recap some of the issues that have emerged so far and to reveal more clearly the philosophical strata underpinning the ideological landscape.

What relationship do ideologies have to truth? This is probably the trickiest of all problems regarding the nature of ideology, because, as Boudon puts it, 'what is knowledge for one person is ideology for another and *vice versa*' (1989: 22). Typically, of course, if one is trying to judge, for example, whether liberalism gives a true picture of the social and political world while socialism gives a false one, then the temptation is to resort to empirical examples. Can we not just look at the world around us in a broadly scientific fashion and discover the truth of the matter? Both classical Marxist approaches and many non-Marxist approaches resort to this strategy. The trouble is that ideologies shape what we see when we look at the social and political world. In this sense, the ideological spectacles are already donned before the social scientific research takes place, and it is by no means clear that a method exists which can either remove or even lessen the distorting effects of ideology on social and political research (despite Althusser's theoretical gymnastics on this issue!). When it is truth that is at stake, when people disagree about what the truth of a situation really is, the attempt to refer to the facts of the situation is likely to dig us deeper into the ideological mire.

In a useful essay on Marx's concept of ideology, Stuart Hall (1983) argues that the 'problem' of truth and falsity in the classical conception can be abated by refusing to think in such 'all or nothing' terms. He suggests that in place of these tough metaphysical categories we think of ideologies as either 'partial' or 'adequate'. Within non-Marxist literature Boudon also suggests that we need some criterion for judging ideologies, even if we will never be able to definitively proclaim one ideology true and the others false. The criterion he plumps for is 'soundness'. It is impossible to prove the truth of an ideology, he argues, but we may assess the soundness of its principles (1989: 202). Interestingly, Freeden's approach to ideology tries to take a step back from even these watered-down attempts at assessing the veracity of different ideologies by focusing instead on the idea that ideologies are to be analysed according to the concepts that they allow or disallow as true or false accounts of political reality. Moving away from the idea that ideologies are more or less 'true', 'adequate' or 'sound' attempts at reflecting the social and political world, he proposes instead that the world we inhabit is 'partly the product of those ideologies, operating as ways of organizing social reality' (1996: 4). The student of ideologies, for Freeden, should pursue their morphologies with a broadly detached attitude to questions of truth and falsity. Of course, one might argue that such detachment masks an ideological agenda, one which fails to call to account the false ideas that distort people's view of the social world around them, and that, therefore, this is an approach which ends up legitimating the status quo. Once again, the philosophical depths of ideology theory are quickly exposed.

Will there ever be a time when there are no ideologies? Although the main features of the well-established debate around the end of ideologies are outlined in the last chapter, answers to this question depend to a large extent on the answer one would give to the previous question. If it is thought that ideologies are false ideas that can be exposed by one form of analysis or another, then the idea of an end to ideology is conceivable. If ideologies are patterns of thought that shape the political world, then this would suggest that, if we accept the timeless nature of political engagement, there will always be ideologies.

What is the relationship between ideologies and political activity? There is a tendency to view ideologies as merely constellations of ideas that do not directly impact on day-to-day political activity. However, the picture is more complex than this view suggests. As discussed above, both Marxist and non-Marxist accounts of ideology recognise that ideologies have a role in shaping political activity, often in unconscious ways. Of course, the everyday machinations of politicians may appear unrelated to the admittedly rarefied discourses of scholars, but this appearance should not cloud the insight that political activity without an ideological frame would be verging on the meaningless. As noted above, however, students of ideology should be wary of a straightforward correspondence between the 'reality' of party politics and the various ideologies they appear to represent, given the way these relationships can change and mutate over time. Many of these changes are traced in the chapters that follow.

Are ideologies really just the ideas of ideologues? From the outset, it was noted that those who hold firm to their view of the political world have been labelled ideologues. This claim presupposes that the real activity of politics is best served by compromise, flexibility and openness, such that any political actor who does not display these features is merely a dangerous ideologue. Classically, this view is associated with Napoleon's condemnation of de Tracy and with Marxist condemnation of apologists for capitalist liberal democracy. More generally, it is found in arguments against those in political life, be they academics or activists, who endorse to some degree the idea that the social and political world should be made to conform to a ready-made ideal. Many conservatives and some liberals, for example, tend to dismiss other ideologies as the rantings of ideologues while, typically, arguing that their own chosen perspective is non-ideological precisely because it is based on pragmatic politics rather than ideals. There are two problems with such views. First, and as the relevant chapters in this book make clear, both conservativism and liberalism contain ideal visions of the good society. Secondly, the attempt to caricature other political viewpoints as the views of ideologues fails to adequately differentiate those ideological views that are commonly held within the political world from those that are the product of manipulative individuals trying to shape those commonly held views. In other words, all ideologies may have their ideologues, conservativism and liberalism included, but the views of ideologues are only a part of the rich and complex network of concepts and activities that constitute any given ideology.

These questions by no means exhaust the interrogation of ideology, but they do serve to remind the student of ideology that the domain of ideologies sits, uncomfortably at times, between the rarefied world of philosophical inquiry and the day-to-day machinations of *realpolitik*. If Freeden is right that it is precisely this condition that makes the analysis of ideologies central to the study of political life, then it is important to navigate a clear path between the rock of Marxist political economy and the hard place of Anglo-American analytical philosophy.

Conclusion: a return to ideology?

The current political milieu is characterised by two interlocking tendencies: the gradual coalescence of ideological positions within liberal democracies and the persistent eruptions of ideological fury around the world. In many respects these two phenomena can be explained, at least in part, with reference to the return of ideology, in the singular.

While for much of the twentieth century parties that reflected deep-seated class divisions dominated politics in liberal democracies, we are now witnessing a form of dealigned politics which means that each of the main political parties is striving to appeal to all 'the people'. This signifies a change, within both left and right political parties, in their perception of the political terrain. It is no longer possible to gain political power by appealing to one section of the community (the work force, for example) by claiming that the views of the other section (the managers and capitalists, for example) are simply false. There is, in other words, an attempt by all parties to occupy a popular terrain that they define as non-ideological. The student of political ideologies can still recognise that this supposedly non-ideological political realm is irreducibly marked by a variety of competing ideological positions. More than this, however, it cannot go unnoticed that the populism of recent political history has brought with it a return of the idea of ideology (in the singular). As outlined at the beginning of this chapter, it may be no coincidence that ideology, as the propagation of false ideas that serve only one section of society, has returned in political debate precisely at the time when some politicians and commentators have announced the end of the age of ideologies.

In the global arena, the political realm is also marked by disagreement over the nature of ideology. Even if those involved in the big ideological battles of the contemporary world are rarely Marxist in outlook, the world of international politics is still replete with those political actors determined to reveal the liberal democratic consensus as *the* ideology that distorts the vision of vast swathes of humanity in the service of the imperialist tendencies of global capitalist powers. Most notably, this criticism lurks behind both the criticisms of 'Western governments' in their attitude to non-Western states and the anti-capitalist protests against multinational corporations. For all the obvious differences between these global movements, both can be said to be pitting a classical conception of *ideology* against the alternative notion of a world of irremovable *ideologies*. If we fail to see this dimension we fail to understand the sources that motivate political actors to turn to radical forms of political expression in pursuit of their objectives. Indeed, that the meaning of ideology is still being contested throughout the world reminds us that the populist consensus within liberal democracies is by no means the end of the matter.

Further reading

One of the most significant recent developments in the study of ideology has been the appearance of Michael Freeden's book *Ideologies and Political Theory* (1996). Although a complicated and demanding text in many ways, the core ideas it contains are well worth the effort of close reading. Important summaries and clarifications can be found in Freeden's *Ideology: A Very Short Introduction* (2003) and his edited collection *The Meaning of Ideology: Cross-Disciplinary Perspectives* (2007). The student of ideology would also do well to examine many of the papers that have appeared in the *Journal of Political Ideologies*, established and edited by Freeden. Of particular interest are Freeden's own editorials, where he clarifies aspects of his own thought as well as summarising and commenting on developments within this growing field of study.

D. McLellan's *Ideology* (1986) provides a brief yet insightful introduction to many of the issues raised in the introduction, and can be usefully complemented by T. Eagleton's *Ideology: An Introduction* (1991), which undertakes a more wide-ranging analysis encompassing recent trends in social theory. There are good discussions of the nature of ideology in the following texts: T. A. van Dijk, *Ideology: A Multidisciplinary Approach* (1998); A. Vincent, *Modern Political Ideologies* (1992); and S. Malesevic and I. MacKenzie (eds), *Ideology after Poststructuralism* (2002). J. B. Thompson's *Studies in the Theory of Ideology* (1984) is an excellent guide to traditional debates while also showing how the terms of these debates have shifted during the course of the twentieth century. For a useful survey of the material on ideology, see M. B. Hamilton's *'The elements of the concept of ideology'* (1987). A very analytical, and at times quite dry, approach to the epistemological problems alluded to above can be found in R. Boudon's *The Analysis of Ideology* (1989). J. Larrain's *The Concept of Ideology* (1979) also provides a study of ideology that is difficult but rewarding.

Interesting, and challenging, accounts of the nature of ideology, at both a theoretical and a practical level, can be found in the collection by the Centre for Contemporary Cultural Studies *On Ideology* (1978), and also in N. O'Sullivan's edited collection *The Structure of Modern Ideology* (1989). R. Porter's *Ideology: Explorations in Contemporary Social, Political and Cultural Theory* (2005) gives an excellent account of 'a critical conception of ideology', articulated through the writings of Zizek, Deleuze and Habermas, that also provides a rich analysis of cultural forms, especially films.

The literature on Marxism and ideology is vast, often very difficult and related to particular debates within Marxism. However, useful starting points are B. Parekh's *Marx's Theory of Ideology* (1982) and J. Larrain's *Marxism and Ideology* (1983). I would also thoroughly recommend S. Hall's 'The problem of ideology – Marxism without guarantees' (1983). For the more adventurous in this area, I. Meszaros's *The Power of Ideology* (1989) is a very long (over 500 pages) Marxist discussion of ideology that can be as frustrating as it is rewarding. A good overall guide to Althusser can be found in A. Callinicos's *Althusser's Marxism* (1976). An excellent account of Althusser's theory of ideology is C. Williams's 'Ideology and imaginary: returning to Althusser' (2002). A. Assiter's *Althusser and Feminism* (1990) is an ambitious attempt to wed Althusserian Marxism with contemporary feminism.

Approaches to ideology that have not been covered in the introduction but would prove interesting in terms of a more detailed look at the debates are K. Mannheim's *Ideology and Utopia* (1936), which provides a useful link between Marxist and non-Marxist accounts of ideology; and E. Shils in 'The concept and function of ideology' in the *International Encyclopaedia of the Social Sciences*, VII (1968), argues, to my mind unconvincingly, that scientific knowledge is gradually eroding ideologies. The best currently available anthology of different perspectives on ideology and political ideologies is M. Kenny and M. Festenstein's edited collection *Political Ideologies: A Reader and Guide* (2005).

References

Althusser, L. (1969) 'Marxism and humanism', in *For Marx*, London: Allen Lane.
Assiter, A. (1990) *Althusser and Feminism*, London: Pluto Press.
Bacon, F. (1855) [1620] *Novum Organon*, Oxford: Oxford University Press.
Boudon, R. (1989) *The Analysis of Ideology*, Cambridge: Polity Press.
Callinicos, A. (1976) *Althusser's Marxism*, London: Pluto Press.
Centre for Contemporary Cultural Studies (1978) *On Ideology*, London: Hutchinson.
Connolly, W. (1983) *The Terms of Political Discourse*, 2nd edn, Oxford: Martin Robinson.

Dijk, T. A. van (1998) *Ideology: A Multidisciplinary Approach*, London: Sage.

Eagleton, T. (1991) *Ideology: An Introduction*, London: Verso.

Fisher, M. (2009) *Capitalist Realism: Is There No Alternative?*, Ropley: Zero Books.

Freeden, M. (1996) *Ideologies and Political Theory: A Conceptual Approach*, Oxford: Oxford University Press.

—— (2003) *Ideology: A Very Short Introduction*, Oxford: Oxford University Press.

Freeden, M. (ed.) (2007) *The Meaning of Ideology: Cross-Disciplinary Perspectives*, London: Routledge.

Gallie, W. B. (1955/6) 'Essentially contested concepts', *Proceedings of the Aristotelian Society*, 56, pp. 167–98.

Hall, S. (1983) 'The problem of ideology – Marxism without guarantees', in B. Matthews (ed.) *Marx: A Hundred Years On*, London: Lawrence and Wishart.

Hamilton, M. B. (1987) 'The elements of the concept of ideology', *Political Studies*, 35, pp. 18–38.

Kenny, M. and Festenstein, M. (eds) (2005) *Political Ideologies: A Reader and Guide*, Oxford: Oxford University Press.

Larrain, J. (1979) *The Concept of Ideology*, London: Hutchinson.

—— (1983) *Marxism and Ideology*, London: Macmillan.

McLellan, D. (1986) *Ideology*, Milton Keynes: Open University Press.

Malesevic, S. and MacKenzie, I. (eds) (2002) *Ideology after Poststructuralism*, London: Pluto Press.

Mannheim, K. (1936) *Ideology and Utopia: An Introduction to the Sociology of Knowledge*, London: Kegan Paul.

Marx, K. and Engels, F. (1974) [1845–46] *The German Ideology*, students' edn, ed. C. J. Arthur, London: Lawrence and Wishart.

—— (2000) [1848] *The Communist Manifesto*, in D. McLellan (ed.) *Karl Marx: Selected Writings*, 2nd edn, Oxford: Oxford University Press.

Meszaros, I. (1989) *The Power of Ideology*, London: Harvester Wheatsheaf.

O'Sullivan, N. (ed.) (1989) *The Structure of Modern Ideology: Critical Perspectives on Social and Political Theory*, Aldershot: Edward Elgar.

Parekh, B. (1982) *Marx's Theory of Ideology*, London: Croom Helm.

Porter, R. (2005) *Ideology: Explorations in Contemporary Social, Political and Cultural Theory*, Cardiff: University of Wales Press.

Shils, E. (1968) 'The concept and function of ideology', in D. L. Sills (ed.) *International Encyclopaedia of the Social Sciences*, VII, New York: Macmillan.

Thompson, J. B. (1984) *Studies in the Theory of Ideology*, Cambridge: Polity Press.

Vincent, A. (1992) *Modern Political Ideologies*, London: Blackwell.

Williams, C. (2002) 'Ideology and imaginary: returning to Althusser', in S. Malesevic, and I. MacKenzie (eds) *Ideology after Poststructuralism*, London: Pluto Press.

Chapter 2

Liberalism

Andrew Shorten

Problems of definition

The emergence of liberalism as a distinctive political ideology has been connected to sources as various as the rise of capitalism and the upheavals of the Reformation. Its intellectual origins are likewise disputed. Although some scholars have identified pre-modern antecedents of key liberal ideas, a more typical approach has been to locate the birth of liberal political thought in the social contract theorists of the seventeenth century and the Enlightenment of the eighteenth century. It was not, however, until the nineteenth century that liberalism was to become consolidated as a self-conscious and distinctive political ideology. It was also at this time that the first political factions were to be identified as 'liberal'. The earliest of these, the *liberales* in Spain, campaigned for freedom of expression and a secular constitution, ideas still endorsed by liberals today. Elsewhere, liberals were to criticise the privileges of aristocratic elites, emphasise the importance of individual rights, advance the cause of free trade, advocate constitutional and limited government, and develop optimistic theories about human nature and social progress. By the end of the century, a 'new' or social form of liberalism began to take shape, linking liberalism to the condemnation of poverty, and influencing the birth of the welfare state.

In the twenty-first century, liberalism has become so deeply permeated into the cultural, economic and political fabric of western societies that it can be difficult to discern where ideology ends and practice begins. The difficulties of defining liberalism have been exacerbated by the flexible usage of the term by both proponents and critics. On the one hand, liberals themselves have often been guilty of defining liberalism 'in such a way that only the very deluded or the very wicked could fail to be liberals' (Ryan, 2012: 22). For instance, liberals will sometimes characterise liberalism as a doctrine that respects the dignity or well-being of individuals, or as a theory that favours freedom, or as an ideology that opposes authoritarianism, none of which is an especially controversial position to adopt. On the other hand, critics of liberalism will often castigate liberal ideas on the basis of shortcomings they locate in existing practices or institutional arrangements, on the assumption that since contemporary societies are described as liberal, liberals endorse these societies and their arrangements *in toto*.

This chapter traces the origins and development of liberalism, and draws attention to two key and contested themes that have remained central to the liberal tradition: individualism and toleration. Liberalism is a thriving and flexible ideology, and the final parts of the chapter will take up some of the issues that divide contemporary liberals and explore the ways in which liberalism overlaps with other traditions in political thought. As will become clear, liberalism is a complex and contested ideology, containing few fixed points of agreement. For example, liberals disagree about matters as varied and important as the legitimate scope of government, the welfare state, the nature of freedom, the possibility of progress, the morality of the marketplace, the significance of private property, and the value of democracy. Perhaps this should be expected of a tradition that takes its name from a word signifying open-mindedness and tolerance.

Origins and evolution

Liberalism is a modern political ideology, which took shape initially in Europe, after the disintegration of feudalism and the weakening of aristocratic privilege. Scholars have offered different explanations about its emergence and spread. One view, prominent amongst Marxists and socialists, is that liberalism is the twin of capitalism (Macpherson, 1962; Arblaster, 1984). On this account, the rise of liberalism is inextricably linked with that of capitalism, and liberalism itself is a capitalist – or bourgeois – ideology. Proponents of this view tend to emphasise liberal sympathy for property rights and the principle of *laissez faire* (the French term *laissez faire* translates literally as 'let do'; in political economy the principle of *laissez faire* stipulates that economic transactions should not be taxed or regulated by the state). Another view about the emergence of liberalism instead connects it to the political and intellectual upheavals that followed the Reformation. For example, John Rawls traces the modern liberal conceptions of 'liberty of conscience and freedom of thought' to this period (1993: xxiv). William Galston similarly identifies the birth of a distinctive theory of liberal toleration in what he calls 'the Reformation Project – that is, the effort to deal with the political consequences of religious differences in the wake of divisions within Christendom' (1995: 525).

Identifying liberalism's philosophical founders is a similarly contentious business. A number of ancient philosophers have been identified as its intellectual progenitors. F. A. Hayek, for instance, described the Roman legal theorist Cicero as 'the main authority for modern liberalism' (1963: 244), on the grounds that he gave expression to the idea that freedom depends on the rule of law rather than the rule of men. John Gray goes back even further, and identifies some 'germs of liberal ideas' (1986: 1), such as universal equality and democracy, amongst the Greek Sophists and Athenian democrats. A more conventional view is that the initial manifestations of some distinctively liberal ideas are to be found in the early modern period, and in particular in the work of two English philosophers.

The first of these is Thomas Hobbes (1588–1679), best known today for his *Leviathan* (1651). Hobbes may strike many readers as an unlikely figure to be found in the pantheon of liberal political theorists. Although he explicitly opposed many of the ideals that liberals later came to cherish – such as freedom of conscience, the separation of church and state, and the doctrine of limited government – Hobbes also helped to develop a mode of theorising about politics that profoundly influenced the subsequent trajectory of liberalism. Leo Strauss made this claim in bold terms, crediting Hobbes with having inaugurated modern political philosophy and describing him as the 'founder of liberalism' (1953: 182). Michael Oakeshott advanced a more nuanced version of this claim, concluding that 'Hobbes, without himself being a liberal, had in him more of the philosophy of liberalism than most of its professed defenders' (1975: 63). Interpretations of Hobbes that place him close to the liberal tradition tend to pick out five ideas: his markedly individualistic conception of society; his claim that individuals are by nature equals; his assumption that constraints on natural freedom must be justified; his view of the state as 'artificial' rather than 'natural'; and his distinctive conception of political freedom, which he locates in those spaces where no rules have been prescribed and the laws are silent.

In contrast to Hobbes, many liberals have been eager to assimilate John Locke (1632–1704) into their tradition, and his *Two Treatises of Government* (1689) is frequently cited as a foundational liberal text, especially in the United States. Locke's *Two Treatises* contains a number of ideas that were to become associated with liberalism. For instance, he rejected political absolutism, advocated limited government, argued that legitimate political power is grounded on consent, insisted that men have natural rights which governments must respect, and included amongst those rights a right to resist arbitrary power. Critics who regard liberalism as a bourgeois ideology emphasise the significance that Locke attributed to property rights, his view that men put themselves under government primarily for the purpose of preserving property, and his restriction of citizenship to the propertied (Macpherson, 1962). Meanwhile, more sympathetic treatments tend to emphasise Locke's political radicalism (Ashcraft, 1986, 1987; Laslett, 1988) and his firm insistence on man's fundamental moral equality (Waldron, 2002).

A number of Lockean themes were taken up by the American revolutionaries, and particularly by Thomas Paine (1737–1809). In his *Common Sense* (1776) the British-born Paine argued that government is created by men to uphold their natural rights, and that people have a right to overthrow a reigning government if it fails to do so. Within months, these ideas were to be stated in an even more compressed form in the famous opening passage of the American Declaration of Independence (1776):

> We hold these truths to be self-evident, that all men are created equal, that they are endowed by their Creator with certain unalienable Rights, that among these are Life, Liberty and the pursuit of Happiness. That to secure these rights, Governments are instituted among Men, deriving their just powers from the consent of the governed; That whenever any Form of Government becomes destructive of these ends, it is the Right of the People to alter or to abolish it, and to institute new Government, laying its foundation on such principles and organizing its powers in such form, as to them shall seem most likely to effect their Safety and Happiness.
>
> (Quoted in Sargent, 1997: 62–3)

Paine's liberal radicalism was given its most systematic expression in his *Rights of Man* (1791), in which he defended the French revolutionaries against their conservative critics, such as Edmund Burke (1729–97). Although the revolutionaries in France took much of their inspiration from ideas outside the liberal tradition, their central document – the *Declaration of the Rights of Man and of the Citizen* (1789) – reflected preoccupations that were shared by liberals of the period, such as the desire to overthrow aristocratic privilege and the project to establish limited government and religious toleration.

Another current of thinking from this period was also to influence both the revolutionaries and the progressive liberals of the nineteenth and twentieth centuries. This is the idea that human affairs can be improved through the unfettered application of reason, which can be found in the writings of a number of Enlightenment *philosophes*, such as Denis Diderot (1713–84) and the Marquis de Condorcet (1743–94), as well as in Immanuel Kant's (1724–1804) famous essay 'What Is Enlightenment?' (1784). According to these authors, science and reason enable us to understand and improve the world, liberating us from custom and tradition. For example, Condorcet's posthumously published *Sketch for a Historical Picture of the Progress of the Human Mind* (1795), written whilst in hiding from the Revolutionary Terror, outlined his vision for a future society based on reason and justice. Similar ideas were also canvassed by radicals in England, such as William Godwin (1756–1836), anarchist and author of *Political Justice* (1798). Although many later liberals lacked the *philosophes'* faith in human progress, a residue of Enlightenment optimism can be found in John Stuart Mill's (1806–73) quintessentially liberal defence of the freedoms of speech and thought. Common to both Mill and his eighteenth-century predecessors are the beliefs that dogma is the enemy of progress and that all moral, scientific and theological views must be subject to ongoing critical scrutiny. The persistence of these ideas within the liberal tradition prompted one commentator to note that liberalism 'is *par excellence* the doctrine of the Enlightenment' (Barry, 1990: 2).

Notwithstanding this, the *term* 'liberal' became an established part of our political lexicon only after the revolutionary moments of the eighteenth century, and one scholar identifies the 1830s as the point at which 'we begin to encounter the fully self-conscious liberal ideology' (Vincent, 2010: 27). The liberalism of this period exhibited an intoxicating blend of ideas, pulling in a number of directions. For instance, England in the nineteenth century has been described as a 'golden age of liberal theory and practice' (Gray, 1986: 26). Certainly, there were some important victories for the liberal movement in the first half of the century, such as the Catholic Emancipation Act (1829), the Reform Act (1832) and the repeal of the Corn Laws (1846). There were ideological developments too, and figures associated with the 'Manchester school', like Richard Cobden (1804–65) and John Bright (1811–89), advanced the cause of free trade by linking economic freedom to the case against aristocratic and monopolistic privilege. Most influentially, Mill's famous *On Liberty* (1859) supplied 'the most eloquent and passionate defence of individual liberty in all political thought' (Seglow, 2002: 180). In this essay, Mill provided a bold defence of individuality, argued against the physical or moral coercion of individuals by either state or society, and insisted that

> the sole end for which mankind are warranted, individually or collectively, in interfering with the liberty of action of any of their number, is self-protection . . . the only purpose for which power can be rightfully exercised over any member of a civilized community, against his will, is to prevent harm to others. His own good, either physical or moral, is not a sufficient warrant . . . Over himself, over his own body and mind, the individual is sovereign.
>
> (1985: 68)

Whilst liberalism in England retained a broadly *laissez faire* character until the end of the century, liberals in France developed a more democratic strand of liberalism (Siedentop, 1979). Although authors such as Mme de Stael (1766–1817) and Benjamin Constant (1767–1830) contributed to this development, the most significant figure is Alexis de Tocqueville (1805–59). In his *Democracy in America* (1835/1840), Tocqueville identified civic virtue and a vigorous associational life as the best safeguards against the dangers of centralised power. In doing so, he drew attention to the importance of diffusing an appropriate set of customs or habits of mind (*moeurs*) if liberal society is to sustain itself.

This 'civic virtue' strand of liberalism was an anathema to many English liberals of the period, such as Herbert Spencer (1820–1903). However, the next generation of liberals in Britain, including T. H. Green (1836–82), L. T. Hobhouse (1864–1929) and J. A. Hobson (1858–1940), did much to establish a link between the liberal tradition and emerging ideas about social democracy. To some extent, this move was anticipated by Mill himself, who opened the door to the redistribution of wealth in his *Principles of Political Economy* (1848). The British Idealist Green took things a step further, and his lecture 'Liberal Legislation and Freedom of Contract' (1881) defended the public provision of health and education on the grounds that both would promote the freedom of the disadvantaged. This social or egalitarian strand within liberalism was deepened by Hobhouse and Hobson, who favoured a wide range of social rights, including pensions for the elderly, a minimum wage for workers and welfare for the unemployed.

By the early years of the twentieth century, liberalism had adapted itself to some of the challenges posed by the socialist movement, and the commitment to the principle of *laissez faire* had been modified by the incorporation of a commitment to social equality. Some critics regard this 'new liberalism' as a revisionary and collectivist deviation from the principles of classical liberalism. For instance, John Gray identifies a 'hubristic rationalism' in the new liberals, in which they 'sought to submit the life of society to rational reconstruction' (1986: 92). Whatever the merits of this claim, liberalism's rapprochement with social democratic politics had two long-term effects. First, the welfare state became a liberal cause. Indeed, the architect of the British welfare state, William Beveridge (1879–1963), had been a member of the Liberal Party, and framed the case in its favour in language that would have not looked out of place in Hobson or Hobhouse. Second, the distribution of wealth and opportunities became an increasingly central concern for liberals. By the end of the twentieth century, under the influence of liberal egalitarian philosophers such as John Rawls (1921–2002), liberalism was to become increasingly identified with the concept of distributive justice.

During the twentieth century, a number of authors – including F. A. Hayek (1899–1992), Karl Popper (1902–94), Isaiah Berlin (1909–97) and Jacob Talmon (1919–80) – developed a distinctive anti-totalitarian argument for liberal institutions. For example, Popper's *The Open Society and Its Enemies* (1945) argued against utopianism in political thought, and instead advocated piecemeal reform within the context of an open, liberal society. Meanwhile, Hayek's *The Road to Serfdom* (1944) revived the case for *laissez faire* liberalism and castigated the central economic planning that had been advocated by social liberals, which he regarded as a step towards tyranny. By the end of the twentieth century, a further variant of *laissez faire* liberalism, now commonly described as neoliberalism, began to attract attention. Influenced by economists, including Ludwig von Mises (1881–1973) and Milton Friedman (1912–2006), neoliberalism has been described as the view that 'human well-being can best be advanced by liberating individual entrepreneurial freedoms and skills within an institutional framework characterized by strong private property rights, free markets and free trade' (Harvey, 2005: 2). In politics, neoliberalism has been most passionately promoted by conservatives and is associated with deregulation, privatisation and rolling back the state. The influence of neoliberalism, particularly at the level of global public policy, has been profound.

Individualism and individuality

Liberals do not share a single view about human nature. However, most liberals have inherited, from Hobbes and Locke, 'a vision of society as in some sense constituted by individuals for the fulfilment of ends which were primarily individual' (Taylor, 1985: 187). This vision can be described as liberal individualism, which is a rich and multifaceted doctrine. In its most general sense, liberal individualism combines the following four ideas: that each individual is equally important; that each individual is a separate unit; that individuals are (in some sense) prior to and more important than society; and that social, political and economic arrangements are to be evaluated according to how well individuals fare within them.

Critics have seized upon liberalism's commitment to individualism. For example, contemporary multiculturalists, such as Bhikhu Parekh, have argued that liberal individualism arrogantly posits a narrow model of human excellence, and in so doing rules out 'traditional and customary ways of life, as well as those centred on the community' (1994: 13). A related line of criticism can be found in feminist writings, and Alison Jaggar thinks that liberals are guilty of 'political solipsism, the assumption that human individuals are essentially self-sufficient entities' (1983: 40). Meanwhile, critics from the political left have connected liberal individualism to acquisitive tendencies associated with commercial society. For example, C. B. Macpherson identifies a theory of 'possessive individualism' within liberalism's seventeenth-century progenitors, in which the individual is conceived 'as essentially the proprietor of his own person or capacities, owing nothing to society for them' (1962: 3). Objections such as these are not a recent phenomenon. For instance, in nineteenth-century France, both socialist and conservative critics connected liberal ideas to the isolation of individuals and the dissolution of society (Lukes, 1971: 45–54). A modern twist on this argument has been suggested by 'communitarian' authors, who worry that liberalism has pernicious effects on people and their communities. On this view, liberalism is 'fragmentation in practice' (Walzer, 2004: 145), because liberal institutions foster social dislocation by inducing introspective and even selfish dispositions amongst members.

Liberals themselves have been divided on two key issues: one concerning the proper relationship between individual, state and society, and another concerning the philosophical grounds for individualism. With respect to the first issue, liberals occupy a broad range of positions. At one end of the spectrum are those who believe that individualism and collectivism are fundamentally in tension with one another. This tends to be a view insisted upon by advocates of the principle of *laissez faire*. For example, in nineteenth-century Britain, a pamphlet produced by the Liberty and Property Defence League claimed that the state regulation of 'social activity and industry' was an 'invasion of individual freedom of action' and represented a 'general movement towards State-Socialism' (quoted in Freeden, 1996: 287). The most prominent ideologue of the League was Spencer, who objected to early manifestations of the welfare state in his illuminatingly titled *The Man versus the State* (1884). Libertarians in twentieth-century America drew a similar conclusion, arguing that redistributive taxation is exploitative because it treats some people as a means to the good of others. For example, Robert Nozick (1938–2002) argued that using a person 'for the benefit of others . . . does not sufficiently respect and take account of the fact that he is a separate person, that his is the only life he has' (1974: 32–3). An even more radical form of anti-collectivist individualism is normative egoism, which has been endorsed by some thinkers associated with the liberal tradition. Normative egoism is the principle that one *ought* to aim only at benefitting oneself. A twentieth-century proponent of this view, Ayn Rand (1905–82), objected to altruism and defended a doctrine called the 'virtue of selfishness'.

At the other end of the spectrum are liberals who deny that individual and collective goods are fundamentally in tension with one another. According to many of these authors, the fierce individualism of some *laissez faire* liberals supplies an unappealing ideal about how things ought to be, neglecting important ideas such as the common good and civic virtue. These positions are nevertheless recognisably liberal, because they do not allocate priority to collective goals over individual ones. For example, the social liberalism that emerged in Britain at the end of the nineteenth century connected the good of the individual to the social provision of welfare. Green emphasised that individual self-realisation occurs within society, and rejected Spencer's view that promoting collective ends frustrates individual freedom. Instead, he argued that the common good was harmonious with individual freedom and that 'freedom in the positive sense' was 'the liberation of the powers of all men equally for contributions to a common good' (1986: 200). Hobhouse advanced a similar position, arguing that 'social liberty' and the 'living equality of rights' will require extending the 'sphere of social control'. He concluded that 'individualism, when it grapples with the facts, is driven no small distance along Socialist lines' (1994: 47). A further example of liberalism's departure from a robust individualism occurred during the latter part of the twentieth century, where a number of liberal authors took an interest in theories of civic virtue, developing Tocqueville's idea that a flourishing political community will require a sense of public spiritedness amongst its members (Macedo, 1990; Galston, 1991).

The second issue that divides liberals with respect to individualism has to do with its philosophical grounds, and two broad camps can be identified. One version of liberalism, prominent amongst contemporary North American liberal political philosophers, has been strongly influenced by the moral philosophy of Immanuel Kant, in which human beings are autonomous and rational agents, to be treated as ends in themselves and never only as means to the ends of others. Translated into a liberal political theory, this means that each individual is entitled to be treated with 'equal concern and respect' (Dworkin, 1977, 1985) and that the good of society – or any other group – should not be placed above that of the individual. Rawls formulated this view as follows: 'Each person possesses an inviolability founded on justice that even the welfare of society as a whole cannot override . . . justice denies that the loss of freedom for some is made right by a greater good shared by others' (1971: 3–4). Liberal individualism of this variety demands that political arrangements respect the 'separateness of persons', an idea described by one contemporary liberal feminist as follows:

> In normative terms, this commitment to the recognition of individual separateness means, for the liberal, that the demands of a collectivity or a relation should not as such be made the basic goal of politics: collectivities, such as the state and even the family, are composed of individuals . . . Each of these is separate, and each of these is an end. Liberalism holds that the flourishing of human beings taken one by one is both analytically and normatively prior to the flourishing of the state or the nation or the religious group; analytically, because such entities do not really efface the separate reality of individual lives; normatively because the recognition of that separateness is held to be a fundamental fact for ethics, which

should recognize each separate entity as an end and not as a means to the ends of others.

(Nussbaum, 1999: 62)

It is important to note that the 'separateness of persons' is compatible with a range of views about distributive justice and the welfare state, and recent Kantian liberals have been divided along lines that in many respects resemble those which divided the earlier British liberals. On the one hand, as we have already seen, libertarians such as Nozick have appealed to the 'separateness of persons' to reach conclusions similar to Spencer. On the other hand, liberal egalitarians have suggested that the 'separateness of persons' is compatible with citizens having substantial duties towards one another, including duties of distributive justice. For example, in his *A Theory of Justice* (1971) Rawls argued that a Kantian theory of the person is compatible with a broadly egalitarian redistribution of wealth and the public provision of welfare services.

A different version of liberal individualism centres on the idea of 'individuality'. A characteristic expression of this line of thought can be found in Mill's *On Liberty*, in which he argued that 'it is only the cultivation of individuality which produces, or can produce, well-developed human beings' (1985: 128). Mill connected the ideal of individuality to the case in favour of liberty, and claimed that individuality (or 'self-development') is an important component of individual well-being. Individuality is threatened wherever there is a widespread tendency for people to believe that 'everybody should be required to act as he, and those with whom he sympathizes, would like them to act' (1985: 64). Therefore, a free society will require not only political institutions that respect the 'separateness of persons', but also a social ethos that values the cultivation of individuality.

Mill offered at least three arguments in support of the claim that 'the free development of individuality' is an essential part of individual well-being. First, individuality fosters social and intellectual progress, and 'the only unfailing and permanent source of improvement is liberty' (1985: 136). His idea was that once individuality is given a free rein, society will acquire a vibrant diversity of practices and ideas. Meanwhile, allowing custom to stifle individuality will lead to mediocrity, suffocating creativity and frustrating human progress. This argument is given its clearest statement in Mill's famous defence of the 'liberty of thought and discussion', where he argues that the best guarantor of truth and progress is a free marketplace of ideas. Secondly, Mill also connected individuality to the cultivation of one's higher nature or best qualities. The idea is that in choosing one's own mode of life, and by considering and testing out 'experiments in living', a person exercises the important human faculties of judgment and perception. By contrast, people who follow the well-trodden path of social expectation will be unable to cultivate some of these human excellences. Thirdly, in some passages Mill also indicates that individuality, and choosing one's own plan of life, is a good in itself. For example, he writes that '[i]f a person possesses any tolerable amount of common sense and experience, his own mode of laying out his existence is best, not because it is the best in itself, but because it is his own mode' (1985: 132–3).

In celebrating individuality and spontaneous self-creation, Mill contrasts these with 'ape-like' imitation, drawing a connection between individuality, character and authenticity. A person has character, on Mill's view, if his 'desires and impulses are his own – are the expression of his own nature, as it has been developed and modified by his own culture' (1985: 124). By contrast, someone whose 'desires and impulses are not his own, has no character, no more than a steam-engine has a character' (1985: 124). Individuality is not only about selecting one's own projects and ambitions, and about resisting the temptation to shape those projects according to the expectations of others. Individuality is also about being true to oneself, listening to one's inner voice, and discovering a way of living that is consistent with one's own authentic nature. This aspect of Mill's case for individuality was influenced by German romanticism, and particularly by Wilhelm von Humboldt (1767–1835), who supplied the epigraph to Mill's essay. Humboldt's *The Sphere and Duties of Government* (written in 1792 but not published until 1851) contains an early version of the liberal argument for scepticism about state interference, justified by reference to the concept of *Bildung* (usually translated as self-development or self-creation). According to Humboldt, the 'true end of man' was 'the highest and most harmonious development of his powers to a complete and consistent whole' (1969: 16), and the ideal society was one in which 'each strives to develop himself from his own inmost nature, and for his own sake' (1969: 19). Humboldt and Mill agreed about the value of originality, spontaneity and self-development. However, they disagreed about what kinds of political arrangements would be conducive to individuality. Whilst Humboldt was sceptical about all forms of state interference, Mill favoured positive government intervention to ensure that all had available to them the preconditions for individuality.

Toleration and religious freedom

Toleration is widely celebrated by liberals and 'constitutes an essential element of the liberal project' (Galeotti, 2002: 23). Indeed, some believe that toleration is *the* fundamental value of liberalism. For example, Chandran Kukathas claims that a 'society or community is a liberal one if, or to the extent that, it is tolerant' (2003: 23). Although the complex roots of toleration pre-date the modern liberal tradition, by the end of the eighteenth century a distinctively liberal conception of toleration had taken shape. Three lines of thought fed into this conception. First is an appreciation of the importance of toleration for social peace. This was to emerge falteringly during the aftermath of the Reformation and the subsequent wars of religion. Second is a principle of respect for religious conscience, which first flowered during the seventeenth and eighteenth centuries, and especially in the writings of some Protestant dissenters. Third is the doctrine of the separation of church and state. This eventually became established as the most viable way to resolve the struggle between political and ecclesiastical authorities that had been unleashed by the Reformation. Taken together, these three strands form the core of a liberal conception of political toleration, in which political stability is secured by removing religious commitments from politics and public contestation, and instead containing them within a private sphere.

During the sixteenth and seventeenth centuries, religious wars were fought across Europe, and Protestant reformers quickly proved themselves to be as adept at persecuting heretics as the Catholic Church. Toleration emerged as a pragmatic solution to the problem of religious conflict. Etymologically, toleration derives from the Latin *tolerare*, which means to bear or to endure, and respite from combat was established by convincing each side to put up with their theological and political rivals. In its earliest guise, toleration required that the warring parties give up their demands to use state power to compel adherence to a particular religious doctrine. Often this was a reluctant gesture on the part of warring parties, and as one historian notes, toleration for the sake of securing peace became 'a retreat to the next best thing, a last resort for those who often still hated one another but found it impossible to go on fighting any more' (Butterfield, quoted in Walsham, 2006: 4).

Some contemporary liberals have extended this rationale for toleration to formulate a general theory of *modus vivendi* liberalism. According to this view, toleration (and by extension, liberalism) is about securing peaceful coexistence in the absence of shared principles. As one proponent describes it, this Hobbesian form of liberalism 'has no truck with the notion of an ideal regime' but only 'aims to find terms on which different ways of life can live well together' (Gray, 2000: 6). The social peace rationale for toleration strikes many as being unsatisfactory and incomplete. For instance, one historian of toleration points out that toleration for the sake of 'political expediency . . . unaccompanied by a genuine belief in and commitment to toleration as something inherently good and valuable, was not enough to bring about a permanent peaceful coexistence between hostile religious confessions in Reformation Europe' (Zagorin, 2003: 12). One reason why toleration for the sake of social peace is not enough is that pragmatic compromises were often unstable. For instance, although the Edict of Nantes (1598) established Catholic toleration of Huguenots and put a temporary end to the bloodshed in France, persecution of the Protestant minority was revived during the seventeenth century, and in 1685 the Edict was revoked, forcing the Huguenots to seek refuge elsewhere. Another reason why toleration for the sake of social peace is inadequate is that this rationale for toleration is compatible with intolerance of religious minorities. For example, the Treaty of Westphalia (1648), which ended the wars of religion in continental Europe, was based on the principle *cuius region, eius religio* ('whose realm, his religion') and did not preclude the suppression of internal heresy.

The second strand of thought that was to shape the liberal ideal of toleration did indeed nourish a 'commitment to toleration as something inherently good and valuable'. This strand connected the case for toleration to the freedom to dissent from orthodox or established religion, which was a passionate cause of many radicals during the seventeenth century. Although similar arguments for religious toleration were also canvassed in Europe – for instance by Baruch Spinoza (1632–77) and Pierre Bayle (1647–1706) – it was in England and amongst the American colonists that these arguments gained their strongest foothold. Three figures in particular are worth picking out: John Milton (1608–74), Roger Williams (ca. 1604–83) and John Locke.

Milton was an English poet who composed a number of tracts on toleration. The most famous of these was his *Areopagitica* (1644), which opposed a recent Parliamentary order requiring printed materials to be approved and licensed prior to publication. This order reinstated government control over printing, which had been suspended following the abolition of the King's Star Chamber in 1641. During this brief interlude of press freedom, pamphleteering had flourished, often attracting vigorous controversy, such as that which surrounded Milton's own tract on divorce. In *Areopagitica* Milton drew attention to the benefits of intellectual contestation, celebrated England's fleeting moment of liberty and argued that censorship hindered the revelation of truth:

> And though all the winds of doctrine were let loose to play upon the earth, so Truth be in the field, we do injuriously by licensing and prohibiting, to misdoubt her strength. Let her and Falsehood grapple; who ever knew Truth put to the worse, in a free and open encounter?
>
> (1959: 561–2)

For Milton, pre-publication censorship was objectionable not only because it frustrated intellectual discovery, but also because it undermined an individual's ability to interpret religious truth for himself and to share his beliefs with the world.

Williams also emphasised the importance of an individual being free to interpret religious truth on his own terms, and published *The Bloody Tenent of Persecution* in the same year that Milton composed *Areopagitica*. Born in England, Williams left for America with the Puritans and eventually founded a colony at Rhode Island, after being banished from Massachusetts (the Puritans, having escaped persecution in England, had quickly established a theocracy in which orthodoxy was imposed and dissent suppressed). In the course of arguing that religious persecution assaults our dignity and is a kind of 'soul or spiritual rape' (2001: 110), Williams developed a sensitive account of the primacy and fragility of individual conscience:

> I acknowledge that to molest any person, Jew or Gentile, for either professing doctrine, or practicing worship merely religious or spiritual, it is to persecute him; and such a person, whatever his doctrine or practice be, true or false, suffers persecution for conscience.
>
> (2001: 33)

Because conscience is a faculty shared by everyone, Williams's case for religious freedom had a wider scope than Milton's. Although Milton supported toleration in the case of 'neighbouring differences', he did not extend this to 'Popery, and open superstition' (1959: 565). Meanwhile, and unlike many other Protestant defenders of religious freedom in the seventeenth century, Williams did not limit freedom of conscience to the different branches of Protestantism. Catholics, as well as non-Christians, should enjoy freedom of conscience, provided they give good assurances of 'civil obedience to the civil state' (Williams, 2001: 124). One historian concludes that Williams's *Bloody Tenent* 'represents the broadest kind of tolerationist thinking to be found in English radical religious culture of the period' (Marotti, 2009: 68).

Locke's *A Letter Concerning Toleration* was published (anonymously) in 1689 and written during his exile in the Netherlands between 1683 and 1688. Locke was an associate of the Earl of Shaftesbury, a leading figure in the Parliamentary opposition during the Exclusion Crisis. Shaftesbury and his 'Whigs' were mindful of the growing absolutism in France and feared the prospect of the Catholic Duke of York succeeding to the throne, which they believed would jeopardise the power of Parliament and lead to greater restraints on religious conscience. Restoration England had already witnessed attacks on religious freedom, and the 'Clarendon Code' of the 1660s had seriously disadvantaged non-Anglicans and gone a considerable distance towards promoting religious uniformity. In the *Letter*, Locke argued that religious coercion was irrational, because religious belief is not subject to the will and cannot be compelled. Further, he argued that governments have no grounds for imposing penalties to ensure religious orthodoxy and are not responsible for the religious beliefs of their subjects:

> care of souls cannot belong to the civil ruler, because his power consists wholly in compulsion. But true and saving religion consists in an inward conviction of the mind; without it, nothing has value in the eyes of God. Such is the nature of the human understanding that it cannot be compelled by any external force. You may take away people's goods, imprison them, even inflict physical torture on their bodies, but you will not achieve anything if what you are trying to do by this punishment is change the judgement of their minds about things.
>
> (2010: 8)

Although Locke's theory provided for a wide degree of religious freedom, he limited toleration in three ways. First, he did not require that the government tolerate otherwise unlawful religious practices, simply because they were religious. Second, he denied toleration to Catholics, because their allegiance to a foreign sovereign (the pope) was a danger to civil authority. Third, he also denied toleration to atheists, on the grounds that '[n]either the faith of the atheist nor his agreement nor his oath can be firm and sacrosanct' and these 'are the bonds of human society' (Locke, 2010: 37).

In Milton, Williams and Locke we find three powerful and distinctive arguments for tolerating religious dissent, even if Milton and Locke failed to appreciate some of the implications of their views. These arguments were to be taken up again by later liberals. For instance, during the nineteenth century Mill was to extend Milton's argument that freedom of speech supports the pursuit of truth. Similarly, the connection that Williams drew between the case for freedom of religious conscience and a principle of respect for the dignity of individuals was to be echoed in the subsequent arguments of Kant and Rawls (see Nussbaum, 2008: 55–8). Meanwhile, Locke grounded his case for toleration on a careful distinction between the scope of civil and religious authorities. It was this aspect of his argument that was to influence the third strand of thought against which the liberal ideal of toleration took shape.

In his *Letter*, Locke laid particular emphasis on the need to distinguish 'political and religious matters' and to 'properly define the boundary between church and commonwealth' (2010: 6). According to him, whilst the state is concerned with temporal matters and the welfare of society, churches are voluntary associations concerned with the spiritual welfare of their members. Neither is entitled to impose religious truth coercively, since this is a matter of individual conscience. The distinction Locke draws between civil and religious jurisdictions is an early version of the doctrine of the separation of church and state, which contains two principles. First, that the state must not promote any version of religion as 'orthodox', and second, that the state must not dictate the terms of religious truth to religious believers themselves.

Perhaps the best-known version of this doctrine is supplied by the First Amendment to the US Constitution, which was part of the Bill of Rights, ratified in 1791. Amongst other things, the First Amendment insists that 'Congress shall make no law respecting an establishment of religion, or prohibiting the free exercise thereof'. The 'free exercise' and 'establishment' clauses gave legal protection to religious freedom and ruled out an established or national church. Like Locke's *Letter*, the First Amendment combined the distinction between civil and religious jurisdictions with an egalitarian reading of the doctrine of natural rights. In Locke's case, toleration of religious dissent (free exercise) was required so that religious minorities were granted 'the rights that other citizens have been granted' (2010: 40). The establishment clause goes further, connecting the idea of equal rights to the case against an established church. This move had been foreshadowed by the *Virginia Statute for Religious Freedom* (1777), which later became the *Virginia Act for Establishing Religious Freedom* (1786). Drafted by Thomas Jefferson (1743–1826), it declared

> that to compel a man to furnish contributions of money for the pro-
> pagation of opinions which he disbelieves is sinful and tyrannical; that
> even the forcing him to support this or that teacher of his own religious
> persuasion is depriving him of the comfortable liberty of giving his con-
> tributions to the particular pastor, whose morals he would make his
> pattern ... Be it enacted by General Assembly that no man shall be

compelled to frequent or support any religious worship, place, or ministry whatsoever, nor shall be enforced, restrained, molested, or burthened in his body or goods, nor shall otherwise suffer on account of his religious opinions or belief, but that all men shall be free to profess, and by argument to maintain, their opinions in matters of Religion, and that the same shall in no wise diminish, enlarge or affect their civil capacities.

(Jefferson, quoted in Sargent, 1997: 69–70)

The ideological context from which the Bill of Rights sprang makes it clear that the intention was to go beyond merely permitting expressions of religious dissent, and was rather to institute something that we would now recognise as secular equality (Nussbaum, 2008: 72–114).

Incorporating a right to religious freedom transformed the practice of toleration. There is a sense in which a constitutional guarantee of religious freedom surpassed the idea of toleration, because it removed the possibility of intolerance. Thomas Paine, for example, believed that in establishing 'universal rights of conscience', the French *Declaration of the Rights of Man and of the Citizen* 'hath abolished or renounced toleration, and intoleration also' (1989: 94). However, another way to interpret a right to religious conscience is as a 'generalization of the ideal of toleration' that 'made possible the notion of the religiously neutral secular state' (Galeotti, 2002: 26). This is an aspect of the separation of church and state that recent philosophical formulations of liberalism have refined. An idea widely endorsed by contemporary liberals is that the liberal state should be 'neutral', which means that 'the state should not reward or penalize particular conceptions of the good life [e.g. ethical and religious traditions] but, rather, should provide a neutral framework within which different and potentially conflicting conceptions of the good can be pursued' (Kymlicka, 1989: 883).

Democracy and constitutions

Despite the preponderance of the compound noun liberal democracy, liberalism does not entail democracy and liberal ideology does not contain a fully fleshed-out theory of democracy. Indeed, despite their emphasis on government by consent, many of the early liberals are best described as ambivalent democrats. Often, liberal reluctance about democracy stemmed from a worry that democratic populism might jeopardise freedom and individuality, as suggested by Tocqueville's 'tyranny of the majority'. In some cases, such as Mill's, enthusiasm for democracy was also tempered by an elitist streak, and a fear that incorporating uneducated voters as political equals might be destabilising or even dangerous. By the end of the nineteenth century, however, democracy had become more firmly established in the liberal imagination, and a distinctively liberal justification for democratic self-government had begun to take root. This can be seen, for example, in Hobhouse's pamphlet *Government by the People* (1910), written for the People's Suffrage Foundation. Here, he concluded that democracy 'is an experiment worth making in a world where no alternative holds out equal hopes of social progress' (1994: 135). The value of democracy, on Hobhouse's account, is not intrinsic but instrumental. In particular, he argues that popular representation 'is the natural guardian of popular rights' and part of 'a much more comprehensive effort towards liberty' (1994: 131). Subsequent liberals have favoured democracy for similar reasons. Generally, liberals are distrustful of direct citizen participation in self-government, and instead prefer a theory of representative democracy, in which political office is distributed by regular elections. A great advantage of representative democracy, for liberalism, is that it protects the interests of individuals by ensuring that government happens in public and by allowing for the expression of a diversity of views.

The liberal theory of government may be ambivalent about democracy, but it is more strongly committed to constitutionalism. Constitutions ensure that government is limited and protect the rights and freedoms of individuals. In addition to the separation of church and state, another important feature of liberal constitutionalism is the separation of powers. This idea, and its connection with political freedom, was given its first clear articulation by Baron de Montesquieu (1689–1755), in his *The Spirit of the Laws* (1748). The crucial thought is that if the judicial, executive and legislative branches of government are separated out, power is less likely to become concentrated. Consequently, liberty is protected and the risk of arbitrary and tyrannical rule is reduced.

Liberal sympathy for constitutionalism also resonates with the way in which liberals understand the relationship between freedom and the law. Liberalism has often been connected with a 'negative' theory of freedom, in which freedom consists in the absence of external obstructions or interference (Berlin, 1969). Someone is free, according to this view, to the extent that they are able to do the things which they want to do, without being blocked by an obstacle or another person. Law thus appears to be an impediment to freedom, since it coerces and constrains. However, law also secures 'negative' freedom, by protecting us against the interference of others (for example, the law might protect your freedom to worship by stopping another person from persecuting you). In his lecture 'The Liberty of the Ancients Compared with That of the Moderns' (1819), Benjamin Constant (1767–1830) distinguished this kind of freedom from the 'liberty of the ancients'. For the ancients, liberty was the freedom to participate in collective self-government, and to deliberate amongst peers about matters of common concern. By contrast, for the moderns, liberty came to mean civil liberty, exercised individually, in the form of being free from arbitrary arrest, to associate with whom one pleases, to choose an occupation, and to profess one's beliefs. Modern or negative freedom ties up with the liberal commitments to toleration and individuality, and is secured by protecting individuals against interference. However, it should be noted that not all liberals endorse this conception of freedom. Green, for example, defined freedom as 'a positive power or capacity of doing or enjoying something worth doing or enjoying, and that, too, something that we enjoy with others' (1986: 199). For him, freedom did not mean merely the absence of constraint, but rather meant being able to do worthwhile things in the company of others.

Contemporary liberalism

Over the last forty years there has been an astounding revival of liberal political theory, inspired in large part by John Rawls's *A Theory of Justice* (1971). Though contemporary liberalism contains a number of diverse strands, two features of the field are especially worth noting. First is liberalism's engagement with the topic of social or distributive justice. In particular, a division has opened up between liberal egalitarians and libertarians, both of whom have claimed to be the proper heirs of the liberal tradition. Second is liberalism's engagement with a number of other ideological traditions, including feminism, nationalism and multiculturalism. Just as the new and progressive strands of liberalism in the first half of the twentieth century successfully accommodated some of the demands of social democrats, so liberals continue to demonstrate the flexibility of their tradition by incorporating ideas from other ideological families.

Social or distributive justice concerns the allocation of the benefits and burdens of social cooperation, including such things as opportunities, resources and welfare. Contemporary liberals disagree both about how these should be distributed and about whether or not justice permits their redistribution. Liberal egalitarians, like John Rawls, Ronald Dworkin (1931–2013) and Brian Barry (1936–2009), believe that there is a presumptive case in favour of an equal distribution, and identify equality (or equality of opportunity) as a core value for liberalism (Dworkin, 1985). Consequently, their work is a counter-example to a longstanding left-wing objection to liberalism, which claims that liberals are indifferent about the distribution of wealth and property.

For example, Rawls's theory of 'justice as fairness' applies to the design of society's major social, economic and political institutions. This 'basic structure' will have an inevitable and pervasive effect upon how well our lives will go, shaping our chances in life and our access to resources and opportunities. Our starting position within this structure is largely a matter of luck, and 'cannot possibly be justified by an appeal to the notions of merit and desert' (1971: 8). Consequently, the basic structure should be regulated by principles of social justice, and Rawls suggests the following two principles, which he ranks in order of priority:

(a) Each person has the same indefeasible claim to a fully adequate scheme of equal basic liberties, which scheme is compatible with the same scheme of liberties for all; and

(b) Social and economic inequalities are to satisfy two conditions: first, they are to be attached to offices and positions open to all under conditions of fair equality of opportunity; and second, they are to be to the greatest benefit of the least-advantaged members of society (the difference principle).

(2001: 42–3)

Whilst the first principle has familiar liberal implications, the second is explicitly egalitarian. The outcome of Rawls's theory is that it may be permissible for society to allow some people to have larger shares of resources than others, but only if doing so really will improve the situation of the least well-off. Moreover, access to well-paid occupations must be open to everyone 'under conditions of fair equality of opportunity', which means both that job applicants should not be subject to discrimination and (more demandingly) that people with similar talents and propensities should have similar prospects of success. Amongst other things, this might require that society prevent the accumulation of wealth from distorting equality of opportunity.

Other liberal egalitarians, including Dworkin, have criticised Rawls for not being egalitarian enough. Regardless of this disagreement, liberal egalitarians agree that equality is a fundamental liberal value, and conclude that a liberal theory of social justice will be broadly egalitarian in character. Meanwhile, libertarians believe that liberal egalitarianism is a perversion of liberalism, because egalitarian theories of social justice are incompatible with freedom. Instead, they favour an account of justice in which property rights play a more prominent role and in which taxation for the purpose of redistributing wealth and opportunities is ruled out.

Robert Nozick was Rawls's best-known libertarian critic, and he developed two important objections to liberal egalitarianism in his *Anarchy, State and Utopia* (1974). First, Nozick believed that liberal egalitarians treated the goods in society like 'manna from heaven' (manna was the food miraculously supplied to the children of Israel in the wilderness). Nozick pointed out that goods are produced by people, who have presumptive rights of ownership over them. As such, they are not 'unattached' and up for redistribution in whatever way the theorist decides. Second, Nozick claimed that 'patterned' principles of justice were incompatible with freedom. He argued that preserving a liberal egalitarian distribution of resources will require that the state 'either continually interfere to stop people from transferring resources as they wish to, or continually (or periodically) interfere to take from some persons resources that others for some reason chose to transfer to them' (1974: 163).

Whilst liberal egalitarians favour an extensive welfare state, libertarians like Nozick favour a minimal – or 'nightwatchman' – state. On the libertarian view, the function of a state is to uphold property rights. The basic idea is that if people have come to acquire legitimate property rights in something, then that thing is theirs, to do with as they please. The state should not interfere in consensual acts and it is not entitled to impose taxes on free exchanges (including paid labour). The role of the state is to protect individuals against theft, fraud and other rights violations, and not to provide instruments of welfare policy, such as a public health or education system. Libertarians believe that the provision of such services should be left to the private and voluntary sectors of society.

The second distinctive feature of contemporary liberalism is the preponderance of hybrid offshoots, such as liberal feminism, liberal nationalism and liberal multiculturalism, some of which have origins that can be traced to earlier modes of liberal political thought. Like other ideologies from the past, liberalism has often neglected gender. An important exception to this was Mary Wollstonecraft's (1759–97) *A Vindication of the Rights of Woman* (1792), a foundational text for both liberal and feminist traditions. Wollstonecraft utilised the radical principles of the Enlightenment to launch a powerful critique of gender inequality in eighteenth-century Britain, objecting to the exclusion of women from the professions and the public sphere. She argued that confining women to the domestic and private realms had a disastrous effect on women's capacity to reason and induced behavioural traits that undermined female independence and autonomy. Another important early liberal feminist text was Mill's *The Subjection of Women* (1869). Mill depicted the subordinate legal status of women in nineteenth-century Britain as a form of slavery and argued against the prevailing conservative view that gender inequality was natural.

In recent years, prominent exponents of liberal feminism, such as Susan Moller Okin (1946–2004) and Martha Nussbaum (1947–), have used the conceptual vocabulary of liberalism – of rights, freedom and equality – to condemn the persistence of gender inequality in modern society. In turn, gender inequality is understood by these authors as a failure to fully implement the values of liberalism (or liberal egalitarianism). Paradigmatic liberal feminist movements include the campaign for universal suffrage and the advocacy of anti-discrimination (or equal opportunity) laws. What makes this kind of politics distinctively liberal is that it aspires to equalise the distribution of rights or opportunities by reforming legal and political arrangements. Although liberal feminism has not garnered much controversy amongst liberals, some feminists have expressed scepticism about the capacity of liberalism to absorb the deeper feminist critique of patriarchy. For example, feminist critics of liberalism (and by implication, of liberal feminism) object to its commitment to individualism (Jaggar, 1983), its inattention to issues relating to power, subordination and domination (MacKinnon, 1989) and its neglect of important virtues such as care (Held, 2006).

Over the last twenty years, a number of liberals have staked out a distinctive theory of liberal nationalism (Gans, 2003; Miller, 1995; Tamir, 1993). Proponents tend to argue for one of two things: either that nationalism or some forms of it are compatible with liberalism, and therefore that liberals can be nationalists, or that important liberal goals (including democracy, social trust and individual autonomy) depend upon the presence of a common national culture, and therefore that liberals should be nationalists. Much of the philosophical and rhetorical energies of liberal nationalists have been directed towards convincing fellow liberals to adopt a more amenable stance towards nationalism. This has proved controversial, as many liberals understand their tradition in universalist or cosmopolitan terms, incompatible with the particularism of nationalism (Nussbaum, 2002). No doubt the scepticism of contemporary liberals has been aggravated by the recent historical experience of xenophobic and chauvinistic versions of nationalism.

During the nineteenth century, many liberals took it for granted that sympathy for the national cause was part of the wider liberal project, compatible with progressive aspirations and humanitarian impulses. Paradigmatic of this is Mill, who in his *Considerations on Representative Government* (1861) argued that 'where the sentiment of nationality exists in any force, there is a *prima facie* case for uniting all members of the nationality under the same government, and a government for themselves apart' (1972: 392). An important aspect of Mill's position was his argument that shared nationality plays an important instrumental role in sustaining democratic self-government:

> Free institutions are next to impossible in a country made up of different nationalities. Among a people without fellow-feeling, especially if they read and speak different languages, the united public opinion, necessary to the working of representative government, cannot exist.
>
> (1972: 392)

Recent philosophical treatments of liberal nationalism have added further arguments to the liberal nationalist repertoire. One common strategy has been to underline the cultural significance of national memberships for individual identity or well-being. This move opens up the possibility of developing a recognisably liberal argument for national self-determination, grounded in a concern for individuals and their rights. The success of such arguments remains contested. Particularly hot flash points between critics and advocates of liberal nationalism concern its implications for difficult questions about immigration, citizenship and global justice.

Whilst recognisably liberal versions of feminism and nationalism have longstanding pedigrees, liberal multiculturalism is of a more recent vintage. Liberal multiculturalists, such as Will Kymlicka, believe that members of minority cultures are entitled to group-differentiated rights in order to allow them to preserve their distinctive identities and ways of life. Without such rights, the fear is that some cultural groups – including national minorities, like the Québécois and the Basques, as well as indigenous peoples and immigrants – might become assimilated into the majority culture. What makes Kymlicka's theory a liberal one is that it is grounded on an appeal to freedom. In his *Multicultural Citizenship* (1995), he develops the claim that 'freedom is intimately linked with and dependent on culture' (1995: 75). To support this, he points out that cultural memberships perform two important functions. First, they supply us with options about how to lead our lives. Second, they make those options meaningful by providing us with the concepts and cultural narratives that we need in order to negotiate those options. The outcome of Kymlicka's argument is that cultural memberships should be treated as a matter of justice. We have a 'right to culture' because without access to our cultural groups we would experience a diminished capacity for autonomy.

Kymlicka's theory has inspired a rich debate, both within and beyond the liberal tradition. To understand the place of liberal multiculturalism within liberal ideology, it is worth noting two objections that have originated from liberal quarters. First, Jeremy Waldron has suggested that Kymlicka is mistaken in claiming that access to a stable cultural structure is a necessary precondition for autonomy, pointing out that many people are able to lead fulfilling lives beyond the confines of their ancestral cultural groups (Waldron, 1995). If Waldron is right, then Kymlicka's liberal case for minority rights is undercut. Second, Okin has argued that cultural rights are often incompatible with gender equality, which (like autonomy) is an important liberal value (Okin, 1998). Since patriarchal practices are often deeply embedded within cultural traditions, preserving the cultural identity of some minority groups will often be contrary to the best interests of women and girls. If Okin is right, then Kymlicka's case for minority rights is incompatible with liberalism.

Conclusion

Liberalism contains a number of different strands, which can make it difficult to identify its distinctive ideological features. For example, liberals occupy a range of places on the left-to-right spectrum, and they disagree about things as varied as the nature and extent of property rights, the role and morality of the marketplace, and the legitimate scope of government. More fundamentally, they also disagree about the ultimate purposes of political association and human life. In some respects, the flexibility of liberalism represents one of its strengths, and liberals have successfully responded to shifting political circumstances through ideological innovation and the formation of hybridised variants. Notwithstanding this, this chapter has identified two recurring themes that crop up in liberal writings, and suggested that each of these captures an important aspect of liberalism as a political ideology.

First, liberals are individualists. Although liberal individualism is nourished by a range of rival intellectual sources, it is their commitment to individualism that unites liberals, and sets their tradition against ideologies that place the good of the collective above that of the individual. Amongst other things, liberal individualism supports a wariness about utopianism in politics, a general preference for piecemeal reform, and an emphasis on the idea of rights. However, the implications of individualism for liberalism are disputed. Some, like Spencer, Hayek and contemporary libertarians and neoliberals, believe that a concern for the freedom of each individual commits liberalism to the principle of *laissez faire* and to a minimal state. Others, like the new liberals and contemporary liberal egalitarians, believe that a concern for the welfare of each individual commits liberalism to principles of distributive justice and a welfare state. This disagreement is not only about the weight or priority that is allocated to individualism, but also about the ways in which individualism is understood to relate to other important values, such as freedom, equality and happiness.

Second, liberals are committed to toleration. Liberal toleration combines two important ideas: that social diversity is better than social uniformity, and that individuals should be granted a wide range of liberty in choosing how to lead their lives. As with individualism, the liberal commitment to toleration flows from a range of different intellectual sources. What makes the liberal theory of toleration distinctive is that it seeks to supply principled grounds for allowing that which we disapprove of, and that it establishes a presumptive entitlement for toleration on the part of the tolerated party. Liberal theories of toleration face two important contemporary challenges. One concerns the limits of toleration, and in particular the difficult question of deciding what behaviours and practices to tolerate. The other concerns whether or not toleration is enough for minority groups, who might be tolerated but nevertheless think it objectionable to be subject to social disapproval. The future relevance of liberalism will depend very much upon the ability of liberals to respond to these challenges, as well as their ability to develop principles of justice appropriate for a globalised economy.

Further reading

Most overviews of liberalism take an historical approach. For example, Michael Freeden's *Ideologies and Political Theory* (1996) and *Liberal Languages* (2005) contain contextually rich and nuanced studies of the key ideological developments within liberalism during the nineteenth and early twentieth centuries. A less contextual though nonetheless stimulating approach is taken by Pierre Manent in his *An Intellectual History of Liberalism* (1996), which adopts a broad view about the origins of important liberal ideas. John Gray's *Liberalism* (1986) locates liberalism's high point in the nineteenth century, and makes a lively case in favour of an individualist version of classical liberalism and against social liberalism. Anthony Arblaster provides a wide-ranging and more critical account of liberalism's development in his *The Rise and Decline of Western Liberalism* (1984). Alan Ryan's *The Making of Modern Liberalism* (2012) collects together a number of his essays about the history, key figures and philosophy of liberalism. Although most historical overviews of liberalism focus on Britain, important recent exceptions to this trend include Richard Bellamy's *Liberalism and Modern Society* (1992), which also discusses France, Germany and Italy, and James Kloppenberg's *The Virtues of Liberalism* (2000), which focuses on America. Classic, somewhat dated but still helpful accounts of the evolution of the liberal tradition include Hobhouse's *Liberalism* (1994), Guido de Ruggiero's *The History of European Liberalism* (1959) and Harold Laski's *The Rise of European Liberalism* (1936).

Philosophical overviews of liberalism often try to identify an underlying theoretical unity to the liberal tradition. Amongst contemporary liberal egalitarians, important recent attempts to do this include Ronald Dworkin's essay 'Liberalism', collected in his *A Matter of Principle* (1985), and Jeremy Waldron's essay 'Theoretical Foundations of Liberalism', collected in his *Liberal Rights* (1993). An accessible book-length account that claims to identify the core of liberal egalitarian political philosophy is Paul Kelly's *Liberalism* (2005). Meanwhile, John Gray's *Two Faces of Liberalism* (2000) defends a minimalist *modus vivendi* liberalism against the universalist ethical aspirations of liberal egalitarians. A more radical 'realist' critique of the pretensions of contemporary liberal political philosophy is advanced by critical theorist Raymond Geuss in his *Philosophy and Real Politics* (2008).

Many liberal philosophers have inspired extensive secondary literatures. An account of Locke's life can be found in Roger Woolhouse's *Locke: a biography* (2007). Helpful overviews of his political theory include John Dunn's *Locke* (2003), Richard Ashcraft's *Locke's Two Treatises of Government* (1987) and David Lloyd Thomas's *Locke on Government* (1995). Meanwhile, a thorough treatment of his theory of toleration can be found in John Marshall's *John Locke, Toleration and Early Enlightenment Culture* (2006). A lively account of Mill's life and work can be found in Richard Reeves's *John Stuart Mill: Victorian Firebrand* (2007). Useful studies of his *On Liberty* include Jonathan Riley's *Mill on Liberty* (1998) and John Gray's *Mill on Liberty: a defence* (1996). John Skorupski's *Why Read Mill Today?* (2006) contains a subtle account of the connections between Mill's political theory and his wider philosophical project.

A number of works have been published on the liberal theory of toleration. Perez Zagorin's *How the Idea of Religious Toleration Came to the West* (2003) is an accessible historical overview, whilst Catriona McKinnon's *Toleration: a critical introduction* (2006) takes a more philosophical approach. Susan Mendus's *Toleration and the Limits of Liberalism* (1989) discusses the arguments of Locke and Mill, whilst Anna Elisabetta Galeotti's *Toleration as Recognition* (2002) provides a sceptical account of liberal toleration. Many of the theoretical and practical challenges of toleration are broached in David Heyd's edition collection *Toleration: an elusive virtue* (1996). Martha Nussbaum supplies an accessible account of religious freedom in the United States in her *Liberty of Conscience* (2008).

Contemporary theories of liberalism have been developed under the shadow of John Rawls. Rawls's most important works are *A Theory of Justice* (1971) and *Political Liberalism* (1993), and his key ideas are given a relatively succinct statement in his *Justice as Fairness: a restatement* (2001). Overviews of his philosophical project abound, and accessible commentaries include Harry Brighouse's *Justice* (2005) and Jon Mandle's *Rawls's 'A Theory of Justice': an Introduction* (2009). Recent intellectual biographies of Rawls by Thomas Pogge (2007) and Samuel Freeman (2007) place his work within the relevant historical and philosophical contexts. Many of the debates that surrounded Rawls's first book are covered in Chandran Kukathas and Philip Pettit's *Rawls: 'A Theory of Justice' and its critics* (1990). Meanwhile, a comprehensive and accessible overview of the liberal–communitarian debate is contained in

Stephen Mulhall and Adam Swift's *Liberals and Communitarians* (1996), and a helpful resource on that debate is Shlomo Avineri and Avner de-Shalit's edited collection *Communitarianism and Individualism* (1992). A sophisticated treatment of the place of individualism within liberal thought is supplied by Colin Bird's *The Myth of Liberal Individualism* (1999).

Liberal theories of multiculturalism have been developed by Chandran Kukathas (*The Liberal Archipelago*, 2003), Jacob Levy (*The Multiculturalism of Fear*, 2000) and Will Kymlicka (*Multicultural Citizenship*, 1995). Brian Barry's *Culture and Equality* (2001) contains a powerful liberal egalitarian critique of multiculturalism. Useful analyses of the relationship between liberalism, feminism and multiculturalism include Cohen, Howard and Nussbaum's edited collection *Is Multiculturalism Bad for Women?* (1999), Sarah Song's *Justice, Gender and the Politics of Multiculturalism* (2007) and Ayelet Shachar's *Multicultural Jurisdictions* (2001). Liberal nationalist theories have been developed by Yael Tamir (*Liberal Nationalism*, 1993), David Miller (*On Nationality*, 1995) and Chaim Gans (*The Limits of Nationalism*, 2003).

References

Arblaster, A. (1984) *The Rise and Decline of Western Liberalism*, Oxford: Blackwell.

Ashcraft, R. (1986) *Revolutionary Politics and Locke's Two Treatises of Government*, Princeton: Princeton University Press.

—— (1987) *Locke's Two Treatises of Government*, London: Allen and Unwin.

Avineri, S. and A. de-Shalit (eds) (1992) *Communitarianism and Individualism*, Oxford: Oxford University Press.

Barry, B. (1990) 'How Not to Defend Liberal Institutions', *British Journal of Political Science*, 20 (1), pp. 1–14.

—— (2001) *Culture and Equality: An Egalitarian Critique of Multiculturalism*, Cambridge: Polity.

Bellamy, R. (1992) *Liberalism and Modern Society: A Historical Argument*, Cambridge: Polity.

Berlin, I. (1969) *Four Essays on Liberty*, Oxford: Oxford University Press.

Bird, C. (1999) *The Myth of Liberal Individualism*, Cambridge: Cambridge University Press.

Brighouse, H. (2005) *Justice*, Cambridge: Polity.

Cohen, J., M. Howard and M. Nussbaum (eds) (1999) *Is Multiculturalism Bad for Women?*, Princeton: Princeton University Press.

De Ruggiero, G. (1959) *The History of European Liberalism*, Boston: Beacon.

Dunn, J. (2003) *Locke*, Oxford: Oxford University Press.

Dworkin, R. (1977) *Taking Rights Seriously*, Cambridge: Harvard University Press.

—— (1985) *A Matter of Principle*, Cambridge: Harvard University Press.

Freeden, M. (1996) *Ideologies and Political Theory: a conceptual approach*, Oxford: Oxford University Press.

—— (2005) *Liberal Languages: ideological imaginations and twentieth century progressive thought*, Princeton: Princeton University Press.

Freeman, S. (2007) *Rawls*, London: Routledge.

Galeotti, A. E. (2002) *Toleration as Recognition*, Cambridge: Cambridge University Press.

Galston, W. (1991) *Liberal Purposes: goods, virtues and diversity in the liberal state*, Cambridge: Cambridge University Press.

—— (1995) 'Two Concepts of Liberalism', *Ethics*, 105, pp. 516–34.

Gans, C. (2003) *The Limits of Nationalism*, Cambridge: Cambridge University Press.

Geuss, R. (2008) *Philosophy and Real Politics*, Oxford: Princeton University Press.

Gray, J. (1986) *Liberalism*, Milton Keynes: Open University Press.

—— (1996) *Mill on Liberty: a defence*, London: Routledge.

—— (2000) *Two Faces of Liberalism*, Cambridge: Polity.

Green, T. H. (1986) *Lectures on the Principles of Political Obligation and Other Writings*, Cambridge: Cambridge University Press.

Harvey, D. (2005) *A Brief History of Neoliberalism*, Oxford: Oxford University Press.

Hayek, F. A. (1963) *The Constitution of Liberty*, London: Routledge and Kegan Paul.

Held, V. (2006) *The Ethics of Care*, Oxford: Oxford University Press.

Heyd, D. (ed.) (1996) *Toleration: An Elusive Virtue*, Princeton: Princeton University Press.

Hobhouse, L. T. (1994) *Liberalism and Other Writings*, Cambridge: Cambridge University Press.

Humboldt, W. (1969) *The Limits of State Action*, Cambridge: Cambridge University Press.

Jaggar, A. (1983) *Feminist Politics and Human Nature*, Maryland: Rowman and Littlefield.

Kelly, P. (2005) *Liberalism*, Cambridge: Polity.

Kloppenberg, J. (2000) *The Virtues of Liberalism*, Oxford: Oxford University Press.

Kukathas, C. (2003) *The Liberal Archipelago: a theory of diversity and freedom*, Oxford: Oxford University Press.

Kukathas, C. and P. Pettit (1990) *Rawls: 'A Theory of Justice' and its critics*, Cambridge: Polity.

Kymlicka, W. (1989) 'Liberal Individualism and Liberal Neutrality', *Ethics*, 99, pp. 883–905.

—— (1995) *Multicultural Citizenship: a liberal theory of minority rights*, Oxford: Oxford University Press.

Laski, H. (1936) *The Rise of European Liberalism*, London: Allen and Unwin.

Laslett, P. (1988) 'Introduction', in J. Locke, *Two Treatises of Government*, Cambridge: Cambridge University Press, pp 3–126.

Levy, J. (2000) *The Multiculturalism of Fear*, Oxford: Oxford University Press.

Lloyd-Thomas, D. (1995) *Locke on Government*, London: Routledge.

Locke, J. (1988) *Two Treatises of Government*, Cambridge: Cambridge University Press.

—— (2010) *A Letter Concerning Toleration*, in R. Vernon (ed.) *Locke on Toleration*, trans. Michael Silverthorne, Cambridge: Cambridge University Press, pp. 3–46.

Lukes, S. (1971) 'The Meanings of "Individualism"', *Journal of the History of Ideas*, 32 (1), pp. 45–66.

Macedo, S. (1990) *Liberal Virtues: citizenship, virtue, and community*, Oxford: Oxford University Press.

MacKinnon, C. (1989) *Toward a Feminist Theory of the State*, Harvard: Harvard University Press.

McKinnon, C. (2006) *Toleration: a critical introduction*, London: Routledge.

Macpherson, C. B. (1962) *The Political Theory of Possessive Individualism: Hobbes to Locke*, Oxford: Clarendon Press.

Mandle, J. (2009) *Rawls's 'A Theory of Justice': an introduction*, Cambridge: Cambridge University Press.

Manent, P. (1996) *An Intellectual History of Liberalism*, Princeton: Princeton University Press.

Marotti, A. F. (2009) 'The Intolerability of English Catholicism', in R. D. Sell and A. W. Johnson (eds) *Writing and Religion in England, 1558–1689*, Farnham: Ashgate, pp. 47–72.

Marshall, J. (2006) *John Locke, Toleration and Early Enlightenment Culture*, Cambridge: Cambridge University Press.

Mendus, S. (1989) *Toleration and the Limits of Liberalism*, Basingstoke: Macmillan.

Mill, J. S. (1972) *Considerations on Representative Government*, Dent: London.

—— (1985) *On Liberty*, London: Penguin.

Miller, D. (1995) *On Nationality*, Oxford: Oxford University Press.

Milton, J. (1959) 'Areopagitica', in D. Wolfe, *Complete Prose Works of John Milton*, volume two, New Haven: Yale University Press.

Mulhall, S. and A. Swift (1996) *Liberals and Communitarians: an introduction*, second edition, Oxford: Blackwell.

Nozick, R. (1974) *Anarchy, State and Utopia*, Oxford: Blackwell.

Nussbaum, M. (1999) *Sex and Social Justice*, Oxford: Oxford University Press.

—— (2002) 'Patriotism and Cosmopolitanism', in J. Cohen (ed.) *For Love of Country?*, Boston: Beacon Press, pp. 3–17.

—— (2008) *Liberty of Conscience*, New York: Basic Books.

Oakeshott, M. (1975) *Hobbes on Civil Association*, Oxford: Blackwell.

Okin, S. M. (1998) 'Feminism and Multiculturalism: some tensions', *Ethics*, 108, pp. 661–84.

Paine, T. (1989) *Political Writings*, Cambridge: Cambridge University Press.

Parekh, B. (1994) 'Superior People: the narrowness of liberalism from Mill to Rawls', *Times Literary Supplement*, 25 February 1994, pp. 11–13.

Pogge, T. (2007) *John Rawls: his life and theory of justice*, Oxford: Oxford University Press.

Rawls, J. (1971) *A Theory of Justice*, Cambridge: Harvard University Press.

—— (1993) *Political Liberalism*, New York: Columbia University Press.

—— (2001) *Justice as Fairness: a restatement*, Cambridge: Harvard University Press.

Reeves, R. (2007) *John Stuart Mill: Victorian firebrand*, London: Atlantic Books.

Riley, J. (1998) *Mill on Liberty*, London: Routledge.

Ryan, A. (2012) *The Making of Modern Liberalism*, Princeton: Princeton University Press.

Sargent, L. T. (ed.) (1997) *Political Thought in the United States: a documentary history*, New York: New York University Press.

Seglow, J. (2002) 'Mill', in A. Edwards and J. Townshend (eds) *Interpreting Modern Political Philosophy*, Basingstoke: Palgrave.

Shachar, A. (2001) *Multicultural Jurisdictions: cultural differences and women's rights*, Cambridge: Cambridge University Press.

Siedentop, L. (1979) 'Two Liberal Traditions', in A. Ryan (ed.) *The Idea of Freedom: essays in honour of Isaiah Berlin*, Oxford: Oxford University Press.

Skorupski, J. (2006) *Why Read Mill Today?*, London: Routledge.

Song, S. (2007) *Justice, Gender and the Politics of Multiculturalism*, Cambridge: Cambridge University Press.

Strauss, L. (1953) *Natural Right and History*, Chicago: University of Chicago Press.

Tamir, Y. (1993) *Liberal Nationalism*, Princeton: Princeton University Press.

Taylor, C. (1985) *Philosophy and the Human Sciences*, Cambridge: Cambridge University Press.

Vincent, A. (2010) *Modern Political Ideologies*, third edition, Oxford: Blackwell.

Waldron, J. (1993) *Liberal Rights: collected papers 1981–91*, Cambridge: Cambridge University Press.

—— (1995) 'Minority Cultures and the Cosmopolitan Alternative', in W. Kymlicka (ed.) *The Rights of Minority Cultures*, Oxford: Oxford University Press, pp. 93–121.

—— (2002) *God, Locke, and Equality: Christian Foundations in Locke's Political Thought*, Cambridge: Cambridge University Press.

Walsham, A. (2006) *Charitable Hatred: tolerance and intolerance in England, 1500–1700*, Manchester: Manchester University Press.

Walzer, M. (2004) *Politics and Passion: toward a more egalitarian liberalism*, New Haven: Yale University Press.

Williams, R. (2001) *The Bloudy Tenent of Persecution, for the cause of conscience, discussed in a conference between Truth and Peace*, Georgia: Mercia University Press.

Woolhouse, R. (2007) *Locke: a biography*, Cambridge: Cambridge University Press.

Zagorin, P. (2003) *How the Idea of Religious Toleration Came to the West*, Princeton: Princeton University Press.

Chapter 3

Conservatism

Stefan Andreasson

> Conservatism does not ask ultimate questions and hence does not give final answers. But it does remind men of the institutional prerequisites of social order.
>
> (Huntington 1957: 473)

Conservatism and change

Whether conservatism is understood as the ideological articulation of a reactionary tendency to defend establishment and social privilege or merely a prudent manifestation of risk aversion and scepticism towards grand schemes for improving society, it has coalesced into a body of thought inseparable from the question of how to manage change. As emphasised in a recent study by O'Hara (2011), conservatives do not simply reject and resist all forms of change in social, political and economic arrangements of any given society. Instead they accept that change is inevitable and have articulated a distinct approach to identifying and understanding circumstances in which change might contribute to resolving contradictions and discord in existing arrangements. In doing so, conservatives aim to aid in the preservation of institutions and practices, rather than rendering them unviable and thus tearing them asunder by rejecting any change at all. As O'Sullivan puts it in his introduction to the 'philosophy of imperfection':

> [c]onservatism as an ideology, then, is characterized in the first instance, by opposition to the idea of total or radical change, and not by the absurd idea of opposition to change as such, or by any commitment to preserving all existing institutions.
>
> (1976: 9)

Willingness on the part of conservatives to accept change where necessary must however be distinguished from accepting any change, or generously promoting it. Neither the radical reactionary nor the progressive mind-set captures the conservatives' outlook on social change. In making any decisions to alter, for instance, the basis for a monarch's authority, the scope of participation by citizens in parliamentary affairs or the extent to which private property can be taxed to provide public goods, a careful balance must be struck between a need to adjust disequilibrium in existing social arrangements and the importance of not overestimating the degree to which the status quo might be improved upon, as opposed to creating worse problems than the ones already at hand: from the French to the Russian and Chinese revolutions, history provides ample evidence of radical change to existing social arrangements producing evils in some instances far surpassing those they succeeded.

From this point of view, conservatism is not a mere negative reaction to social change, brought on in the modern era by the ideational and socio-economic transformations of, respectively, the Enlightenment and industrial revolution. Burke, for instance, supported the claims of American colonists against King George III and argued for the easing of the Penal Laws against Catholics in Ireland partly for the purpose of maintaining the British Empire. By compromise and accepting the necessity of some significant change to existing arrangements, he aimed to protect an established order against further disruption (O'Brien 1992). On this view, conservatism constitutes a positive engagement with change to mitigate its destructive potential and to preserve established ways of societies as they actually exist and wherein, in Burke's words, the living bear responsibilities not only to their own generation, and not merely contractual ones, but to those generations past and those still to come. In this emphasis on obligations transcending the individuals immediately involved in societal interactions we can perceive an early divergence within the otherwise intertwined origins of conservatism and liberalism in Britain: key conservative concepts such as social discipline, deference and corporate solidarity were ones that, according to Wolin (2001: 55), 'liberal thinkers beginning with Hobbes and Locke and continuing in the English Utilitarians were unable to generate from liberal assumptions about free, equal and consciously consenting individuals'. The idea, then, is to conserve to the extent possible, but not absolutely.

Most notably, the preference for society as it actually exists places in the conservative's mind the burden of proof for showing how the benefits of alterations to an existing order will outweigh the potential costs of doing so on those who advocate change, whether they be Jacobin revolutionaries or the social planners that Hayek expected would lead modern society to serfdom. Oakeshott (1962: 196) speaks of 'a world of fact, not poetic image . . . a world inhabited by others besides ourselves who cannot be reduced to mere reflections of our own emotions'. An existing society with all its accumulated knowledge and complexity cannot simply be judged by the standards derived from abstract theories based on *a priori* assumptions of how society ideally should function, a sentiment vividly invoked by Sir Walter Scott:

> An established system is not to be tried by those tests which may with perfect correctness be applied to a new theory. A civilized nation, long in possession of a code of law under which, with all its inconveniences, they have found a means to flourish, is not to be regarded as an infant colony on which experiments in legislation may, without much danger of presumption, be hazarded. A philosopher is not entitled to investigate such a system by those ideas which he has fixed in his own mind as the standard of possible excellence.
>
> (Quoted in O'Hara 2011: 64)

Implicit in this attitude towards change is also an 'epistemological doctrine' of conservatism (O'Hara 2011: 24). Unlike liberal and, in particular, socialist approaches to social change, conservatives are less inclined to assume that sufficient information required to successfully undertake large-scale and top-down reforms is readily available to government planners and social engineers. It is with Hayek, in the wake of World War II and the emerging Soviet challenge to liberal order in the West, and with the comprehensive reorganisation of British society by means of government planning and intervention, that the question of epistemology is brought to the centre of political analysis. While Hayek's relationship to conservatism remains complicated, there is a similar epistemological scepticism present in Burke's notion of government being inevitably 'shrouded in mystery' and later also in Oakeshott's critique of 'rationalist' social engineers.

An important distinction must also be made between what Quinton (1978) and O'Hara (2011) understand as two very different types of change: organic and artificial. The former, which the conservative would be inclined to accept, refers to change in societal arrangements that can be conceived of as bottom-up, in that it is driven by voluntary decisions made incrementally by large populations, such as the increasing acceptance in twentieth-century Britain of women's role in the work force and a multi-ethnic society. The latter refers to top-down change implemented by a small number of political leaders or planners to which a general population must, often in a relatively short period of time, simply adapt, the archetypal example of which would be the Leninist notion of a vanguard party – or a 'New Class' of experts, or technocrats – claiming for itself the right to interpret and implement the will of the people. Thus we can conceive of organic change as 'demand-driven' and artificial change as 'supply-driven' (O'Hara 2011: 74); conservatives in Britain who in recent years have attempted to legislate against the grain by, for instance, suggesting that 'major behavioural trends' such as the 'permissive society' and mass migration ought to be reversed are therefore arguably reacting against organic change and thus acting in a manner that is 'futile, wrong-headed and ultimately counterproductive' (2011: 97). The temptation to legislate against the grain finds some self-styled conservatives, including many Conservative Party politicians in the Thatcherite mould as well as neo-conservative Republicans in America, challenging rather than channelling a long-standing Anglophone conservative tradition.

The inherently sceptical attitude towards artificial change is the reason why conservatives sometimes wish to eschew the very notion that conservatism is an ideology. The (positive) definition of an ideology suggests an *a priori* set of values from which general principles and even specific societal arrangements can be derived, and on the basis of which politicians and other decision-makers ought to act through relevant institutions and by available means of persuasion in order to align society with those principles. In the case of the Enlightenment ideologies, these are principles understood to be universally applicable. Ideology thus implies positive action. Where for O'Hara (2011: 6) ideology 'mediates between philosophy and action', for MacKenzie (2003: 2) all ideologies embody accounts of reality and how it can be bettered. The argument, for those reluctant to acknowledge that conservatism is an ideology, is that conservatism does not entail or imply the derivation of specific schemes for how society ought to be organised and that it entails a negative rather than positive view of action. While, as suggested by Huntington in this chapter's epigraph, conservatism gives us an idea about what institutional arrangements are likely to ensure societal order (and, possibly, which ones will not), implying furthermore that order is a fundamental requirement for any legitimate polity, it lacks a positive vision. However, E. H. Carr noted that '[t]o denounce ideologies in general is to set up an ideology of one's own' (quoted in Drolet 2011: 15). Indeed, it is possible to derive from conservatism a general set of beliefs about social change – if any, it should be gradual – and about the virtue of some social arrangements over others, that is, those in tune with tradition rather than those aiming to reject it. Because policy prescriptions can be inferred from conservative values, just as from liberal and socialist ones, conservatism can profitably be treated as a political ideology standing alongside its main ideological competitors.

An examination of the historical origins of modern conservatism in the wake of the Enlightenment and its crowning achievement, the French Revolution, and of a conservative critique of grand schemes for social transformation based on assumptions of a melioristic character about human nature and the existence of universal values, suggests a consistent approach to change which sets conservatism apart from liberalism and socialism, its rival ideological alternatives in the modern era. If the defining features of a conservative body of political thought are to be discerned, they must be examined in comparison with, and in contrast to, the ascendant radical and progressive ideological forces of that era.

> At least five major schools of radical thought have competed [with conservatives since Burke] for public favour ...: the rationalism of the *philosophes*, the romantic emancipation of Rousseau and his allies, the utilitarianism of the Benthamites, the positivism of Comte's school, and the collectivistic materialism of Marx and other socialists.
>
> (Kirk 1995: 9)

Liberalism embraces, indeed it constitutes a core component of, the Enlightenment and its attendant belief in an ability to improve society by means of harnessing human capacity for reason, to identify and clearly state universally valid principles and rights on the basis of which an improved society can be organised – (individual) freedom and equality being pre-eminent among these. A dominant strand of socialism conceives in a teleological fashion of a perennial conflict between classes throughout history as inevitably resulting in a final revolution that transcends previously existing class-based societies, however vaguely the nature of that classless end-state may have been articulated by socialists themselves. In contrast to those promoting these two competing visions of how society could best be organised in accordance with Enlightenment values, conservatives emphasise the inherent value of existing social arrangements and the importance of ensuring that any change is gradual, with those in charge clearly cognisant of the risks involved in departing from what is tried and tested.

The anti-revolutionary sentiment

When considering conservatism not only as a body of political thought, but as an ideology with concrete implications for actual political developments across time and space, there is perhaps no other issue through which we can better perceive the conservative ideology in action than the conservative's response to revolutionary social change.

Originating in the radical challenges to established order in Europe, conservatism is for Huntington (1957: 458) 'the product of intense ideological and social conflict', where 'men are driven to conservatism by the shock of events' (470). The important role played by (the prospect of) revolution in shaping conservatism is also central to Freeman's (1980) highly critical account of Burke and his defence of the *ancien régime* in France. Huntington (1957: 470) is, however, arguing in a somewhat counterintuitive manner about the origins of the conservative mind-set when insisting that 'conservatism comes from the challenge before the theorist, not the intellectual tradition behind him', and as a consequence 'conservative thinkers of one age . . . have little influence on those of the next'. This argument jars with a general conservative reverence for tradition whereby 'one generation links with another', the necessity of which Burke so eloquently spoke of and without which '[m]en would become little better than the flies of a summer' (Burke 1986: 193).

This is, however, only a problem if one accords history unduly great determining powers over future events. Clearly the past, that is, actually lived experiences transmitted over generations, is crucial for any conservative's considerations of whether a contemporary polity is good or bad, and whether proposed change ought to be considered as promising or dangerous. But *contra* Marx's argument in *The Eighteenth Brumaire*, the history and tradition of dead generations does not, for conservatives, have to weigh like a nightmare on the minds of the living. Conservatives clearly cannot rely on the discounting of history by means of which liberals can proceed to deduce from axiomatic notions of the public good fundamental principles of how society ought to be organised. But because conservatism is inherently pragmatic in terms of the social outcomes produced by an established order, and because it also rejects deterministic conceptualisations of history that hamper flexibility in adjusting to new and unforeseen events that inevitably crop up, the conservative is as capable intellectually to adapt to events as they occur as he is to recognise the merits in what has gone before. Following Tacitus, custom does adapt itself to experience.

The revolutionary vision stands in sharp contrast to the conservative sentiment, and is indeed its anti-thesis. Before descending into a Reign of Terror, the French Revolution proclaimed the universal Rights of Man and a future to be defined by liberty, equality and fraternity. A new world order was to be ushered in, so complete in its rupture with the *ancien régime* that even a new way of keeping time had to be introduced, whereby the Gregorian calendar was replaced by a new Republican one. The supposed *tabula rasa* created by revolution and regicide was designated Year One (later echoed in Pol Pot's Year Zero, marking the Khmer Rouge takeover of Cambodia) to symbolise a total rejection of the past. Thus Jacobinism and the French Revolution were the very embodiment of radicalism as a means to transformation, a persistent theme echoed in many revolutions since. Half a century later, Marx and Engels's *Communist Manifesto* called on the working men of all countries to unite in overturning the history of all civilisation, by transcending past epochs of class struggle between freeman and slave, patrician and plebeian, lord and serf, a struggle later conceived of as one between capitalists and workers, to usher in the inevitable and classless society of communism by means of a revolution to end all revolutions. Thus, the major social and political ruptures of the modern era, beginning with the French Revolution in the late eighteenth century (if not earlier with the sixteenth-century Protestant Reformation), transitioning through the abortive European revolutions of the nineteenth century and culminating in the Russian revolution of the early twentieth century, all constitute violent reactions against established order that in each case were based on radical premises and utopian aspirations.

The modern revolution is, moreover, a peculiarly Western phenomenon subsequently exported enthusiastically across the world.

> Revolutions, in the grand sense, are, as Friedrich says, 'a peculiarity of Western culture.' The great civilizations of the past – Egypt, Babylon, Persia, the Incas, Greece, Rome, China, India, the Arab world – experienced revolts, insurrections, and dynastic changes, but these did not 'constitute anything resembling the "great" revolutions of the West.' . . . More precisely, revolution is characteristic of modernization. It is one way of modernizing a traditional society . . . [and] is the ultimate expression of the modernizing outlook, the belief that it is within the power of man to control and change his environment . . .
>
> (Huntington 1968: 264–5)

Where revolutionaries succeeded in bringing down existing order, radicalism habitually gave birth to terrors greater than those which revolutionaries sought to end. As Madame Guillotine terminated a moment of volatile freedom in France, so did Stalin's Great Terror (an intensification of activities begun by Lenin's secret police) end the dreams of those who had hoped that Russians could free themselves from centuries of autocracy and despotism they had hitherto endured. Similarly, revolutionary premises would later underpin nationalist movements and waves of decolonisation sweeping across the European empires in Africa and Asia. The Congo's first elected leader, Patrice Lumumba, proclaimed on the eve of independence in 1960, less than a year before his murder at the hands of Belgian and Congolese officers, the beginning of a new struggle for the Congolese, and Africans generally, that would culminate in the fulfilment of all that was aspired to in the Declaration of the Rights of Man.

Correspondingly grand proclamations, promptly betrayed, and with hindsight not feasible to begin with, were articulated by leaders across the formerly colonised world. As with previous revolutions, those who managed to cast off the yoke of European colonialism often found themselves saddled with governments and rulers every bit as oppressive as those they had previously endured. Contemplating for instance the legacies of Amin, Bokassa and Mengistu in Africa, and post-colonial leaders elsewhere similarly willing to employ violence and provoke economic ruin in pursuit of personal power, it is not difficult to argue that conditions indeed changed for the worse. At a fundamental level, psychological as much as it is socio-cultural or political, it is the sense of horror when contemplating revolutions degenerating into destruction, even nihilism, which animates the conservative aversion to radicalism and to those grand projects which promise comprehensive change and an end to the ills of contemporary society. The conservative perspective on social change does not hold that any and all change is necessarily ruinous. It is possible to improve conditions of life, but the revolutionary road will not provide deliverance. Indeed, revolution becomes for the conservative something 'unthinkable', tantamount to, in Scruton's (2001: 11) rather gruesome analogy, 'murdering a sick mother out of impatience to snatch some rumoured infant from her womb'.

The origins of conservatism

The roots of an Anglophone intellectual tradition of conservative thinking – contrasting developments in Britain and America with a more reactionary, and radical, form of conservatism emerging in Europe in response to the French Revolution as represented by Maistre and the other so-called Clerical philoso-phers, Bonald and Chateaubriand – are present already in the Elizabethan theologian Richard Hooker's late sixteenth-century magnum opus, the *Laws of Ecclesiastical Polity*. Huntington (1957: 480) suggests that in Hooker's *Laws*, written two centuries before Burke's *Reflections on the Revolution in France*, are 'delineated every significant strand of Burkean thought'. As demonstrated by Wolin (1953) and Quinton (1978), this is nevertheless a con-servative tradition most profoundly shaped by the eighteenth-century Anglo-Irish statesman Edmund Burke, most palpably by his experience of the ideational and societal transformations in Europe prompted by the Enlighten-ment and culminating in the French Revolution and the violent end to the Bourbon monarchy of Louis XVI. In this sense, Burke's *Reflections* stands as the seminal contribution to what has become an Anglophone tradition of con-servatism, the exponents of which are '[united] in identifying Edmund Burke as the conservative archetype and in assuming that the basic elements of his thought are the basic elements of conservatism' (Huntington 1957: 480). In its Burkean form, O'Sullivan (1976) describes it as a tradition broadly characterised by scepticism and pragmatism in its approach to political and social reform.

It constitutes, according to Kekes (1997a: 356), a 'via media between the dangerous extremes of Utopian [and rationalistic] politics and the [fideistic] repudiation of reason' and stands in stark contrast to the universalism and progressivism on which its rival ideologies, liberalism and socialism, are based.

While Anglophone conservatism is Burkean in its origins, it must also be recalled that this tradition contains within itself considerable variation, even within its articulation in an English context. In tying his conservative position in the *Reflections* closely to a specific time and place, Burke espoused rather excited notions of the exceptional nature of the English and their supposedly innate conservatism (and in contrast to the national character of the French, which, on his account, revolutionary fervour had debased):

> Thanks to our sullen resistance to innovation, thanks to the cold sluggishness of our national character, we still bear the stamp of our forefathers. We have not ... lost the generosity and dignity of thinking of the fourteenth century; nor as yet have we subtilized ourselves into savages. We are not the converts of Rousseau; we are not the disciples of Voltaire; Helvetius has made no progress amongst us ... We fear God; we look up with awe to kings; with affection to parliaments; with duty to magistrates; with reverence to priests; and with respect to nobility.
>
> (Burke 1986: 181–2)

The contrast between Burke's grandiloquence and Oakeshott's subtle elucidation of merely a 'conservative disposition' almost two centuries on is significant. For Oakeshott (1962: 183), conservatism is not in the end about any particular religious belief in a providential order or an organic theory of human society tied to a belief in 'a primordial propensity of human beings to sin'. Nor is it, in the English context, about an inevitable connection to Royalism and Anglicanism. Oakeshott's conservative disposition is about 'certain beliefs about the activity of governing and the instruments of government'. In its concrete manifestation it becomes a politics averse to rationalist approaches where 'to govern is to turn a private dream into a public and compulsory manner of living'. It is a vision of government as an umpire of interests in a plural society and not an imposer of uniformity, whether this is uniformity along the lines of a socialism concerned with equality in outcomes or that of a liberalism deducing a system of government from a specific set of ideal values.

> Government, then, as the conservative in this matter understands it, does not begin with another, different and better world, but with the observation of the self-government practiced even by men of passion in the conduct of their enterprises; it begins in the informal adjustments of interests to one another which are designed to release those who are apt to collide from the mutual frustration of a collision.
>
> (Oakeshott 1962: 188)

It is important to note also that key contributors to this Anglophone conservative canon, from Burke to the twentieth-century American political scientist Samuel Huntington, were not primarily philosophers, nor were they straightforwardly conservative in their political allegiances. Burke was immersed in the parliamentary politics and intrigues of his day on behalf of the Whig Party. Indeed, Burke is more appropriately thought of as a statesman, politician and orator than as a philosopher per se. Lock (1985: 1) considered Burke 'not primarily a writer or thinker, but a party politician' whose 'rhetorical genius [and] ability to generalise' was such that his *Reflections* continue to be read 'as a classic of conservative political thought'. Even Sternhell (2010: 28), a sternly critical judge of Burke and his intellectual legacy as constituting the primary obstacle to the realisation of Enlightenment ideals, supposedly begetting even the twentieth-century fascist reaction to liberal democracy, considers Burke 'one of the first great intellectuals to make a profession of politics'. Huntington considered himself a strong defender of America's explicitly liberal tradition, and his scholarship extended far beyond the realm of political philosophy into historical and empirical studies of political change, most notably his seminal study *Political Order in Changing Societies* (1968). Both Burke and Huntington are emblematic of the eclectic and empirically rooted nature of conservatism, by contrast to which a scientific theory of socialism or a Rawlsian theory of justice are in their very exposition fundamentally alien to the ways in which scholars have attempted to formulate the basic contours of conservatism and key tenets of conservative political thought.

The relationship to liberalism

To fully understand the emergence of a discernible body of conservative political thought, and a conservative ideology constituting a distinct political approach to social and political change, it is necessary to also examine the relationship between classical liberalism and conservatism and the important early linkages between the two ideologies. This remains in both the British and American contexts a very complex relationship. One reason why this relationship is often overlooked, and differences between the classical liberal and the conservative often exaggerated in political discourse, is that conservatism becomes conflated with Toryism, and liberalism, certainly in its postwar incarnation, becomes defined primarily by its emphasis on individualism and negative freedom. This tendency is in the case of liberalism exaggerated by a selective reading of Adam Smith's *The Wealth of Nations* which ignores important caveats to the abstracted individual (what in recent times comes to define the 'neo-liberal' Smith) in his earlier and less widely read *Theory of Moral Sentiments*. Hence Preece's (1980: 3) reference to Smith as the 'most commonly maligned and misrepresented of thinkers'.

Understanding the conservative tradition in Britain as merely defined by its dominant Tory elements, that is, its emphasis on organism, corporatism and collectivism combined with a defence of monarchy, makes it difficult to understand the relationship between (small-c) conservatism and a Conservative politics as championed by many in the Conservative Party since the ascent of 'Thatcherism' in the 1970s, and by the New Right with which the Thatcherite project became associated in the 1980s. Concepts like organism and corporatism are clearly discordant with the neo-liberal tendencies of the New Right. Conversely, when conservatism in America becomes defined as merely a *laissez-faire* liberalism based on an abstracted reading of Locke (and Smith), ignoring the Locke who by invocation of the 'ever judicious [Richard] Hooker' defends English medieval tradition (Preece 1980: 16), it becomes difficult to discern the fact that British and American strands of conservatism, each with a complex relationship to, and anchoring in, classical (Whig) liberalism, have more in common than is generally assumed. It is this anchoring in Whig liberalism which, for Preece, ultimately sets the 'Anglo-Saxon' nations apart from other Western societies.

On this reading of the interwoven history of 'Anglo-Saxon' liberalism and conservatism, the key historical context and ideological move out of which conservatism emerges is the desire to conserve the (Whig liberal) values and arrangements of the Glorious Revolution rather than those of the *ancien régime* and absolutist monarchy. To conserve this settlement in Britain, a proto-conservative like Burke was to some extent obliged to defend a set of classical liberal values. In fact,

> English conservatives no less than English liberals accepted the important role for Parliament established in the settlement of 1689 – in their case more because they valued continuity than because they had confidence in popular self-government.
>
> (Lakoff 1998: 441)

This places Burke closer to Locke than his liberal detractors give him credit for and remains insufficiently recognised by many conservatives in the modern American tradition who trace the values of the American republic back to a controversial and one-dimensional understanding of Locke's liberalism. In this context, Lakoff (1998: 442) argues that Burke, like Tocqueville, can best be described as a 'liberal conservative . . . leery of abstract dogmas and of all else that smacked of *l'esprit de système*'.

> In Britain, where ideas of divine right had held little sway . . . what was being conserved was the orderly institutionalization of Whig ideas of the Glorious Revolution of 1688 . . . the England which Montesquieu [for whom Burke expressed great admiration] had described as the nation *par excellence* of constitutional liberty . . . [E]ven the most Tory Duke of Wellington recommended government 'on liberal principles' and numbered *The Wealth of Nations* among his favourite books.
>
> (Preece 1980: 8)

Leading Tory thinkers of that time – Burke, the Marquis of Halifax, Lord Bolingbroke – all 'wrote in the new liberal context expressed most completely by John Locke' (Preece 1980: 9). What the exponents of this emerging conservative tradition had in common was a 'desire to reconcile liberty and authority'; they 'admired . . . the principles of the Lockean constitution' but were also 'concerned to limit its potential excesses' (Preece 1980: 10). Concerns shared by these British conservatives and Whig liberals are important, as they make it possible to understand how attempts by one ascendant grouping of modern conservatives – 'dries' in Thatcher's Conservative Party and neo-liberals in Reagan's Republican Party – to realign economic policymaking in Britain and America more closely with classical liberal principles need not be understood as a radical rejection of the status quo. That status quo was the collectivist settlement emerging out of World War II, subscribed to in Britain by both One Nation Tories and Gaitskellites, and the broad consensus in favour of the New Deal in America emerging in the wake of the Great Depression and attendant progressive policymaking following the war (during decades of Democratic domination of Congress and the White House). The aims of these modern conservatives were rather generated by a desire to rediscover classical liberal principles originally shaped in symbiosis with industrialisation and expanding capitalist power, and on which stable democracy was deemed to ultimately depend.

Zuckerman (2008), in his recent study of the history of American conservatism, is wrong to suggest that attempting to 'subvert and overturn' the New Deal legacy in America is driven by radical rather than conservative sentiments. After all, the New Deal emerged out of a modern American liberalism manifested in the work of Dewey, channelling T. H. Green and Hobhouse rather than Locke and Smith: a modern liberalism which, through Bentham, becomes 'a friend of radical rationalism' and, through Mill, 'an ally of relativist social democracy' (Preece 1980: 19). The ways in which the New Deal era transformed the meaning of liberalism in America, from a liberalism denoting its classical origin into one signifying egalitarian progressivism and even social democracy, explains why the post-war conservative project in America is considered more radical than it really is. This remains the case even if aspects of the Reaganite programme (similarly to the Thatcherite programme) were unduly influenced by the 'rationalist version of Locke's studiously complex philosophy' as represented by the French and American Enlightenment (1980: 20).

The at times close affinity between an Anglophone conservatism and strands of liberalism represented by Lakoff's 'conservative liberals' is furthermore illustrated by the Kantian notion, popularised in a rather different liberal context by Isaiah Berlin, of the 'crooked timber of humanity', which no genuine conservative would aim to straighten. It remains a complex and at times contradictory relationship, as evidenced by both Conservatives and Republicans in recent decades aiming for a radical restructuring of existing society and the socio-economic organisation on which it is based. Therefore it is also necessary to consider the question of whether Conservative Party politics following

Thatcher, and Republican Party politics following the ascent of first the Reaganites and then the neo-conservatives, can be considered legitimate heirs to the long-standing tradition of Anglophone conservatism.

Core components of conservatism

To define the nature of a conservative ideology it is necessary to confront a formidable scholarly scepticism regarding the pedigree and merits of conservatism as a coherent body of thought. This is a scepticism originating in the fact that, according to Wilson (1941: 40), conservatism is a political ideology 'weak in its statement of purpose'. Disregarding at this stage political developments specific to Britain's Conservative Party and John Stuart Mill's slight about it being the 'stupid party', it is important to note that normative accounts of conservatism, and of conservatism's standing in the pantheon of political thought, as put forth by conservatives themselves often begin on the defensive. Symptomatic of this approach is Scruton's *The Meaning of Conservatism* (2001). He notes in the very first paragraph of this widely referenced text the commonplace criticisms of conservatism as being devoid of genuine essence, core beliefs and vision. According to such criticism, conservatism constitutes instead an attitude of 'mere reaction . . . procrastination . . . [and] nostalgia.' According to Honderich (1990), the conservative is ultimately lacking in morality on account of his utter selfishness, an accusation echoed in Eccleshall's (2003: 54) claim that conservatives 'all favour a society in which certain inequalities are preserved, and in condemning purposive politics their intention is to ridicule the egalitarian ideals of their opponents'.

In response, Scruton maintains that conservatism is in fact both coherent and 'reasonable', and not merely a poor substitute for a systematic theory of politics – what Lionel Trilling (1950: ix), in reference to American conservatives, memorably dismissed as 'irritable mental gestures which seem to resemble ideas'.

> Conservatism may rarely announce itself in maxims, formulae or aims. Its essence is inarticulate, and its expression, when compelled, sceptical. But it is capable of expression, and in times of crisis, forced either by political necessity, or by the clamour for doctrine, conservatism does its best, though not always with any confidence that the words it finds will match the instinct that required them. This lack of confidence stems not from diffidence or dismay, but from an awareness of the complexity of human things, and from an attachment to values which cannot be understood with the abstract clarity of utopian theory.
>
> (Scruton 2001: 1)

This tendency to define conservatism in defensive terms, by arguing against its purported deficiencies, implies an ideology quite distinct from both liberalism and socialism. It suggests to a much greater extent a pragmatic and even tentative approach or, as Oakeshott would have it, disposition to politics and societal organisation generally. This defensiveness comes about because, arguably, conservatism lacks a 'substantive ideal', making it in Mannheim's (1953: 120) memorable phrase 'a politics without ideals' (*Wunschbilder*). In a similar vein, Huntington (1957: 457–8) suggests that '[n]o political philosopher has ever described a conservative utopia'.

For conservatives, however, avoiding the articulation of any prescribed and specific order or set of preferences that are universally applicable is not an inherent weakness. Rather it equips conservatism with a sensitivity and adaptability which, as an ideology, makes it particularly suitable to account for politics in culturally and socially diverse settings very different from those in which the Enlightenment ideologies arose and where, in a state of flux, momentous decisions are forced. Indeed, the essence of conservatism is articulated more forcefully and lucidly in times of crisis when the status quo is fundamentally challenged, as in Burke's *Reflections* and Huntington's *Social Order*, perhaps even in the cultural criticism of Scruton's *England: An Elegy*. For conservatives there is, in this sense, clarity in the inherent pragmatism of their approach to politics, which arguably provides an advantage in adapting to changing circumstances and in remaining a relevant ideological approach across a range of socio-cultural settings. Conservatism becomes particularly suitable for accommodating cultural and political diversity in ways that liberalism and, especially, socialism cannot. This is notably the case if we extend our view beyond Western societies and examine conservatism as it applies to the rapid changes that have transformed the formerly colonised world.

Postcolonial societies have in many ways remained resistant to modernisation. Despite continual attempts at transformation, they are still in many important respects characterised by traditional attributes such as deference to authority and hierarchy, the imperatives of religious duties and familial obligations and a lingering respect for traditional knowledge and ways of social and official conduct. They retain conservative principles more so than they have ever come to approximate ideals of liberal individualism, socialist collectivism or other variations on the ideological and political themes of progressivism. Thus, conservatism offers a framework for understanding and engaging with the formerly colonised world that is very different from the liberal and Marxist foundations on which Western thinking about colonialism initially depended, as in the ambivalent views on imperialism found in the works of Mill and Marx and in the unequivocal critiques by Hobson and Lenin. Compared to liberalism, with its focus on the (abstracted) rational individual and universal values, and socialism, with its reliance on an inevitable march of history towards a communist utopia in the context of a rationalist collectivism, conservatism can accommodate a wide range of polities and societal characteristics, where, for Kekes (1997b), most of the values constituting modern liberalism are actually incompatible with a genuine commitment to pluralism.

Conservatism's ability, as a pragmatic rather than universalist ideology, to accommodate diversity can be traced back to Burke, who

> defended Whig institutions in England, democratic institutions in America, autocratic institutions in France, and Hindu institutions in India. Indian institutions, he warned, must be based upon 'their own principles and not upon ours,' denouncing those ... who 'subverted the most established rights and the most ancient and most revered institutions of ages and nations'.

(Quoted in Huntington 1957: 463)

But in order to move beyond the commonly acknowledged scepticism and pragmatism, as well as a general aversion to radicalism, inherent in conservatism as a 'disposition', the hallmark components of a conservative ideology, without which we lack a clear and positive understanding of the concept itself, must be identified. In synthesising a range of existing definitions into a coherent whole, Huntington (1957) evaluates three theories of conservatism: the aristocratic, the autonomous and the situational. According to the aristocratic theory, conservatism is fundamentally a reaction to a unique historical moment, that is, the reaction of the late eighteenth-century 'feudal-aristocratic-agrarian classes' to the French Revolution. The autonomous definition does not connect conservatism to any specific class. Rather it defines conservatism as an 'autonomous system of ideas' based on 'universal values such as justice, order, balance, moderation'. The situational definition, which is the one Huntington ultimately favours, understands conservatism as originating in a 'distinct but recurring type of historical situation' in which an established order is fundamentally challenged and where conservatism 'is that system of ideas employed to justify [that] social order' (Huntington 1957: 454–5).

Lest this situational definition be understood as a justification for *any* social order, we should note that conservatives in the Anglophone tradition would and could not endorse absolutist monarchy or totalitarian rule in the way that Maistre and other proponents in Europe of a reactionary anti-liberalism could in principle justify the unfettered Divine Right of Kings and even theocracy (Maistre's ultramontanism). The origins of Burkean conservatism in a Britain shaped by the Glorious Revolution effectively rendered meaningless any such justification for absolutist rule. After all, Wood (1991: 98) described Britain as the European monarchy with 'the most republican constitution' – what Montesquieu called 'a republic disguised under the form of monarchy'. The main advantages of the situational definition are that it avoids the aristocratic theory's inability to accommodate forms of conservatism, including non-Western ones, unrelated to the historical and cultural context of the French Revolution, and also that it avoids the difficulty arising with the autonomous definition, which makes it impossible to draw a proper distinction between conservatism and its rival ideologies on the issue of universal values.

What Huntington (1957: 456) identifies as six core components of 'the conservative creed', and which he suggests also constitute the 'essential elements of Burke's theory', remain useful as a general definition of conservatism and for evaluating its relevance as an analytical approach to, and normative prescription for, a conservative politics. First, '[m]an is basically a religious animal, and religion is the foundation of civil society'. From archetypal conservatives like Burke to modern ones like Alasdair MacIntyre and Robert George, legitimate social order is sanctioned by the divine. The anchoring of society in a divine order serves to check the inevitable hubris encouraged by (Enlightenment) ideologies placing mankind at the centre, or on top, of an order which man himself ultimately sanctions. Second, '[s]ociety is the natural, organic product of slow historical growth'. When deformed by revolutionary fervour and thus divorced from the accumulated wisdom of the ages – Burke's 'bank and capital' – institutions lose legitimacy and cannot last. Likewise '[r]ight is a function of time', in the sense that rights cannot simply be proclaimed, as have been rights proudly issued forth by supranational organisations like the United Nations and the European Union. As Scruton (1991) argues, legitimate and therefore enduring rights can only be derived from the traditions and customs of a society in which people live and which they can therefore hope to properly understand and genuinely accept. For conservatives, the local and national tend always to carry more weight than do the supranational and universal. This in turn has important implications for conservatives' preferences as regards international politics and foreign policy in an increasingly globalised world, of which Britain's persistent scepticism towards the EU project and America's tendency towards unilateralism are recent examples.

Third, '[m]an is a creature of instinct and emotion as well as reason'. The excessive faith placed by Enlightenment thinkers in rationality provokes hubris and encourages reforms doomed to fail, as they are predicated on unrealistic and overly optimistic assumptions about a human nature which is inherently fallible and characterised by a propensity for evil (Kekes 1990). The fallibility of human nature is for most (Western) conservative thinkers rooted in the Christian teachings of the Fall of Man and Original Sin, reflecting a perennial pessimism about human nature that is characteristic of the conservative mind-set and evident in works as diverse as Sophocles's *Antigone*, Thucydides's *History of the Peloponnesian War*, Machiavelli's *The Prince* and *Discourses*, Montaigne's *Essays*, Bradley's *Ethical Studies* and Santayana's *Dominations and Powers* (Kekes 1997a). 'Prudence, prejudice, experience, and habit' are, according to Huntington, superior foundations on which to build a durable social order because '[t]ruth exists not in universal propositions but in concrete experiences'. Fourth, '[t]he community is superior to the individual'. Because 'rights of men derive from their duties', it is not possible to pass judgement on any social arrangement merely by asking how it conforms to a set of universal ideals. Rather it is the case that each society, each regime and each particular situation must be judged on its own merits, that is, in the context of its specific historical development and in the context of the duties and obligations, as well as rights and expectations, inherent in that historical context.

Fifth, '[e]xcept in an ultimate moral sense, men are unequal'. Social arrangements inevitably produce complex hierarchies (formal and informal) including classes, orders and groups. These are, following Michels's 'iron law' of organisations, an inevitable characteristic of all social organisations. Political philosophies that cannot accommodate inequality are unable to account for societies as they actually exist and always have existed. *Contra* Eccleshall, this recognition is not primarily about vindicating inequality but about the ability of conservatism, as an ideology and as politics, to engage with perennial features of human societies as they exist through the ages. Sixth, following Burke, '[a] presumption exists "in favour of any settled scheme of government against any untried project"'. Because, as Wilson (1941: 42) so succinctly states, '[m]an's hopes are high, but his vision is short', it is necessary to accommodate an intrinsic risk aversion in any account of social action and proposed reform of an existing order. The higher the reach of ambition and the bolder the promise of improvement, the greater the risk of failure. While arguments in favour of changing the world, as famously made by, for example, Marx in his *Theses on Feuerbach*, can certainly be justified, they must be based on realistic, as in empirically grounded and historically sensitive, expectations and not an *a priori* reasoning from which derives abstractions such as *Homo Oeconomicus* and the Rights of Man.

The language and terminology preferred by conservatives has changed, as have modern societies. The religious tenor has faded, but the conservative's concern about how to forge legitimate order in societies inhabited by fallible human beings, and where grand projects for improving life's conditions are bound to fail, remains the key concern. Thus, it is within the broad historical and ideational parameters of this Anglophone conservatism as outlined by Huntington that a diverse range of British and American conservatives attempt to articulate a conservative politics in the twenty-first century.

Conservatism today

With massive social change throughout the twentieth century, produced by technological advances, world wars, decolonisation and secularisation, came inevitably also significant changes to modern interpretations of conservative traditions, including conservative politics in Britain and America. These two strands of modern conservatism are useful for illustrating how conservatism has remained a complex and sometimes contradictory body of political thought as it has adapted to changing social and political circumstances on both sides of the Atlantic. The main challenge for British and American conservatives has revolved around how it is possible to articulate a vision for a supposedly radical reorganisation of society and the economic foundations on which it is based, that is, the neo-liberal and market-driven reforms associated with conservative politics during the Thatcher and Reagan eras onwards, while at the same time claiming the mantle of conservatism and the centuries-long tradition on which it is based. While in some instances there has been continuity in sentiments and policies, there have also been sharp breaks with traditional conservative beliefs.

Writing in the dying days of Major's Conservative government, when a terminal crisis of British conservatism was regularly predicted and which the subsequent landslide election victory of Blair's New Labour in 1997 seemed to confirm, Gamble (1995) argues that modern conservative policies since Thatcher have undermined the very pillars of a Tory hegemony which had ensured that the Conservative Party dominated British politics for most of the twentieth century. This was a Tory hegemony defined by a defence of state (which included in the post-war years its substantial provision of welfare and security), union, property and empire, its 'characteristic ideological themes' being constitutionalism, unionism, anti-socialism and imperialism (Gamble 1995: 9). For Gamble, the defeat of Heath and ascent of Thatcher resulted in a likely irreversible repudiation of this tradition, thus 'hollowing out' the very pillars of Tory England. The new Conservatives showed much less inclination than did their Tory predecessors 'to be bound by precedent and convention', turning instead established state institutions into a major target for reform. They paved the way for devolution and saw the electorally important link with Ulster Unionists crumble, thus placing the future of union under a cloud of uncertainty. Their sharp turn towards neo-liberal economic policies not only produced confrontation with the political opposition and public sector workers but caused internal rifts inside a Tory party often in the past inclined towards protectionism and the 'corporatist bias' characteristic of Macmillan's and Heath's One Nation Toryism. The already pronounced decline of empire forced the Thatcherites into a difficult position internationally, attempting a fine balance between an increasingly subordinate reliance on its crucial alliance with America and an increasingly difficult relationship with Europe.

These developments make it increasingly problematic to claim that British conservatism as defined by Conservative Party policies represents, rather than breaks with, a greater Anglophone tradition of conservatism. And it is not at all clear whether there is a way back from this break, to reconnect with that longer-standing tradition.

> The old trajectory of Conservative politics is burnt out and cannot be revived. Thatcher was right in her perception of this. What is not clear is whether her fifteen-year reign over the Party has provided the basis for an alternative tradition that can in the future restore Conservative political hegemony. The Thatcherite revolution may not have been radical enough. Many of the old institutions were assailed but few were fundamentally changed. Most are still in place and are hostile towards the Thatcherite project. But the strength of the Thatcherite legacy is that, although it is

now strongly criticized from almost every side, there are few coherent programmes for undoing it or going much beyond it.

(Gamble 1995: 24)

This verdict remains instructive to this day, not least in the sense that leading British politicians, from Blair and Brown to Cameron and Clegg – 'Thatcher's children', as Simon Jenkins famously styled them – have been seen to maintain rather than challenge the new political landscape forged during the Thatcher years. The Conservative Party's electoral fortunes have since of course revived, bringing the party back into power in 2010, albeit in coalition with Liberal Democrats. But two years into the first Conservative-led government since the New Labour victory in 1997, after which followed the longest period in modern times for Conservatives in the political wilderness, it remains difficult to see exactly how Cameron's Conservatives could effectively reconnect with that older tradition of British conservatism which in the past ensured political dominance. The fact that the Conservative Party is at present reliant on the Liberal Democrats for staying in government makes the likelihood of such a prospect even less clear and further serves to confirm the notion that post-Thatcher politics have become increasingly ideologically muddled.

In America, the recent tribulations of the Republican Party, and of the eclectic and wide-ranging forms of popular conservatism from which it draws its main electoral strength, suggest a similarly confusing situation as regards the future of a coherent and distinct American conservative ideology. Long before the upheaval caused in Republican ranks by the populist and ideologically incoherent Tea Party movement, as well as by the increasing rightward shift of Republicans in Congress which has been the primary cause of increasing political polarisation in Congress over the last decade, American conservatism had experienced a series of important shifts and transformations. President Franklin D. Roosevelt's New Deal constituted a watershed moment in American politics, heralding a generation of Democratic and progressive domination of national politics and transforming the social and political landscape in the process. The traditional conservatives of the 'pre-New Deal' era, most prominently represented in the staunch opposition to the New Deal by Senator Robert Taft of Ohio, receded from the forefront of national politics. For conservatism to make a comeback at the end of the turbulent 1960s, amidst cultural counter-revolution at home and war abroad in Vietnam, it would have to reinvent itself.

While it is important to acknowledge a shared cultural and historical heritage of British conservatives and their counterparts in the American colonies, as most notably chronicled by Kirk's *The Conservative Mind* (1995), it is also important to recognise the vast differences between the socio-cultural contexts in which a conservative ideology develops on either side of the Atlantic, thereby avoiding attempts to crudely graft a British Tory tradition onto a wholly different society in America. Beyond some similarities in sentiments, vastly different social circumstances inevitably made for divergent intellectual and, especially, political developments in Britain and America in the twentieth century. Charting the American conservatives' quest to identify a 'viable heritage' on which to draw strength intellectually and to thereby promote a plausible political ideology, Nash quotes the conservative German émigré William Schlamm on the immense task facing American conservatives in this respect:

> The specifically *American* experience of life . . . is indisputably a fierce yen for institutionalized 'progress' by utopian legislation and industrial gadgetry. Individual Americans, like Calhoun and Adams, may have known better; the American *species* (to the extent that there really is such a thing) is, of course, populist rather than conservative – and for this very forceful reason: America happens to be the only society in creation built by *conscious* human intent, . . . and developed, by Europeans *tired* of Europe's ancient commitments, and determined, . . . each in his own way, on a 'new beginning'.
>
> (Nash 2006: 291)

As such, the American soil was never suitable for a mere transplantation of the British conservative tradition.

Key events in reshaping and defining the modern American conservative mind-set, producing by the late twentieth century a near-hegemonic and ideologically heterodox neo-conservatism, are for Drolet (2011) the great social and economic changes ushered in with the New Deal in the 1930s and culminating in the counter-cultural eruption of the 1960s whereby the very foundations of America's society seemed blatantly challenged by radical progressives and socialists, civil rights activists, anti-war protestors and others advocating a subversion of the (conservative) social norms characterising the, by comparison, socially stable 1950s. Whereas conservatism up until World War II can primarily be characterised by a combination of localism and populism at home and isolationism in its approach to international affairs, coexisting rather tenuously with an East Coast big business or 'country club' conservatism (later the so-called Rockefeller Republicans), it grew increasingly radical from the 1960s onward. Indeed, when considering the post-war development of a modern American conservatism, it makes sense to think of it as 'counter-revolutionary' (Nash 2006: 295–6), given that American conservatives aimed to roll back the progressive (as opposed to classical) liberal state erected since the New Deal. In this sense, modern American conservatives share an attitude towards politics, as well as a rationale for action, that is comparable to that of Thatcherite conservatives in Britain attempting to radically reform or uproot the collectivist institutions and Keynesian intellectual underpinnings of the British post-war settlement.

However, the significant libertarian strand of politics introduced into American conservatism with Arizona Senator Barry Goldwater's Republican primary election triumph against the moderate New York Governor Nelson Rockefeller in 1964 (although followed by a disastrous presidential election in which he lost by a landslide to the incumbent Democratic President Lyndon B. Johnson), and the subsequently successful conservative populism of the Nixon and Reagan administrations, lacks any similarly powerful counterpart in British politics, even when considering the fundamental challenge to Tory tradition posed by Thatcher and her co-ideologues. The neo-conservatism of the G. W. Bush administrations of the early twenty-first century, as well as the recent impact of the Tea Party in producing a more combative conservatism amongst the grass-roots activists across the country and in Congress, further exemplify the distinctness, if also increasing ideological incoherency, of an American conservatism today. While too marginal a phenomenon to triumph electorally, conservative libertarianism remains influential, as evidenced by the significant minority of conservatives supporting Texas Congressman Ron Paul in his presidential bid during the 2011–12 Republican primary campaign.

Finally, it is also necessary to recognise an important European link to modern American conservatism, distinguishing America from a British context in which One Nation Toryism and an Oakeshottian 'disposition' exert a residual influence even into the era of the New Right. Post-war American conservatism became profoundly influenced by European émigré scholars who had fled following the demise of liberal democracy in Weimar Germany and across Europe in the interwar years. Leo Strauss is perhaps the most important among these émigrés, considering his significant intellectual and political influence on a whole generation of American 'neo-conservatives', many of them influential in the foreign policy of Republican administrations from Reagan to G. W. Bush (see Drolet 2011). The ranks of these neo-conservatives were bolstered by a Trotskyist Left disillusioned by Stalinism, and also by anti-communist Democrats like Norman Podhoretz and Jeanne Kirkpatrick, who abandoned a Democratic party they saw as increasingly weak in the face of the Soviet threat abroad and 'anti-American' cultural subversion at home. The neo-conservatives infused American conservatism with a more radical and perhaps even crypto-reactionary character. This remains a serious and frequently raised accusation which has its origins in the intellectual indebtedness of Strauss to Carl Schmitt, the prominent and later infamous scholar of Weimar and Nazi Germany. It is in post-Cold War American foreign policy that the legacy of a much popularised (and vulgarised) Straussian neo-conservatism might best be discerned. While this aspect of modern conservatism is less relevant for understanding foreign policy developments in Britain, given the decline of empire, it constitutes a vital ideological component of America's rise to superpower status in the context of the Cold War, of the triumphalism defining the post-Cold War era and of the 'War on Terror' following the terrorist attacks of 9/11. It has been said that, for neo-conservatives, 'it is always 1939', suggesting an urgency and determination in the American disposition and conduct of foreign policy that is shaped by a traumatic historical experience and has promoted a tendency towards

American 'exceptionalism' characterised by a ready reliance on military might and unilateral action in international affairs.

The ideological ambiguity that has come to characterise both British and American conservatism was perhaps an inevitable outcome of the eclectic and historically contingent nature of conservatism both as a body of political thought and as a political ideology. Even though conservatism can be considered as an approach to managing change and preserving tradition, rather than a mere vindication of inequality, it remains by comparison to liberalism and socialism hampered by a lack of a positive vision according to which the ideology can be clearly evaluated, which contributes to a sense of ideological, if not necessarily intellectual, elusiveness. Whether or not this is the case, conservatism's historical lineage is well established, its judgement on revolution and radicalism for conservatives themselves vindicated by history, and its import as an alternative understanding of modernity and social change to that offered by the triumphant ideologies of the Enlightenment undeniable.

Further reading

Three seminal contributions that are useful introductions to conservatism and the history of conservative political thought are O'Sullivan's (1976) *Conservatism*, Quinton's (1978) *The Politics of Imperfection* and the sections on 'the adaptability of conservatism' in Freeden's (1996) *Ideologies and Political Theory*. Green's (2004) *Ideologies of Conservatism* is a more recent analysis of conservatism in the twentieth century which also belongs to a core of texts anyone wishing to familiarise themselves with conservatism ought to read.

Scruton's (2001) *The Meaning of Conservatism* ranks among the most vigorous and important defences of (an Anglo-Saxon) conservatism by a self-styled conservative thinker, whereas Honderich's (1990) *Conservatism* is one of the most accessible critical accounts rejecting the essential arguments put forth by conservative thinkers. Holmes's (1996) *The Anatomy of Antiliberalism* and Sternhell's (2010) *The Anti-Enlightenment Tradition* are particularly illuminating accounts of reactionary undertones in conservative thinking, and in anti-liberal and anti-Enlightenment thought more generally. While these accounts target primarily the reactionary conservatism emerging in Europe, and therefore speak less directly to the pragmatic Anglophone tradition of conservatism outlined in this chapter, they are valuable in that they highlight key liberal concerns about a slippery slope in conservative ideology towards reaction.

Given Burke's prominence in Anglophone conservatism, his biography is central to the development of conservative political thought. O'Brien's (1992) *The Great Melody* is an unconventional and empirically rich biography providing important insights into Burke's thoughts on colonial Ireland, America and India. Lock's (1985) *Burke's Reflections on the Revolution in France* engages with Burke's thought in the context of arguably the most important, formative event in the history of conservatism as ideology – the French Revolution.

A longer perspective on conservative politics in Britain is provided in Charmley's (2008) *A History of Conservative Politics Since 1830*, and Bale's (2011) *The Conservative Party* charts the transformation of the Conservative Party from the Thatcher years to its return to power under Cameron's leadership. Jenkins's (2007) *Thatcher & Sons* is a valuable account aimed at a broader readership of the legacy of Thatcherism as manifest in the politics not only of the Conservative Party but also of New Labour. O'Hara's (2011) *Conservatism* contains a recent elaboration on the conservative worldview that can be traced from Burke to Oakeshott, emphasising the central task of conservatism as that of managing change. Özsel's (2011) edited volume, *Reflections on Conservatism*, contains an up-to-date examination of the intersection between conservative thought and politics from a pan-European perspective.

In the American context, Kirk's (1995) *The Conservative Mind* attempts to produce a 'canon' of conservative thinkers from Burke to Eliot that can ground and therefore give meaning to a conservative mind-set in the New World. Nash's (2006) *The Conservative Intellectual Movement in America* explores important developments in post-war American conservatism. These two books remain the pre-eminent contributions to the history of conservatism in America. Gottfried (2009) provides a provocative and heterodox account of a traditionalist American conservatism which has been eclipsed by the neo-conservatism characterising recent Republican administrations and post-New Deal politics more generally. Drolet's (2011) *American Neoconservatism* provides an up-to-date history of neo-conservatism, its philosophical foundations and its implications for politics beyond America's borders.

References

Bale, T. (2011) *The Conservative Party from Thatcher to Cameron*, Cambridge: Polity Press.

Burke, E. (1986 [1790]) *Reflections on the Revolution in France*, London: Penguin.

Charmley, J. (2008) *A History of Conservative Politics Since 1830*, 2nd ed., Basingstoke: Palgrave Macmillan.

Drolet, J.-F. (2011) *American Neoconservatism: The Politics and Culture of a Reactionary Idealism*, London: Hurst and Company.

Eccleshall, R. (2003) 'Conservatism', pp. 47–72 in R. Eccleshall, A. Finlayson, V. Geoghegan, M. Kenny, M. Lloyd, I. MacKenzie and R. Wilford (eds), *Political Ideologies: An Introduction*, 3rd ed., London: Routledge.

Freeden, M. (1996) *Ideologies and Political Theory*, Oxford: Clarendon Press.

Freeman, M. (1980) *Edmund Burke and the Critique of Political Radicalism*, Oxford: Blackwell.

Gamble, A. (1995) 'The Crisis of Conservatism', *New Left Review* 214: 3–25.

Gottfried, P. E. (2009) *Conservatism in America: Making Sense of the American Right*, New York: Palgrave Macmillan.

Green, E. H. H. (2004) *Ideologies of Conservatism: Conservative Political Ideas in the Twentieth Century*, Oxford: Oxford University Press.

Holmes, S. (1996) *The Anatomy of Antiliberalism*, Cambridge: Harvard University Press.

Honderich, T. (1990) *Conservatism*, London: H. Hamilton.

Huntington, S. P. (1957) 'Conservatism as an Ideology', *American Political Science Review* 51 (2): 454–73.

—— (1968) *Political Order in Changing Societies*, New Haven: Yale University Press.

Jenkins, S. (2007) *Thatcher & Sons: A Revolution in Three Acts*, London: Penguin Books.

Kekes, J. (1990) *Facing Evil*, Princeton: Princeton University Press.

—— (1997a) 'What Is Conservatism?', *Philosophy* 72 (281): 351–74.

—— (1997b) *Against Liberalism*, Ithaca: Cornell University Press.

Kirk, R. (1995) *The Conservative Mind: From Burke to Eliot*, 7th ed., Washington, DC: Regnery Publishing, Inc.

Lakoff, S. (1998) 'Tocqueville, Burke, and the Origins of Liberal Conservatism', *Review of Politics* 60 (3): 435–64.

Lock, P. F. (1985) *Burke's Reflections on the Revolution in France*, London: George Allen and Unwin.

MacKenzie, I. (2003) 'The Idea of Ideology', pp. 1–16 in R. Eccleshall, A. Finlayson, V. Geoghegan, M. Kenny, M. Lloyd, I. MacKenzie and R. Wilford (eds), *Political Ideologies: An Introduction*, 3rd ed., London: Routledge.

Mannheim, K. (1953) 'Conservative Thought', in P. Kecskemeti (ed.), *Essays on Sociology and Social Psychology*, London: Routledge and Kegan Paul.

Nash, G. H. (2006) *The Conservative Intellectual Movement in America: Since 1945*, thirtieth-anniversary ed., Wilmington: ISI Books.

Oakeshott, M. (1962) 'On Being Conservative', pp. 168–96 in *Rationalism in Politics: And Other Essays*, London: Methuen.

O'Brien, C. C. (1992) *The Great Melody: A Thematic Biography and Commented Anthology of Edmund Burke*, London: Sinclair-Stevenson.

O'Hara, K. (2011) *Conservatism*, London: Reaktion Books.

O'Sullivan, N. (1976) *Conservatism*, London: J. M. Dent and Sons.

Özsel, D. (ed.) (2011) *Reflections on Conservatism*, Newcastle: Cambridge Scholars Publishing.

Preece, R. (1980) 'The Anglo-Saxon Conservative Tradition', *Canadian Journal of Political Science* 13 (1): 3–32.

Quinton, A. (1978) *The Politics of Imperfection: The Religious and Secular Traditions of Conservative Thought in England from Hooker to Oakeshott*, London: Faber and Faber.

Scruton, R. (ed.) (1991) *Conservative Texts: An Anthology*, Basingstoke: Macmillan.

—— (2001) *The Meaning of Conservatism*, 3rd ed., Basingstoke: Palgrave.

Sternhell, Z. (2010) *The Anti-Enlightenment Tradition*, London: Yale University Press.

Trilling, L. (1950) *The Liberal Imagination: Essays on Literature and Society*, New York: Viking Press.

Wilson, F. G. (1941) 'A Theory of Conservatism', *American Political Science Review* 35 (1): 29–43.

Wolin, S. S. (1953) 'Richard Hooker and English Conservatism', *Political Research Quarterly* 6 (1): 28–47.

—— (2001) *Tocqueville Between Two Worlds: The Making of a Political and Theoretical Life*, Princeton: Princeton University Press.

Wood, G. S. (1991) *The Radicalism of the American Revolution*, New York: Vintage Books.

Zuckerman, M. (2008) 'American Conservatism in Historical Perspective', *Early American Studies: An Interdisciplinary Journal* 6 (2): 464–80.

Chapter 4

Socialism

Vincent Geoghegan

Problems of definition

The key problem in defining socialism, as with all ideologies, is that of adequately capturing similarity and difference: showing what unites socialists without minimizing the tremendous differences which separate them. Two dangers have to be avoided: 'essentialism' and 'historicism'. Essentialism reduces the richness of the socialist tradition to a few very general 'essential' or 'core' characteristics. These 'essential' characteristics will be few because once one starts eliminating those many areas over which socialists disagree, relatively little common ground will remain. For example, socialists disagree in their conceptualizations of the state: some see it as a reformable and ultimately beneficial instrument of social change, whilst others see it as a prop to capitalist society which will eventually wither away. Attitudes to the state cannot therefore form one of the 'essential' elements of socialism. Likewise, since some socialists look forward to the end of private property, whilst others consider it as a necessary feature of any conceivable society, socialism cannot be defined in terms of a 'core' theory of property. As a consequence, very few concepts or beliefs will be left to provide the definition of socialism. Those core ideas that do remain will be at a high level of generality; for the more specific one becomes, the greater the risk of resurrecting the major differences which separate socialists. Hence it is true to say, for example, that (except for some very early examples) socialists undoubtedly believe in equality, but when asked what they mean by equality, they have responded with a variety of definitions, from equality of opportunity to levelling uniformity. Thus whilst it is true to say that most socialists do believe in equality, this bald statement conceals more than it reveals. In short, the desire to find common ground uniting all socialists will often result in a rather meagre collection of very abstract 'essential' propositions.

One reaction to essentialism is a flight into 'historicism': namely the reduction of the socialist tradition to mere historical narrative, where an account is given of all those over the centuries who have called themselves, or have been deemed by others to be, socialists. A procession of utopian socialists, Marxists, Christian Socialists, social democrats, and so forth passes by leaving little sense of what has brought them all together. Difference is registered by this approach, but any attempt to isolate similarities is all but abandoned, and one is left with a mass of dates, personalities and theories.

Any attempt to provide a definition of socialism which avoids the two dangers of essentialism and historicism is inevitably going to involve an element of compromise. It is, in other words, necessary to have a certain definitional modesty. It will not be possible to produce a definition of socialism which does full justice to similarity and difference: generalities will have to be qualified (as in 'this of course does not apply to socialism brand x'); saving phrases will constantly appear (such as 'most socialists', or 'there was a tendency amongst socialists', or 'socialists by and large'). So long, therefore, as a degree of flexibility is employed, it will be possible to make general statements about socialism without assuming an underlying essential identity. The philosopher Ludwig Wittgenstein sought to capture similarity and difference with his theory of 'family resemblance'. In an analysis of what united games (board games, card games, ball games, Olympic games), he concluded that they had a series of overlapping similarities and dissimilarities, which united them into a *family* of games. Family members are not identical, but they clearly belong together: 'games form a *family* the members of which have family likenesses. Some of them have the same nose, others the same eyebrows and others again the same way of walking; and these likenesses overlap' (1972: 17). In a similar fashion, one can point to overlapping family resemblances in socialism. Wittgenstein argued that no common features could be found in his 'families'; the view taken in this chapter is that, given the compromises mentioned above, it is possible to make general statements about the nature of socialism.

What is socialism?

Let us begin at a very general level. Socialists are engaged in three funda- mental activities: they offer a critique, an alternative and a theory of transition; that is, they reveal defects in a society, suggest better arrange- ments and indicate how these improvements are to be achieved. Of course the relative importance of these activities vary amongst socialists: some, for example, have a highly developed critique of capitalism, but only a fairly cursory theory of transition; whilst others may have sophisticated analyses of both, but are unwilling to engage in advanced 'speculation' about a future socialist society.

The critique is usually grounded in some form of egalitarianism. Some early socialists were not egalitarian, some socialists have been egalitarian in theory but not in practice, others have considered equality to be a 'bourgeois' value, and yet others have defined egalitarianism so as to allow a deal of inegalitarianism. Nonetheless, most socialists have viewed capitalism, which historically has been their main target, as a fundamentally unequal economic system, concentrating wealth and power in the hands of a minority and condemning the majority to absolute, or relative, poverty and impotence. Socialists stress the unacceptable differences between life chances in such divided societies, and contrast capitalist notions of constitutional and market equality with the widespread inequality found in everyday life. They echo Anatole France's remark in *Le Lys Rouge* (1894) that 'The law in its majestic equality forbids the rich as well as the poor to sleep under bridges, to beg in the streets, and to steal bread.'

A second element usually found in the critique is a denunciation of those practices and institutions which undermine or stifle sociability and co-operation. Capitalism is criticized for the isolated, selfish individuals it encourages; too little care is shown for others, who tend to be seen either as irrelevant to one's 'private' sphere, and therefore not worthy of genuine concern, or as competitors, and as such a threat. The result is a stunted individual unable to achieve the humanity that flows only from a genuine community. Socialists agree with the words of John Donne:

> No man is an island entire of itself; every man is a piece of the continent, a part of the main; . . . any man's death diminishes me, because I am involved in mankind; and therefore never send to know for whom the bell tolls; it tolls for thee.
>
> (Donne, 1623)

A contrast is thus drawn between the rhetoric of community promoted by capitalism, with its images of togetherness and belonging, and the fact of isolation and marginality.

Third, the critique operates with a conception of freedom which makes it highly critical of liberal free-market formulations. The classical liberal definition of freedom as absence of constraint is deemed to be contradictory and shallow. It is contradictory because the liberty of the free market tends to undermine both the freedom enshrined in constitutional rights and the actual free activity of the individual: poverty flows from free markets and poor people cannot be fully free. The contrast here is between the complacent claim of the advocates of capitalism that it is a free society and the reality of a large measure of unfreedom in such a society; or as David McLellan has paraphrased an old sentiment, 'it was no use having the right of access to the Grill Room at the Ritz if you couldn't afford the bill' (1983: 145). It is shallow in that genuine liberty is not mere freedom *from* external pressures but freedom *to* develop fully as an individual among other free individuals, to be not a mere isolated unit ('free' from all that is most satisfying) but a well-rounded, fulfilled human being, delighting in the free use of all one's faculties.

Thus in their critique, socialists have echoed, and conceptualized in their own particular way, the great rallying call of the French Revolution – liberty, equality and fraternity – rendering it into equality, community and liberty. These values are deemed to be both goals to be achieved and individual attributes. A future society embodying equality, community and liberty would simply not be possible if these values were not in some sense grounded in contemporary humanity. In arguing this way, socialists deploy a variety of empirical propositions and ethical characterizations. Thus whilst very few socialists would argue that individuals are equal as regards ability, character, and so forth (i.e. possessing *identical* characteristics), most would posit a common humanity composed of human capacities, needs and entitlements. Shylock's words in the *Merchant of Venice* come to mind: 'Hath not a Jew eyes?/Hath not a Jew hands, organs, dimensions, senses, affections, passions? . . . if you prick us, do we not bleed?' The deep inequalities of capitalism are deemed to be an affront to this fundamental level of equality. Likewise, whilst acknowledging the lack of genuine community in capitalist society, socialists do argue that people are at some basic level social or sociable, or have the ability or the need to become so. Freedom too, though absent in its full form in capitalism, is held to be a deeply rooted human aspiration or need. Even socialists who are hostile to theories of human nature in which fixed or essential characteristics are assumed, and who stress the changing nature of humanity over history, would nonetheless recognize the continuing presence of the human capacity for equality, community and liberty. Socialists therefore claim that their critique isn't mere abstract aspiration, but is, rather, rooted in human experience.

The critique is, as we have seen, a far from seamless whole. Important differences exist between socialists. What is the status, for example, of the constitutional rights and values of liberal capitalist societies? Many Marxists have considered that the equality, community and liberty offered by such societies is not merely bogus, but actually harmful, because it mystifies true relationships and thereby neutralizes the revolutionary proletariat; social democrats and democratic socialists, on the other hand, have considered them to be genuine, if flawed, gains, which need to be built upon and perfected. Socialists have also weighted these values differently, some emphasizing equality and community over liberty (as in certain forms of Asian communism), others liberty over equality and community (as in Western libertarian socialism), and so on and so forth. Much of the diversity of the socialist movement arises from these differing emphases.

Tensions between the three values have been identified both within the socialist movement and by critical outsiders. Is it not unfair, it has been asked, to criticize capitalism for failing to combine equality and liberty, when any conceivable economic system is likely to have immense problems in reconciling them? Does not the drive for equality act as a drag on the development of freedom? Are the freedom and equality of the employer to count for nothing? Are not community and liberty also pulling in different directions? Is not a vital component of liberty the right to develop apart from or even against the community? When can the needs of the community legitimately override one's individual liberty? These problems have led many to reject the socialist critique – perhaps capitalism, if not an ideal system, is nonetheless the least worst! They have also prompted many socialists to conclude that some form of accommodation with capitalism is necessary.

Turning from the socialist critique to the socialist alternative, we are again confronted with great diversity. Socialists have found it impossible to function without posing an alternative but have embraced the activity with varying degrees of warmth. Thus although an outline of communist society can be reconstructed from Marx's writings, he was worried that speculation about the future would distract the working class from freely creating such a society themselves. William Morris, on the other hand, was an enthusiastic utopian who thought that it was a duty of socialists to show how and why their alternative was superior to capitalism (on this issue within Marxism see Geoghegan, 1987). A strong rationalist current in socialism has given socialists the confidence to pose alternatives. Reason is deemed to be a faculty and a norm, and therefore people can distinguish truth from error and construct a rational alternative to an unsatisfactory (and therefore irrational) reality. Socialism, like liberalism, is heir to that great period of questioning in the seventeenth and eighteenth centuries, which most graphically manifested itself in the Enlightenment and the French Revolution. Ideologies such as conservatism which argue that reality is too complex to be adequately grasped by the mere individual (let alone criticized by the individual) are rejected by socialists as false and repressive. Some socialists, it should be said, do not base their alternatives in rationalism: some have confidence in faculties such as intuition or feeling and develop non-rational (though not necessarily irrational) visions (Sorel's espousal of myth, for example, or the sex/drug-based visions of the US New Left); others look to inspired texts for their grounding, as in certain forms of Christian Socialism.

The many and varied alternatives which emerge from this process necessarily reflect the values underpinning the critique. Socialists have favoured redistribution of wealth or abolition of private property to overcome inequality; various forms of co-operative production and radical town planning have been suggested to overcome competition and isolation; and new work and education patterns have been proposed to promote the growth of free individuality. They have varied in degrees of radicalism, from reformist amelioration of existing structures to root-and-branch revolutionary transformation, or have taken a stages form of a short-term minimum programme leading in time to a more ambitious maximum programme. They have been presented in a variety of forms: manifesto commitments, five-year plans, full-scale utopian blueprints, and so on, and so on.

A recurring theme is the democratic nature of the alternatives – genuine democracy is seen as embodying the unity of equality, community and liberty: all are equal in a democracy; the democratic will is a communal will; and democracy is grounded in the free choice of the individual. In its earliest days socialism was not democratic – many utopian socialists looked to elites such as intellectuals, philanthropists and statesmen to bring about social transformation. Later socialists, especially those who feared the effect of 'bourgeois indoctrination' on the working class, have also been prepared to modify democracy with more authoritarian elements – the Marxist–Leninist organizational principle of 'democratic centralism', for example. These are exceptions to the predominant conception of socialism as democratic to its core.

Many socialists also claim that their alternatives embody the best of liberalism, liberalism at a higher stage, stripped of its association with the worst aspects of capitalism. Eduard Bernstein, for example, when discussing liberalism, asserts that 'socialism is its legitimate heir, not only in chronological sequence, but also in its spiritual qualities' (1961: 149). Socialism is seen as providing a climate in which the great, and historically revolutionary, values of liberalism can flourish, unlike capitalism, which in practice causes these values to wither. This is what Andrew Gamble means when he writes: 'As a doctrine socialism is not so much a call to reject the principles of liberalism as a claim that it alone can fulfil them' (1981: 100). There are of course socialists who are irredeemably hostile to the liberal legacy both in theory and in practice (Pol Pot and the Khmer Rouge, for example), but such intense hostility is an exception. The critique of liberalism, and the routine abuse directed towards it by socialists, should not be taken as wholesale rejection.

The criticism directed towards socialist alternatives, especially the most radical of these alternatives, recalls the types of argument long levelled at 'utopian' schemes in general: namely, that they are impractical and unrealistic. Often this is couched in terms of theories of human nature: individuals are essentially imperfect as regards intellect and morality and therefore cannot fulfil the sorts of role which socialist society demands. Thus, it is argued, individuals lack the mental ability to plan the immense complexities of a socialist society ('what cannot be known cannot be planned'; Hayek, 1988: 85), and cannot be trusted to act altruistically in such structures; whereas capitalism, by contrast, with its market converting private greed into public utility, merely requires humans, not angels. Such criticism has drawn sustenance from the sorry record of so-called socialist societies from the Soviet Union onwards, despite the claims of many that the socialist credentials of these societies were or are bogus. Friedrich Hayek, one of the most influential critics of socialism, sees the socialist project as based on ignorance and vanity, and doomed to failure due to the inevitable constraints of the real world:

> The intellectuals' vain search for a truly socialist community, which results in the idealisation of, and then disillusionment with a seemingly endless string of 'utopias'. . . should suggest that there might be something about socialism that does not conform to certain facts.
>
> (1988: 85–6)

The socialist alternative is thus damned as a factual impossibility.

Socialists clearly disagree in their critiques and alternatives, but it is over the question of transition that the greatest and most intense disagreement occurs. Whereas the alternatives do reflect the values of the critique, the theories of transition may have a more complicated relationship with such values. Many socialists believe that there is a continuity of values from critique to transition to alternative. They argue that the socialist end must be operative in the socialist means. Thus, since the goal of socialism includes peace, respect for others, truth and integrity, these qualities must be apparent in the transition to socialism. This is justified on both ethical and prudential grounds – socialists *should* incorporate their values in the transformation, and are more likely to be ultimately successful if they do so. Other socialists, however, argue that the resistances to socialism are so great in society that the transformation may require the use of methods which, in the interim, fall short of the value system of socialism. Thus the use of violence may be necessary, though the goal is a society without violence; or there may be the need for elite leadership, though a society without elites is desired. The justification is usually in terms of 'political realities': the goal will never be achieved without the use of these 'regrettable' methods – 'one cannot make an omelette without breaking eggs'. The two approaches condemn one another from these perspectives – the latter sees the former as naively idealistic, and the former views the latter as cynical and manipulative.

A wide range of transitions have been advocated over the years: amongst these are general strikes, mass insurrections and parliamentary roads, effected either singly or in concert. Underlying beliefs inform the choice of method. Social democrats have believed that it is possible, through parliament, to turn the state into the cutting edge of socialism; revolutionary Marxists assumed that ruling classes would use any means to cling to power, necessitating the use of violent revolution; ethical socialists believed that fundamental transformations had to occur in the hearts of individuals; Fabians maintained that under the guidance of experts, socialism would gradually but inevitably evolve out of capitalism. Some see the political arena as the main site of transformation, others the industrial; yet others seek to combine the two. Some look for transformation top down, *via* the state, others from the bottom up, *via* trade unions, co-operatives and other 'grass-roots' institutions. The variations and combinations make classification extraordinarily difficult.

The moral and practical problems involved in the various theories of transition are themselves multitudinous. Moral questions come spilling out. When is radical political action legitimate? Can the present generation be sacrificed for the good of future socialist citizens? Conversely, is an ethical, reformist strategy a betrayal of the interests of future generations? When is it right to break the law in pursuit of the socialist goal? When can violence be used? Questions on the effectiveness of strategy and tactics are as old as the ideology itself. Who is to be the transforming agency? The working class; a part of the working class; the working class with sections of the bourgeoisie; 'the people'; 'the nation'? What is to be the role of political parties, or of intellectuals? Can socialism be brought about in one country? Who are the enemies of socialism? Does participation in government de-radicalize socialist parties? Socialists have agonized over these questions from the start.

This therefore is a good point to move from considering these more general issues to looking at the actual history of socialism. Whilst the focus will be on the British experience, this will necessarily also involve discussion of the broader international context.

The emergence of socialism

Socialism emerged with the development of industrial capitalism at the start of the nineteenth century. It is, however, possible to identify precursors in Britain as far back as the fourteenth century which whilst not socialist, are of interest in that: they represent the earliest radical response to the growth of capitalism in Britain; later socialists have declared an affinity with them, so that understanding of the former is assisted by knowledge of the latter; and in a striking fashion, they advocate, embody or discuss beliefs and visions which lie at the heart of socialism and are thus of abiding interest. A good starting point is the Peasants' Revolt of 1381, which formed part of the complex break-up of English feudalism and the emergence of those social relations which would eventually produce industrial capitalism. In the pages of the medieval chronicler Froissart we can read of the radical cleric John Ball and his sermon to the rebellious peasantry at Blackheath on the proverb 'Whan Adam dalf and Eve span wo was thanne a gentilman', with its image of a golden age of equality before the Fall. By the sixteenth century the capitalist penetration of agriculture was such as to help stimulate a major critical work: Thomas More's *Utopia* (1516). In this work More developed a trenchant critique of private property, and speculated about an imaginary island where property was common, where distribution was based on need not wealth, and where 'with the simultaneous abolition of money and the passion for money, how many other social problems have been solved, how many crimes eradicated!' (1965: 130). In the following century, during the turbulent events of the English Civil War, Gerrard Winstanley proposed political democracy and economic communism, and set up a short-lived 'Digger' colony to put these ideas into practice. 'A man', he wrote, 'had better to have had no body than to have no food for it; therefore this restraining of the earth from brethren by brethren is oppression and bondage' (1973: 295–6).

The words 'socialism' and 'socialist' began to appear in Britain and France from the late 1820s to early 1830s. The earliest usage of the term 'socialist' was in an 1827 issue of the *Co-operative Magazine*, a journal associated with the man who many see as the founder of British socialism, Robert Owen (1771–1858). Owen's life highlights the Janus-face of Britain's industrial revolution: on one side the tremendous increase in productivity and wealth which enabled Owen, the son of a humble tradesman, to make a fortune as a manufacturer; on the other the human costs experienced by large sections of the population, which propelled Owen in the direction of philanthropy and socialism. The remedy he proposed rested on a small number of basic ideas which he stubbornly broadcast to whomever would listen, certain that he had discovered the fundamental levers of human happiness. Since for Owen character was determined by the environment, he proposed that the environment be manipulated so as to replace its negative traits with positive ones:

> any community may be arranged . . . in such a manner as, not only to withdraw vice, poverty, and, in a great degree, misery, from the world, but

also to place *every* individual under such circumstances in which he shall enjoy more permanent happiness than can be given to *any* individual under the principles which have hitherto regulated society.

(Morton, 1962: 73)

Owen attempted to put this theory into practice in a number of ventures: he commenced fairly successfully with a reform of working and living conditions at his New Lanark mill, and much less successfully in the more ambitious schemes (like the community of New Harmony in the United States) which were envisaged as prototypes for a radically new co-operative form of existence. Owen displayed both a naïve rationalism and a deeply engrained elitism. He believed that he could convert conservative governments and land-owners, not merely to his minimal quasi-philanthropic enterprises (which could have seemed attractive to ruling circles worried by labour unrest), but to his maximal socialist schemes; ideas of class struggle were alien to his nature. He saw reform in terms of expert planning from above, and saw ordinary men and women as objects of benevolence rather than as creative subjects.

From the 1830s to the 1880s the energy of the working class in Britain was mainly channelled through movements such as co-operation, trade unionism (in both of which Owen played a role) and Chartism. There was little native development in socialist theory, unless one counts the Christian Socialists, a group of predominantly middle-class reformers such as Frederick Maurice and Charles Kingsley, who considered the competition engendered by capitalism to be contrary to Christian principles. Britain did, however, become home to undoubtedly the most influential theorists in the socialist tradition, Karl Marx (1818–83) and Friedrich Engels (1820–95). In his early work (some important texts of which remained unpublished in his lifetime – particularly the *Economic and Philosophical Manuscripts* of 1844) Marx developed a critical synthesis of German Idealist philosophy (centred on the work of Hegel), British political economy (including Adam Smith and Ricardo) and utopian socialism (notably the French theorists Fourier and Saint-Simon, and Owen himself). In the resulting new theoretical system a critique of capitalism was formulated highlighting the deleterious effects of alienation, communism was posited as the alternative, and the proletariat were entrusted with bringing about the transition. In his mature work, much of it growing out of his studies in the British Museum, and part of it published in his lifetime as the first volume of *Capital* (1867), Marx produced an anatomy of capitalist society intended to demonstrate that the internal logic of the capitalist mode of production was impelling it towards its own destruction.

Engels's residence in Britain predated Marx's own arrival. In 1845 Engels had produced *The Condition of the Working Class in England*, which contained a graphic and horrifying account of the physical and mental suffering inflicted on working people by industrial capitalism. As a member of a German mill-owning family with a factory in Manchester, Engels proved a valuable collaborator for Marx in his studies of capitalism (though the precise nature of the Marx–Engels theoretical relationship is the source of scholarly controversy). Their most influential collaborative political text, the *Manifesto of the Communist Party* (1848), was confident that 'what the bourgeoisie ... produces, above all, is its own grave-diggers. Its fall and the victory of the proletariat are equally inevitable' (McLellan, 2000: 255). Engels produced a number of independent texts which developed, popularized (and some would say distorted) what was becoming known as Marxism; after Marx's death in 1883 he was of great importance in the burgeoning Marxist movement. In the wake of the failure of the 1848 revolutions, London had become a centre for exiled revolutionaries, and it was here in 1864 that a body seeking international working-class unity, the International Working Men's Association (the First International) was established; Marx's inaugural address ended with the rallying call 'Proletarians of all countries, unite!'. This organization, which lasted until 1876, provided an arena for the development and propagation of socialist ideas, strategy and tactics, and also the forum for a vicious ideological battle between Marxism and anarchism.

During the last two decades of the nineteenth century, in a climate of periodic slump and depression, Britain experienced a socialist renaissance. A number of theorists, most notably William Morris, Eleanor Marx and Edward Carpenter, sought to broaden socialists' concerns to include areas of human experience relatively neglected in earlier theorizing. William Morris (1834–96) infused his socialism with insights drawn from his experiences as an artist and art critic. Capitalism, he argued, condemned the bulk of the population to labour which is fundamentally dehumanizing; only in a socialist society could genuine creative activity be generalized. He drew on Victorian medievalist notions to compare the days before the triumph of capitalism when 'all men were more or less artists' (Morton, 1973: 61) with current conditions in which the instincts for beauty were thwarted. Lack of fulfilment was not confined to the working class, though they were the most abject victims – the aristocracy's idleness and the sham work of the bourgeoisie were part of a pervasive condition of waste and ugliness. He had no inhibitions about depicting a future socialist society, and when the American Edward Bellamy produced an influential, high-tech, centralized utopia, *Looking Backward*, Morris responded with his own *News from Nowhere* (1890), which combined respect for the supposed simplicity and creativity of the past with the political and economic arrangements of the Marxist vision of communism.

Marx's daughter, Eleanor Marx (1855–98), jointly with her lover Edward Aveling, produced work on the relationship between capitalism and the exploitation of women. Socialist feminism had emerged in the days of Owen, and included the Irish socialist William Thompson (1785–1833) and a number of women connected with the Owenite movement whom feminist historians are now beginning to bring to light: Anna Wheeler (1785–?), Fanny Wright (1795–1852) and Emma Martin (1812–51) (see Taylor, 1983). By the time Eleanor Marx and Aveling came to write 'The Woman Question from a Socialist Point of View' in 1886, the Owenite feminists had been forgotten. This article, which was a review of August Bebel's *Woman in the Past, the Present and the Future*, drew explicitly on the Marxist perspective of this work, and of Engels's *Origins of the Family, Private Property and the State*, to point to the ultimately economic basis of women's oppression in capitalism and to argue that the need for women to organize themselves was a necessary component of the struggle for human emancipation: 'both the oppressed classes, women and the immediate producers, must understand that their emancipation will come from themselves' (1886: 21). In a socialist society (which, like many of the Marxists of the time, they saw as an inevitable, certain event) men and women will communicate as equals; women will have the same educational and other opportunities as men; marriage – in its present commercial form – will disappear; sexuality will lose its burden of shame and prostitution will vanish. In short: 'there will no longer be one law for the woman and one for the man' (1886: 22).

An even more radical perspective is to be found in the work of Edward Carpenter (1844–1929). His vision of socialism is of a society in which people have overcome not merely economic and political oppression but also the sexual and emotional repression which permeates capitalist society. Carpenter, however, unlike Eleanor Marx and Aveling, who spoke of the 'natural horror' people experienced on encountering 'the effeminate man and masculine woman', displayed much greater sensitivity to the diversity of human behaviour and relationships. Carpenter's defence and advocacy of same-sex relationships (a brave act in the wake of the Oscar Wilde scandal) was one aspect of a call for individuals to regain their sensual/spiritual unity. He therefore saw such relationships (which he termed the 'Uranian spirit', emanating from 'the intermediate sex') as a type of vanguard in the struggle against capitalist society: 'the advance guard of that great movement which will one day transform the common life by substituting the bond of personal affection and compassion for the monetary, legal and other external ties which now control and confine society' (1984: 238).

This period also saw the emergence of socialist groups and parties. One might note the role of Henry Mayers Hyndman (1842–1921), whose contribution lay not in the field of theory (his work was a rather undistinguished and highly derivative mixture of Toryism and Marxism) but in the foundation in 1884 of Britain's first modern socialist party – the Social Democratic Federation. Morris, Eleanor Marx and Aveling were all sometime members (Carpenter had some association), and although splits occurred (partly due to Hyndman's high-handedness), a climate was created in which socialist theory, strategy and tactics could be discussed and, to a limited extent, put into practice.

The year 1884 also saw the foundation of the Fabian Society, an exclusive debating and propaganda group whose cultured and highly individual membership (including George Bernard Shaw, Sidney and Beatrice Webb, Annie Besant and Graham Wallas) defies easy characterization. The Fabians were committed to a policy of gradualism, which was evoked in the society's name and motto, part of which read: 'For the right moment you must wait, as Fabius did most patiently, when warring against Hannibal, though many censured his delays.' They stressed steady, piecemeal progress, a gradual replacement of capitalist institutions by socialist ones, and eschewed revolutionary, catastrophic conceptions – 'the inevitability of our scheme of gradualness', as Sidney Webb put it. Although committed to democracy, the Fabians were strongly elitist, viewing themselves as an intellectual vanguard: not a mass political party, but a powerhouse of select socialist thinkers, whose role was to inculcate sound scientific views which would promote rational action by a benign state. The second part of the Fabian motto, 'but when the time comes you must strike hard, as Fabius did, or your waiting will be vain, and fruitless', prompted George Lichtheim to remark that there was no historical record of Fabius having ever 'struck hard', and that 'malicious critics of Fabianism have been known to hint that there may have been something prophetic, or at least symbolic, in this misreading of history' (Lichtheim, 1975: 65).

The twentieth century

In the spring of 1902 Lenin (1870–1924) arrived in London for what turned out to be a year's stay. The previous year Eduard Bernstein (1850–1932) had returned to Germany after spending more than a decade in the British capital. Lenin gained no new insight from his visit – London merely confirmed his views of the stark class division of capitalism – and his commitment to revolutionary Marxism was not affected. Nadezhda Krupskaya, his wife, recalled visits to areas in which squalid and lavish housing coexisted, where Lenin 'would mutter through clenched teeth, and in English: "Two nations!"' (1970: 65). Bernstein, by contrast, was changed by his period of residence, and, although Rosa Luxemburg's remark that 'Bernstein has constructed his theory upon relationships obtaining in England. He sees the world through English spectacles' (quoted in McLellan, 1979: 23) is an exaggeration, it is true that his experience in Britain was an important factor in the development of his 'revision' of Marxism. These two men were to be significantly associated with what became the two dominant forms of socialism in the twentieth century – communism and social democracy.

Controversy has long raged on the nature of the relationship between Marx, Lenin and Stalin. Whereas anti-Marxist critics portray a malign trinity, Stalinists arrange the three into a form of revolutionary apostolic succession. Marxist anti-Bolsheviks distinguish the admirable Marx from the corrupting duo of Lenin and Stalin, whilst Bolshevik anti-Stalinists reject any continuity between the monstrous Stalin and revolutionary founders Marx and Lenin. In the case of Lenin, the debate has been fuelled by the theoretical diversity of his voluminous writings and the complexities of his political life. These complications makes it very difficult, or even impossible, to portray an essential Lenin; however, and ironically, the boldness of some of his statements and acts encourages people to do precisely this (especially when important interests are at stake). Communism (known also as Leninism or Marxism–Leninism) was developed under Stalin's aegis, and drew much of its theoretical sustenance from the events surrounding, and the ideas expressed in, Lenin's *What Is to Be Done?* (1902). In this work Lenin had argued for a tightly disciplined, exclusive party of professional revolutionaries dedicated to bringing socialist consciousness to, and helping to organize, a working class who, unaided, would merely develop sub-socialist trade-union consciousness. It was at the 1903 Second Congress of the Russian Social Democratic Labour Party (held in Brussels and London) that Lenin had eventually managed to get a majority for his conception against a much broader conception of the party developed by Martov (Lenin's group thus got the name 'Bolsheviks' or Majoritarians, while Martov's group acquired the name 'Mensheviks' or Minoritarians). This conception became the centrepiece of Stalinist communism, though used in a way Trotsky had feared in 1904:

> In the internal politics of the Party these methods lead . . . to the Party organisation 'substituting' itself for the Party, the Central Committee substituting itself for the Party organisation, and finally the dictator substituting himself for the Central Committee.
>
> (n.d.: 77)

Lenin attempted to combine discipline with democracy in the party's organizational principle of democratic centralism: relatively free discussion and criticism until a decision is taken when it becomes binding on the party. The failings in Lenin's own use of this principle were dwarfed by those of Stalin, who merely paid it lip service; in reality the democratic element was dissolved. Stalin, *via* a cult of the leader, came to dominate party, class, state and international communism. Drawing on an idea of Marx, Lenin had, prior to the 1917 October Revolution in Russia, argued for a temporary proletarian dictatorship after the revolution in order to root out residual hostile elements. He had however conceived this dictatorship as distinct from the party. Stalin's equating of the two (anticipated, let it be said, by developments while Lenin was in power) generated a party state. The party also came to control the world communist movement *via* the nominally independent Third International, enforcing the Bolshevik party model and the latest Moscow line.

The Communist Party of Great Britain, founded in 1920, for the first two decades of its existence shared the Soviet party's hostile stance on 'the parliamentary road to socialism'. The Second Congress of the International (Comintern) explicitly rejected a parliamentary road, considering that, at best, parliament was an arena for propaganda and agitation, whereas socialism, as in Russia, was to be brought about primarily by insurrectionary means.

The Communist Party of Great Britain did, over the years, attract militant elements of the working class and, in the 1930s, numbers of anti-fascists. It also had internal factions and oppositional currents. But although the party was able to foster a lively intellectual culture, including an influential and distinctive school of socialist historians (amongst others, Christopher Hill, E. P. Thompson and Eric Hobsbawm), party ideology, in the hands of Central Committee/Politburo members such as R. Palme Dutt (1896–1974), largely consisted of theoretical and policy acrobatics to shadow developments in Moscow: most dramatic of these was the rapid volte-face on fascism in the wake of the Nazi–Soviet Pact of 1939. With the death of Stalin in 1953, and in the cold light of revelations of the grim, inhuman past of Stalinism, and the continuing oppressive present (witnessed in the invasion of Hungary in 1956), democratic currents within many Western communist parties became much more prominent. In the 1970s eurocommunism represented an attempt, by principally the French, Spanish and Italian parties, to develop a strategy which took democratic, parliamentary aspirations into consideration. By the 1980s, time was running out for the world communist movement. The coming to power of Gorbachev in the Soviet Union in 1985, with his watchwords of *glasnost* (openness) and *perestroika* (restructuring), saw a final, doomed attempt to reform Soviet communism from within, which actually led to the complete unravelling of the Soviet system in the USSR and Eastern Europe. In Britain the party – whose journal *Marxism Today* had been part of a desperate search for a reinvigorated Marxism in the 1980s – shattered into hard-line splinters and a 'democratic left' residue which sought to jettison all the remaining baggage of the communist period – not least, the thoroughly compromised name 'communist'.

In conceiving of the Third International, Lenin had sought a radical replacement for the Second International (founded in 1889), which had effectively collapsed amidst the ferocious jingoism at the start of the First World War. Prior to this debacle, however, the Second International had been convulsed by the revisionist controversy: superficially a mere squabble within Marxism but in fact, amongst other things, a landmark in the development of social democracy. Eduard Bernstein, the most notable exponent of revisionism, developed a critique of a number of Marxist orthodoxies which involved rejecting revolutionary insurrectionism in favour of a gradualist, parliamentary approach. The beast capitalism, he argued, was being tamed: property-holders and shareholders were increasing, small and medium agriculture was growing, wages were rising and prosperity was becoming more widespread. All this was reflected in an increasingly complex class system which belied orthodox expectations of a polarization between a small, wealthy bourgeoisie and a massive, impoverished proletariat. At the political level, the working class was gradually, through parliament, gaining a say in the organization of society. In short, Bernstein held that a bloody revolution was not only unlikely but unnecessary. He emphasized present realities and the foreseeable future, and sought achievable, if unspectacular, advances and not some supposed, fanciful millennium. Moreover, the liberal notions of freedom with which he was imbued made political democracy valid in absolute terms, and not merely as a tactic, and further, this democracy enjoined both limitations on majorities and respect for minority rights; proletarian dictatorships were entirely ruled out: 'In this sense one might call socialism "organizing liberalism"' (Bernstein, 1961: 153–4).

Much of this type of thinking has informed modern social democracy. The British Labour Party (founded in 1900 as the Labour Representation Committee) has always been a broad church, but this very broadness, insofar as it reflects underlying social realities, has encouraged a social-democratic approach amongst its leadership. According to Ramsay MacDonald the fact that the party was called 'Labour' and not 'Socialist' indicated the parameters within which any sensible left-wing party would have to operate for the conceivable future: 'Under British conditions, a Socialist Party is the last, not the first, form of the Socialist movement in politics' (quoted in Crick, 1987: 70). It was not, of course, German revisionist Marxism but existing native reformist currents, including Fabianism, which provided the main intellectual input into British social democracy, and made most of the running.

Between the two World Wars, Labour could point to successes and failures. Its goal of using the existing rules of the parliamentary game to win power was achieved, and the Fabian Sidney Webb could enjoy cabinet office under Ramsay MacDonald. Once in power, however, the party found itself in a double bind: not only did it face the classic socialist dilemma (its state role was to stabilize society, and therefore capitalism, whilst its party role was to overcome capitalism), but this dilemma was aggravated by both its unwillingness to depart from a narrow constitutionalism and its desperate desire to be seen as a 'respectable' party. The world economic depression brought matters to a head in 1931, when Ramsay MacDonald formed a National Government with Tories and Liberals to introduce cuts in pay and unemployment benefit demanded by international bankers – but opposed by important sections of his own party. The ensuing election saw the Labour vote plummet, leaving the party in opposition for the rest of the decade.

In the period of economic prosperity between the 1950s and the early 1970s, the 'revisionism' of Anthony Crosland (1918–77) represented a highly optimistic reformulation of the social democratic case. It was a theory appropriate to a reformist practice – Labour social democracy had given up the idea that socialism was fundamentally distinct from capitalism, in favour of the notion of the interpenetration of the two. Crosland argued in *The Future of Socialism* (1956) that in Britain 'Capitalism has been reformed almost out of recognition'. There was now a caring and effective state, strong trade unions, businesses increasingly run by socially aware managers rather than bloated plutocrats, and the likelihood of continuous and largely crisis-free prosperity. The existence of private ownership of the means of production was no longer to be seen as a barrier to socialism; remaining inequalities and social injustices could be removed in the context of a mixed economy and a parliamentary democracy – thereby reconciling equality with liberty and efficiency.

With the collapse of economic prosperity in the 1970s, Croslandite optimism became unsustainable. The New Right onslaught, enshrined in government from 1979, left the Labour Party badly split. The social democrats, too, split. A resurgent left drove frightened social democrats like Shirley Williams and David Owen out of the party altogether, and into attempts, *via* the Social Democratic Party, at restructuring the centre-left in Britain; ultimately, most regrouped with their natural ideological allies in the Liberal Party. Under Neil Kinnock and John Smith, the Labour Party began a process of 'modernization', which sought to update party policy and structures, and thereby make Labour more electable. The left was marginalized, and, at the policy level, there was a good deal of implicit acceptance of elements of the Thatcherite agenda. Under Tony Blair (1953–), this overhaul of the party gathered even greater momentum. In a sustained charm offensive, reassurance was the fundamental objective. The markets were to be convinced that the party was not hostile to their interests but rather welcomed a healthy private sector. Previously supportive social groups who had defected to the Conservatives were to be won back, new bases of support acquired and bedrock support retained. To carry off this ambitious project, particularly nimble ideological and rhetorical footwork was required. Appeals to social justice rubbed shoulders with 'prudent economics', toughness on crime with toughness on the causes of crime, minimum wages with welfare reform. From the perspective of the left, and even amongst some social democrats, Blair's plans for 'New' Labour involved a clear distancing from socialism. Blair himself argued that his policies were rooted in the traditional socialist values of the party, but that modern problems require modern methods; he portrayed himself as a principled pragmatist. The most notable, sympathetic attempt to give this new direction a degree of theoretical coherence was to deem it a 'Third Way' between social democracy and neo-liberalism. It proved to be a winning strategy, with four straight electoral defeats giving way to a crushing victory in 1997.

Some, however, might wish to press the claims of an earlier and very different 'third way' – democratic socialism – distinct from both communism and social democracy. Not all commentators would accept the validity of this procedure. Anthony Wright, for example, has been sceptical about the distinction between social democracy and democratic socialism, viewing it as a largely untheorized piece of Labour left rhetoric:

> the distinction ... was not accompanied by any serious attempt to explore the theoretical pedigrees of these traditions in order to establish what distinction (if any) there actually was, apart from the fact that one sounded more muscular than the other.
>
> (1983: 24)

Bernard Crick (1987), on the other hand, subsumes much of what would be considered social democratic into a very broad category of democratic socialism, including, amongst others, Anthony Crosland, Ramsay MacDonald and Beatrice and Sidney Webb. Undoubtedly, problems do exist in maintaining this distinction. Can one describe as a democratic socialist someone who patently did not use this term as a self-description? Furthermore, how is a history to be written of a tradition that was not really aware of itself as a tradition? There will also be the inevitable boundary disputes as to where social democracy ends and democratic socialism begins. Nonetheless, the distinction is worth persevering with, for it does help to illuminate genuine points of difference in the socialist movement.

Democratic socialism can be seen as trying to steer a third way between communism and social democracy: an attempt to synthesize the best elements of the two other traditions, whilst rejecting the objectionable features of both. Democratic socialism shared with communism (or more precisely, with the Marxist core professed by the adherents of communism) a similar analysis of the basic anatomy of capitalism. Democratic socialism therefore criticized social democracy for its naïve reading of capitalism – for its blindness to entrenched interests and the inherent instability of the system. This, it argued, issued in a shallow liberal conception of the institutions and personnel of exploitation and oppression. On the other hand, democratic socialism shared with social democracy a thorough-going critique of the authoritarianism of communism – the rhetorical praise for, but actual stifling of, genuine participation at all levels of society. Democratic socialism could therefore be seen as a form of synthesis of these two strands or traditions: namely an attempt to combine a real move towards socialism with authentic democracy. In the British context this involved a combination of radical social analysis with genuine respect for the strengths of the liberal constitutional system.

Within the British Labour Party, a fierce attack on social-democratic assumptions was precipitated by the 1931 crisis. The whole episode served to confirm to democratic socialist critics just how capitalist interests could successfully protect themselves against a Labour government – a situation which called for a hard look at traditional Labour views. This stance was adopted by a body within the party called The Socialist League and in the writings of one of its leading members – Harold Laski (1893–1950). Laski's work provided a critique of both social democracy and communism. In *Democracy in Crisis* (1933), he argued that vested economic interests prevent the people from advancing from formal political control to real economic and political power. Using Marxist conceptions of state and society, Laski rejected the thesis that the great institutions of society (the courts, the press, the educational system, the armed forces, *etc.*) were genuinely neutral, as opposed to merely formally so; they were firmly in a bourgeois camp which showed every willingness to resort to whatever means were required, including violence, to protect its privileged position. Laski feared that people's understandable frustration would lead to violent revolution, resulting either in defeat and chaos or in the establishment of a Soviet-type dictatorship which would be essentially alien to British liberal-democratic traditions. Instead he hoped that a future Labour government would push through a thorough socialist transformation. However, the crisis of 1931, and the rise of fascism, had demonstrated how ruthless capitalist interests could be; and thus a radical Labour government would have to be prepared to make a significant departure from traditional constitutional practice to protect its policy: it 'would have to take vast powers, and legislate under them by ordinance and decree; it would have to suspend the classic formulae of normal opposition' (1933: 87). This theme was reiterated by another prominent Socialist Leaguer, Sir Stafford Cripps, who envisaged a Labour government placing before Parliament 'an Emergency Powers Bill to be passed through all its stages in one day' which would allow rule by ministerial orders 'incapable of challenge in the Courts or in any way except in the House of Commons' (quoted in Bealey, 1970: 137–8). The Laskian perspective graphically demonstrates both the character of and the problems inherent in British democratic socialism. A radical (in Laski's case, Marxist) analysis of capitalism is combined with a profound belief in the continuing utility and validity of liberal-democratic values and institutions; yet these latter can only be preserved by actions which would appear, to many, to be a flagrant violation of liberal democracy. Laski himself was on the National Executive of the Labour Party, and, due to the complexities of Labour Party organization and certainly not to any hegemony in the party, found himself Chairman of the Labour Party during Labour's 1945 landslide election victory. The new government rapidly found its party chairman's radical criticisms an embarrassment, resulting in Attlee's famous rebuke that 'a period of silence on your part would be welcome'!

A later expression of democratic socialism can be found in the work of Tony Benn (1925–). At the height of his influence amongst the Labour left, in the late 1970s and early 1980s, he produced a stream of essays analyzing the state of British society, and British socialism. Reflecting on his time as a cabinet minister in the 1970s, he recalled a cabinet meeting at which Anthony Crosland reluctantly accepted the humiliating terms set by the International Monetary Fund as the price for assistance; this, Benn argued, displayed the utter bankruptcy of Crosland's social-democratic vision of a humanized capitalism: 'That was the moment when social-democratic revisionism died in the Labour Party. It was killed, not by the Left but by the bankers' (1982: 33). Of particular concern for Benn was Britain's imperfect democracy: its formal inadequacy, covert checks and external constraints – all major obstacles to the achievement of socialism. Formal problems included 'the unfinished business of 1688', for example, the lack of a written constitution, the powers of the House of Lords and the residual personal prerogatives of the monarch, plus new impositions such as the growth of ministerial and prime ministerial government at the expense of parliament. To this is added the effect of powerful vested interests, the civil service, judiciary, armed and security services, media, city and others who directly and indirectly sabotage socialist initiatives. Finally there are the external pressures from the USA, international capital and, a particular *bête noire* of Benn's, the then EEC. Like Laski, Benn wished to see the election of a government committed to a radical socialist agenda. Legitimate extra-parliamentary activity included: 1) the right of the labour movement to organize itself to promote a Labour victory at the polls; 2) the right to limited civil disobedience where ancient and inherited rights are threatened; and 3) the right to protect a Labour government from a coup by force if necessary. If the Labour Party was to be successful, it had to reform its own internal structure, particularly in the area of inner-party democracy; higher levels of the party had to become accountable to lower, and all had to become accountable, whether in power or in opposition, to the electorate. It was therefore none too surprising that Benn's brand of democratic socialism won him few friends amongst the great and the good in the Labour Party. He viewed this growing marginality as an opportunity to speak out, untrammelled by party institutional constraints.

The death of socialism?

By the mid-1990s, claims that socialism was dead or dying were commonplace (on this see Geoghegan, 1996 and Pierson, 1995). Socialism was deemed to be an exhausted ideology totally lacking any significant electoral appeal. Diagnoses varied, but four themes predominated: changes in the working class, globalization, the collapse of communism and postmodernism. As regards the working class, it was claimed that significant sections had abandoned socialism, and that the class itself was declining in both numbers and social significance. Socialism was therefore losing its social base. In the case of globalization the claim was that national states could no longer develop truly independent policies. This was considered particularly damaging for socialism, for capital would withdraw its resources from states that attempted to introduce socialist policies. Third, the abject failure of 'actually existing socialism' in the Soviet Union and East Europe, as well as the scramble for capitalist relations of production, also took their toll. The bitter Soviet joke '"What is socialism?" "The long road from capitalism to capitalism"' hit a nerve. The collapse of communism, it was argued, put a question mark over the whole ideology of socialism. Finally, influential postmodernist perspectives claimed that the great 'modernist' ideologies, which included socialism, were no longer credible. Socialism, with its grand theoretical claims, was a dinosaur, the product of an age surpassed. All four of these explanations pointed starkly in one direction – socialism's day had gone. As Joseph Stiglitz wrote in 1994: 'if I were to claim that socialism as an ideology can now be officially declared dead, I do not think it would be an exaggeration' (1994: 279).

This rather gloomy appraisal, however, did not have the field to itself. Not everybody found the various explanations convincing. Doubts were cast on the extent of the decline of the working class, which, it was claimed, retained a significant presence in modern society. Furthermore, socialism, it was argued, had never been able to take working-class support for granted, and in Britain had always had to battle for this support against the rival charms of liberalism and conservatism. Nor had socialists rested content with wooing merely the working class: the importance of cross-class support had not been lost on earlier generations. Necessarily so, for, outside of Britain, the manual working class had never been a majority of the workforce. Socialism from its inception had to deal with sociological and ideological changes in the working class, and this had acted as a spur to theoretical and strategic innovation. In the case of globalization, there was some scepticism as to the power and penetration of this phenomenon: the fact that there were some global checks on domestic policies in no way implied that social democratic states had no basis for constructive economic policy. In addition, it was argued, the inflated claims for globalization ignored the pragmatic nature of capital, which is driven by the need for profit, not ideological purity, and the fact that corporations may actually prefer a social democratic state if their plants require an effective infrastructure and a healthy and educated workforce. For some forms of socialism, notably Marxism, globalization seemed to confirm theoretical assumptions; capital had indeed become global, and if centre and periphery were now more closely integrated, there was also the possibility of the periphery significantly striking back. As to the collapse of communism, much of the damage by association for socialism predated the collapse. Indeed, the right lost a valuable weapon in its ideological onslaught on the left, whilst in the East itself the experience of the brutal realities of the rapid introduction of markets was to give a new lease of life to socialist parties. Finally, the postmodern critique was challenged as inaccurate and of very limited impact. It was charged with caricaturing modernity, including socialism, and of having little explanatory or predictive power. An argument was made that socialism was not dying but changing; that like all long-established ideologies, socialism had a protean quality; that major challenges in the past had encouraged premature obituaries for the whole ideology: the defeat of the revolutionary wave of 1848, the collapse of the Second International in 1914, and the neutralization of socialism by prosperity in the early 1960s had seemed, to some, to sound the death-knell of socialism itself, and in each case socialism survived, having learnt valuable lessons from its trials and tribulations.

Socialism, neo-liberalism and looking forward

> When the capital development of a country becomes a by-product of
> the activities of a casino, the job is likely to be ill-done.
> John Maynard Keynes, *The General Theory of*
> *Employment, Interest and Money* (1936)

> It will, of course be said that such a scheme as is set forth here is quite unpractical, and goes against human nature. This is perfectly true . . . This is why it is worth carrying out, and that is why one proposes it . . . [I]t is exactly the existing conditions that one objects to.
>
> Oscar Wilde, *The Soul of Man Under Socialism* (1891)

New Labour's Third Way rhetoric claimed that it was steering clear of neo-liberalism, but in reality neo-liberalism became central to the socio-economic policy of the New Labour governments, as the doctrine of the limitless self-generating benefits of free-market capitalism became globally a seemingly unstoppable force. And then, beginning in 2006 and 2007, and especially after 2008, the gaping chasm that separated the ideal and the reality of neo-liberalism became catastrophically evident. What began as a huge surge of house foreclosures in the USA (the 'subprime mortgage crisis') rapidly developed into a tidal wave of an economic crisis that swept huge banks and financial institutions away, plunged whole economies into recession, triggered the 'sovereign debt crisis' in the Eurozone, and seemed close to generating global financial meltdown; it was in David Harvey's words 'undoubtedly the mother of all crises' (2011: 6). Many critics made the point that with the ensuing bailout of the banks the 'freedom' of the free market was patently abrogated, for whilst profits remained privatized, risk was socialized – a condition of socialism for the rich, and capitalism for everybody else.

In Britain, Gordon Brown, chancellor of the exchequer and eventual prime minister, in the New Labour years of power, was central to the neo-liberal agenda of the party. In his 2010 memoir of the economic crisis, he recalls his own visceral response to the run on the Northern Rock bank in 2007:

> In one day, Northern Rock depositors withdrew £1 billion in the first run on a British bank since Overend, Gurney and Company collapsed in 1866, some 141 years before. Most people watched in complete disbelief as our TV screens showed hitherto unbelievable pictures of a bank run in a modern economy. I was at Downing Street watching long queues outside branches of a British high street bank. It was like a scene in a film or a picture in a history textbook, but not something I had ever expected to see in my lifetime or under my watch.
>
> (2010: 21–2)

Brown's own chancellor, Alistair Darling, equally conveys the shock of the unthinkable happening when he got an urgent phone call from the chairman of the financially troubled Royal Bank of Scotland, Sir Tom McKillop, in 2008:

> He sounded shell-shocked. I asked him how long the bank could keep going. His answer was chilling: 'A couple of hours, maybe.' . . . I put the phone down and told my officials: 'It's going bust this afternoon.' I felt a deep chill in my stomach. If we didn't act immediately, the bank's doors would close, cash machines would be switched off, cheques would not be honoured, people would not be paid. . . . If RBS closed its doors, the banking system would freeze, not just in the UK but around the globe.
>
> (Darling, 2012: 153–4)

Amongst the reasons Brown gives for having opposed the eventual interim solution to the Northern Rock's problems – nationalization – was that he preferred a private-sector buyout, adding 'Tony Blair and I had spent twenty years building New Labour on the foundation of market competition, private enterprise, and economic stability and I was not prepared to undermine that painstaking work with one instant decision' (2010: 23). However, the speed and depth of the crisis meant that very rapidly the Labour government was forced to nationalize to varying degrees, and among those institutions to be nationalized were, it insisted, temporarily, Northern Rock and both the Royal Bank of Scotland and HBOS-Lloyds TSB. Brown's own broader solutions to the economic crisis boiled down to a call for the international management of the problems that beset globalization (his preferred analytical category for the world economic system) and for the entrenchment of morality in the economic system. After Brown's fall from power following defeat in the 2010 general election, the Labour Party under its new leader, Ed Miliband, seems bereft of new ideas.

To others, particularly those of a Marxist disposition, the economic crisis revealed capitalism in its true colours as an inherently oppressive and unstable system. The crisis, they argued, would strip the capitalist system of the pretence that it is a natural phenomenon and reveal it for what it is, an historical project rooted in selfish interests. In Terry Eagleton's words: 'You can tell the capitalist system is in trouble when people start talking about capitalism' (2011: xi). Indeed, Marx's reputation as a thinker, which had gone into relative decline in the 1980s and 1990s (when compared to the 1960s and 1970s), has experienced a veritable efflorescence, with the publication of a spate of new books extolling his anatomy of the self-destructive tendencies of capitalism. However, few expect that neo-liberalism, though battered, is on the way out, given the powerful forces behind it; as George Monbiot has argued: 'The complete failure of this world-scale experiment is no impediment to its repetition. This has nothing to do with economics. It has everything to do with power' (2013). In this vein, David Harvey quotes Warren Buffett, the US investor and one of the wealthiest people on the planet: 'There's class warfare, all right, but it's my class, the rich class, that's making war and we're winning' (Harvey, 2011: 261).

The rejection of the capitalist present, as we saw earlier in the discussion of socialist alternatives, raises the issue of the nature of a socialist future. This is a matter that simply will not go away, though there are those in the socialist tradition, as we have also seen, that are thoroughly uncomfortable with this territory, fearing that the land in question might be called utopia. Here the strategy of embracing the insult might be genuinely fruitful, for opposition to the sophisticated dystopianism of current capitalism may need the intellectual and imaginative power of the utopia; to use Roberto Unger's phrase: 'We must be visionaries to become realists' (Unger, 1998: 74). This is also the import in David Harvey's speculations about a post-capitalist society: 'Of course this is utopian! But so what! We cannot afford not to be' (Harvey, 2011: 231; on utopianism see Levitas, 2013).

Further reading

General

The classic history of socialism is G. D. H. Cole's *A History of Socialist Thought* (1953–60), although its five volumes only go up to 1939. A fine concise history is provided by George Lichtheim's *A Short History of Socialism* (1975), and there is also Michael Newman's *Socialism: A Very Short Introduction* (2005); see also on European socialism *One Hundred Years of Socialism* (2010) by Donald Sassoon and *Modern European Socialism* (1994) by Lawrence Wilde. Good discussions of the basic themes of socialism are R. N. Berki's *Socialism* (1975); Bernard Crick's *Socialism* (1987); Anthony Wright's *Socialisms: Theories and Practices* (1987); chapters 11 and 12 in Michael Freeden's influential book *Ideologies and Political Theory* (1996); and Donald Sassoon's article 'Socialism in the twentieth century: an historical reflection' (2000). For a philosophical defence of socialism see G. A. Cohen's *Why Not Socialism?* (2009). An old history of British socialism, which is very good on origins, is Max Beer's *A History of British Socialism* (1929); an illustrated one-volume edition was published by Spokesman in 1984. For an account of socialism in late nineteenth-century Britain, see Mark Bevir's *The Making of British Socialism* (2011); see also John Callaghan's *Socialism in Britain since 1884* (1990).

Texts

A wide range of British extracts, with a useful introduction, can be found in Anthony Wright's *British Socialism* (1983). The following are works on individual authors: Robert Owen – *A New View of Society and Other Writings* (1991); Karl Marx – McLellan's edited volume *Karl Marx: Selected Writings* (2000); William Morris – Morton's edited volume *Political Writings of William Morris* (1973); Edward Carpenter – *Selected Writings, Volume 1: Sex* (1984); the Fabians – G. B. Shaw's edited volume *Fabian Essays in Socialism* (1889); V. I. Lenin – *Selected Works* (1969); Eduard Bernstein – *The Preconditions of Socialism* (1993); C. A. R. Crosland – *The Future of Socialism* (1956); Harold Laski – *Democracy in Crisis* (1933); Tony Benn – *Arguments for Socialism* (1980).

Commentaries

For Owen and Owenism see J. F. C. Harrison's *Robert Owen and the Owenites in Britain and America: the Quest for the New Moral World* (1969) and Gregory Claeys's *Citizens and Saints: Politics and Anti-Politics in Early British Socialism* (1989). From the vast literature on Marx, Engels and Marxism, three useful introductions are George Lichtheim's *Marxism* (1961), David McLellan's *The Thought of Karl Marx* (1971) and Lesek Kolakowski's *Main Currents of Marxism*, in three volumes (1978); there is also a new biography of Marx: Jonathan Sperber's *Karl Marx: A Nineteenth-Century Life* (2013). William Morris is served by E. P. Thompson's *William Morris: Romantic to Revolutionary* (1977), Edward Carpenter by Shelia Rowbotham's *Edward Carpenter: A Life of Liberty and Love* (2008), and Eleanor Marx by the two-volume *Eleanor Marx*, by Yvonne Kapp (1979); for the Fabians there is A. M. McBriar's *Fabian Socialism and English Politics 1884–1918* (1966).

A good commentary on Lenin is provided by N. Harding's *Lenin's Political Thought* (1983), and on Bernstein by Peter Gay's *The Dilemma of Democratic Socialism: Eduard Bernstein's Challenge to Marx* (1962). For Crosland see David Lipsey and Dick Leonard's edited volume *The Socialist Agenda: Crosland's Legacy*, (1981); for Laski, Isaac Kramnick and Barry Sheerman's *Harold Laski: A Life on the Left* (1993); and for Benn, Jad Adams's *Tony Benn: A Biography* (1992). On Blair, New Labour and the Third Way, see Alan Finlayson's *Making Sense of New Labour* (2003) and John Rentoul's biography *Tony Blair: Prime Minister* (2013); see also Anthony Giddens's *The Third Way: The Renewal of Social Democracy* (1998). On the 'death of socialism' debate see the first three chapters in *Socialism after Communism* by Christopher Pierson (1995); see also Vincent Geoghegan's 'Has socialism a future?' (1996). For neo-liberalism, capitalism and socialism, see David Harvey's *The Enigma of Capital and the Crises of Capitalism* (2011). For considerations on Marx as a valuable thinker for the contemporary world, see Jonathan Wolff's *Why Read Marx Today?* (2002), Terry Eagleton's *Why Marx Was Right* (2011) and, from a US perspective, Charles Derber's *Marx's Ghost: Midnight Conversations on Changing the World* (2011).

References

Adams, J. (1992) *Tony Benn: A Biography*, London: Macmillan.
Bealey, F., ed. (1970) *The Social and Political Thought of the British Labour Party*, London: Weidenfeld and Nicolson.
Beer, M. (1929) *A History of British Socialism*, London: Bell.
Benn, T. (1980) *Arguments for Socialism*, Harmondsworth: Penguin.
—— (1982) *Parliament, People and Power*, London: Verso.
Berki, R. N. (1975) *Socialism*, London: Dent.
Bernstein, E. (1961) *Evolutionary Socialism*, New York: Schocken.
—— (1993) *The Preconditions of Socialism*, Cambridge: Cambridge University Press.
Bevir, M. (2011) *The Making of British Socialism*, Princeton and Oxford: Princeton University Press.
Brown, G. (2010) *Beyond the Crash*, London: Simon and Schuster.
Callaghan, J. (1990) *Socialism in Britain since 1884*, Oxford: Blackwell.
Carpenter, E. (1984) *Selected Writings, Volume 1: Sex*, London: GMP.
Claeys, G. (1989) *Citizens and Saints: Politics and Anti-Politics in Early British Socialism*, Cambridge: Cambridge University Press.
Cohen, G. A. (2009) *Why Not Socialism?*, Princeton and Oxford: Princeton University Press.
Cole, G. D. H. (1953–60) *A History of Socialist Thought*, 5 vols, London, Macmillan.
Crick, B. (1987) *Socialism*, Milton Keynes: Open University Press.
Crosland, C. A. R. (1956) *The Future of Socialism*, London: Cape.
Darling, A. (2012) *Back from the Brink*, London: Atlantic Books.
Derber, C. (2011) *Marx's Ghost: Midnight Conversations on Changing the World*, Boulder and London: Paradigm Publishers.
Donne, J. (1623) 'Meditation XVII'. Available online at http://en.wikisource.org/wiki/Meditation_XVII.
Eagleton, T. (2011) *Why Marx Was Right*, New Haven and London: Yale University Press.
Finlayson, A. (2003) *Making Sense of New Labour*, London: Lawrence and Wishart.
Freeden, M. (1996) *Ideologies and Political Theory*, Oxford: Clarendon Press.
Gamble, A. (1981) *An Introduction to Modern Social and Political Thought*, London: Macmillan.
Gay, P. (1962) *The Dilemma of Democratic Socialism: Eduard Bernstein's Challenge to Marx*, New York: Collier.
Geoghegan, V. (1987) *Utopianism and Marxism*, London and New York: Methuen; reissued with new introduction, Oxford and Bern: Peter Lang (2008).
—— (1996) 'Has socialism a future?', *Journal of Political Ideologies*, 1 (3), pp. 261–75.
Giddens, A. (1998) *The Third Way: The Renewal of Social Democracy*, Oxford: Polity.
Harding, N. (1983) *Lenin's Political Thought*, London: Macmillan.
Harrison, J. F. C. (1969) *Robert Owen and the Owenites in Britain and America: the Quest for the New Moral World*, London: Routledge.
Harvey, D. (2011) *The Enigma of Capital and the Crises of Capitalism*, London: Profile Books.
Hayek, F. (1988) *The Fatal Conceit: The Errors of Socialism*, London: Routledge.

Kapp, Y. (1979) *Eleanor Marx*, 2 vols, London: Virago.

Kolakowski, L. (1978) *Main Currents of Marxism*, 3 vols, Oxford: Clarendon.

Kramnick, I. and Sheerman, B. (1993) *Harold Laski: A Life on the Left*, London: Hamish Hamilton.

Krupskaya, N. K. (1970) *Memories of Lenin*, London: Panther.

Laski, H. (1933) *Democracy in Crisis*, London: Allen and Unwin.

Lenin, V. I. (1969) *Selected Works*, London: Lawrence and Wishart.

Levitas, R. (2013) *Utopia as Method: The Imaginary Reconstitution of Society*, London: Palgrave Macmillan.

Lichtheim, G. (1961) *Marxism*, London: Routledge.

—— (1975) *A Short History of Socialism*, Glasgow: Fontana.

Lipsey, D. and Leonard, D. (eds) (1981) *The Socialist Agenda: Crosland's Legacy*, London: Cape.

McBriar, A. M. (1966) *Fabian Socialism and English Politics 1884–1918*, Cambridge: Cambridge University Press.

McLellan, D. (1971) *The Thought of Karl Marx*, London: Macmillan.

—— (1979) *Marxism after Marx*, London: Macmillan.

—— ed. (1983) *Marx: The First 100 Years*, London: Fontana.

—— (2000) *Karl Marx: Selected Writings*, 2nd edn, Oxford: Oxford University Press.

Marx Aveling, E. and Aveling, E. (1886) 'The woman question from a socialist point of view', *Westminster Review*, 49, pp. 207–22.

Monbiot, G. (2013) 'If you think we're done with neoliberalism, think again', *The Guardian*, 14 January. Available online at www.guardian.co.uk/commentis free/2013/jan/14/neoliberal-theory-economic-failure (accessed 10 June 2013).

More, T. (1965) *Utopia*, Harmondsworth: Penguin.

Morton, A. L. (1962) *The Life and Ideas of Robert Owen*, London: Lawrence and Wishart.

—— ed. (1973) *Political Writings of William Morris*, London: Lawrence and Wishart.

Newman, M. (2005) *Socialism: A Very Short Introduction*, Oxford: Oxford University Press.

Owen, R. (1991) *A New View of Society and Other Writings*, Harmondsworth: Penguin.

Pierson, C. (1995) *Socialism after Communism*, Oxford: Polity.

Rentoul, J. (2013) *Tony Blair: Prime Minister*, London: Faber and Faber.

Rowbotham, S. (2008) *Edward Carpenter: A Life of Liberty and Love*, London and New York: Verso.

Sassoon, D. (2000) 'Socialism in the twentieth century: an historical reflection', *Journal of Political Ideologies*, 5 (1), pp. 17–34.

—— (2010) *One Hundred Years of Socialism*, London: I. B. Tauris.

Shaw, G. B., ed. (1889) *Fabian Essays in Socialism*, London: Fabian Society.

Sperber, J. (2013) *Karl Marx: A Nineteenth-Century Life*, New York and London: Liveright.

Stiglitz, J. E. (1994) *Whither Socialism?*, Cambridge, MA: MIT.

Taylor, B. (1983) *Eve and the New Jerusalem: Socialism and Feminism in the Nineteenth Century*, London: Virago.

Thompson, E. P. (1977) *William Morris: Romantic to Revolutionary*, London: Merlin.

Trotsky, L. (n.d.) *Our Political Tasks*, London: New Park Publications.

Unger, R. M. (1998) *Democracy Realized: The Progressive Alternative*, London and New York: Verso.

Wilde, L. (1994) *Modern European Socialism*, Aldershot: Dartmouth.

Winstanley, G. (1973) *The Law of Freedom and Other Writings*, Harmondsworth: Penguin.

Wittgenstein, L. (1972) *The Blue and Brown Books*, Oxford: Basil Blackwell.

Wolff, J. (2002) *Why Read Marx Today?*, Oxford: Oxford University Press.

Wright, A. (1983) *British Socialism: Socialist Thought from the 1880s to 1960s*, Harlow: Longman.

—— (1987) *Socialisms: Theories and Practices*, Oxford: Oxford University Press.

Nationalism

Alan Finlayson

Introduction

Nationalism presents a challenge to theorists and analysts of political ideology. Socialist or conservative ideology has been reflected upon, revised and developed by theorists in many different historical, cultural and geographical contexts. Each has sought to draw on an initial body of theory, and to apply it to its particular circumstances. There are many variants of socialism and conservatism, but these ideologies clearly possess a recognizable set of core themes and propositions. In contrast, nationalists the world over don't hold colloquia or congresses, form think-tanks or create international confederations dedicated to sharing, refining and spreading the doctrine of nationalism. There seem to be as many nationalisms as there are nationalist movements, and their similarities – consisting of very general claims – are far outweighed by all the differences. In short, nationalism seems not to possess a substantial conceptual core in the way other ideologies do.

Because it seems so thin, nationalism has often been neglected by political theorists. It has been more of a concern for historians and sociologists, who understand it as a form of social or political movement rather than as a political ideology. However, this chapter will show that nationalism is an extremely important part of political ideologies. In fact, it will argue that we can't properly understand other ideologies unless we also understand nationalism and how it fits together with them. It will also show that, despite 'globalization' and 'cosmopolitanism' – perhaps because of them – nationalism might play a big role in the politics of the future. Indeed, some political theorists are returning to the nation, seeing it as a way to give real shape and meaning to values of mutual responsibility.

We will begin by examining some of the problems – and opportunities – of studying nationalist ideologies. We will then explore how nationalism has been understood as the product of a particular period of social change and the alternative view that contemporary nationalisms are rooted in ancient historical experiences. We will then look in more detail at how nationalism is often joined (or 'articulated') with other political ideologies and consider what this might tell us about how ideology works. Next we will consider some recent developments in political theory which have posited nationalism as a viable way of providing solidarity or community. Before concluding we will address the question of what might happen to nationalism in the future.

Nationalism and the theory of ideologies

As you will have seen in earlier chapters of this book, it is not difficult to pull out the main tenets of ideologies such as socialism, conservatism and liberalism. They are complex and contested philosophies, but, nevertheless, we can fairly easily say something about how they understand human nature, how they think about the state, their moral claims, and so forth. Although disputed, these themes provide points of reference. They are co-ordinates which mark out the ways in which an ideology differs from others and they structure debates between adherents. Can we say the same of nationalism? Can we identify the core propositions that shape its manifestations? According to the influential analyst Elie Kedourie, the doctrine of nationalism:

> holds that humanity is naturally divided into nations, that nations are known by certain characteristics which can be ascertained, and that the only legitimate type of government is national self-government.
>
> (Kedourie, 1960: 12)

According to Kedourie, then, three important political claims are made by nationalists: nations are a natural unit of social and political organization; such units are identifiable because each possesses specific characteristics; and only when government is connected to units of this kind can it be legitimate.

These are important, substantive and far-reaching claims. The first is a proposition about human nature. Where liberalism proposes that we are first and foremost individuals who choose to enter into social relations, nationalism proposes that we are naturally part of social groups. Socialism might agree that we are social beings but insist that the social group which matters most is our economic class or the entirety of humanity. In contrast, nationalism proposes that the important unity of community is geographically and politically limited: the nation. That claim leads into a second proposition – that such communities are identifiable because they each have specific characteristics. That is, nations are not merely units of administrative convenience. Communities possess particular attributes that belong to them and not to others. Nationalism thus makes a claim that is simultaneously universal and particular. It says something meant to be true about all of us everywhere (that we naturally belong to nations) but also says that each of these groups is particular or unique. And from that claim, the nationalist makes a third, with immense political implications: that only when political organization is in harmony with our natural division into nations can it be legitimate.

These are claims about political fundamentals: how we are naturally; the relationship between this and political organization; the basis of governmental legitimacy. But while nationalism makes large and important claims about these essential elements of any serious political ideology, things seem to stop here. Nationalism outlines something about the structure and basis of political rule but does not say much about its content. There are still many questions about how to identify nations. For instance, what are the characteristics which specify nations? Language is an important way in which communities are distinguished, but nobody thinks that all the English-speaking people of the world should be one nation. People may claim to share a history or traditions, but the latter often turn out to be very recent inventions (see Hobsbawm and Ranger, 1992) and the former, history, is rarely free from disruption, population changes and all kinds of social transformation. Politicians often talk about the distinct values of a nation, but these are often not very distinct at all and almost always contested. Nor is it clear how the boundaries to a nation are fixed. Who is and is not included within one? What about different communities within a nation? And the claim that the only legitimate government is one which is attached to a nation says little about how exactly that government should be arranged. Must it be a single sovereign state or can it be legitimate for a nation to be part of a large multinational or federal state? Must it be a democracy or is a monarchy appropriate? These questions arise before we get to more specific issues: equality, property rights, economics, and so on.

At this level it is not immediately clear that the propositions of nationalism distinguish it at all. The socialist critique of private property is something that cannot be shared by conservatism or liberalism and is thus one of the things that makes socialism a relatively distinct ideology. Similarly, the conservative defence of elitism cannot be shared by liberalism or socialism and makes conservatism relatively distinct. But conservatives and liberals need not find it difficult to endorse the view that nations are central to political organization. Socialists, even those keen to emphasize the importance of an international structure of class oppression and the need for universal liberation, have happily supported struggles for national independence and self-determination. Nationalism can be in contradiction with socialism or conservatism, but it doesn't seem to be the case that it is necessarily so. What, then, is distinctive about nationalism?

Because of the generality of the claims of nationalism, the political theorist Michael Freeden calls it a 'thin' ideology: it offers an outline of how politics should work but doesn't add any of the necessary layers. Each core concept of nationalism, he explains:

> logically contains a number of possible meanings . . . [and they may be] attached to as many adjacent and peripheral concepts as there are interpretations of nationalism . . . the core concepts of nationalism cannot rival the possibilities available to mainstream ideologies such as conservatism, liberalism or socialism – all of which have core conceptual structures which permit a far fuller range of responses to socio-political issues.

> (1996: 752)

That is to say, while the 'big three' ideologies provide a rich set of ideas, concepts and arguments on which to draw when addressing a particular political problem or situation, nationalism does not. For instance, it is not immediately clear how nationalist ideology might orient us in relation to a political dilemma such as euthanasia or how it might help us think about the balance between spending cuts and tax rises in a time of high government debt. Liberalism, socialism and conservatism don't provide single or immediate responses to these issues, but they do present a framework within which we may develop them. Nationalism does not. However, this thinness means that nationalism is very flexible. The fact that it can be allied to conservatism or to socialism might not be a weakness but a strength.

According to Freeden, ideologies 'enable meaningful political worlds to be constructed' (1996: 749), and they do so by providing identifiable sets of meaning or 'conceptual configurations'. Nationalism, he suggests, doesn't provide such a unique constellation. It is composed of a 'restricted core' and a narrow range of political concepts. Often it is a component of other ideologies. But he adds two important points to the three elements identified by Kedourie: the first is that any particular nationalist ideology does not propose only that nations are central to human relationships but that a *particular* nation is *particularly* important; the second is that nationalism is always marked by strong emotions and attachment to history as a story about the continuous existence or persistence of a people, and to a territory understood as the place where that history has been, and should continue to be, played out (1996: 751–4).

Nationalism as a broad claim about the naturalness of nations and their connection to political legitimacy doesn't propose very much. But very few people – and no nationalist activists – propose only these broad claims. They propose the self-determination of a *particular* nation or people, and in so doing they specify things about that people: their history; the key events that shape and define them; their values, perhaps including their attitude towards property rights, the proper form of government, euthanasia, taxes and spending. It then becomes quite a substantive and extensive ideology, and one that is able to appeal to our emotions and sense of identity. What this suggests is not that nationalism in some way fails to be a proper political ideology, but that it is one that works in a very specific way.

Benedict Anderson opens his renowned and important study of nationalism by declaring that it is less like ideologies such as liberalism and fascism than it is like 'kinship or religion'. What he means is that we should think of it not as a framework within which we propose how a community should be organized but as a way of thinking about that community in the first place. A nation, Anderson says, is an 'imagined community'. Its members cannot possibly know or even hear of all their fellows, 'yet in the minds of each lives the image of their communion' (Anderson, 1991: 6; see also Finlayson, 2011). Furthermore, that community is 'imagined as both inherently limited and sovereign' (Anderson, 1991: 5). It is limited because all nations consider themselves to have boundaries beyond which are other nations (perhaps against which the nation is defined); and it is sovereign because nationalists demand that the nation should occupy the centre-stage of political arrangements, standing in the place where once we would have found divinely ordained monarchs.

What Anderson means is that nationalism is a very particular way of thinking about our relationship to each other. We could think of ourselves as connected by some kind of direct kinship (like a clan). We could think of ourselves as all part of one God-made family. But nationalism proposes that we are parts of bounded communities and that these particular kinds of community are the source of political authority and legitimacy. At this level it is not a single coherent, doctrinal ideology (like socialism, liberalism or conservatism) but a kind of governing principle that gives order, meaning and significance to social relations and political structures. Scholar of nationalism Walker Connor argues that the essence of a nation is 'a psychological bond that joins a people and differentiates it, in the subconscious conviction of its members, from all other people in a most vital way'. What is significant, he argues, 'is not *what is* but *what people believe is*... a nation is a matter of attitude and not of fact' (1994: 93). What Connor means is that nationalism is an attachment to a certain way of experiencing the world. In that respect it is a kind of social theory of how the world works – of what gives us a place in it, of how we should think of our relations with other people and of how we should be politically organized. But it is also a way of giving that theory emotional colour and depth. As Freeden points out: 'All ideologies... carry emotional attachments to particular conceptual configurations, both because fundamental human values excite emotional as well as rational support, and because ideologies constitute mobilizing ideational systems to change or defend political practices' (1996: 754). Nationalism, because it is rooted in everyday experiences, is able to do this in very powerful ways.

The peculiarities of nationalism perhaps teach us something about ideologies. They indicate the extent to which political ideologies are not merely abstract philosophies of the world but attempts to encourage us to act in particular ways within it. As well as providing explanations and justifications, ideologies also provide us with a way of interpreting what is going on around us, a sense of identity and a motivation to act. In fact, one of the things ideologies do is join explanations and ideologies to motivations and identities. And that might be why nationalism matters. It may be rather thin on its own, but it can be connected with a wide variety of political claims and even other ideologies. It can provide them with emotional resonance and motivational force which supply it with substantive claims that help it answer questions about how to specify a nation and how it will work. To understand more about this we need first to look at debates about the historical emergence of nationalism.

Nationalism and modernization

All ideologies have their roots in particular historical social conditions. Liberalism, conservatism and socialism can all point to ancient precedents, but they emerge at reasonably clear moments in modern history: the latter two attain definition in responses to the French Revolution and the upheavals of industrialization (see chapters 3 and 4). Liberalism grows out of the culture of Protestantism and the rise of social groups with an interest in restraining monarchical power (see chapter 2). And in this respect, nationalism is no different. It too has its roots in historical development and social change. The common assumption that outbursts of nationalist fervour are indicative of a kind of latent tribalism, a primordial trait of human nature, is misleading. It may well be that some sort of group loyalty has always been intrinsic to human social organization. But the particular ideas associated with nationalism are recent developments. Kedourie remarked that 'Nationalism is a doctrine invented in Europe at the beginning of the nineteenth century' (1960: 12). Historian Hugh Seton-Watson declared that 'the doctrine of nationalism dates from the age of the French Revolution' (1977: 27). But another historian, Liah Greenfeld, states that the 'original modern idea of the nation emerged in sixteenth-century England, which was the first nation in the world' (1992: 14). There is no uniform scholarly opinion on the exact origins of nationalism, and there is considerable argument about the extent to which it grows on historic roots. But all agree that the fulcrum of this dispute is the idea of 'modernization'.

When political and social scientists talk of modernization or modernity, they mean the shift from simple and traditional forms of social organization to industrialized societies based around the complex interaction of the economy, large-scale state bureaucracies and mass communication systems: the long process that brought larger and larger groups of people into contact with each other and established all sorts of social connections between them. This is a process, not a moment in history, and it takes place at different speeds in different places. Indeed, some places on our planet have not become fully modernized, while others, some claim, are now postmodern. The argument of some scholars of nationalism is that the conditions of upheaval and dislocation wrought by modernization lead to a situation in which the reproduction of everyday social life and culture cannot be taken for granted. The ways in which people are used to doing things, their habits, their traditions, their prejudices, are all thrown off kilter. That could lead to a total breakdown in society, but nationalism helps to integrate populations into this new social context.

For example, Ernest Gellner (1983) traces the sources of nationalism to the transformation of societies from a predominantly agricultural economy to an industrial one. He characterizes agrarian societies as predominantly local in their orientation, hierarchical in structure and, crucially, semi-literate. That is to say, they were fairly closed and rigid forms of social organization with limited variation between people in any particular social unit. In agrarian societies literacy is not a widespread skill but one monopolized by clerics. The ruling class, of nobles and monarchs, exists in rigid separation from the peasantry. People are, in short, limited in their social as well as geographical mobility.

Industrialization, Gellner argues, alters all this. People move through society and get mixed up much more. Industrial society is open-ended and always developing, demanding flexibility. Modern industrial societies don't prosper if people want to stay in the same place and always do the same thing. They need people to move about, for instance from the country to the city, where there are new kinds of work for them to do, or, as industries die out, from one city to another. For Gellner, nationalism is born out of this upheaval, out of 'a certain kind of division of labour, one which is complex and persistently, cumulatively changing' (1983: 24). In industrial society, he writes:

> notwithstanding its larger number of specialisms, the distance between specialisms is far less great. Their mysteries are far closer to mutual intelligibility, their manuals have idioms which overlap to a much greater extent and re-training though sometimes difficult is not generally an awesome task.
>
> (1983: 26–7)

What Gellner means is that as society gets more complex it also demands and creates more homogeneity. Because people have to move about more, their social roles change and keep changing, such that 'culture' becomes an important part of social organization. It is what binds them together. People need to share a common training in literacy and numeracy because this facilitates their practical communication with each other and over time they develop a set of shared cultural reference points, expectations and assumptions. My work as an academic includes all sorts of specialist terms and actions, as does the work of my friend who is a mechanic. Nevertheless, we can explain ourselves to each other, our lives and experiences are not so far apart and, substantially, we share the same culture. The institutionalization and organization of such a culture, Gellner argues, is something only the modern state can provide. It is, he says, the body that possesses the monopoly on legitimate education: the capacity and authority to produce and maintain a culture in the context of modernization. Consequently culture and the state become linked. If cultures are to survive, they need to have their own 'political roof', their own state which can promote that culture, train people in it and defend it. This, for Gellner, is the origin of nationalism: the genesis of a cultural principle of political organization lies in a historic transformation of social structure.

This is what scholars call the 'modernization thesis' of nationalism. While Gellner is an exemplar of this approach, he is not alone in articulating it. Many social scientists and political theorists have adopted something like a modernization-based approach, though their precise rendition of it may vary. Benedict Anderson's proposal that nations are 'imagined communities' rests on the claim that the possibility of imagining a national community required the spread of literacy and the development of a competitive, capitalist, market in printed materials. In standardizing languages and creating a new sort of market which it satisfied through newspapers, periodicals, novels, and so forth, print-capitalism not only brought individuals information about others in the same linguistic community but also created the experience of living in the same moment as them (Anderson, 1991). In the newspaper we can read about people on the other side of the country who have the same sorts of feelings and preoccupations as we do (and with whom we may experience a kind of affinity, even though we will never meet them). Other Marxist writers have drawn attention to the way in which nationalism lends legitimacy to the capitalist state, obscuring what should be the international consciousness of the working class (see Nimni, 1994).

However, there are a number of criticisms that may be made of the modernization thesis. Not the least is that such theories are often taken to imply that the era of nationalism has passed. This may have looked like the case at one stage, but it certainly doesn't look like that now. Recent decades have seen a resurgence of nationalist and ethnic conflicts in all parts of the globe, including Central and Eastern Europe. A second criticism is that it is not wholly clear whether advocates of the modernization thesis are proposing that nationalism is an outcome of the modernization process or a necessary condition for its emergence. Does it make it possible for societies to industrialize or is it something that industrialization produces? A third, and perhaps the most serious, challenge to the modernization thesis is the argument that historically nationalism has not always emerged alongside industrialization. The historian Marc Bloch has argued that national consciousness is apparent in France and Germany as far back as 1100 – long before 'modernization' (Bloch, 1961: 436). By contrast, Eugen Weber (1979) has demonstrated that some people living in rural France did not consider themselves 'French' as late as the end of World War I. They lived in isolation from the rest of the country, spoke distinct regional vernaculars and generally had little to do with urbanized 'modern' France. As Walker Connor concludes, it is hard to date the precise emergence of a nation, since an elite may be attached to national consciousness long before there is any record of what the mass of people thought. A nation is formed through a long process, and there is no single point when it is definitively completed (see Connor, 1994: 210–26; also Williams, 1991).

This is why Anthony Smith stresses that nationalism cannot be explained through the modernization process alone. Ideas such as self-determination are indeed quite recent, and national*ism* is of eighteenth-century origin. But Smith reminds us to be careful not to confuse *state* formation with *nation* formation. A national identity, he argues, can't be invented out of nothing at all (let alone the ideology and the state that flow from it). Nations and nationalism develop only on the basis of an already existing 'ethnic core' or *ethnies* (French for 'ethnic communities'). Historical experiences such as prolonged warfare with other ethnic groups produce a strong bond of ethnicity and a sense of belonging to an immemorial community and provide the basis for the deeply held sentiments of nationhood. 'If nationalism is modern and shapes nations', writes Smith, 'then this is only half the story. Specific nations are also the product of older, often pre-modern ethnic ties and ethno-histories' (1998: 195).

Smith is not arguing that nations are formed out of actual kinship. Rather than physical descent, what binds people is a 'sense of continuity, shared memory and collective destiny' (Smith, 1991). Their longevity relies on myths, persistent traditions and shared symbols. These then provide the resources for modern nationalists to shape nationalisms. For example, there is much truth in the claim that ethno-religious identification in Northern Ireland persists because of the instrumental manipulation of political elites. But this manipulation works only because history has bequeathed to that region the elements of such identities. They are not unchanged over time, but neither are they total fabrications (see Whyte, 1990).

Smith's approach is a corrective to the more cavalier modernization theories that can be too general in their search for laws of development rather than ways of looking at the importance of contexts that are not simply incidental. As he makes clear, it is not impossible to combine a modernization thesis with the recognition of such historicity (Smith, 1998). Nationalist intellectuals and activists may expend a great deal of effort recovering (perhaps inventing) traditions, folk tales, languages, songs, and so forth (see Hobsbawm and Ranger, 1992). But they do so on the basis of existing materials. Although nationalism has some objective causes of the sort that modernization theorists point to, it also has important subjective components. The analysis of nationalism is haunted by the opposition between objectivity and subjectivity. The historian Hugh Seton-Watson declared, in a tone that sounds somewhat exasperated: 'All that I can find to say is that a nation exists when a significant number of people in a community consider themselves to form a nation, or behave as if they formed one' (1977: 5). In a famous lecture in 1882 the French philosopher and biblical scholar Ernest Renan asked the question 'Qu'est-ce qu'une nation?' – 'What is a nation?' – answering that it is 'a spiritual principle', constituted by 'possession in common of a rich legacy of remembrances' and by 'the desire to live together, the will to continue to value the heritage which all hold in common'. It is, he said, founded on a 'tangible deed' of consent: 'a daily plebiscite' (Renan, 1990). Renan is suggesting not that we really do vote to accept our nationality, but that there can be nations and nationalism only because the people of a given nation continually will it – they accept the idea, believe in it and act in accordance with it. This is not a view that many today would wholly endorse. But it is hard to see how nations, although made possible by objective criteria such as a shared and accessible print culture, can exist without the addition of some kind of feeling, a consciousness of being part of one nation and not of any other.

And this is where we can return to political ideologies in general. What the study of nationalism reminds us is that ideologies are not only abstract propositions about the world, but tools for acting upon it. Those tools are forged through long and ongoing historical effort. They help us make sense of the political world, act within it and persuade others. An ideology cannot take root where there is no fertile ground, and to succeed it must be capable of being adapted to the situation at hand. That means it must be capable of connecting with people's subjective experiences and outlooks. And in these respects nationalism is extremely effective. Indeed, its thinness is an advantage. It provides a reason to think of some people as having a connection with each other. It connects that to the claim that they should have their own distinct political system. It draws on new material conditions (for instance, the spread of literacy and print capitalism) but is shaped by the longer local historical context and advances propositions that help to solve social and intellectual problems thrown up by modernization. Yet because these are not highly detailed, it is capable of being connected with all sorts of other political arguments.

As societies have become more complicated, the need for a clear principle of integration becomes pressing. Social unity is no longer an automatic and unconscious result of necessity, derived from the fact that without the group we can't survive or that we all live in almost exactly the same sort of way. In the contemporary culture of individualism our communality is, not entirely but to a significant degree, a matter of will and choice (a daily plebiscite in which we could, at any moment, change our 'vote'). But the form community takes cannot be just anything. It is always dependent on circumstances, on a history (albeit partly mythical and partly invented) that we believe ourselves to share and want to continue. Nationalism has been the most successful example of the formation and maintenance of identity and communal feeling, enabling states to set in place the kinds of institutions that create the experiences and propagate the history that in turn supports the nationalist case. Indeed, it has been so successful that other political ideologies want, as it were, a piece of the action.

The articulations of nationalism

Historian Liah Greenfeld argues that in sixteenth-century England the concept of the nation became very important as a new kind of synonym for 'the people'. Thought of as a nation, the idea of 'a people' lost the negative connotations of terms such as 'rabble' and 'mob'. Hitherto, the 'people' had been those who were not the nobility, whereas as 'the nation' the people became a kind of elite, sharing in something that elevated them all (Greenfeld, 1992: 7). In England, she writes, the assertion of the nationality of the English polity went hand in hand:

> with the insistence on the people's right of participation in the political process and government through Parliament. In fact in this case 'nation', England's being a nation, actually meant such participation. The representation of the English people as a nation symbolically elevated it to the position of an elite which had the right and was expected to govern itself, and equated nationhood with political citizenship.
>
> (Greenfeld, 1992: 30)

Nationalism, then, was joined to the idea of popular sovereignty or democracy. In order to 'think' democracy, people also needed to think of themselves as already united and connected with each other. Imagining themselves to be part of an ancient nation with ancient rights helped them do this. Thus the ideologies of English democracy and English nationalism were, for a time, inseparable and mutually supporting.

The concept political theorists and analysts use to help them think about this joining of different ideologies is 'articulation'. It combines two meanings of the word: that of 'joining' or 'linking' (as in 'articulated lorry'); and that of speaking, expressing or simply making sounds. One of the things people do in politics is 'articulate': they express and communicate viewpoints on the world and in doing so they join together concepts with each other and with people's experiences, everyday habits, feelings, and so on (see Hall, 1985; Laclau, 1977; Laclau and Mouffe, 1985; Slack, 1996; Therborn, 1999: 32–3). For instance, we might say – following Greenfeld's comments – that a growing experience of connectedness was 'articulated' with the idea of Englishness to create a sense of nation-ness and that this in turn was articulated with claims about equality and participation: a version of democracy. Such articulations give very particular meanings to the concepts that are joined. When Englishness and equality are articulated, both concepts are changed. What is produced is a conception of equality that is specific to those who count as English (and not to everyone) and also a concept of being English that puts it at odds with certain elitist assumptions.

Because of this sort of phenomenon, Freeden is led to ask, 'are democracy and community glosses on nationhood, or are nationhood, and nationalism more generally, a gloss on ideologies in which democracy and community play a crucial part?' (1998: 759). Perhaps, paradoxically, the answer to this question is both and neither. That is, the articulation of these elements can at one time emphasize one side and then, later, the other. Then again, maybe we shouldn't think of them as being different elements: once joined they form a distinct whole ideology. And one of the things that is interesting – and perhaps peculiar – about nationalism is the variety of ways in which it is articulated with other ideologies across the political spectrum. Elements of nationalism can contribute to all sorts of other ideologies, giving them a much needed context and a claimed legitimacy.

As Breuilly shows, nationalism 'arises out of the need to make sense of complex social and political arrangements' (1982: 343). Since the modern state developed by basing its claims to legitimacy on the sovereignty of the people, rather than of the monarch, the problem arose of which people exactly were sovereign, and 'Once the claim to sovereignty was made on behalf of a particular territorially defined unit of humanity it was natural to relate the claim to the particular attributes of that unit' (1982: 343). In other words, it made sense to justify political arrangements by finding them to be in accordance with the nature or spirit of the people, the national community. Nationalism helped answer some questions posed by democratization. And many ideologies can find nationalism useful in this way, their persuasiveness enhanced through their association with national character or sentiment. This is not to suggest that nationalism is always consciously employed by unscrupulous and manipulative politicians as a strategy for maintaining power. It may just be that politicians or ideologues, in trying to make sense of the world and to sustain their own arguments, find themselves seeing things in national terms.

For instance, think of the extent to which British politicians routinely refer to the good of the nation or the national interest; they portray themselves as being more in tune with the national spirit than their opponents (see Billig, 1995). In this way the claims of, say, conservatism (which often advocates an organic notion of some sort of unified community to which we owe allegiance) may combine with nationalism (which of course also advances a notion of a naturally unified community). But socialism can also combine with nationalism, particularly in the case of populist anti-colonial nationalisms, because the two ideologies share the idea that the people, their common interest, is the source of legitimacy. We might also make mention of ecologism, which, given that it seeks in part to protect the landscape, is quite capable of being used by nationalism and of using nationalism and national sentiment as justification for opposition to certain kinds of social change.

There is also an important relationship between feminism and nationalism. Feminism, like nationalism, often forges a relationship to another ideology – liberalism or socialism, for instance. But the claims of feminism are sometimes related to those of nationalism, especially in the context of national liberation struggles, in which women often play a crucial part. The incorporation of gendered symbolization within nationalisms has been astutely analyzed and criticized by feminist scholars. They point out how nations are often imagined in mythic form as female figures. We speak of Britannia and paint her as a woman. In France, Joan of Arc is a key female national icon and France itself is imagined as female. But this often means that the land or the country is being figured as a nurturing mother whose warrior sons must always be ready to defend her. Her daughters can consequently be instructed to continue the work of reproducing the nation both biologically and culturally. In fact a whole range of gendered and sexualized imagery almost always goes along with nationalism (see e.g. Yuval-Davis, 1997; Walby, 1996; Mosse, 1985), and appeals to nationhood may be one way in which a certain form of anti-feminism is promoted.

These are all examples of the 'articulation' of ideologies. Articulating political claims with nationhood gives them a sense of belonging with the people, as something natural and everyday, part of our identity. For instance, Tony Blair often made the argument, when promoting a skills- and knowledge-based economy, that he was simply returning to an emphasis on the natural inventiveness and talent of the British people (see Finlayson, 2003). More recently, David Cameron has promoted his vision of 'the big society' (of people taking over responsibilities once assigned to government), saying:

I know the British people and they are not passengers – they are drivers. I've seen the courage of our soldiers, the spirit of our entrepreneurs, the patience of our teachers, the dedication of our doctors, the compassion of our care workers, the wisdom of our elderly, the love of our parents, the hopes of our children.

(Cameron, 2010)

This list of different kinds of people (but also only some kinds of people), all of whom are 'ours' (that is, they belong to 'us' the community), is an excellent example of an attempt to have us imagine a community and to see that community in terms that both derive from and add to very particular propositions about how the government should work and how society should be organized. This is exactly the work of nationalism.

Nationalism and liberal community

We have not yet considered the articulation of nationalism with liberalism. Because liberalism champions a pre-social individual, and proposes a political regime designed to protect her liberty from the impositions of collectivist ideologies, we might well presume that nationalism and liberalism are antagonistic ideologies. Certainly, nationalism has not been widely admired by liberal political theorists. Isaiah Berlin, for example, while he understood the potency of the romantic ideal of the organic community, criticized nationalism precisely because of the way in which it privileges the interests of that community over those of smaller groups or individuals (Berlin, 1979: 333–55). But Berlin made the common distinction between national*ism*, the ideology, and nationality or 'mere national consciousness – the sense of belonging to a nation' (1979: 346). Other liberal scholars have done the same thing – separating good nationalisms from bad ones, sometimes through a contrast between 'civic' and 'ethnic' conceptions of the nation (see Geertz, 1963; Plamenatz, 1976; Ignatieff, 1993). For 'civic nationalism', the nation is primarily a 'political' unit with some sort of civic tie between a set people that fosters duties, rights, responsibilities and obligations. By contrast, 'ethnic' nationalisms are understood as interpreting the nation as bonded through some kind of blood tie or through a powerful shared historical or cultural consciousness, as chapter 6 in this volume, on fascism, explores (see also Kohn, 1944; Plamenatz, 1976). Other versions of this distinction are 'civic-territorial' versus 'ethnic-genealogical' (Smith, 1991) and 'individualistic-libertarian' versus 'collectivist-authoritarian' (Greenfeld, 1992).

This sort of division of nationalism has enabled liberalism to find in the nation a way of imagining community and then using it to sustain claims about individual rights, legal equalities and the legitimacy of government. John Stuart Mill, the archetypal liberal thinker, believed that free government was virtually impossible in multinational states. It was, he thought, necessary for a governed people to feel some connection and solidarity with each other. Increasingly, contemporary liberal political theorists and ideologists are beginning to see ways in which a sense of nationality remains important. In part this has been stimulated by the criticisms of what is known as communitarianism. Communitarian thinkers have argued that liberalism is insufficiently attentive to the need of individuals to be part of a wider substantive community. They argue that values such as tolerance, justice, fairness, and so forth take on meaning for people only within the context of an embedded, shared culture within which they can feel themselves a part of something (see Mulhall and Swift, 1992; Kenny, 2003).

A leading proponent of the articulation of liberalism with nationalism is the political theorist David Miller. He does not see himself as promoting nationalism but, rather, defending the 'principle of nationality' (Miller, 1995). His motivation is partly a sort of realism. Miller simply thinks it unlikely that people will suddenly decide that their sense of nationality was a big fiction and give up on it. Better then to think within nationality and see how it may fit with liberal, civic, principles. In any case, many political philosophers already assume something like a national community, a body of people with a sense of shared history, continuity, and so forth, when they begin to theorize about the nature of concepts such as justice and rights.

Miller's arguments are not based solely on such realism. He also argues that it need not be thought irrational or indefensible to claim that national identity is a part of one's identity. Nations are ethical communities providing a basis for meaningful moral values (Miller, 1995). To see oneself as belonging to a national community is to see oneself as having a particular and meaningful relationship with some other people (though this need not mean that we owe no ethical obligations to those beyond our nation or no special ethical obligations to a smaller unit such as our family). This gives rise to a politics of nationality that Miller opposes to a narrow 'politics of identity'. A civic national identity does not impose itself upon other identities. It is a framework for a common identity within which other identities may make legitimate claims. Ethnic or cultural minorities within a liberal state have a right to expect that the state will make some effort to accommodate them, but they too must accept their responsibility to be loyal to the national state. It is reasonable for liberals to think that they have some special and greater responsibility for co-nationals than for just anybody, although this is not a reason to forgo all global responsibilities (Miller, 2005, 2007).

Miller's arguments have come in for criticism on the grounds that they are thought to lead to support for the status quo (for the nations that already exist rather than those yet to be formed) and thus downplay the extent to which the grievances of a minority may be severe and rooted in the unjust nature of present political arrangements which the principle of nationalism can only make worse. It has also been argued that Miller does not fully appreciate the interrelationship of civic and ethnic conceptions of nationalism, the fact that they provide each other with support (see O'Leary, 1996; Smith, 1998). But of most interest to students of political ideologies is the fact that Miller is an example, or a proof, of the way in which the ideology of nationalism can be articulated with another set of political claims in a way that changes both. His philosophy leads to a form of civic nationalist ideology because he articulates liberalism with nationalism. That is something quite different to the violent or racist forms we find articulated with (or as) fascism. But it is also a form of liberalism that is different to that promoted by political philosophers keen to promote global cosmopolitan and universal rights and philosophies (e.g. Archibugi, 1998; Caney, 2005).

A nationalist future?

Today, we are living through some kind of 'globalization': supra-national political institutions such as the European Union and the World Trade Organization have assumed powers, albeit on an agreed basis, previously exercised by single nations. Multinational corporations, international non-governmental organizations and transnational protest movements are all vital forces in global politics. Increasingly, as governmental institutions become detached from national communities, political and social theorists are proposing ways of formalizing a global cosmopolitanism, giving it institutional but also cultural and ideological legitimacy (e.g. Brown and Held, 2010; Held, 2010), although others suggest that this may be nothing other than a way of legitimating 'interventions' motivated by economic or political self-interest (see Archibugi, 2003; see also discussion in Fine, 2007).

Of particular significance for nationalism are transformations in the organization of communication. As we have seen, many theories of nations and nationalism emphasize the importance of systems of communication that enable the formation and maintenance of nationhood. Anderson, for instance, emphasized literature, literacy and the trade in printed materials, and Gellner the cultivation of a shared idiom. Karl Deutsch emphasized that the kind of communication important for nations entails not only language but also 'systems of writing, painting, calculating etc. . . . information stored in the living memories, associations, habits, and preferences . . . material facilities for the storage of information such as libraries, statues, signposts and the like' (1966: 96). In the twentieth century national media systems (especially cinema and television) promoted national cultures. Governments regulated the right to broadcast through a licensing system and often sought to limit the involvement of corporations not based in the nation. Television was understood by its own creators as a means of integrating millions of domestic family units into the rhythms and experiences of a national imagined community (Ang, 1996: 5), and the mass media, far from simply reflecting national experiences, create them. Be it the coronation of a monarch, the swearing in of a president or a 'national' event (sports, a famous person's funeral, a grisly crime), media events can 'integrate societies in a collective heartbeat and evoke a renewal of loyalty to the society and its legitimate authority' (Dayan and Katz, 1992: 9).

But in the twenty-first century the media are increasingly internationalized and fragmented. It is now less and less likely that people will all simultaneously watch the same event at the same time, despite wide access to such media (although there can be *global* audiences for events like 9/11, the Olympic Games and the football World Cup). Media products and markets have become globalized (in both their production and dissemination), leading to what some call a 'de-territorialization' of cultural space (that is, cultural creations are not rooted in specific locations) and individuals (through the internet we go where we want, when we want). Furthermore, claims Douglas Kellner, a theorist and analyst of the politics of global media:

> a new global culture is emerging as a result of computer and communications technology, a consumer society with its panorama of goods and services, transnational forms of architecture and design, and a wide range of products and cultural forms that are traversing national boundaries and becoming part of a new world culture.
>
> (n.d.)

This might herald the emergence of a global imagined community, some measure of emotional affinity with those who are otherwise distant, a kind of 'popular cosmopolitanism' (Nash, 2003).

However, despite these forces, what seems to be happening is in fact the proliferation of 'new' or resurgent nationalisms. In the United Kingdom, for example, devolution in Scotland and Wales is actually reinforcing nationalism or national sentiment, in England as well as in the devolved nations (see Aughey, 2007), where there is also opposition to the integration of the nation into the EU. On the continent of Europe, smaller regions such as the Basque Country and Catalonia in Spain continue to fight their cause. From the other side, we may look at the attempts by some supranational organizations to try to generate a supranational identity. The European Union has tried to develop common cultural and media policies and seeks to fund, for example, film projects which it hopes may add to a sense of shared culture and identity across the countries of Europe. In a sense this reproduces the activities of the nation state, as understood by someone such as Gellner, in developing a shared 'high culture' across a territory.

The growth of communication technologies doesn't only homogenize or standardize the world population; the individualization of media consumption also makes it possible for people to maintain their sense of cultural identity and specificity regardless of territorial factors. For instance, global diasporas may remain in regular, even permanent, contact with their home countries, living under one state while consuming and producing the imaginary of another. As media theorist Marie Gillespie has noted: 'improved access to, speed and effectiveness of transport, communication and information systems has enabled a strengthening of transnational kinship, religious, economic and political networks, leading to powerful globalizing alliances as well as troubling polarizations' (2002: 174). Indeed, parts of a diaspora may, despite living apart from a national state, still exercise influence upon its domestic politics, acting as what Jean Seaton has termed 'external republics ... groups of immigrants who remain fiercely committed to the communities from which they have come, and the ways of life they leave behind' (1999: 256). This is a kind of 'nationalism at a distance' and can be a powerful influence, especially in conflict situations (see also Appadurai in Nash, 2000: 110–14).

Despite much upheaval and challenge, the idea of nations and the feeling of attachment to them continues to shape our everyday understanding of political order locally, regionally and internationally. The independent and largely homogeneous nation with its own state is still the primary shape of the otherwise varied political structures under which most of us live. Our cultural habits and attitudes may be changing, but arguments about them still take place primarily within nations. And, significantly, we still think of the world largely in terms of nations and national peoples. Our 'mental map' of the globe divides it into sovereign states and classifies people, albeit loosely, according to their nationality. It is part of our everyday common sense or mental shorthand to speak of 'the French' or 'the Germans' or 'the Russians' as meaningful entities with national characteristics of which we are all aware. If nationalism, as Kedourie put it, 'holds that humanity is naturally divided into nations, that nations are known by certain characteristics which can be ascertained, and that the only legitimate type of government is national self-government' (1960: 12), are we not all, mostly and still, nationalists?

It seems likely, then, that nationalism, and more generally the grounding of political claims in an experience or a sense of community, is likely to continue to be a major part of the future ideological landscape. Contemporary social and technological changes may change the shape of such nationalism but not eradicate it. Yet nationalism still raises more questions than it answers. Pressing questions for the future concern the ways in which national communities cope with the continued – and in some cases growing – presence of substantial minorities; the rights of nations to protect themselves from globalizing pressures (economic, cultural and political); and the possibilities (as well as threats) of global cosmopolitanism. As these questions are resolved, by our social and political actions as well as by philosophical reflection, nationalism will be articulated and rearticulated with political positions across the spectrum.

Conclusion

In this chapter we have looked at nationalism in a slightly unusual way. Rather than treat it as an isolated political doctrine, we have considered the interaction of nationalism with other ideologies and touched on what this may tell us about the nature of ideology. We have seen how ideologies can be understood in terms of 'articulation', the way in which they are joined together and in the process transformed into something new. Nationalist ideology is not just or only a doctrine composed of certain core claims. It is a set of conceptual tools that contribute to a larger 'world view' and which may be drawn on by a range of political actors and thinkers in different ways, at different times and in different contexts. Furthermore, it makes possible a connection between such a world view and our sense of identity and our emotional attachments. But this connection, this articulation, is not one-way, and ideologies that join with nationalism are changed by it as much as they change nationalism.

Nationalism makes a claim as to the basis of human sociality and relationships. It gives reasons for why we should (or shouldn't) feel obliged to others. It advances a case for what makes the best form of legitimate government and suggests something about citizens' relationship to the state. But these claims can be articulated with a range of others. When it comes to advancing a case about the distribution of wealth, for example, or about the way in which an economy should be run, nationalism may be found to imply a kind of equality between all fellows, but it may also advocate a hierarchical and authoritarian form of government. But this variability should not blind us to the fact that nationalism is an ideology the central function of which is to provide an incontestable answer to the question of why we should think of ourselves as living together in certain ways. This, surely, is the fundamental question of any political theory, and perhaps it is what all ideology tries to answer: what is our relationship to each other? Why should I want to have anything to do with you? On what basis can I trust you or enter into any sort of collaboration with you?

Without an answer to these questions there can be no society. Political theory has provided answers to these questions in ways that are different from nationalism. In world history there have been other solutions to them too. Because nationalism answers these questions in ways that are often exclusivist, hostile to some people in order to favour others, some have sought to establish better and more open ways of answering these fundamental political questions, while others have tried to 'co-opt' nationalism to their cause. Perhaps in the future we will develop yet more answers. If our world is to become more successful in managing interdependence between the varied peoples of the globe, it will need to think of ways of under-standing that interconnection that do not just rely on homogeneity, exclusivity and territorial boundaries. But, because no other ideology has yet succeeded in providing, on its own, an answer of sufficient emotional force, in institutionalizing it and making it last, we are all, still, nationalists.

Further reading

Anyone undertaking the study of nationalism should start by reading 'the big three': Benedict Anderson's *Imagined Communities* (2006); Ernest Gellner's *Nations and Nationalism* (1983 and the 2006 reissue, with an interesting and important essay by John Breuilly); and of the many great works by Anthony Smith, *Nationalism: Theory, Ideology, History* (2010) provides a good starting point. Students should not hesitate to explore the key journal in the field, *Nations and Nationalism*.

For quick bites, *Nationalism: A Very Short Introduction* by Steven Elliott Grosby (2005) is worth a look, while the best compilation of short extracts from many of the major writers on this topic is still *Nationalism: A Reader* (1994), edited by A. D. Smith and John Hutchinson.

The debate stimulated by David Miller's endorsement of the 'principle of nationality' is well represented by the special issue of the journal *Nations and Nationalism* (see O'Leary, 1996) and by the special issue of the *Critical Review of International Social and Political Philosophy* (2008) addressing his 2007 book *Nationalism and Global Justice*. For an introduction to the debate about nationalism and cosmopolitanism, readers should look to *The Cosmopolitan Reader*, edited by David Held and Garret Brown (2010), and pay particular attention to the extracts 'Nationalism and Cosmopolitanism' by Kok-Chor Tan and 'Patriotism and Cosmopolitanism' by Martha C. Nussbaum. Also of use in this context is Daniele Archibugi's edited collection *Debating Cosmopolitics* (2003).

References

Anderson, Benedict (1991) *Imagined Communities*, 2nd edition, London: Verso.
—— (2006) *Imagined Communities*, revised edition, London: Verso.
Ang, Ien (1996) *Living Room Wars: Rethinking Media Audiences for a Postmodern World*, London: Routledge.
Archibugi, Daniele (ed.) (2003) *Debating Cosmopolitics*, London: Verso.
Archibugi, Daniele, Held, David and Kohler, Martin (eds) (1998) *Re-imagining Political Community: Studies in Cosmopolitan Democracy*, Cambridge: Polity Press.
Aughey, Arthur (2007) *The Politics of Englishness*, Manchester: Manchester University Press.
Berlin, Isaiah (1979) 'Nationalism: Past Neglect and Present Power', in *Against the Current: Essays in the History of Ideas*, London: Hogarth Press.
Billig, Michael (1995) *Banal Nationalism*, London: Sage.
Bloch, Marc (1961) *Feudal Society, Volume 2: Social Classes and Political Organisation*, Chicago: University of Chicago Press.
Breuilly, John (1982) *Nationalism*, Manchester: Manchester University Press.
Brown, Garrett Wallace and Held, David (2010) *The Cosmopolitanism Reader*, Cambridge: Polity.
Cameron, David (2010) 'Speech to Conservative Party Conference', Birmingham (available online at www.britishpoliticalspeech.org/speech-archive.htm?speech= 214).
Caney, Simon (2005) *Justice Beyond Borders: A Global Political Theory*, Oxford: Oxford University Press.
Chatterjee, Partha (1986) *Nationalist Thought and the Colonial World*, London: Zed Books.
Connor, Walker (1994) *Ethnonationalism: The Quest for Understanding*, Princeton NJ: Princeton University Press.
Critical Review of International Social and Political Philosophy (2008), special issue, 'Nationalism and Global Justice: David Miller and His Critics', 11 (4).

Dayan, Daniel and Katz, Elihu (1992) *Media Events: The Live Broadcasting of History*, Cambridge, MA: Harvard University Press.

Deutsch, Karl (1966) *Nationalism and Social Communication*, Cambridge, MA: MIT Press.

Fine, Robert (2007) *Cosmopolitanism*, London: Routledge.

Finlayson, Alan (2003) *Making Sense of New Labour*, London: Lawrence and Wishart.

—— (2011) 'Imagined Communities', in Kate Nash and Alan Scott (eds) *Blackwell Companion to Political Sociology*, revised and updated second edition, Oxford: Blackwell.

Freeden, Michael (1996) *Ideologies and Political Theory*, Oxford: Oxford University Press.

—— (1998) 'Is Nationalism a Distinct Ideology?', *Political Studies*, 46 (4), pp. 748–65.

Geertz, Clifford (1963) 'The Integrative Revolution: Primordial Sentiments and Civil Politics in the New States', in C. Geertz (ed.) *Old Societies and New States: The Quest for Modernity in Asia and Africa*, New York: Free Press.

Gellner, Ernest (1983) *Nations and Nationalism*, Oxford: Blackwell.

—— (2006) *Nations and Nationalism*, 2nd edition, Oxford, Blackwell.

Gillespie, Marie (2002) 'Dynamics of Diasporas: South Asian Media and Transnational Cultural Politics', in Gitte Sald and Thomas Tufte (eds) *Global Encounters: Media and Cultural Transformation*, Luton: University of Luton Press.

Greenfeld, Liah (1992) *Nationalism: Five Roads to Modernity*, Cambridge, MA: Harvard University Press.

Grosby, Steven (2005) *Nationalism: A Very Short Introduction*, Oxford: Oxford University Press.

Hall, Stuart (1985) 'Signification, Representation, Ideology: Althusser and the Post-structuralist Debates', *Critical Studies in Mass Communication*, 2 (2), pp. 91–114.

Held, David (2010) *Cosmopolitanism: Ideals and Realties*, Cambridge: Polity.

Hobsbawm, Eric and Ranger, Terence (1992) *The Invention of Tradition*, Cambridge: Cambridge University Press.

Ignatieff, Michael (1993) *Blood and Belonging: Journeys into the new Nationalism*, London: Chatto and Windus.

Kedourie, Elie (1960) *Nationalism*, London: Hutchinson.

Kellner, Douglas (n.d.) 'Globalization and the Postmodern Turn'. Available online at www.gseis.ucla.edu/faculty/kellner/.

Kenny, Michael (2003) 'Communitarianism', in Alan Finlayson (ed.) *Contemporary Political Thought: A Reader and Guide*, Edinburgh: Edinburgh University Press.

Kohn, Hans (1944) *The Idea of Nationalism: A Study of Its Ideas and Background*, New York: Macmillan.

Laclau, Ernesto (1977) *Politics and Ideology in Marxist Theory*, London: New Left Books.

Laclau, Ernesto and Mouffe, Chantal (1985) *Hegemony and Socialist Strategy*, London: Verso.

Linklater, Andrew (1998) *The Transformation of Political Community: Ethical Foundations of the Post-Westphalian Era*, Cambridge: Polity Press.

Mill, John Stuart (1995 [1861]) *On Representative Government*, Oxford: Oxford University Press.

Miller, David (1995) *On Nationality*, Oxford: Clarendon Press.

—— (2005) 'Reasonable Partiality Towards Compatriots', *Ethical Theory and Moral Practice*, 8 (1), pp. 63–81.

—— (2007) *National Responsibility and Global Justice*, Oxford: Oxford University Press.

Mosse, George (1985) *Nationalism and Sexuality: Middle Class Norms and Sexual Morality in Modern Europe*, Madison, WI: University of Wisconsin Press.

Mulhall, Stephen and Swift, Adam (1992) *Liberals and Communitarians*, Oxford: Blackwell.

Nash, Kate (ed.) (2000) *Readings in Contemporary Political Sociology*, Oxford: Blackwell.

—— (2003) 'Cosmopolitan Political Community: Why Does It Feel So Right?', *Constellations*, 10 (4), pp. 506–18.

Nimni, Ephraim (1994) *Marxism and Nationalism: Theoretical Origins of a Political Crisis*, London: Pluto Press.

O'Leary, Brendan (ed.) (1996) 'Symposium on David Miller's *On Nationality*', *Nations and Nationalism*, 2 (3).

Plamenatz, John (1976) 'Two Types of Nationalism', in Eugene Kamenka (ed.) *Nationalism: The Nature and Evolution of an Idea*, London: Edward Arnold.

Renan, Ernest (1990) 'Qu'est-ce qu'une nation?', in Homi Bhaba (ed.) *Nation and Narration*, London: Routledge.

Seaton, Jean (1999) 'Why Do We Think the Serbs Do It? The New "Ethnic" Wars and the Media', *Political Quarterly*, 70 (3), pp. 254–70.

Seton-Watson, Hugh (1977) *Nations and States: An Enquiry into the Origins of Nations and the Politics of Nationalism*, London: Methuen.

Slack, Jennifer Daryl (1996) 'The Theory and Method of Articulation', in David Morley and Kuan-Hsing Chen (eds), *Stuart Hall: Critical Dialogues in Cultural Studies*, London: Routledge, pp. 112–30.

Smith, Anthony D. (1991) *National Identity*, London: Penguin.

—— (1998) *Nationalism and Modernism*, London: Routledge.

—— (2001) *Nationalism: Theory, Ideology, History*, Cambridge, Polity.

Smith, Anthony and Hutchinson, John (eds) (1994) *Nationalism: A Reader*, Oxford: Oxford University Press.

Therborn, Goran (1999) *The Ideology of Power and the Power of Ideologies*, London: Verso.

Walby, Sylvia (1996) 'Woman and Nation', in G. Balakrishan (ed.) *Mapping the Nation*, London: Verso, pp. 235–45.

Weber, Eugene (1979) *Peasants into Frenchmen: The Modernisation of Rural France, 1870–1914*, London: Chatto and Windus.

Whyte, John (1990) *Interpreting Northern Ireland*, Oxford: Clarendon.

Williams, Glyn A. (1991) *When Was Wales?*, Harmondsworth: Penguin.

Yuval-Davis, Nira (1997) *Gender and Nation*, London: Sage.

Fascism

Rick Wilford

> Fascist movements and regimes were characterized more by what they were against than what they were for – a Manichean division of the world into the forces of good and evil.
>
> (Eatwell, 1995)

Introduction

Almost seventy years after the end of the Second World War seems a secure vantage point from which to do little more than look over the remains of fascism. After all, the dictatorial regimes that constituted the fascist Axis were utterly defeated and their satellites or puppets vanquished.

Militarily, 1945 represented a consummate victory for the Allied forces, and yet, while the fascist regimes were themselves crushed, the rag-bag of ideas upon which they were based continued to be – and indeed still are – peddled by their adherents. Such adherence is expressed in a variety of forms, including the desecration of both Jewish cemeteries in Belgium and mosques in Italy, arson attacks on immigrant hostels in Germany, the bombing of a gay bar in London's West End and the continuing publication of 'Holocaust denial' literature. Each is a symptom of the continued existence of neo-fascist groups and their propensity to engage in anti-Semitic, anti-Muslim, racist and homophobic violence. The calculated murders of seventy-seven (mostly young) people in Norway in July 2011 by Anders Breivik – whose self-styled 'manifesto' celebrated his Islamophobia, anti-feminism and anti-Marxism, and envisioned a Europe from which all Muslims would be deported – stoked memories of earlier fascist movements and parties, and tactics. What these and Breivik share is a hatred of both difference and those who celebrate diversity.

Another symptom of the resilience of fascist ideas is that across Europe, including in countries formerly subjugated by Nazism, neo-fascist and radical/extreme right parties attract in some cases significant levels of electoral support. Such parties, which articulate xenophobic, exclusive forms of nationalism, include France's *Front National* (FN). In 1995, the FN candidate and then party leader, Jean-Marie Le Pen – who has described the Holocaust as 'a mere detail in history' – polled 15 per cent of the national vote in the first round of the presidential election. In 2002 he increased his vote share to just under 17 per cent, coming second in the poll ahead of the socialist candidate, thereby guaranteeing him a straight fight with the incumbent (and emphatic winning) candidate, Jacques Chirac, in the second and final presidential ballot. In 2012, Le Pen's daughter, Marine, the new leader of the FN, secured almost 18 per cent in the first round of the presidential election, attracting over 6 million voters, and the party subsequently returned to the French Parliament for the first time since 1998.

The electoral support for neo-fascist parties is not confined to France. In Austria, the Freedom Party – established by a former member of the SS – was formerly led by Jorg Heider, a man who had extolled the employment policies of the Nazi era. In 1999 it emerged as the joint second largest party in the national election, its level of support enabling it to form a coalition government with the Austrian People's Party. Now led by Heinz-Christian Strache, the subject of disputed neo-Nazi allegations, its candidate was runner-up in the 2010 presidential election, having emerged as the country's third largest party at the 2008 National Council (parliamentary) election. By contrast, in the UK the neo-Nazi British National Party has fared dismally at parliamentary, devolved and local elections, but did win two seats at the UK's European parliamentary elections in 2009, attracting just under a million votes.

Such electoral evidence, including support for Greece's neo-fascist 'Golden Dawn' party, implies that an obituary of fascism would be premature. But why, for some, does such a discredited ideology retain its appeal?

'Appeals' of fascism

Part of the answer lies in the ability of fascists to simplify the complexities of political life. Characteristically, its ideologues divide peoples and nations into two irreconcilable camps, 'them' and 'us': those who are not of, or for, 'us' are the enemy. 'They', whether Jews, Blacks, Muslims or 'foreigners' in general, are responsible for the ills besetting 'us'. This feature of the doctrine alerts us to its exclusivity, its 'either-or-ism'. But this is much more than a simple dualism. The bifurcation is predicated upon a hierarchy of value: 'they' are not just different from, but inferior to, 'us'. The notion of superior and inferior peoples – in Nazi terms, *Ubermenschen* and *Untermenschen* – justified a relationship of domination and subordination that led, ultimately, to the death camps of Europe. Whether couched in terms of a superior state, as in Mussolini's Italy, or a 'master race', as was the case in Hitler's Germany, fascism was and is both exclusivist and inegalitarian.

Its stress on superiority rather than mere difference distinguishes fascism from nationalism, with which it does have an affinity. But, whereas nationalism (see chapter 5) can be inclusive, co-exist with other doctrines and respect the integrity of other self-governing nations, fascism neither tolerates ideological competitors nor recognizes a fundamental equality among nations. This basic intolerance is also signalled by its celebration of militarism. Fascism is a belligerent form of nationalism, contemptuous of the rights of both individuals and other nations, seeking proof of its vitality in the ability to subject others to its thrall. The pursuit of its goals – whether national glory or racial supremacy – was conducted not through the power of argument but rather through the argument of power, and its armed forces became the instrument of national honour and the agency of redemption.

Fascism did of course flourish in the inter-war period, initially in Italy and subsequently in Germany, and was mimicked by parties and movements elsewhere in Europe, including Britain. To that extent it appeared as and, according

RICK WILFORD

to its exponents, was the new doctrine for the new age of the twentieth century, representing a break with the past by consigning other doctrines to the dustbin of history. Yet, while extolling its novelty, the ideologues of fascism were mindful of the past. In that respect, it is a Janus-like doctrine, looking both forward and backward, seeking to revivify some imagined, pre-industrial sense of community and belonging, whether it was the romanticized Roman Empire or the image of a sylvan mediaeval Germany. Moreover, fascism was and is a counter-revolutionary ideology, seeking to subvert the civilizing effects of the Enlightenment that had displaced myth and superstition in favour of rationalism and secularism.

Already we can sense something of the duality of fascism's appeal. While celebrating those aspects of a re-imagined past its adherents considered inspiring, it also rejected other traditions and ideas that encumbered its primary mission: that of national redemption. Conservatism (see chapter 3), while sensitive to the past, was regarded by fascists as unequal to the task of national re-awakening and rebirth. For fascist ideologues the attachment of conservatism to emergent democratic norms rendered it powerless to confront the universalizing ambitions of competing ideologies: national regeneration required the defeat of conservatism and its vested interests, which were perceived as a brake on the wheel of history. Moreover, service in the cause of national re-awakening required not the pursuit of individualism prescribed by liberalism, or the realization of an egalitarian society promised by socialism, but the rebirth of the nation as the living community to which all true peoples belonged. A recovered national identity would transcend the individual and unite all classes in a common enterprise. As Sternhell (1979: 368) observes, fascist doctrine offered 'a vision of a coherent and reunited people [and] waged an implacable war against anything which stood for diversity or pluralism'.

Plotting a definition

Though we inevitably associate fascism with the regimes of Hitler and Mussolini, it did not appear entirely unannounced with Mussolini's march on Rome in 1922, but emerged from an eclectic range of ideas that long pre-dated the twentieth century. Yet, tracing the provenance of those ideas is not a simple task. As Paul Hayes (1973: 19) has observed, 'fascist theory is not a tightly knit bundle of ideas. It is, in fact, rather untidy and inchoate . . . composed of a large number of diverse ideas, drawn from different cultures'.

These ideas were unscrupulously pillaged from other traditions, cultures and doctrines. Moreover, there is no *locus classicus* akin, say, to the *Communist Manifesto* for Marxists, which supplied inspiration for fascist leaders and thinkers. Rather, fascist thought flowed from a variety of sources which later surged into the mainstreams of Italian fascism and German National Socialism.

To plot the course of the evolution of fascism, this chapter provides a set of organizing themes that recur in the writings of its precursors, exponents and followers, namely: statism, racialism, imperialism, elitism and national socialism. These interact and overlap and vary in their significance across the various fascist parties and movements, each of which was influenced by its peculiar national history, traditions, cultures and prejudices. Thus, while acknowledging that there were distinctive national variations, the argument of this chapter is that fascism can be understood by focusing upon its intellectual heritage. The exploration of these origins thereby provides a framework within which each of the variations can be accommodated. What the chapter offers is not, therefore, an unambiguous definition of fascism, but rather an exploration of its key themes.

Besides the difficulties of tracing these themes to their sources, there is another problem confronting the examination of fascism. The heavy and fatal emphasis upon racialism that paved the way to the death camps does, in the view of some scholars, set Nazism apart from other fascist movements. From this perspective, the systematic practice of mass genocide renders National Socialism as unique, and not an exaggerated variation of fascism. While in no way diminishing this argument, the purpose here is to identify the ideas that supplied the pretext for the 'Final Solution', whereby the manufacture of death became a (self-financing) way of life. Moreover, to imply that other fascist regimes were not implicated in the Holocaust is to turn a blind eye to their complicity in transporting Jews and others to certain death in Auschwitz and elsewhere.

While the exponents of fascism sought to celebrate its modernity, none of the various elements that they fashioned into a body of doctrine were new in themselves. It was, however, the assiduity with which those elements were implemented – mass mobilization, mass propaganda and mass murder – that leant fascism its modernizing claim. Its novelty lay in the execution of ideas – and of people – rather than the ideas themselves. Fascism, then, owed much to an intellectually pillaged past. Most immediately, the fascist movements and regimes of the inter-war period inherited their ideas from a mood of revolt that was current in Europe towards the end of the nineteenth century and which had developed throughout its course. This mood is our starting point, not least because it embodied the antithetical nature of fascist doctrine.

A starting point

The labelling of historical periods in terms of a prevailing mood or climate is a tempting but risky undertaking, invariably concealing as much as it reveals. Nevertheless, one can characterize the European intellectual climate towards the end of the nineteenth century as one of revolt. Just as the regimes of Mussolini and Hitler emerged from economic and political crises, the embryonic ideology of fascism was one outcome of an intellectual upheaval that become more apparent as the nineteenth century drew to a close. Initially, this upheaval took the form of an assault upon liberal doctrine.

The development of liberalism, as chapter 2 indicates, was associated with Enlightenment optimism, its proponents stressing the importance of individual judgment as the guide to action. Enlightenment thinkers demanded a new political system that would liberate individuals from the shackles of feudalism. Their portrayal of society as an aggregate of rational individuals, possessed of natural rights, challenged conservatism's pessimistic and hierarchical view of human nature. The liberal belief that individuals in interaction would produce a natural harmony of interests was opposed to the conservative belief in the necessity for order imposed by a natural hierarchy. Whereas conservatives espoused a paternalistic conception of society, emphasizing duty and deference, liberals stressed individual rights and a belief in self-government.

However, the advance of liberalism in Europe was uneven, and initial opposition to it was sporadic. Yet, by the 1880s and 1890s, a generation of thinkers had developed a body of work that constituted a challenge to what they perceived as the outmoded character of liberal ideas. It is within the context of this revolt against liberalism that the more immediate precursors of fascism can be located.

The rational individualism of liberal doctrine – its belief in diversity, pluralism and tolerance – led, so these critics argued, to insecurity, instability and mediocrity. Their focus was not the individual but the wider community, commonly represented as a self-regarding, organic whole. Collectivism and conformity, rather than individualism and choice, was their preferred social order. Moreover, the liberal emphasis on reason as the guide to action was supplanted by a preference for non-rational motives – instinct, descent, heredity and race – which were celebrated as the primary forces driving human behaviour.

Such thinkers, some of whom owed their inspiration to a perverse reading of Charles Darwin's (1809–82) *Origin of Species* (1859) and have been dubbed 'social Darwinists', portrayed individuals as unreflective, amoral creatures, spurred by the instinctive fight for survival. Darwin himself did not, however, draw any normative lessons from the theory of natural selection in order to apply them to human society. Indeed, the very phrase 'the survival of the fittest' – coined not by Darwin, but by the British philosopher Herbert Spencer (1820–1903) – was seized upon eagerly by proto-fascist thinkers because it imparted a simplifying gloss to the theory of evolution.

Such contorted thinking provided a radical alternative to liberalism's emphasis upon deliberate, rational choice as the basis of human action. Spencer's belief, shared by other social Darwinists – that society pro-gresses through a harsh struggle for survival and that the weak suffer from their own incompetence – contributed to the assault upon liberalism's values. Moreover, the muscular philosophy of social Darwinism fostered an anti-intellectual climate within which racialist 'theories' flourished.

Race and state

Pseudo-scientific 'theories' of racialism, partly inspired by a wilful misreading of Darwin's ideas, were but one manifestation of a much longer current of thought. For instance, during the late eighteenth and early nineteenth centuries the theme of racial superiority surfaced in Germany with the popularization of the *Volk*. At a literal level this concept translates as 'the people', but it also has a more abstract meaning – a system of absolute values and an immutable metaphysical ideal of peoplehood. As George Mosse (1971: 8) puts it: 'Just as individual men had a soul, so there existed a *Volk* soul which, like man's soul, gave the *Volk* its unique and unchanging character'. The task for Germans was to recover and liberate their collective soul, which was 'wild and dynamic, based on emotions rather than on a tortured intellectualizing'.

An early exponent of this abstract interpretation of the *Volk* was Johann Fichte (1762–1814), who, like his contemporary Johann Herder (1744–1803), depicted the German nation as a natural whole united by descent, language and culture. At the beginning of the nineteenth century Fichte propagated the belief that Germany, though disunited and militarily humiliated by France, would eventually prevail because of the *natural* superiority of its people. In his *Addresses to the German Nation* (1807–8) he portrayed the Germans as an archetypal *Volk*, in whom was invested a special mission on behalf of mankind: that of leading a cultural struggle against 'Western', primarily French, influence.

Such beliefs, allied to a sense of mission, provided a source of brooding consolation for nascent Germans, one that was nourished by Herder. He purported to trace the origins of the *Volk* to mediaeval Germany, envisaged as a close-knit rural society wherein the *Volkisch* 'spirit' or 'soul' had been freely expressed. In the writings of both thinkers, the *Volk* was presented in romantic terms: it connoted a happy, rural idyll, an organically whole national community in which the interests of the individual were subordinated to the national 'spirit'. Moreover, and crucially, both asserted that the German 'spirit' was superior to that of other peoples.

This emphasis upon the organic nature of the state was also characteristic of Georg Hegel (1770–1831). Unlike Fichte, however, Hegel did not equate the state with an ethnic or natural conception of the *Volk*, although he did address the issue of German unification. In *The German Constitution* (1803) he lamented the disintegration of the nation into a hotchpotch of rival petty prince-doms, thereby depriving it of the collective sentiment he believed to be the foundation of statehood. He elaborated these and other ideas in *Philosophy of Right* (1821), in which history was presented as a dynamic process whose engine was the conflict or dialectic of ideas. In his view the state was the ultimate idea, the realization of spirit or reason in history. Unlike Fichte and Herder, however,

Hegel was preoccupied not by the search for German statehood but rather by the 'idea' of the state, which he believed to be based upon 'the power of reason actualizing itself as will'.

Hegel's intention was not to subordinate the individual to the whole, but to illustrate how the state supplied its inhabitants with a common focus: a set of institutions and values with which all could freely associate. It was through their common membership of the state that individuals could move beyond their own private interests and identify with the common good. Yet Hegel's ideas, like those of Darwin, were to fall prey to the avid search by fascists for an intellectual tradition.

Hegel's portrayal of the state as the culmination of history was to infatuate Mussolini and his leading ideologue and arbiter of cultural policy, Giovanni Gentile (1875–1944). But, whereas Hegel recognized the relationship between civil society and the state to be one of mutual dependence, in fascist Italy state and society were conflated: 'Everything for the State, nothing outside the State'. The quest for a renewed Roman Empire required a cloak of philosophical respectability, and this Mussolini and Gentile purported to find in Hegel's idea of the state as an end in itself. This, however, was a perversion of the work by Hegel, who became another casualty in the search for an intellectual tradition that could fuel national regeneration. By contrast, as we shall see, German National Socialism did not require even a distorted interpretation of Hegel. Unlike Mussolini, Hitler regarded the state not as an end in itself but as a means to assure racial superiority. It was Fichte who had laid the basis of the *Volkisch* ideology that was to become a core principle of Nazism.

The belief in a superior German culture charged with a mission to overcome 'Western' influences gathered pace throughout the nineteenth century. In Germany, Friedrich Jahn (1778–1852) furthered the idea of a natural organic community and extolled the superiority of an anti-liberal, authoritarian Germanic political tradition. In *German Nationhood* (1810) he defined the basis of nationhood as racial purity and asserted the uniqueness and superiority of all Germans. His goal was a greater German 'people's democracy', encompassing Austria, Holland, Switzerland and Denmark, from which all foreign influences would be expunged.

Jahn prized collective national sentiment and nationhood above both individual rights and universalism and as such supplied a motive for a struggle against 'the West', that is, against liberal precepts. It was a message that became increasingly strident at the turn of the nineteenth century, as intellectuals from different national backgrounds sought a 'third way' between Enlightenment values and the growing challenge of socialism.

By the mid-nineteenth century the concept of racial superiority was firmly established in European thought and was by no means confined to the works of German thinkers. An early exposition of racial 'theory' was provided by a French diplomat, Count Arthur Gobineau (1816–62), whose *Essay on the Inequality of Races of Man* (1853–5) proclaimed the superiority of white 'races' over non-whites and Jews as well as the primacy of 'race' above individual and nation. Furthermore, he asserted degrees of racial purity among whites: those possessing the highest levels of purity carried the potential to advance civilization, whereas those less richly endowed transmitted racial decay. In the former category lay the Teutons, whilst Slavs and Celts were consigned to the latter group.

The attempt to invent a racial hierarchy within which Jews occupied the lowliest position can be placed within a tradition of anti-Semitism that long pre-dates Gobineau. Stereotypes of Jews were commonplace throughout much of European history and, during the later eighteenth and the first half of the nineteenth century, were expressed primarily in the form of religious antagonism towards Judaism. This cultural prejudice, widely propagated in contemporary popular literature, supplied a spurious rationale for anti-Semitism and assisted in creating a receptive climate for the ideas of Gobineau and certain of the social Darwinists.

It had earlier been contended that the 'Jewish problem' could be solved by re-socializing Jews, encouraging them to shed their religious beliefs, which served to set them apart from the dominant cultures of their 'host' societies. By engaging in 'honest toil', Jews would acquire new roots and thus become deserving of assimilation into their adopted countries. However, as the essentially irrational *Volkisch* nationalism began to take root, Jews came to be regarded not merely as non-assimilable but as constituting a *racial* rather than a cultural threat to the German nation.

This transformation from cultural to biological anti-Semitism was stimulated by social Darwinism. One English thinker who contributed to this metamorphosis was Houston Stewart Chamberlain (1855–1927), son-in-law of the German composer Richard Wagner. Asserting that the fittest were those who were racially pure, Chamberlain developed the notion of the 'Aryan folk nation', which, he believed, was 'destined to triumph because of its superior genetic gifts' (Hayes, 1973: 23ff.). On this basis, inter-racial marriage (miscegenation) was scorned as an unnatural evil, since it diluted the purity of the blood. Moreover, egalitarianism, internationalism and pacifism were dismissed by Chamberlain on the ground that they offended the natural order of things. In their place, war and the struggle for survival by the fittest were extolled as evidence of a race's vitality. Destiny belonged to those confident of their inherent superiority, a pre-eminence bestowed by a presumed racial purity.

National imperialism

During much of the nineteenth century, nationalism, through its association with the French Revolution, was understood by many as an agent of emancipation and freedom. However, under the impact of a racially defined conception of statehood, a new European nationalism began to develop: one nourished by the conviction that the unification of both Italy and Germany was the outcome of an intoxicating mixture of 'blood and iron'. The growing belief in a racial state spanning generations and existing frontiers and the advocacy of struggle by Spencerite social Darwinists merged to provide a rationale for imperialism. This found expression in the principle of *Machtpolitik*. Loosely translated, it means power politics, but more to the point, it was the belief that might was right.

The creed of *Machtpolitik* was exemplified by the German general Friedrich von Bernhardi (1843–1930):

> might gives the right to occupy or conquer. It is at once the supreme right and the dispute as to what is right is decided by the arbitrariment of war. War gives a biologically just decision, since its decisions rest on the very nature of things.
>
> (Bernhardi, 1914)

Here lay the pretext for national expansion: racial superiority and the naturalness of conflict provided a perverse normative guide. In this worldview, power and morality were fused: the interests of the nation took priority over the rule of international law, and so the belief in the universal rights of man was disdained.

The interlacing of power politics with nationalism and racialism is equally explicit in the works of Chamberlain and his fellow Englishman Karl Pearson (1857–1936). Pearson regarded the exercise of might as a moral injunction: 'when wars cease there will be nothing to check the fertility of the inferior stock' (1905: 27). Chamberlain shared this grotesque view. Presenting the process of history as a 'race struggle', and arguing that only the 'Aryans' were capable of creating culture, he declaimed: 'the power of might is the destiny of selected races . . . it is their duty to conquer and destroy the impure and inferior' (quoted in Hayes, 1973: 115).

This, in effect, meant that the advocacy of war and suppression was a 'moral' duty. Support for the equation of race with statehood and for the primacy of national as opposed to individual interests began to converge towards the later part of the nineteenth century. A 'natural' national greatness, imbued with a spiritual mission, was harnessed in order to supply the motive for imperialism.

Elitism and leadership

The growing emphasis upon race, coupled with the idea of an imperial mission, required leadership of a special character: a figure who embodied the claimed virtues of the race. The disdain for egalitarian principles shared by social Darwinists led them to reject democratic forms of government. Not only did they postulate a natural hierarchy among 'races', but they also asserted the existence of naturally superior individuals within racial groups. Here lay the justification for leadership by an elite.

One exponent of elitism was Friedrich Nietzsche (1844–1900). Some of his ideas and much of his rhetoric were to be appropriated by fascists, and yet he too fell foul of their search for a philosophical tradition. Nietzsche affirmed the irrational 'will to power' as the mainspring of personality, and deemed the value of life to be measured by perpetual struggle: 'Life itself is essentially appropriation, infringement, the overpowering of the alien and the weaker, oppression, hardness, the imposition of one's own form, assimilation and, at the least and mildest, exploitation' (Hayes, 1973: 34). This virile prescription demanded an elite of the tough and the strong that would lead the 'lower orders', whose instincts were slavishly to defer to their natural leaders and betters.

His portrayal of the leader figure took on heroic proportions: a 'Superman', a 'magnificent blond beast', who would trounce the weak, the decadent and the mediocre. Equality had no place in this vision, and in its stead was a conception of hierarchy, at the top of which strode the naturally superior. This credo was to prove irresistible to later fascist leaders: in Nazi Germany it was enshrined as the *Fuhrerprinzip*, and in Italy it was personified in the cult of *Il Duce* – in short, dictatorship.

Yet, as already implied, Nietzsche's albeit equivocal reputation was sullied by fascism. Although a proponent of the irrational, he did not advocate the organic society favoured by proto-fascists, but instead celebrated rugged individualism. Nor did he embrace nationalism, and, far from decrying miscegenation, he considered it to be the crucible in which great culture was forged. He was, however, opposed to the Judeo-Christian tradition, labelling Christianity a 'slave religion' that, along with its secular successors, humanism and socialism, 'encouraged a false sense of universalism, tending to promote pity for the weak rather than respect for the strong' (Eatwell, 1995: 8). It was the appeal of his wilder rhetorical flourishes – the imagery of blond beasts animated by the will to power – that proved compelling to the would-be 'Supermen' of Nazi Germany and Fascist Italy. As with Hegel and Darwin, the appropriation of Nietzsche as a progenitor of fascism was testimony to the selective looting of ideas engaged in by its ideologues.

The advocacy of elitism was shared by many of Nietzsche's contemporaries. At a time when the fitful movement towards mass suffrage was occurring, fear of the implications of democracy encouraged numerous thinkers to devise arguments for the maintenance of leadership by the few. The Italian academic Vilfredo Pareto (1848–1923), for instance, in a number of works extolled the virtues of elite leadership (*Les Systemes Socialistes*, 1902, and *The Mind and Society*, 1916–19). He likened society to a pyramid, at the apex of which stood a gifted minority fit to govern, and below which sprawled an acquiescent, pliant and mediocre mass. Such ideas bore the hallmark of social Darwinism, as did Pareto's theory of history, which he understood as the story of conflict between warring elites. So popular were his views that in 1922 Mussolini made him a member of the Italian Senate.

Disdain for 'the masses' was shared by the French theorist Gustave Le Bon (1841–1931). His *Psychology of Crowds* (1865), later cited with approval by Mussolini, offered a justification for elitism and authoritarianism. In Germany, Julius Langbehn's (1851–1907) *Rembrandt as Educator* (1891) echoed Le Bon's contempt for mass democracy. Langbehn postulated race as the determining factor in history: the 'power of blood' was, he claimed, supreme and transcended the nation. His preferred elite was the hereditary aristocracy, which he urged to mobilize the masses in order to crush those he considered guilty of propounding liberal, democratic and socialist ideas: the bourgeoisie and assimilated Jews.

Though their precise roles as progenitors of fascism differed, Nietzsche, Pareto, Le Bon and Langbehn did help to foster the 'baleful creed' of permanent struggle, elitism and unreason. In that respect each contributed to the climate of irrationalism that characterized Europe in the later nineteenth century. The cult of elitism, the emphasis on power, struggle and authoritarianism, and the stress on feeling and instinct were pitted against the rational individualism of the liberal world. In the developing mass societies of late nineteenth-century Europe, the portrayal of the individual as an integral part of an organic whole, valued only inasmuch as she or he served that whole, was a direct challenge to liberalism. Moreover, the defiant critique of Enlightenment values supplied by social Darwinists led them to prize inegalitarianism. The celebrants of unreason regarded the people as an unthinking, irrational mass, responsive to the appeals of emotion and feeling orchestrated by those Nietzsche had characterized as 'the highest specimens'.

National Socialism

The appeal of the prophets of unreason was further enhanced by their explanation of worsening material conditions confronting Europe. The severe economic depression in the last quarter of the nineteenth century weakened the belief in both *laissez-faire* economics and free trade; as such liberalism's claim to be the guarantor of economic progress came under increasing strain. Furthermore, the Prussian rise to ascendancy in Germany, the Piedmont ascendancy in Italy and the defeat of France in 1870 by the Prussian army appeared to demonstrate the law of the strong advocated by some social Darwinists. The conjunction of these economic and political events underpinned the threat to liberal values. But the shock troops of the doctrinal assault against Enlightenment values, armed with their irrational remedies for national renewal, also had to confront the growth of socialism.

Socialism sought to divide nations on the basis of class interests and to promote international workers' solidarity, ideas that were anathema to proponents of elite-led *Machtpolitik* intent on imperial conquest and expansion. In order to confront both liberalism and socialism, a 'third way' needed to be fashioned between these competing ideologies. Part of the answer lay in the promotion of economic self-sufficiency (autarky).

In German thought, the idea that national resources should be marshalled for the national purpose was well established. Fichte, for instance, had advocated a planned economy, the reduced reliance on imports and the restriction of external trade, as the means to cohere the state. His prescriptions amounted to a highly regulated economy that was wholly at odds with the tenets of economic liberalism advanced by his contemporary Adam Smith (1732–90). Moreover, Fichte proposed the expansion of Germany to its 'natural boundaries', as did another apostle of autarky, Friedrich List (1789–1846). List advanced imperial expansion and the regulation of capital and labour by the state: in short, a planned economy founded upon a Germany that incorporated both neighbouring states and overseas territories.

In Germany during the nineteenth century, economic self-sufficiency came increasingly to be seen as necessary for the development of state power, and that goal entailed imperial expansion. In an atmosphere suffused with *Machtpolitik*, the espousal of internationalism by socialists was equated with cowardice, whereas the exercise of power politics demanded the appropriation of resources. In domestic terms, autarky was deemed to require loyalty, obedience and service in the national interest, not the rights of liberty, equality and fraternity. Liberal political economy was rejected because of its opposition to state intervention and its advocacy of free trade, while socialism was spurned because it was seen to weaken the nation by advocating class conflict, championing egalitarianism and promoting internationalism.

In Britain the case for autarky was voiced both by Joseph Chamberlain (1836–1914), during the tariff reform campaign, and the *fin de siècle* advocates of social imperialism, including George Bernard Shaw (1856–1950). What they had in common was, as Robert Skidelsky (1975: 57) notes, a belief in 'the national community as a value to be defended against free-trade internationalism on the one side and working class internationalism on the other'. These themes of protectionism, imperial preference and a belief in a technocratically managed economy were to be revisited by Oswald Mosley (1896–1974), the leading British fascist of the inter-war period.

While autarky did not take root in Britain, it flourished in Germany and Italy and was intimately related to the corporate state. Corporatism asserted that the array of social institutions, including the family, the region and, above all, the nation, enjoy a higher value than the individual. Its exponents claimed that the development and security of the individual depended upon the well-being of these institutions and their ability to foster social, economic, emotional and spiritual solidarity. As such, their interests transcended those of the individual. From this perspective, the health of the wider community, commonly represented as a living and dynamic organism, was paramount: all its constituent parts were required to serve this higher purpose.

It was no accident that Mussolini chose an organic metaphor to characterize Italy under fascism: 'A society working with the harmony and precision of the human body. Every interest and every individual is subordinated to the overriding purpose of the nation' (Walker, 1977: 17). Here lay the third way between liberal capitalism and socialism. 'Liberalism', wrote Mussolini, 'denies the state in the interests of the individual', while 'socialism . . . ignores the unity of classes established in one economic and moral reality in the state' (Lyttelton, 1973: 42).

Keenly aware of the mobilizing appeal of nationalism and persuaded of the necessity of conflict to secure change, Mussolini attempted to fuse nationalism and socialism. The means lay in corporatism, which exhorted all classes to collaborate in building the fascist state. Instead of fighting among themselves on the basis of class interests, or of lending primacy to the pursuit of individual interests, Italians were urged to engage in a common external struggle: that between proletarian and bourgeois nations. This would rescue Italy from its status as the poor relation of Europe, secure social cohesion and restore national greatness.

In devising this corporatist formula, Mussolini appropriated and perverted syndicalist ideas (Roberts, 1979; Gregor, 1979a). Originating in France, syndicalism had advocated the creation of autonomous worker organizations (syndicates) as the basis for proletarian revolution. Syndicalists believed that through direct action at the workplace the revolutionary transformation of capitalism could be achieved. An ex-socialist (he had edited the socialist journal *Avanti!*), Mussolini was familiar with the syndicalist vision. When he came to power, and especially after 1925 when he consolidated his dictatorship, he began to install a system of corporations modelled loosely on these ideas. But, whereas revolutionary syndicalists had envisaged their organizations as worker monopolies, Mussolini's corporations encompassed both workers and employers. Moreover, though notionally equal, the spokesmen of capitalist interests were relatively unfettered, while labour representatives became mere puppets of his regime: the authentic voices of the working class were stifled by imprisonment, exile or death.

The exertion of centralized control over these corporations signals a crucial distinction between the syndicalist vision and Mussolini's. Whereas syndicalists were profoundly anti-statist, he elevated the state to a position of dominance:

> For Fascism the State is an absolute before which individuals and groups are relative. Individuals and groups are 'thinkable' only in so far as they are within the State . . . when one says Fascism one says the State.
> (Lyttelton, 1973: 53, 55)

Here lay the crude attempt to fuse nationalism with socialism. Italian fascism emphasized duty, sacrifice and obedience in the service of the nation-state. The compelling interest was that of the nation, served by the rigidly organized and hierarchically controlled corporations that were bereft of autonomy. The fusion of nationalism with socialism was served by a brutally simplistic formula: the nation is the community to which all belong, thus all classes must serve the interests of the nation.

The pursuit of autarky also led to the imposition of a centralized and planned economy in Germany. While corporatism was less fully developed than in Italy, the crushing of independent trade unions and their replacement in 1933 by the 'Labour Front' was couched in organic terms. Workers and employers were exhorted to serve, in Hitler's words, 'only one interest, the interest of the nation; only one view, the bringing of Germany to the point of political and economic self-sufficiency' (Noakes and Pridham, 1974: 405).

In Nazi Germany, as in Italy, the claim to socialist credentials was baseless. A belief in the common ownership of the means of production or in the abolition of wage slavery, for instance, held no place in Hitler's worldview. In *Mein Kampf* (1925–6) Hitler purported to define the 'socialist' aspects of Nazism in quite vacuous terms, such as 'nationalizing the masses' or 'giving the broad masses back to their nation'. To be 'social' was to share in a sense of 'feeling and destiny' in the national community.

As Robert Cecil observes, in Hitler's view the only acceptable form of socialism was that of the 'front line' which had developed in the trenches of the First World War. This was characterized by Alfred Rosenberg (1893–1946), a leading ideologue of Nazism's racial 'theory', in the following terms: 'Out of the battlefield, the men in grey brought back something new: a feeling for the social and national cohesiveness of the different classes' (Cecil, 1972: 57). The camaraderie of soldiers – Mussolini coined the word 'trenchocracy' to convey the same sentiment (Griffin, 1995: 28–9) – and the common bonds forged in battle became the spurious metaphor for socialism.

The 'Twenty-Five Point Programme' of the Nationalist Socialist German Workers Party published in 1920 (Noakes and Pridham, 1974: 405) included such ostensibly impeccable socialist goals as the nationalization of large corporations, the abolition of unearned incomes, the confiscation of war profits and the prohibition of land speculation. But the commitment to such an agenda wore increasingly thin, despite the fact that Hitler was keenly aware of the need to counter the growth of support among workers for socialism, itself portrayed as a 'Jewish Marxist conspiracy'.

By the later 1920s the relative failure of the Nazi Party to secure mass support among the working classes led it to re-orientate its appeal to capitalists, small businessmen, farmers and white-collar workers. While there were those in the Nazi Party, like the Strasser brothers, Gregor and Otto, and the leader of the SA (the Brownshirts), Ernst Rohm, who sought to promote more tangible material benefits for the working class, they were progressively marginalized. The persistence of Gregor Strasser and of Rohm in seeking to sustain and develop gains for workers led, ultimately, to their murders in 1934. Their 'purge', during the 'night of the long knives', on the pretext that they were engaged in a plot against Hitler, also effectively purged the Nazi Party of an already threadbare socialist programme.

Consistent with his unwavering belief in racial hierarchy, egalitarianism was anathema to Hitler, whether within or among peoples. What mattered was the moulding of a common unity among Germans as nationalists, thereby transcending the alternative appeals of class and individual interest. Like Mussolini, Hitler subscribed to an organic conception of society. Individuals mattered only insofar as they served the whole: 'If we consider the question, what in reality are the state-forming or even state-preserving forces, we can sum them up under one single head: the ability and will of the individual to sacrifice himself for the totality' (1969: 140).

Fascist corporatism also supplied the means to mobilize and control the working population, ostensibly serving to integrate the working class into a national organic whole. The encouragement of improved working conditions through the 'Beauty of Labour' scheme, the organization of leisure activities by the 'Strength through Joy' movement, and the reduction in high levels of unemployment achieved by a massive programme of rearmament: all were deployed to win over industrial workers.

Yet, while expressing socialist pretensions, corporatism in inspiration and practice was nothing more than state capitalism. Individuals were perceived as expendable means to be used in pursuit of a regenerated national community. The grotesque simplicity of the national socialist dimension of fascism was epitomized by the British fascist Oswald Mosley: 'If you love our country you are national and if you love our people you are socialist' (1938: 41).

Interim summary

The disparate elements of a nascent fascist worldview were apparent in Europe by the later nineteenth century. The emphasis which each of these elements – statism, racialism, elitism, imperialism and national socialism – received varied in accordance with the diverse traditions of those nations which produced fascist regimes, movements or parties. In Italy, Mussolini stressed statism. It was not until 1938, for instance, that racialism in the form of anti-Semitic laws was introduced. Five years earlier he had praised Italian Jews for their military service in the First World War and their exemplary roles in society and economy (Fermi, 1961: 290–1). The abrupt about turn was a cynical move by Mussolini: from being celebrated as 'good citizens', Jews of Italian birth became pawns unscrupulously used as a means of consolidating the Axis with Nazi Germany. There was, though, far less rigour in implementing anti-Semitism in Italy and much opposition to the implementation of the 'Final Solution', so that, according to Eatwell (1995: 68), four out of five Italian Jews survived the regime and the war, most in hiding.

Though Mussolini was to adopt biological racialism, proclaiming Italians to be 'Aryans of Mediterranean type', his key preoccupation was the renewal of the Italian state. The introduction of corporatism provided the means of instilling the will and of securing the resources to embark on the imperial regeneration of the fascist state, through for instance the invasion of Abyssinia in 1935–6. Portraying Italy as a living organism supplied the rationale for imperialism: just as healthy, individual organisms develop and grow, so too must the state. War and conquest were symptoms of its health: 'For Fascism the tendency to Empire . . . is a manifestation of its [the state's] vitality: its opposite, staying at home, is a sign of decadence . . . War alone puts the stamp of nobility upon the peoples' (Lyttelton, 1973: 53, 56). From this perspective, the renewal of empire was testimony to the fitness of the state.

In Nazi Germany, the goal was racial supremacy. Hitler was a racial nationalist, obsessed by a fanatical belief in the redemptive power of blood. For him history was the record of the rise and fall of biologically determined racial groups. Humankind, he asserted, fell into three categories: creators of culture, bearers of culture and destroyers of culture. The Aryans comprised the first group, Chinese and Japanese the second and Jews the last. To re-establish the primacy of the Aryans, their blood had to be repurified – and this required the elimination of 'the Jewish threat'.

Hitler explained Germany's collapse at the end of the First World War as the outcome of the progressive degeneration of its people's blood, which had eroded national resolve and purpose. The responsibility for this degeneracy lay with the Jews. By promoting doctrines – liberalism and Marxism – that celebrated individualism, egalitarianism or internationalism, they had engineered the cultural acceptability of miscegenation and subverted the national solidarity of Germans. Not only had the resulting dilution of the racially pure blood stock left Germany enfeebled, but 'international Jewry' had kept its own blood pure and was therefore poised to achieve world domination.

In Nazi Germany, racial policy was twofold. First, Aryan blood had to be repurified, and, second, those who threatened its purity had to be eradicated. The introduction of racial laws in 1933 and their acceleration thereafter was an early indication of the path destined to lead to mass genocide. The laws were accompanied by an unrelenting propaganda campaign that depicted Jews as the enemy within. In *Mein Kampf*, Hitler had portrayed Jews in terms which resonated with the conception of Germany as a 'national organism': 'virus', 'bacillus', 'parasite' and 'vampire' were some of his preferred metaphors. Such imagery was recycled, whether in official proclamations or popular literature, presenting Jews as carriers of disease. Without the removal of 'the Jewish menace . . . all attempts at German reawakening and resurrection are . . . absolutely senseless and impossible' (1969: 103).

The representation of Jews as the embodiment of evil was one side of the racial policy equation: the other was an array of measures designed to promote 'racial hygiene'. Thus, while Jews and other 'lesser races' were to be exterminated and the 'hereditarily ill' (the mentally and physically handicapped) and the 'asocial' (certain criminal offenders and homosexuals) either compulsorily sterilized or killed (see Noakes and Pridham, 1988: 997–1048), 'positive' measures were introduced to improve and purify German blood.

Selective breeding programmes were implemented favouring those who personified 'Aryanism', typically the SS (*Schutzstaffel*). Its members were ordered to 'produce children of good blood' through a union with racially pure women, whether within or outside marriage. Children from countries occupied by Germany who were deemed to exhibit Aryan characteristics were abducted and returned to 'the Fatherland', where they were to be 'Germanized' within 'racially acceptable families'. Such were the means that were adopted to create 'a community of physically and psychically homogeneous creatures' (1969: 357). This task was, moreover, invested with divine mission by Hitler: 'I believe that I am acting in the sense of the Almighty Creator: by warding off the Jews, I am fighting for the Lord's work' (1969: 60).

Such policies were also said to be consistent with what Hitler styled 'the aristocratic principle of Nature' (1969: 60) – that the fittest, the strongest and the most racially pure would always prevail. This 'principle' was also employed to justify dictatorship: 'leadership and the highest influence . . . fall to the best minds [and] builds not upon the idea of the majority, but upon the idea of the personality' (1969: 408). On this basis Hitler erected the *Fuhrerprinzip*: 'absolute responsibility unconditionally combined with absolute authority . . . the one man alone may possess the authority and right to command' (1969: 409). Democracy was rejected as a 'sin' against the 'aristocratic principle: the authority of the individual' (1969: 403).

Whereas in fascist Italy imperialism was the test of the vitality of the state, in Nazi Germany it was a measure of racial superiority. The conquest and occupation of neighbouring countries designed to procure resources – including slave labour – and living space (*Lebensraum*) symbolized the restoration of the 'natural order'. 'Nature', declared Hitler, 'knows no political boundaries . . . soil exists for the people which have the force to take it' (1969: 123). In this respect, the two dictators subscribed to opposed theories of the state. Mussolini, as we have seen, regarded the state as an end in itself. By contrast, in *Mein Kampf* Hitler portrayed it as a means to the end of racial supremacy:

> the state must regard as its highest task the preservation and intensification of the race . . . We, as Aryans, can conceive of the state only as the living organism of a nationality . . . We must distinguish between the state as a vessel and the race as its content.
>
> (1969: 358)

The heavy and fatal emphasis on biological racialism within Nazism does perhaps set it apart from Italian fascism. But rather than trying to draw a distinction between them on the basis of their ideological priorities, the preferred approach here is to represent the doctrine in fluid rather than solid terms. Thus, while its national varieties may have stressed differing elements, each fascist movement drew upon a common set of ideas that had long been current in European political thought. One such idea exemplifying the inegalitarian core of fascism was its treatment and representation of women.

Fascism and women

In the essay on feminism (chapter 8) we will note the pervasive dualism that has underpinned Western political thought. This both assigned women to a different realm from that inhabited by men and elevated the activities and the assumed attributes of men. The distinction between the private, female 'world' and the public, male sphere was not just implicit in fascism; it was openly promoted. On this issue there was nothing to distinguish the beliefs of Hitler from those of Mussolini.

Both exemplified patriarchal attitudes, asserting that the natural sphere for women was that of home and family. Hitler distinguished between the 'greater world', monopolized by men, in which affairs of state, politics and war were conducted, and the 'smaller world', which was the domain of women: 'her world is her husband, her family, her children and her home' (2002: 182). The enfranchisement of women, which had occurred in Weimar Germany, was 'invented only by Jewish intellectualism' and distracted women from the 'duties which nature imposes' (2002: 182, 183). Such 'duties' were summarized by Hitler's propaganda chief, Joseph Goebbels (1897–1945): 'The mission of woman is to be beautiful and to bring children into the world . . . the female prettifies herself for her mate and hatches the eggs for him' (Noakes and Pridham, 1974: 363).

The natural superiority of men was axiomatic within fascist ideology. This was conveyed in the popular Nazi slogan *Kinder, Kirche, Kuche*. Respectively, this confined women to bearing children, attending church and working in the kitchen. The clear boundary drawn between the public and private worlds was founded upon the assertion of intrinsic differences between the sexes: 'Man and Woman represent two quite different characteristics: in Man understanding is dominant [which] is more stable than emotion which is the mark of Woman' (Baynes, 1969: 531).

The recurring view peddled by Hitler was of the naturally dependent and submissive woman, prone to passion and outbursts of jealousy. Preserving the public realm for men was represented as a chivalrous act preventing women from making an exhibition of themselves:

> I detest women who dabble in politics . . . There she is, ready to pull her hair out, with all her claws showing. In short, gallantry forbids one to give women an opportunity of putting themselves in situations that do not suit them. Everything that entails combat is exclusively men's business. There are so many other fields in which one must rely upon women. Organizing a house, for instance.
>
> (1973: 251–2)

In Italy, Mussolini retailed similar attitudes, yet his views on women followed a more serpentine course than those of Hitler. In 1919 the fascist programme advocated female suffrage and three years later endorsed equal rights for women. Mussolini's own support for female enfranchisement seems, though, to have been less than principled. His ambition to institute corporatism led him to favour occupational suffrage rather than the enfranchisement of individuals electing representatives to a democratic assembly. Moreover, from the early 1920s the party's support for female suffrage waned and, increasingly, patriarchal policies prevailed.

As in Nazi Germany, legislation was introduced barring women from certain occupations and exhorting them to produce children. Echoing Hitler's gendered perception of 'greater' and 'smaller worlds', Mussolini asserted that 'War is to man what motherhood is to women' (1939b: 54). From the mid-1920s, under the slogan 'Woman into the home', measures were introduced that encouraged women back into the domestic realm, where they would be prized as the pillars of the family. Such measures were utterly consistent with the views of the Vatican. In 1930 Pius XI issued his encyclical *Casti Connubi*, which urged women to perform their natural roles as wives and mothers, closeted within the hearth and home (Cannistraro, 1982: 203).

Mussolini's stated opinions on women were disdainful. He regarded them as a 'charming pastime, when a man has time to pass, a means of changing one's trend of thought . . . but they should never be taken seriously, for they themselves are rarely serious' (quoted in Koon, 1985: 25). In *Talks with Mussolini* (1933), Emil Ludwig reports that the dictator stated: 'while a woman must not be a slave . . . in our state women must not count' (see Ludwig, 1933: 170).

In one essential respect, of course, women – or, rather, acceptable women – did count in both Nazi Germany and fascist Italy: as bearers of children. Women's reproductive role was vital to both regimes. In Hitler's design, Aryan women were to be the bearers of the master race, while Mussolini needed a growing population to people his planned renewed empire. Incentives were introduced in both countries to increase the birth rate (see for example Frevert, 1990: 205; Burleigh and Wippermann, 1991: 249ff.; Stephenson, 1996: 173ff.; Durham, 1998), reducing acceptable women to little more than nationalist wombs in the service of the state. In Germany the laws governing marriage and fitness to reproduce were minutely governed by racialism; in Italy the preoccupation was with the sheer necessity for population growth, itself a signal of the vitality of the state. In 1933, Paula Siber, the acting head of the Nazi Party's Association of German Women, set out the role for the 'new German woman':

> To be a woman means to be a mother . . . a woman belongs at the side of man, not just as a person who brings children into the world, not just as an adornment to delight the eye, not just as a cook and cleaner. Instead woman has the holy duty to be a life-companion, which means being a comrade who pursues her vocation as a woman with clarity of vision and spiritual warmth. To be a woman in the deepest and most beautiful sense of the word is the best preparation for being a mother . . . the highest

calling of the National Socialist woman is not just to bear children, but . . . to raise children for her people.

(See Griffin, 1995: 138–9)

The message was clear: women were valued only insofar as they submitted to a subordinate role within their lesser domain; they were to bear children, socialize them into the brave new fascist world, and dutifully support their menfolk. The sexing of both Italy and Germany as the 'Fatherland' epitomized the patriarchal thinking that lay at the heart of the doctrine.

British fascism in the inter-war years

We have already noted the contribution of two English thinkers – Pearson and Chamberlain – to the evolution of fascist ideas, but the development of the doctrine in Britain is most closely associated with Oswald Mosley.

In 1932 Mosley founded the British Union of Fascists (BUF), having previously been a Conservative, an Independent Conservative, an Independent and a Labour MP. His transition from the Labour Party, from which he was expelled in 1931, to fascism was by way of the 'New Party', a short-lived parliamentary-based all-party group that was launched primarily to advance protectionist economic policies.

Mosley, following a visit to Italy in 1932, was convinced of the need for the pursuit of autarky. Like Hitler and Mussolini, he presented fascism as a youthful, vigorous movement propounding novel ideas for a new age: 'Italy has produced not only a new system of government but a new type of man who differs from politicians of the old world just as men from another planet' (Walker, 1977: 287). Yet, like those he sought to emulate, there was little that was original in his thought. Mosley merely packaged fascist themes into a form he believed acceptable to 'the British character'.

Racialism

Initially Mosley denied that the BUF subscribed to racialist ideas or harboured anti-Semitic beliefs, and yet the latter were evident from the former, despite the fact that they were expressed in coded terms. Thus: 'we have within the nation a power, largely controlled by alien elements, which arrogates to itself a power above the State' (Nugent, 1977: 149). In 1933, he banned Jews from joining the BUF, and in the same year the Irishman William Joyce, one of Mosley's chief aides (later to achieve notoriety as 'Lord Haw Haw'), in his BUF pamphlet characterized Jews as 'little sub-men' and stated that 'only through the defeat of Jewry can Britain be free' (Joyce, 1933).

From the mid-1930s Mosley's anti-Semitism became more pronounced. The Jews were presented as a subversive 'state within the state' seeking to engineer war with Germany. A signal of the growing centrality of these beliefs was the change in 1936 of the name of his movement to the British Union of Fascists *and National Socialists*. Anti-Semitism, though couched in oblique terms ('the money power' or 'international finance'), bulked ever larger in Mosley's speeches, and allegations that Jews were manipulating the established political parties became routine. Only his movement could root out 'alien influences', since it alone was free of their 'money power'.

His rhetoric recalls that of Hitler. In musing on his preferred 'final solution' to 'the Jewish problem', Mosley proposed the creation of an artificial homeland 'in one of the many waste places of the world' where Jews could languish 'and cease to be the parasite of humanity' (1938: 43). Such a ghettoizing option had been contemplated by Mussolini, but, as we noted above, the introduction of racial laws in Italy did lead to the deaths of Italian Jews in Europe's concentration camps. It is not implausible to suggest that Mosley, who shifted his allegiance to Hitler in 1936, would have followed the same genocidal route had a fascist regime secured power in Britain.

Corporatism

Mosley's infatuation with the corporate state in his earlier writings deepened following his Italian excursion. His advocacy of this model of economic and political organization dovetailed the themes of statism and national socialism. In 1932 he argued that Britain's economic crisis was the result of the stubborn attachment of the 'old gangs' of politicians to *laissez faire* at home and free trade abroad: attachments which reflected the influence and power of 'international finance'. The remedy was the 'rationalization' of the economy through the imposition of the corporate state.

In the place of minimal government and a free market economy, he prescribed planning and protectionism. In advancing such measures, his remarks were virtually indistinguishable from those of Mussolini. Emphasizing the need to introduce corporatism so as to reconcile 'individual initiative with the wider interests of the nation', he verged on plagiarism: 'it means a nation organised as the human body, with each organ performing its individual function but working in harmony with the whole' (Mosley, n.d.). The national organism was paramount, its interests superseding the individualism celebrated by liberals and the class interests prized by socialists. Here lay the attempt to dovetail nationalism and socialism. Yet, of course, his scheme for a 'third way' between competing doctrines extinguished autonomy and freedom and quashed democratic politics. 'There will', he stated ominously, 'be no room in Britain for those who do not accept the principle "All for the State and the State for All"' (Mosley, n.d.).

Internally, Britain would be run on authoritarian lines with pride of place given to the virtues of obedience, order and discipline: all would be bent to 'the national purpose'. To ensure self-sufficiency he proposed 'insulation'. This entailed a ban on the importation of all goods that could be produced in Britain and a closed imperial economy wherein the colonies would supply resources and markets for British products. Here there are echoes of Social Imperialism's autarkic design, amplified by a racially inspired argument. The colonies were to be denied independence both because they would be susceptible to 'alien influences' and because Mosley considered the colonial 'races' to be unfit for the task of economic development.

Elitism and leadership

Mosley's apocalyptic vision of impending economic collapse, allied to his conviction that the 'old gangs' had succumbed to the machinations of 'the money power', led him to justify the need for political authoritarianism. In the first edition of *The Greater Britain* (1932) he appeared to favour collective leadership since it was better suited to 'the British character'. Two years later his view had changed: 'Leadership in fascism may be an individual or a team, but single leadership in practice proves the most effective instrument. The leader must be prepared to shoulder absolute responsibility for the functions clearly allocated to him' (1934: 31).

Mosley's dictatorial ambitions, encoded as 'Leadership', were clear from his plans to promote 'a creed of effective government in strong con-tradistinction to the present decadence of the Parliamentary system ... Whatever movement or party be entrusted with Government must be given the absolute power to act' (1934: 27, 28). The first fascist parliament would invest the government with the power to impose the corporate state by order, leaving the executive free from scrutiny. While parliament would, at this stage, possess the authority to dismiss the government through a vote of censure, thereafter that power would be denied. Political parties would be banned, an occupational franchise introduced, and the House of Lords abolished and replaced by a new second chamber comprising a technocratic elite charged to assist in the implementation of the corporate state.

To supplement the occupational franchise, Mosley proposed to introduce a series of plebiscites or referendums. The population would be invited to express their support for the fascist programme through this populist device. Party-based democratic politics would cease: 'In such a system there is no place for parties and politicians. We shall ask the people for a mandate to bring to an end the Party system and the Parties. We invite them to enter a new civilization. Parties and the party game belong to the old civilization which has failed' (Skidelsky, 1975: 315).

Mosley's blighted vision, his readiness to employ violence to realize it – 'by one road or another we are determined that Fascism will come to Britain' – and his parroting of themes common to Hitler and Mussolini places him squarely in the fascist retinue. His initial enthusiasm for corporatism, though it never waned, was complemented by his later alignment with Hitler:

> the struggle of a National Socialist Movement is a necessary preliminary to the exercise of power, because the bitter character of that struggle gives to the people an absolute guarantee that those who have passed through that test unbroken will not betray their people or their country. Thus alone is forged the 'instrument of steel' to save and then serve the people.
>
> (Mosley, 1938: 8–9)

Contemporary British fascism

The election of a member of the neo-Nazi British National Party (BNP) to the local council in Tower Hamlets, London, in 1993 and the level of support accrued by its parliamentary candidates in Oldham's two constituencies in 2001 provided a disturbing reminder of the resilience of fascist ideas.

The East End of London, including Tower Hamlets, was a favoured stamping ground of Mosley and his erstwhile stormtroopers, the Blackshirts. In the 1930s, these uniformed thugs engaged in street fights with the area's Jewish population and others, notably communists and socialists, in the attempt to inflame prejudice against 'outsiders' and 'alien influences'. Mosley's efforts to rekindle fascism in the area following his release from wartime internment proved to be singularly unsuccessful. In his wake other groups, notably the National Front, emerged to promote fascist ideas, seeking to exploit ill-founded concern over non-white immigration.

The National Front was created in 1967, though it was to split in 1982. One faction of it, led initially by John Tyndall, was to form the British National Party, itself flanked by a number of other British neo-fascist organizations, including Third Way, Blood and Honour, and the paramilitaristic organizations Combat 18 and White Wolves. The latter two, among others, claimed responsibility for the three bomb attacks in London (Brixton, Brick Lane and Soho) in the summer of 1999, which left three dead and more than a hundred injured. Each seeks to garner support by fomenting anti-immigrant feeling directed against black and brown Britons and, more recently, asylum seekers from eastern Europe and, in the wake of September 11, 2001, Muslims everywhere. Irrespective of ethnic differences, all are lumped together as 'them', an amorphous mass said to represent a fundamental threat to 'the British way of life'.

It is no coincidence that such groups seem to secure support at times of political and economic insecurity. Pressure on economic resources and atavistic feelings of British – more usually, English – supremacy are mixed into a potent formula which lays the blame for all social ills on a culturally or physically distinctive community, be it Jewish, Black, Asian or eastern European. The construction of 'them' as folk-devils, responsible for perceived social decline, is a simplistic, populist and opportunistic response to material insecurity and political uncertainty. The experience of high unemployment in western Europe, the advent of globalization and the accompanying porosity of national borders has contributed to the revival of electoral support for neo-fascist parties. Their arousal of anti-immigrant feeling was the stock-in-trade of Tyndall, whose career in fascism left little doubt about the lineage of the BNP.

Prior to founding the BNP, Tyndall had been involved with a number of neo-Nazi groups. In 1961 he co-founded the World Union of National Socialists, which acknowledged the 'spiritual leadership of Hitler' and included among its objectives 'the promotion of Aryanism'. A year later he joined the National Socialist Movement, whose journal, asserting 'the correctness of Nazi ideology', exhorted its readers to 'join a movement which could ideologically and . . . physically smash the Red Front and Jewry' (Walker, 1977: 45). En route to the NF and the BNP, Tyndall co-founded the Greater Britain Movement, which advocated racial laws prohibiting inter-marriage between Britons and 'non Aryans' and the compulsory sterilization of the physically and mentally handicapped. In his *The Eleventh Hour: A Call for British Rebirth*, Tyndall reiterates his view that non-whites are 'unassimilable', rejects miscegenation and insists upon the need to 'build the foundations of a healthier and fitter British Race' (1998: 302–3). Among other things, Tyndall insists on a 'firm polarity' between men and women, a phrase redolent of the unapologetic sexism characteristic of Fascism, and extols physical exercise, reminiscent of Mosley's injunction that the British must 'live like athletes' (1934: 51).

Biological racialism was a consistent feature of Tyndall's beliefs. The recycling of Hitler's ideas concerning 'racial hygiene' and anti-Semitism has marked all the groups with which he has been associated. Though the anti-Semitic character of these ideas tends, as with the BUF, to be expressed in euphemistic terms – 'money power', 'loan capitalism' or 'finance capitalism' – it lies at the core of current fascist groups in Britain. While they are associated primarily in the public mind with attacks on Black British communities and Islamophobia, below the surface the ideologues of fascism also encourage racially inspired attacks on Jews.

As with Hitler, what grips their fevered imagination is a belief that Jews are engaged in a global conspiracy whose aim is to establish a world tyranny. By exercising their 'money power' so as to subvert Britain's economic independence, fostering internationalism through their support for both Marxist ideas and the European Community, and 'polluting' the 'race' by promoting both inward migration and miscegenation, Jews will erode 'the British will to resist' and Jewish world domination will be achieved. The remedies, like the analysis, are wearyingly familiar. Autarky, corporatism, elite leadership, racialism, the primacy of the nation and the submissiveness of the individual to the state. Naturally, men will monopolize the public realm, while women will, in Tyndall's terms, be consigned to 'the feminine role – wife, mother, homemaker' (see *Spearhead*, 1977): if not barefoot then certainly pregnant in the fascist kitchen.

In 1999 Tyndall was dumped as the BNP's leader and replaced by Nick Griffin, its general election candidate in Oldham West in 2001. Griffin, much younger than his predecessor, appears in the guise of the modernizer, the new man for the new millennium, an alternative to the explicit neo-Nazism of the party's past. Hence the BNP's *public* adoption of a policy of voluntary rather than compulsory repatriation for non-whites, and the formation of its 'ethnic liaison committee', ostensibly created to forge links with members of ethnic minority groups, including those opposed to Islam. But this is just window-dressing: to mix metaphors, a case of old racist wine in a redesigned fascist bottle. In 1998 Griffin was tried and found guilty of distributing material likely to incite racial hatred. He also routinely referred to the Holocaust as 'the Hoax of the twentieth century'. A former editor of the BNP's publication *Spearhead*, until sacked by Tyndall, he is reported to have told supporters in 1996 that the party 'needs to be perceived as a strong disciplined organization with the ability to back up its slogan "Defend Rights for Whites" with well directed boots and fists'. He continued, in a phrase worthy of Hitler or Mussolini, 'When the crunch comes, power is the product of force and will, not of rational debate' (see Stop the BNP, n.d.).

Following the electoral flop in the 2010 General Election, when it polled less than two per cent of the vote, the BNP has been riven with internal disputes and conflict, not least between Griffin and his fellow MEP, Andrew Brons. This split has led to rumours of the formation of a new neo-fascist party, itself flanked by erstwhile competitors, including the English Defence League and the British Freedom Party. Indeed, the far right in the UK is littered with splinter groups, each seeking to capitalize on the relative electoral success of neo-fascist parties and the growth of anti-Islamic groups across Europe, epitomized in the person of Anders Breivik. While Islamophobia has become the focus of such groups, the pulse of anti-Semitism remains vital (see the website of Searchlight, the leading anti-fascist monitoring organization: www.searchlight.com).

Conclusion

Proponents of fascism have proven adept at rummaging around in intellectual history in order to fashion their doctrine. In this undertaking they have been able to draw upon themes and ideas whose longevity is, I hope, evident. Such ideas began to become palpable in the later eighteenth century as a reaction against the Enlightenment. Fascism's explicit intolerance of difference and its corresponding preference for a monolithic unity, whether defined in national or racial terms, represented a counter-revolution against Enlightenment values. Later, its precursors drew upon the same or related sources when faced by the ideological challenge from socialism in the later nineteenth century.

The antithetical character of the doctrine is clear from the following remarks of, respectively, Mussolini and Goebbels. Referring to the values of liberty, equality and fraternity bestowed by the French Revolution, their target was clear: 'We stand', stated the Italian dictator, 'for a new principle in the world . . . sheer categorical definitive antithesis to the world which still abides by the fundamental principles laid down in 1789' (Mussolini, 1932). In a 1933 radio broadcast Goebbels was more succinct: 'The year 1789 is hereby eradicated from history' (quoted in Moyn, 2010: 55).

The sheer hubris of such remarks is breathtaking. With one rhetorical gesture, the inspiration for – and the legacy of – the French Revolution was to be swept from the stage of history.

While fascists asserted the novelty of their ideas, the mainsprings of their beliefs were pre-modern. Lamenting a lost past, whether the Roman Empire, the agrarian society of mediaeval Germany, or some other imagined community, fascism proposes a 'barbarous utopia' in which all diversity, individualism and pluralism will be extinguished. Now, as in the past, fascists seek to exploit the emotive simplicities of a national or a racial myth and to impose a numbing conformity upon all. Mussolini set this tone and approach in 1922:

> We have created our myth. The myth is a faith, a passion. It is not necessary for it to be a reality. It is a reality in the sense that it is a stimulus, is hope, is faith, is courage. Our myth is the nation, our myth is the greatness of the nation! And to this myth, this greatness, which we want to translate into a total reality, we subordinate everything else.
>
> (Griffin, 1995: 44)

However its exponents have fashioned the doctrine, whether in the past or in the contemporary world, at root fascism was and is profoundly non-rational. Despite, or indeed because of, this feature of its thought, it should not be lightly dismissed. The arousal of emotion, fostered by the mass marches of troops, flag-bearing youth or torch-bearing girls, was epitomized by the Nuremberg rallies: a mass, moving in unison and from which all individuality was expunged, save for that of the leader, aloft on a monstrous dais, orchestrating all in pursuit of national redemption. At one level, such events appear as little more than street theatre: but it was drama with a sinister purpose. Deaden the intellect, crush the critical spirit, demand blind obedience and eliminate moral uncertainty. As the Italian author and Auschwitz survivor Primo Levi cautioned: 'the memory of what happened in the heart of Europe, not very long ago, can serve as a warning' (1987: 397).

Further reading

I found the following three books to be of real use in understanding fascist ideology: Roger Eatwell and Anthony Wright's edited volume *Contemporary Political Ideologies* (1993), Andrew Vincent's *Modern Political Ideologies* (1995) and Roger Eatwell's *Fascism: A History* (1995). Roger Griffin's *Fascism* (1995) provides a compelling collection of documents written by fascist ideologues, critics and analysts, including more contemporary writings. Neil Gregor's *Nazism* (2001) supplies an equally impressive companion reader. A more recent collection, *The Oxford Handbook of Fascism* (2009), edited by R. J. B. Bosworth, includes contributions by over thirty leading scholars in a truly magisterial volume. Kevin Passmore's *Fascism: A Very Short Introduction* (2002) is a gem of a book, with a wide geographical span.

As someone who is not primarily a political theorist, originally I had to plot my way through a large number of books in order to gain a purchase on the evolution of fascist ideas. Revisiting the chapter for the new edition confirmed my debts to the following authors: Zeev Sternhell ('Fascist Ideology', 1979), Karl Dietrich Bracher (*The German Dictatorship*, 1973), Arno Mayer (*The Persistence of the Old Regime*, 1981), George Mosse (*Crisis of German Ideology*, 1964) and Eugen Weber (*Varieties of Fascism*, 1964). Also recommended are Zeev Sternhell's *The Birth of Fascist Ideology* (1995) and George Mosse's *Towards the Final Solution* (1978).

Michael Burleigh's *The Third Reich* (2001), on Nazi Germany, marries scholarship and accessibility in an enviable way, providing a gripping account of the implementation of fascist ideas in the Nazi state. His co-authored work, with Wolfgang Wippermann, *The Racial State* (1991), is instructive on the pre-history of fascism and contains much primary material written by the executors of the Nazi project. Burleigh has also written on the genocide in Nazi Germany in *Ethics and Extermination* (1997) and 'euthanasia' in *Death and Deliverance* (1994). Fellow historian Ian Kershaw's 2000 work *The Nazi Dictatorship* is also recommended.

On Italy, see Adrian Lyttelton's 'Italian Fascism' (1979), David Roberts's *The Syndicalist Tradition and Italian Fascism* (1979) and A. James Gregor's *Italian Fascism and Developmental Dictatorship* and *Young Mussolini and the Intellectual Origins of Fascism* (1979a and 1979b). Philip Cannistraro has produced a useful source of reference on both the major figures and institutions of Mussolini's regime in *The Historical Dictionary of Fascist Italy* (1982).

Paul Hayes's *Fascism* (1973) is especially informative on the role of British thinkers in the doctrine's development, and it supplies brief notes on key figures. Roger Griffin's 1993 study *The Nature of Fascism* is also recommended, as is his edited reader (1995). On the varieties of social Darwinism see Greta Jones, *Social Darwinism and English Thought* (1980).

On British fascism see Robert Skidelsky's *Oswald Mosley* (1975), Neil Nugent and Roger King's edited volume *The British Right* (1977) and Robert Benewick's *The Fascist Movement in Britain* (1972). Two studies of the National Front are Martin Walker's *The National Front* (1977) and Stan Taylor's *The National Front in British Politics* (1982). See also Kenneth Lunn and Richard Thurlow's edited volume *British Fascism* (1980). The London-based organization Searchlight maintains a watching brief on British and other neo-fascist groups and is a helpful source of information. Its website – www. searchlight.com – includes articles from its journal and has extensive links to other monitoring groups in Europe and elsewhere. It is especially good on tracking the activities of the BNP, English Defence League and more paramilitary-style neo-Nazi groups.

Hitler's *Mein Kampf*, with an introduction by D. C. Watt (1969), is a key primary source, although it is a debilitating read. See also W. Maser's *Mein Kampf: An Analysis* (1970). The one-volume *Documents on Nazism, 1919–1945* (1974),edited by Jeremy Noakes and Geoffrey Pridham, is a compelling selection with commentaries by the editors. The same authors have also edited an indispensable four-volume series on Nazism (see, e.g., Noakes and Pridham, 1988) published under the aegis of Exeter University's 'Exeter Studies in History'. *Hitler's Table Talk, 1941–1944* (1973), translated by Norman Cohen and R. H. Stevens, with an introduction by Hugh Trevor-Roper, provides numerous glimpses into the dictator's obsessions. Norman Baynes (1969) has translated and edited *The Speeches of Adolf Hitler, April 1922 – August 1939*. On Hitler, see also Max Domarus's *Hitler: Speeches and Proclamations* (1990) and Neil Gregor's edited volume *Nazism* (2001). Mussolini's own works are more expansive. Shorter works appeared in English in 1933 and 1935, his auto-biography in 1939 and his book *My Rise and Fall* in 1988. Key biographies of Hitler are Alan Bullock's *Hitler: A Study in Tyranny* (1973) and Joachim Fest's *Hitler* (2002), while Denis Mack Smith (1981) addresses Mussolini in *Mussolini*. Mosley's ideas appeared in 1934 and 1936 and his autobiography in 1968.

The final works I would like to cite are by Hans Fallada (2009) and Primo Levi (1987, 1988, 1989 and 1995). Fallada's novel *Alone in Berlin* conveys in an utterly compelling manner the all-consuming fear inspired by the Nazi dictator-ship and was described by Levi as 'the greatest book ever written about the German resistance to the Nazis' (see Fallada, 2009: inside cover). Turning to Levi, his canon includes works dedicated to an attempt to understand the men-tality of those who ran the death camps of Europe. He is an apt choice as an author: an Italian Jew, a chemist by profession, and a partisan, he was captured and sent to Auschwitz, where he was incarcerated for a year and which, in one sense, he survived. His *If This Is a Man* and *The Truce* provide accounts of, respectively, his period in the camp and his liberation, made all the more moving by his tone of controlled passion. Other works recount the resilience of the inmates of Auschwitz and demonstrate that even in the most dire of circum-stances common humanity could not be wholly extinguished. In 1987, Levi took his own life. His works are a poignant and accessible reminder of the horrors that fascism visited upon so many.

References

Baynes, Norman (ed.) (1969) *The Speeches of Adolf Hitler, April 1922–August 1939*, New York: Fertig.

Benewick, Robert (1972) *The Fascist Movement in Britain*, London: Allen Lane.

Bernhardi, Friedrich von (1914) *Germany and the Next War*, London: Arnold.

Bosworth, R. J. B. (ed.) (2009) *The Oxford Handbook of Fascism*, Oxford: Oxford University Press.

Bracher, Karl Dietrich (1973) *The German Dictatorship*, Harmondsworth: Penguin.

Bullock, Alan (1973) *Hitler: A Study in Tyranny*, London: Hamlyn.

Burleigh, Michael (1994) *Death and Deliverance: 'Euthanasia' in Germany, 1900–1945*, Cambridge: Cambridge University Press.

—— (ed.) (1996) *Confronting the Nazi Past: New Debates on Modern German History*, London: Collins and Brown.

—— (1997) *Ethics and Extermination: Reflections on Nazi Genocide*, Cambridge: Cambridge University Press.

—— (2001) *The Third Reich: A New History*, London: Pan Books.

Burleigh, Michael and Wippermann, Wolfgang (1991) *The Racial State: Germany, 1933–1945*, Cambridge: Cambridge University Press.

Cannistraro, Philip (ed.) (1982) *Historical Dictionary of Fascist Italy*, London: Greenwood Press.

Cecil, Robert (1972) *The Myth of the Master Race*, London: Batsford.

Domarus, Max (1990) *Hitler: Speeches and Proclamations, 1932–1945: The Chronicle of a Dictatorship*, London: I. B. Tauris.

Durham, Martin (1998) *Women and Fascism*, London: Routledge.

Eatwell, Roger (1995) *Fascism: A History*, London: Chatto and Windus.

Eatwell, Roger and Wright, Anthony (eds) (1993) *Contemporary Political Ideologies*, London: Pinter.

Evans, Richard (2001) *Lying about Hitler: History, Holocaust and the David Irving Trial*, New York: Basic Books.

Fallada, Hans (2009) *Alone in Berlin*, London: Penguin.

Fermi, Laura (1961) *Mussolini*, Chicago: University of Chicago Press.

Fest, Joachim (2002) *Hitler*, London: Penguin.

Frevert, Ute (1990) *Women in German History: From Bourgeois Emancipation to Sexual Liberation*, Oxford: Berg.

Gregor, A. James (1979a) *Italian Fascism and Developmental Dictatorship*, Princeton, NJ: Princeton University Press.

—— (1979b) *Young Mussolini and the Intellectual Origins of Fascism*, Berkeley, CA: University of California Press.

Gregor, Neil (ed.) (2001) *Nazism*, Oxford: Oxford University Press.

Griffin, Roger (1993) *The Nature of Fascism*, London: Routledge.

—— (ed.) (1995) *Fascism*, Oxford: Oxford University Press.

Hayes, Paul (1973) *Fascism*, London: Allen and Unwin.

Hitler, Adolf (1969) *Mein Kampf*, trans. Ralph Mannheim, London: Hutchinson.

—— (1973) *Hitler's Table Talk, 1941–1944: His Private Conversations*, intr. Hugh Trevor-Roper, trans. Norman Cameron and R. H. Stevens, London: Weidenfeld and Nicolson; repr. London: Enigma Books, 2000.

—— (2002) Speech to the National Socialist Women's Organization, in Roderick Stackelberg and Sally A. Winkle (eds) *The Nazi Germany Sourcebook: An Anthology of Texts*, New York: Routledge.

Jones, Greta (1980) *Social Darwinism and English Thought: The Interaction between Biological and Social Theory*, Brighton: Harvester.

Joyce, William (1933) *Fascism and Jewry*, London: BUF.

Kershaw, Ian (2000) *The Nazi Dictatorship: Problems and Perspectives of Interpretation*, London: Arnold.

Koon, Tracy (1985) *Believe, Obey, Fight: Political Socialization of Youth in Fascist Italy, 1922–1943*, Chapel Hill: University of North Carolina Press.

Levi, Primo (1987) *If This Is a Man*, London: Sphere Books.

—— (1988) *The Drowned and the Saved*, London: Joseph.

—— (1989) *Moments of Reprieve*, London: Abacus.

—— (1995) *The Truce*, London: Abacus.

Ludwig, Emil (1933) *Talks with Mussolini*, Boston: Little, Brown and Company.

Lunn, Kenneth and Thurlow, Richard (eds) (1980) *British Fascism*, London: Croom Helm.

Lyttelton, Adrian (ed.) (1973) *Roots of the Right: Italian Fascism from Pareto to Gentile*, London: Cape.

—— (1979) 'Italian Fascism', in Walter Laqueur (ed.) *Fascism: A Reader's Guide*, Harmondsworth: Penguin.

Maser, W. (1970) *Mein Kampf: An Analysis*, London: Faber.

Mayer, Arno (1981) *The Persistence of the Old Regime*, London: Croom Helm.

Moseley, Ray (2000) *Mussolini's Shadow: The Double Life of Count Galeazzo Ciano*, New Haven, CT: Yale University Press.

Mosley, Oswald (1934) *The Greater Britain*, London: BUF.

—— (1936) *Fascism: 100 Questions Asked and Answered*, London: BUF.

—— (1938) *Tomorrow We Live*, London: BUF.

—— (1968) *My Life*, London: Nelson.

—— (n.d.) *Blackshirt Policy*, London: BUF.

Mosse, George (1964) *Crisis of German Ideology*, New York: Grosset and Dunlap.

—— (1971) *Germans and Jews*, London: Orbach and Chambers.

—— (1978) *Towards the Final Solution: A History of European Racism*, London: Dent.

—— (ed.) (1979) *International Fascism: New Thoughts and Approaches*, London: Sage.

Moyn, Samuel (2010) *The Last Utopia: Human Rights in History*, Cambridge, MA: Harvard University Press.

Mussolini, Benito (1932) 'The doctrine of Fascism', in *Fascism: Doctrine and Institutions*, Rome: Ardita.

—— (1933) *The Political and Social Doctrine of Fascism*, London: Leonard and Virginia Woolf.

—— (1935) *Fascism: Doctrine and Institutions*, Rome: Ardita.

—— (1939a) *My Autobiography*, London: Hutchinson.

—— (1939b) Speech to the Italian Chamber of Deputies, 28 April, in Dennis Mack Smith (1976) *Mussolini's Roman Empire*, London: Longman.

—— (1988) *My Rise and Fall*, ed. Max Ascoli, Cambridge, MA: Da Capo Press.

Noakes, Jeremy and Pridham, Geoffrey (eds) (1974) *Documents on Nazism, 1919–1945*, London: Cape.

—— (1988) *Nazism, 1919–1945, Volume 3: Foreign Policy, War and Racial Extermination*, Exeter: University of Exeter Press.

Nolte, Ernst (1969) *Three Faces of Fascism*, New York: Mentor.

Nugent, Neil (1977) 'The ideas of the BUF', in Neil Nugent and Roger King (eds) *The British Right*, Farnborough: Saxon House.

Nugent, Neil and King, Roger (eds) (1977) *The British Right*, Farnborough: Saxon House.

Passmore, Kevin (2002) *Fascism: A Very Short Introduction*, Oxford: Oxford University Press.

Pearson, Karl (1905) *National Life from the Standpoint of Science*, London: Black.

Roberts, David (1979) *The Syndicalist Tradition and Italian Fascism*, Manchester: Manchester University Press.

Skidelsky, Robert (1975) *Oswald Mosley*, London: Macmillan.

Smith, Denis Mack (1981) *Mussolini*, London: Weidenfeld and Nicolson.

Spearhead (1977) BNP publication, January.

Stephenson, Jill (1996) 'Women, motherhood and the family in the Third Reich', in Michael Burleigh (ed.) *Confronting the Nazi Past: New Debates on Modern German History*, London: Collins.

Sternhell, Zeev (1979) 'Fascist ideology', in Walter Laqueur (ed.) *Fascism: A Reader's Guide*, Harmondsworth: Penguin.

—— (1995) *The Birth of Fascist Ideology*, Princeton, NJ: Princeton University Press.

Stop the BNP (n.d.) 'Profile of Nick Griffin'. Available online at www.stopthebnp.org.uk/uncovered/pg03.htm.

Taylor, Stan (1982) *The National Front in British Politics*, London: Macmillan.

Tyndall, John (1998), *The Eleventh Hour: A Call for British Rebirth*, 2nd edn, Hove: Albion Press.

Vincent, Andrew (1995) *Modern Political Ideologies*, 2nd edn, Oxford: Blackwell.

Walker, Martin (1977) *The National Front*, London: Fontana.

Weber, Eugen (1964) *Varieties of Fascism*, New York: Van Nostrand Reinhold.

Woolf, Stuart (ed.) (1968a) *European Fascism*, London: Weidenfeld and Nicolson.

—— (1968b) *The Nature of Fascism*, London: Weidenfeld and Nicolson.

—— (1981) *Fascism in Europe*, London: Methuen.

Chapter 7

Green Political Theory

John Barry

Introduction

Ecologism or green political theory is the most recent of schools of political thinking. On the one hand, it focuses on issues that are extremely old in politics and philosophical inquiry, including the relationship between the human and nonhuman worlds, the moral status of animals, what is the 'good life', and the ethical and political regulation of technological innovation. Yet on the other, it is also characterised as dealing with some specifically contemporary issues, such as the economic and political implications of climate change, peak oil, overconsumption, resource competition and conflicts, and rising levels of global and national inequalities. It is also an extremely broad school of political thought covering a wide variety of concerns, contains a number of distinct sub-schools of thought (here sharing a similarity with other political ideologies), and combines normative and empirical scientific elements in a unique manner, making it distinctive from other political ideologies.

First a word about definitions. There are a number of terms used to describe green political theory, ranging from 'ecologism' to 'environmentalism' or ecological political theory or environmental political theory (Barry and Dobson, 2003). This chapter uses the term 'green political theory' on the grounds that both ecological and environmental labels, while certainly conveying one of the key distinguishing features of green political theorising – namely its focus on both the material/metabolic dimensions of human–nonhuman relations and the ethical and political status of the nonhuman world – can offer a rather narrow understanding of green politics. What I mean by this is that ecologism, or environmental political theory, as a way of categorising green politics is too focused on these issues of nature and human–nature relations and does not, at least in my view, allow sufficient scope for the 'non-ecological' and 'non-nature related' principles of green politics. This is particularly the case in respect of understanding and appreciating the specifically intra-human dimensions of green political theory.

There is a common distinction often made in the literature between 'environmentalism' and 'ecologism' (Dobson, 2007), with environmentalism denoting a form of 'single issue' green politics solely concerned with, for instance, pollution and resource management, and ecologism denoting a fully fledged political ideology with views on non-resource and non-environmental concerns. In this respect, what is offered here is closer to ecologism than environmentalism, but nevertheless uses green political theory as the appropriate term, since even ecologism conveys a definite sense (at least on first sight) that green politics is largely or exclusively concerned with the non-human world and human–nonhuman relations. Thus, while it may seem to be simply a pedantic issue, this chapter uses 'green political theory' instead of 'ecologism' as a more appropriate, inclusive categorisation of green politics, which fully acknowledges the uniqueness of its focus on nature while also stressing its radical approach to the organisation of human social, economic and political relations, consistent with, but not exclusively tied to or derived from, its focus on the metabolic/material relationship between humans and nature.

Some origins of green political thinking

Some origins of green theory can be identified and summarised as follows:

- the 'romantic' and negative reactions to the Industrial Revolution, from working-class and peasant resistance to capitalism, mechanisation and the factory production system, the enclosure of the commons, and the despoliation of the countryside;
- the positive reaction to the unfinished project of the French (democratic) Revolution;
- a negative reaction to 'colonialism' and 'imperialism' in the nineteenth and twentieth centuries, and a related concern with global ecological injustice, the 'ecological debt' owed by the minority/'developed' world to the majority/'underdeveloped' world and minority–majority world relations of inequality and power;
- the emergence of the science of ecology and Darwin's evolutionary theory, and later the integration of science, ethics and politics in diagnosing and providing answers to socio-ecological and related problems;
- issues around the resource, pollution and especially energy foundations for human social, economic and political organisation, lifestyles and realisable conceptualisations of the 'good society' and 'good life';
- growing public perception of an 'ecological crisis' in the 1960s, claims of 'limits to growth' from the 1970s onwards, the emergence of 'global environmental problems' in the 1980s and 1990s, and peak oil and climate change in the early part of this century;
- transcending the politics of 'industrialism' (organised on a left–right continuum) by a politics of 'post-industrialism' (beyond left and right);
- increasing awareness of and moral sensitivity to our relations with the nonhuman world (from the promotion of 'animal rights' and animal welfare to ideas that the Earth is 'sacred' and/or has intrinsic value);
- the integration of progressive social, political and economic policies with the politics of transition to a sustainable society, principally the universal promotion of human rights, socio-economic equality, democratisation of the state and the economy. (Barry, 2007)

Of particular importance is the central concern of green theory and practice to overcome both the separation of 'human' from 'nature' and also the misperception of humans as above or 'superior' to nature. Green political theory can be seen as an attempt to bring humanity and the study of human society 'down to earth'. The science of ecology played an important part in arguing that humans as a species of animal (that is, we are not just *like* animals, we *are* an animal species) are ecologically embedded in nature, and exist in a web-like relation to other species, rather than being at the top of some 'great chain of being'. It is crucial to note the significance of green political and social theory having a strong basis in the natural sciences (mainly ecology, evolutionary and environmental psychology, the biological life sciences and thermodynamics), because, as will be suggested below, this gives us a strong indication of what the 'greening' of social theory may involve.

A second and related point is that green social theory, in transcending the culture/nature split, begins its analysis with a view of humans as a species of natural being, which like other species have particular species-specific characteristics, needs and modes of flourishing (and non-flourishing). Central to green theory, unlike other forms of political theory, with the exception of feminism, is a stress on the 'embodiedness' of humans as ethically and politically significant.

A third issue which green political theory raises is the way in which social–environmental relations are not only important in human society, but also *constitutive* of human society. That is, one cannot offer a theory of society without making social–environmental interaction, and the natural contexts and dimensions of human society, a central aspect of one's theory. In its attention to the naturalistic bases of human society, the green perspective is 'materialistic' in a different and arguably much more fundamental way than within Marxist theory, for example. Unlike the latter, green political theory concerns itself with the external and internal natural conditions of human individual and social life, whereas the 'material base' for Marx is primarily economic, not natural. Hence, a green understanding of the metabolism (a particularly evocative and appropriate term used by both greens and Marxists) includes the economic transformative process, but also more importantly the ecological, natural biodiversity, resource and energy flows and stocks that underpin all human economic activity. The economy is thus of particular interest from a green perspective since it is at the centre of the material metabolism between the human and nonhuman. And as will be seen, a key feature of green political theory in this respect is the re-casting of how we understand the 'economy' and the 'economic'.

At the same time, this materialist reading of green social theory questions the 'post-materialist' character often ascribed to green politics and issues, as in Inglehart's popular explanation of green politics as 'post-materialist' (Inglehart, 1977) and, therefore, a mainly middle-class, European/Western phenomenon. This characterisation of green politics is one that Marxists have drawn attention to and used to demonstrate the 'anti-working class' interests of green politics. However, both this Marxist critique and Inglehart's thesis fail to explain the 'environmentalism of the poor' (Martinez-Alier, 2001), the class, ethnic and race dynamics of the environmental justice movement (Schlosberg, 2009), or 'resistance ecofeminism' (Shiva, 1988). The Eurocentric perspective of Inglehart's analysis is of course problematic, as is the empirically weak connection he makes between wealth/income levels and post-materialist values

(Cudworth, 2003: 71). He also limits 'environmental concern' to aesthetic/ amenity interests rather than material or productive interests people have with their environments, both as resources (such as land) and as a sink for pollutants/waste.

A fourth issue to note about green theory is its moral claim about our relationship to the natural environment. What makes green moral theory distinctive is that it wishes to extend the 'moral community' beyond the species barrier to include our interaction with the nonhuman world as morally significant, as well as extending the moral community temporally into the future in its focus on the rights of generations yet to be born and concerns, notably expressed in the idea of 'sustainability', of intergenerational justice.

Waves of green political theorising

One way of understanding the development of green political theory is in terms of waves, much as feminism (see chapter 8) is often categorised in terms of its evolution. 'First wave' green political theory was primarily concerned with articulating the distinctiveness of 'ecologism' as an ideology and green political theory as a distinctive approach to politics (Porritt, 1984; Pepper, 1984; Spretnak and Capra, 1985; Dryzek, 1987; Dobson, 1990; Eckersley, 1992; Paehlke, 1989; Hayward, 1995). 'Second wave' ecological thought was characterised by a concern with debates between green political theory and other schools of thought such as liberalism, feminism, critical theory and socialism, as well as focusing on some key concepts within political thought such as democracy, justice, the state and citizenship (Barry, 1999; Mellor, 1997; Salleh, 1999; Wissenburg, 1998; de-Shalit, 1996; Doherty and de Geus, 1996; Sakar, 1999; Lafferty and Meadowcroft, 1996).

Recent developments in what can be termed 'third generation' green political thought are noticeable for their explicitly interdisciplinary and applied focus. Indeed, on one level it is intellectually difficult to reflect on the many issues of concern to green political theory without venturing into and combining disciplines and bodies of knowledge outside politics, political science and political theory. Related to this interdisciplinary focus, third generation scholarship on green politics and sustainability tends to be informed by a much wider range of disciplines integrated with practical, empirical research. Examples of third way green political theory include my own work, *The Politics of Actually Existing Unsustainability* (Barry, 2012), Molly Scott-Cato's *Green Economics* (Scott-Cato, 2008), Andy Dobson's *Environmental Citizenship* (Dobson, 2003), Mathew Humphrey's *Ecological Politics and Democratic Theory* (Humphrey, 2008), Graham Smith's *Deliberative Democracy and the Environment* (Smith, 2003), Simon Hailwood's *How to be Green Liberal* (Hailwood, 2004) and Tim Hayward's *Constitutional Environmental Rights* (Hayward, 2005). Tim Jackson's *Prosperity without Growth* (Jackson, 2009) has done much to publicise long articulated green economic ideas (especially in relation to questioning conventional 'economic growth'), at a time when such ideas are needed more than ever in our public debate about and responses to the current global economic recession. Other examples are the research, publications and policy briefs from think tanks such as the New Economic Foundation, the incubator of many green political and economic ideas, ranging from its prescient and path-breaking *Green New Deal* report in 2008 (Green New Deal Group, 2008) to the more recent publication of Boyle and Simms, *The New Economics* (Boyle and Simms, 2009).

Green politics, applied theory and state, market and community

Green political theory can be understood as a form of applied political theory, and it shares this feature with other ideologies, all of which seek to make a difference and change the world or society according to their particular political principles. The task of an applied approach to political theory is to analyse some basic political or ethical principles – democracy, justice and citizenship, for example – and see what follows from them given the empirical 'reality of the situation' that faces humanity today, or a particular human society. That is, to explore how public policy can best be implemented, consistent with principles and empirical facts, as well as to contemplate how best to institutionalise the achievement of those principles. In particular, the institutional focus of the applied political theory approach centres on the appropriate ordering and respective roles of and relationships between what can be considered to be the three basic governance/political or order-producing institutions of human societies: the state, the market and the community.

The identification of these three institutions is important in that one can get a good, if basic and rough, idea of different political ideologies by looking at the relative weight and role accorded to state, market and community in both the ideology's analysis of the current political situation and its suggestion for how it should be improved and what its ideal society would look like. For example, the political ideologies of conservatism and liberalism tend to favour the free and self-regulating market, that is, capitalism, as the best institutional form for governing the human economy. What this means is that they favour the free market for ordering and governing the human metabolism with the nonhuman world, including resources, energy sources and waste sinks. On the other hand, the political ideologies of Marxist forms of socialism would tend to favour state-based forms of economic organisation and regulation. Here greens, in keeping with dominant strains of anarchism, differ in favouring the community as a preferred locus of economic (and political) organisation.

Green political theory favours, and prioritises, the community and communal forms of economic, cultural and political organisation and regulation. This can be seen in the long-standing green interest in and support for initiatives based on the principle of 'small is beautiful' (Schumacher, 1973) where appropriate; 'human scale' technology and less centralised forms of political democratic institutions (Sale, 1980); a suspicion of bureaucratised and professionalised/elite modes of meeting human needs (Illich, 1973); more local, grassroots forms of economic and political initiatives such as Transition Towns (Hopkins, 2008); and support for more localised and cooperative forms of economic activity (Scott-Cato, 2008). Perhaps the clearest instance of this privileging of the community is the strong preference for the 'social economy' over and above both market/private and state/public forms of economic life and associated notions of the economy being embedded in, rather than completely divorced from, human social life and social norms (Barry, 2012).

From the perspective of green political theory, the state and market are therefore best regarded as instrumental in supporting community-based forms of political and economic organisation and ways of life. That is, from a green political point of view, we should judge, assess and think about the state and the market (and associated principles and ideas such as private property, modes of economic organisation and the democratic regulation of the state, and state–citizen relations) in relation to their contribution to ensuring that political, economic and cultural life is organised by the community and at the level of community. Thus, while most greens (with the exception of eco-anarchists) do not reject the state, and while they are profoundly suspicious of the concentration and centralisation of power within and by the state, they do see a role for a more democratised and decentralised state in regulating the market to prevent the latter from undermining key green values such as social solidarity, high levels of well-being, human-scale connectedness and the intrinsic values of work (and here greens do not conflate work with formally paid employment). Above all, there is a role for the state in regulating any market-based organisation of human economic relations to prevent the emergence and maintenance of high levels of socio-economic inequality, since the latter not only is corrosive of key green values that are constitutive of community itself, but, as Wilkinson and Pickett (2009) demonstrate, undermines key aspects of the transition from unsustainability (see also Barry, 2012).

Green politics and actually existing unsustainability

While completely accepting the need for, and importance of, more abstract, conceptually based theorising, we can say that there is a major difference between debates about a *theory or theories of justice* (which dominate contemporary liberal political theory) and a debate that accepts the fact that, sociologically speaking, it is *injustice, not justice*, that characterises the world. One gets a very different form of theorising when one begins from where we are in terms of conditions of injustice, rather than seeking to develop compelling and intellectually coherent but abstract benchmarks or criteria against which we can judge present-day, real-world conditions of injustice. The fight against injustices is not necessarily the same as a fight for some positive conception of justice. As Simon rightly suggests, 'injustice has a different phenomenology from justice. Understanding injustice constitutes a separate theoretical enterprise from constructing a theory of justice. . . . injustice takes priority over justice' (Simon, 1995: xvii; Shklar, 1990; Wolgast, 1987). Using a similar line of argument, there are good reasons for recasting green political theory as a *politics of actually existing unsustainability* rather than a *politics for (future) sustainability*. This perspective implies that the analysis of actually existing unsustainability should take priority over the analysis of sustainability.

A politics of unsustainability addresses our attention to the reality of what can be called *actually existing unsustainability*, and the identification of those underlying causes of the continuation of that unsustainability or unsustainabilities. From this perspective, then, the first aim of green politics ought to be to identify the drivers and causes of unsustainability and seek to reduce existing unsustainability as a precondition for the articulation and achievement of future sustainability or to map some future sustainable development path (Barry, 2012).

Indeed, we may have done better since the 1992 Rio Earth Summit – the first international articulation of 'sustainability' and 'sustainable development' – if we had focused attention on a politics of actually existing unsustainability rather than sustainability. The time and debate taken to develop an agreed conception of sustainability has actually 'sustained unsustainability', as it were. One could be forgiven for thinking that from the point of view of those profiting and benefitting from the continuation of actually existing unsustainability, the ideal way for this system to continue relatively unchanged, while acknowledging its unsustainability, would be to focus on the pressing and urgent need to develop a workable and agreed-on conception of sustainability and sustainable development to guide us, complete with associated policies and strategies.

This rather cynical/realistic view of the official politics of 'sustainable development' is where the work of Blühdorn and others on 'simulative green politics' connects with the conception of green political theory outlined in this chapter (Blühdorn, 2000; Blühdorn and Welsh, 2008). It suggests that just as the rich will do everything to help the poor except get off their backs, likewise those benefitting from unsustainability (which simply put is the exploitation of people and planet) are willing to do everything to realise sustainability except stop their unsustainable lifestyles and transform the underlying social and economic dynamics that cause unsustainability. Think of the proliferation of academic, government, NGO and corporate documents about 'sustainability' and 'sustainable development'. What would such documents contain if, instead of being framed and focused around the future achievement of some understanding of sustainability, they were framed and focused around the reduction of unsustainability here and now? What would the policy implications be of a strategy for reducing 'unsustainable development'?

Returning to this focus on actually existing unsustainability and the argument for the priority of an account of injustice over any theory of justice, we can note that, according to Simon, we can identify injustice without recourse to a theory of justice (that is, injustice cannot be reduced to meaning the lack or absence of justice), largely through the ideas of suffering and harm. As he puts it:

> It makes a difference whether we describe our political actions as part of a *fight against injustice, against other people's suffering*, or as a contest for justice. The two labels do not constitute different ways of talking about the same thing . . . Justice beckons us to create the positive in the future whereas injustice frantically yells at us to eradicate the negative in the present.
>
> (Simon, 1995: 1; emphasis added)

An interesting and important point Simon makes concerning the separation of considerations of injustice from considerations of justice is that from a green perspective a critique of the current unsustainable economic system does not, and should not, depend for its validity on the specification of some positive sustainable alternative. That is, while from a political point of view one might wish, when persuading people of one's position, to develop a worked-out alternative, this should not be a requirement for the critique to be politically considered and taken seriously in public policy debate. As he notes:

> the negative recommendation stands on its own, without the inclusion of a positive alternative . . . *Requiring that negative recommendations depend upon positive alternatives has the effect of undermining the negative recommendations.* We need to listen to the negative recommendations, irrespective of whether the negative criticisms also contain positive proposals.
>
> (Simon, 1995: 14; emphasis added)

This prescription relates to many green arguments concerning the need to challenge practices and institutions that promote unsustainability on the grounds that it is *their* responsibility to disprove the charge of unsustainability, as opposed to green objectors having to prove unsustainability (usually based on some notion of sustainability). This is a central issue of the precautionary principle (see O'Riordan and Jordan, 1995), the application of which is compatible with the politics of unsustainability outlined here, namely in that it 'turns the table' in the debate by requiring proponents of the status quo to disprove unsustainability.

As Simon notes, it is the identification of harm (which does not have to have any referent to a theory of justice or what a person is due under such a theory) that enables one to develop an account of injustice conceived as independent from an account of justice. He is explicit in seeing the importance of the acceptance of a 'health metaphor' in defending a theory of injustice. For him, 'Justice relates to injustice in the same way that health relates to disease.

We cannot have informative definitions or analyses of each specific disease only according to what form of health the disease rules out' (Simon, 1995: 12). It is because we can identify harm and suffering without recourse to a theory of justice that we can say the experience of injustice cannot be reduced to not being treated in accordance with some account of justice.

Green politics and human flourishing

If we accept this health metaphor, this represents a distinctive green view of ethics and politics (Barry, 2012). It enables us to understand the urgency of actually existing unsustainability and its associated exploitation of people, the abuse of the planet and the continuing degradation of the nonhuman world. One of the features of this health/suffering/flourishing perspective, and perhaps the one that results in some being critical of its use, is its potential for abuse by whoever or whatever authority determines what is and what is not 'human flourishing'. This is a legitimate concern, since anyone or any institution that determines one's health can potentially do so without any reference to you. That is, such objective forms of determining what is good for people can fall foul of the 'shoe pinching objection'. This is the objection that only the person wearing the shoe can know if and where it pinches: this cannot be determined by some external authority. It can have non-democratic results in that relations between people governed on the basis of 'expert knowledge' are usually (and often legitimately) non-democratic. The classic example here is a patient's relationship to her or his doctor: we do not typically view this relationship as one that necessarily has to be structured by democratic norms. The application of democratic norms is usually viewed as inappropriate in this case (and other similar cases). However, notwithstanding these important considerations, I do not think that making a health, or suffering, or harm, focus central to one's political position necessarily leads to such undemocratic and unjust results. Another concern is 'perfectionism', which is the concern that such a quasi-objectively determined sense of human flourishing could result in non-democratic, individual-insensitive intrusions which would 'force' people to 'flourish' along a particular pattern over which they had no control or to which they did not lend their consent or approval.

A final concern is that this account of the human person, and the associated conception of human flourishing, is homogenous, that is, there is one determinate view of the 'good life' for humans. This would mean a politics that reduced the variety of views of the good life available to individuals and groups. One response to this (liberal) objection would be to point out the empirical experience of how contemporary liberal capitalist societies promote one dominant view of the good life, namely a consumerist one. My contention is that against the backdrop of the crushing uniformity and homogeneity often attendant upon contemporary consumerist culture, there would be *more, not less variety* in views of the good in a post-growth, post-capitalist social order.

A shift away from the dominance of the 'goods life' (Doran, 2006) could open up more, not less, possibilities for a variety of forms of human flourishing. Another response would be that green politics does not require that people 'be or think green', or 'be sustainable' in some determinate sense, but rather that they stop 'being unsustainable' (or be less unsustainable), which both is less contentious and does not have the liberty- or pluralism-reducing effects of 'forcing people to be sustainable'. Relatedly, given the focus on structures and political economy dynamics that underpin green political economy, the issue in respect to unsustainability and its reduction is primarily structural and political, not necessarily to do with individual agents. Therefore, while of course having an impact on individuals, green politics is less interested (though not uninterested) in the behaviour of individuals than in ensuring that what Rawls (1971) called the 'basic structure of society' does not contain structures that enable, encourage or oblige/force individuals to engage in actions and practices which perpetuate actually existing unsustainability.

From this negative Aristotelian perspective, a focus on human flourishing denotes the identification of those features that undermine the range within which being a healthy person, viewed holistically, is possible. The aim, therefore, of a green politics of actually existing unsustainability is the speedy removal of those features, structures, cultural norms and institutional arrangements of the present social order which prevent the realisation of this range of human flourishing for as many people as possible. Thus, negative Aristotelianism is not the promotion of some narrow and determinate sense of the human good – that the good life necessarily requires active citizenship – rather it is the proposition that we can specify those aspects of an individual's particular social structure (social context, milieu, environment) that are actively undermining their realisation of that range of human flourishing.

This negative Aristotelianism of green politics tries on the one hand to avoid or minimise the charge of 'perfectionism' while on the other retaining a quasi-objective account of the conditions of human flourishing, thereby enabling the determination and, hopefully, removal or reduction of those obstacles which constrain more people from realising that range of human flourishing. That is, the aim of a green republicanism of actually existing unsustainability is primarily negative and defensive: to reduce if not eliminate those external and internal features that prevent people from flourishing.[1] Here, green political theory has affinities with both the emancipatory politics of critical theory and utopianism, though re-cast as a form of 'concrete' rather than 'abstract' utopianism (Barry, 2012).

From the account of green political theory articulated here, human flourishing can be understood in a quasi-objective manner, akin to trying to specify those features that together constitute a 'healthy human'. And a green politics of actually existing unsustainability suggests we need to begin our search by developing a view of the human person as someone who is both socially and ecologically embedded, biologically embodied and dependent, biographically, at different points in his or her life. In the 'circumstances of unsustainability' that currently prevail we need a conception of human flourishing that is cognisant of the finite planet and its resources. This is why one short-hand summary of green political goals is 'the achievement of low-carbon, high-quality-of-life forms of human flourishing'. In this way what is needed is to improve the resource- and eco-efficiency of human flourishing, not the eco-efficiency of conventional economic productivity and orthodox economic growth. Or, rather, we can only make decisions and judgements about productivity and economic growth in relation to how they contribute to the primary goal of human flourishing. How can we, in short, secure maximum human flourishing within the regenerative capacities and thresholds of the sustainable use of the ecological resources of our finite planet?

Thus, a key goal of this negative Aristotelianism within green politics is the removal of those external and internal obstacles preventing human flourishing. So what are these? We can identify the following from a green political theory perspective:

- the narrowing of human identity and interests by debt-based consumerism and the deformities of human life due to poverty, insecurity and malnutrition;
- the axiomatic presentation of orthodox, undifferentiated economic growth as a permanent rather than contingent feature of an economy;
- increasing levels of socio-economy inequality;
- the sequestering of our dependent natures and needs;
- the corralling of 'work' into formally paid 'employment' and the imperatives for economic growth;
- the gendered inequalities of necessary reproductive work;
- the 'crowding out' of socially embedded forms of provisioning by the state and market.

When these obstacles are removed the outlines of a green conception of human flourishing begins to emerge. It is based on 'post-consumerist', but not anti-materialist, forms of human identity; the centrality of public policy based on the identification of thresholds beyond which specific macro-economic policies, such as economic growth, hinder rather than facilitate meeting human needs and flourishing; establishing 'rough equality' between people; fully recognising our vulnerable and dependent natures as they change over a lifetime; focusing on promoting work and not just orthodox 'employment'; greater recognition and support for more gender-equal reproductive work; and the enhancing of both the social economy and social solidarity, alongside reformed state and market forms of economic production and provisioning.

This focus on actually existing unsustainability can also be connected to viewing green politics as a form of 'concrete utopianism': a politics of hope for a self-transforming present, one orientated towards the here and now (hence its 'applied theory' character). The movement away from unsustainability is perhaps more practical, as there is more chance of political agreement on what is unsustainable than what is 'sustainable', much in the same way that, as Simon notes, 'We can find agreement more readily over what constitutes injustice than over what constitutes justice' (Simon, 1995: xvii). Thus, there may be strategic reasons why we might want to consider re-casting green politics as a politics of actually existing unsustainability, thereby improving its chances of making a political difference.

Green politics is vulnerable, as are all oppositional and radical perspectives, to the charge of being impatient for change and the accusation that it is perfectionist. That is, in aiming for the 'perfect' it promotes a sense of sustainability where all the inter-related issues of the internal relations between people, and between people, place and planet, have been 'solved'. The 'good life' here is the 'good enough' life: the identification and removal or reduction of those current external-structural and internal features of the human condition that are systematically causing harm, suffering and exploitation and thus preventing human (and nonhuman) flourishing.

On the one hand, there is no 'solution' that 'sustainability' represents, in that (especially from an ecological perspective) any equilibrium 'solution' will always be provisional and dynamic. On the other, a green politics focused on the achievement of sustainability, as indicated above, is liable to spend too long and expend too much energy on developing some agreed account of sustainability, at the expense of devoting time and attention to tackling unsustainability. That is, a politics of sustainability can constrain movement on reducing currently existing unsustainability, since this way of thinking means that we cannot tackle unsustainability until we have a clear and agreed sense of sustainability. While harsh, this is a reasonable overview of the debate and politics around 'sustainability' and 'sustainable development' since the Rio Earth Summit in 1992.

A green politics orientated around analysing and reducing actually existing unsustainability also seems to have the advantage of perhaps mobilising people. That is, when both the realities and causal dynamics of actually existing unsustainability are revealed to people, they connect more easily to the emotional and motivational resources of injustice than the more distant and cold dispositions of both sustainability and justice. A major issue here is that in the contemporary world the realities of unsustainability, and their causal relations, are systematically 'sequestered' and occluded under contemporary patterns of industrial globalisation (Barry, 2012). A key feature of green politics is thus 'de-sequestering' such relations, thereby (re)politicising them (Barry and Ellis, 2010). When the realities and causal relations of unsustainability – such as the exploitation of vulnerable people in other parts of the world, the suffering of people and animals, and the sheer injustice of avoidable, premature deaths – are 'seen', the emotional and psychological responses to these need little encouragement. Sympathy and empathy are entirely ethically appropriate and much-needed ways of looking at the world, especially a world so full of needless suffering. In industrial societies, there are reasons other than cost, aesthetics and health and safety why abattoirs do not have glass walls.

But the movement away from unsustainability is more 'practical' in another sense. It may turn out that making societies less unsustainable is a matter more of *not doing something* than of doing something new, such as consuming *less* of both commodities and energy. This is another central feature of green political theory: the sense that the achievement of a less unsustainable, green society is not so much about getting from 'here' to 'there', but about 'letting go' and showing that it is the unsustainable 'here' that is utopian and unrealistic that needs to be challenged (Mellor, 1995). This does not mean that such a transition is easy, but it does indicate that the state and public discourse should be perhaps directed more towards eliminating existing forms of consumer 'lock-in' to unsustainable and perhaps non-well-being-enhancing practices than necessarily towards unleashing the power of the wind or the atom. That is, reducing actually existing unsustainability may be more about reducing and scaling back existing practices than proposing something new.

People cannot stand too much reality: the emergence of 'hard green' ecological realism

The anthropologist Marshall Sahlins pointed out that every human culture (and nonhuman culture, for that matter) is a 'gamble played with nature' (1972: ix), and like any gamble it can be won or lost. One of the contemporary zeitgeists we can observe is an interlocking and complex sense of anxiety about the future. This zeitgeist is principally driven by fears about life in a climate-changed and carbon-constrained world in the aftermath of 'peak oil' and dangerous climate change, and it has multiplied under the current global economic crisis since 2008. It is an anxiety that our current globalised, carbon-fuelled capitalist system is coming to the end of the line. This chapter was written against the backdrop of a profound (and disturbing) sense of growing doom and frustration at the lack of progress on the social mobilisation, or institutional planning, for the transition to a low-carbon or post-carbon society and economy. *And for greens this transition is inevitable.*

However, what is striking about some recent thinking on the unsustainability of current dominant ways of life are those voices, discourses and works which one might categorise as 'ecological realist'. The 'hard green' analyses tend often to paint the near-future of large sections of humanity in extremely negative and stark terms. Think of Cormac McCarthy's *The Road*, together with the peer-reviewed science of the Intergovernmental Panel on Climate Change, and mix in the complete failure of political leadership by the majority of the most powerful countries on the planet and mainstream political parties. This hard green discourse is peppered with terms such as 'peak oil', 'climate chaos', life in a 'carbon constrained world', 'climate and food (in)security' and climate-imposed 'triage'. Moreover, it is gripped by a profound sense of urgency, as seen in the New Economics Foundation announcement in October 2008 that we had '100 months to save the planet' (Simms, 2008). This ecological realist analysis articulates a green storyline that, on the face of it, could not be more removed from an idealist, hope-filled account of green political theory.

The sheer scale, rapidity and incontrovertible evidence of humanity becoming more 'locked-into' unsustainability, the liquidation of the planet's life support systems and the negative impact on the nonhuman community of life on the planet is matched only by the prevarication of governments and other influential groups, especially business, and the passiveness of the consumer population. In particular, we could point to large corporations and other key sectors of the business community that have lobbied actively against policies and legislation to reduce pollution, funded climate change denial and engaged in 'greenwash' instead of cleaning up their production processes, thereby maintaining unsustainability. Or, relating the discussion to Blühdorn's work referred to above, we could examine the 'cognitive dissonance' displayed by millions of citizens who proclaim to know and accept that their energy-intense, high-consumption and high-mobility lifestyles (and associated economic system and technological infrastructure) are the root causes of global and local ecological breakdown, but who either refuse or are unable to change their lifestyles to enable 'one-planet living'. As Schellenberger and Nordhaus (2006: 9) put it, 'while public support for action on global warming is wide it is also frighteningly shallow'. George Monbiot observes:

> As people in the rich countries – even the professional classes – begin to wake up to what science is saying, climate change denial will look as stupid as Holocaust denial or the insistence that AIDS can be cured by beetroot. But our response will be to demand that the government acts while hoping it doesn't. *We will wish our governments to pretend to act.* We get the moral satisfaction of saying what we know to be right, without the discomfort of doing it. My fear is that the political parties in most rich nation countries have already recognized this. They know we want tough targets, but that we also want those targets to be missed. They know that we will grumble about their failure to curb climate change, but that we will not take to the streets. *They know that nobody ever rioted for austerity.*
>
> (2003: 41–2; emphasis added)

So far, so good for 'simulative green politics' (Blühdorn and Welsh, 2008; Blühdorn, 2000), which constitutes an updated version of St Augustine's request that 'God grant me chastity and temperance, but not just yet'.

In response to Monbiot's reasonable observation, green political theory does, however, suggest that people may riot for their own happiness. Seen from a negative Aristotelian perspective, what they may riot for is the removal of demonstrable obstacles to human (and nonhuman) flourishing. As indicated earlier, green politics argues that the case for 'post-growth' rests on the argument that it is possible to achieve simultaneously a low-carbon, low-resource use and a high-well-being society. Green politics thus offers a far more positive and attractive vision of a sustainable society than those (invariably non-greens) who present a green or sustainable society in terms of a discourse of 'loss', 'sacrifice' and/or 'regress' (Meyer and Maniates, 2010). In many respects, what greens seek is to promote the serious consideration that orthodox 'economic growth' has largely 'done its job' in the developed world (Wilkinson and Pickett, 2009). Moreover, they seek to communicate that its continuation as an uncontested cultural myth or state imperative, or as the underpinning of our modern 'social contact' in high-carbon, high-consumption societies, is systematically undermining human well-being, as well as liquidating the life-supporting systems of the planet. What a post-growth position needs to present is a vision of a better, improved and more advanced society: one in which social innovation is as important as technological innovation, in which time begins to replace money and commodities, in which sufficiency replaces maximisation and in which 'economic security' for all replaces unequally distributed economic growth. It is a better world, not some impoverished, regressive or indeed abstract utopian/dystopian vision of the future. It is the outworkings of a self-transforming present, hence its 'concrete utopian' character, with most of the necessary technological, social and indeed economic practices and innovations already in existence and ready to be mobilised. That most of these are small-scale, under-recognised or un-recognised does not detract from their importance and the powerful fact that they *do* exist. All that is required, and of course this is a big 'all', is the political will and personal and collective courage to learn about and experiment with them, and explore new ways of *living more lightly* on the planet. Particularly in the 'overdeveloped' world, we are asked to slim down, not starve, ourselves in order to address actually existing unsustainability. The issue is this: in the context of the inevitable (and hopefully 'just') transition to a less unsustainable society, it is not what we may lose that is moot, but what we gain.

Given the centrality of the 'limits to growth' to any understanding of green politics, an ecological realist discourse could be viewed as the return to, or vindication of, that earlier green analysis and discourse in a new guise (Meadows *et al.*, 1972). While some contemporary critics dismissed the limits to growth report as 'Malthus with a computer' (Freeman, 1973), this new and improved ecological realist perspective could be viewed as 'limits to growth with PowerPoint'. Other indications of this ecological realism include (in the UK and Ireland) the emergence of initiatives such as the 'Dark Mountain' project founded by 'recovering environmentalists' (Hine and Kingsnorth, 2010), the growth and more general acceptance of the analyses of the once marginal 'peak oil movement', and the emergence of what may be termed 'collapse' authors and thinkers, such as Dimity Orlov (2011) and David Korowicz (2010). As Thomas Friedman notes:

> The world also has a problem: It is getting hot, flat, and crowded . . . In particular, the convergence of hot, flat, and crowded is tightening energy supplies, intensifying the extinction of plants and animals, deepening energy poverty, strengthening petro-dictatorships, and accelerating climate change. How we address these interwoven

global trends will determine a lot about the quality of life on earth in the twenty-first century.

(2008: 5)

While a corpus of books and films have popularised green thinking and certainly raised awareness of our unsustainability, they have also rendered green politics in a negative and unappealing frame. One of the main points Schellenberger and Nordhaus (2006) make in their 'immanent critique' of the US environmental movement is how counter-productive it is to stress and amplify environmental problems (particularly within a technocratic or technological frame), without seeking to outline an attractive and compelling vision which attaches itself to peoples' values and aspirations. Simply put, the green movement has been and continues to be extremely good at highlighting the problems, but less good at articulating its vision for a less unsustainable society, or how the principle of 'sustainability' can relate to a positive future. Perhaps one answer lies, as suggested above, in the green movement moving beyond a 'sustainability' frame to focusing on becoming a politics of 'actually existing unsustainability'.

James Lovelock is perhaps the most well-know environmentalist to capture this ecological realist mood. His most recent work (Lovelock, 2009) claims that there is no point in trying renewable energy or CO_2 emissions trading systems or attempting to negotiate international treaties on reducing CO_2, recycling or any of the other usual components of 'sustainable development'. Lovelock foresees crop failures, drought, death on an enormous scale and massive social disruption right across the globe. The population of this hot, barren world could shrink from about seven billion to one billion by 2100 as people compete for ever-scarcer resources. As he put it in an interview, 'It will be death on a grand scale from famine and lack of water. It could be a reduction to a billion (people) or less' (Griffiths, 2009). According to Lovelock, the human species should be ideally adopting a clear 'survivalist' perspective and investing in efforts to create safe havens in areas which will escape the worst effects of climate change. He puts it bluntly: 'we have to stop pretending that there is any possible way of returning to that lush, comfortable and beautiful Earth we left behind some time in the 20th century' (2009: 68). And, in an even more chilling statement: 'The Earth, *in its but not our interests* may be forced to move to a hot epoch, one where it can survive, though in a diminished and less habitable state. If, as is likely, this happens, we will have been the cause' (ibid.: 3; emphasis added).

Other, more 'post-humanist' but equally pessimistic/realistic writers such as John Gray have rushed to celebrate and endorse Lovelock. In a review of Lovelock's book, Gray writes:

Gaia has no particular concern for humans, and will not be propitiated by empty gestures such as carbon trading or limits on air traffic. What is needed, in fact, is virtually the opposite of the standard Green mix of wind turbines and organic farms, which could at best enable an overblown human population to eke a precarious living from an overtaxed Earth. If there is a sustainable future it is in a compact, high-tech civilisation with far fewer people.

(2009: 1)

We can discern here the outlines of a new vision of a 'sustainable society', and one markedly at odds with the various accounts that pepper green political theory.

Gray's curt and cursory dismissal of green politics as wildly utopian, that is, not only unrealistic but dangerous and counterproductive, is matched by an equally provocative suggestion that we should concentrate on policies for a 'sustainable retreat' in the face of inevitable ecological degradation and resource collapse (Lovelock, 2005; Gray, 2006). This vision is a 'hard ecological' view and has clear resonances with certain Malthusian strains within green politics (Barry, 2007, 1999). It is a vision of a technological 'survivalist' society, one which is orientated towards saving what elements of civilisation we can. It is basically a vision of sustainable society in which we have nuclear power, energy from waste incinerators, genetically engineered crops and medicines, centralised power production, big cities and urban conurbations (though perhaps relocated inland to escape the rising seas), but at the price of social progress, justice and democracy. It is a techno-optimistic progressive sustainable society that is at one and the same time socially regressive.

Another prominent author here is Jeffrey Sachs, director of Columbia University's Earth Institute, who in his 2007 BBC Reith Lectures follows Giddens, Gray and Lovelock (and Al Gore) in promoting a techno-centric and techno-optimistic vision for approaching the challenges we face. For Sachs, the solution to our current 'triple crunch' of climate crisis, economic meltdown and energy insecurity (Green New Deal Group, 2008) is not 'a massive cutback in our consumption levels or our living standards' but 'smarter living . . . to find a way for the rest of the world . . . to raise their own material conditions as well' (Sachs, 2007). At times it is hard to know which is the more unsettling: the cosy and comforting accounts of reformist 'optimists' such as Sachs, Gore and Giddens or the shocking and frightening views of radical 'pessimists' such as Lovelock, Demitri Orlov (2011), James Howard Kunstler (2005) and David Korowicz (2010).

The solutions suggested by such 'hard ecologists' are, in a very important respect, at odds with green political theory, and not just in the obvious sense that many of the solutions proposed are antithetical to green principles, not least in their authoritarian character. An equally significant way in which such solutions are inconsistent with green political theory is that they are often *non-political* techno-fixes, and as such present the analysis of, and transition from, unsustainability in ways that resolutely avoid the quintessentially *political* (including ethical) causes of, and therefore responses to, unsustainability. However, there is a very significant issue all these writers raise, and one central to green politics. That issue, in a word, is *vulnerability*. What all of these gloomy/realist/hard ecological analyses share is a profound sense of the vulnerability of humanity, particular human lifestyles and ways of life to natural limits and resource, energy or sink scarcities. For this reason, vulnerability is central to green politics, and here it perhaps shares much with feminist political thinking on this foundational issue.

Conclusion

What we can say is that the analyses outlined by the new 'ecological realism' expose the fundamental vulnerability of modern technologically advanced industrial societies to a spectrum of problems, ranging from climate change and food production, water and energy insecurity to the epidemics of obesity, declining mental health and well-being within an increasingly climate-changed, crowded, profoundly unequal, unsustainable and carbon-constrained world (Barry, Mol and Zito, 2013; Barry, 2012). Yet, unlike in hard green analyses, the dominant trend within green political theory is to begin from the position that there is little to be gained from the continuing pursuit of the 'malestream' technological fantasy of invulnerability, control and mastery over nature. This project and orientation to the world based on control, human invulnerability and domination of the earth, as critical theorists such as Horkheimer, Adorno, Fromm and Marcuse have long pointed out, leads not to liberation and emancipation but wage and consumer enslavement (of self) and exploitation of others, including nonhuman others. The fantasy of invulnerability, control and conquest culminates in what Marcuse brilliantly diagnosed as the 'repressive tolerance' and disfigured subjectivities of liberal democracy within capitalism (Marcuse, 1964).

In many respects green political theory is faced with the need to provide analyses and responses to multiple socio-ecological dilemmas. This context for green politics has been outlined by Thomas Homer-Dixon, and his contention in a *New York Times* op-ed article in 2010:

> *Policy makers need to accept that societies won't make drastic changes to address climate change until such a crisis hits*. But that doesn't mean there's nothing for them to do in the meantime. When a crisis does occur, the societies with response plans on the shelf will be far better off than those that are blindsided. The task for national and regional leaders, then, is to develop a set of contingency plans for possible climate shocks – what we might call, collectively, Plan Z. We need a much more deliberate Plan Z, with detailed scenarios of plausible climate shocks; close analyses of options for emergency response by governments, corporations and nongovernmental groups; and clear specifics about what resources – financial, technological and organizational – we will need to cope with different types of crises. (Emphasis added)

We are facing inevitable ecological, resource and socio-economic challenges, and we are singularly unprepared for them. At the very least, we should be thankful to these 'hard greens' both for reminding us of the fragility and contingency of our current civilisation and ways of life and for forcing a response to the often grim issues and scenarios they raise. Above all else, green political theory takes from them the importance, noted by Homer-Dixon, of the need for societies to plan for a number of future scenarios as well as actively taking steps to avoid the most negative ones.

This is the promise of recasting and understanding green political theory as a politics of actually existing unsustainability. In some ways, this reading of the 'hard green' position is actually closer to the 'soft green' position outlined by E. F. Schumacher: 'We never know when the winds of change will blow, but when they do we must always have our sails at the ready' (in Rosen, 2002: 181). To sustain this metaphor, we can draw on a Chinese proverb: 'When the winds of change come, some people build walls, others build windmills'.

Further reading

Short, introductory overviews of green political theory can be found in J. Barry's 'Environmentalism' (2002), J. Barry and A. Dobson's 'Green Political Theory: A Report' (2003), J. Barry's 'Green Political Theory' (2001), S. Young's *The Politics of the Environment* (1992), R. Garner's *Environmental Politics* (1995) and E. Cudworth's *Environment and Society* (2003).

Classic early and foundational accounts of ecological/green thinking and green ideas can be found in R. Carson's *Silent Spring* (1962), E. F. Schumacher's *Small Is Beautiful: Economics as if People Mattered* (1973), E. Mishan's *The Costs of Economic Growth* (1968), D. Meadows, D. Meadows and J. Randers's *The Limits to Growth* (1972) and I. Illich's *Tools for Conviviality* (1973).

Current examples of analysis based on the 'limits to growth' include Jared Diamond's *Collapse: How Societies Choose to Succeed or Fail* (Diamond, 2005), Thomas Homer-Dixon's *The Upside of Down* (Homer-Dixon, 2006), Alister McIntosh's *Hell and High Water: Climate Change, Hope and the Human Condition* (McIntosh, 2008), Derrick Jensen's *The Culture of Make-Believe* (Jensen, 2002), the Odums' *A Prosperous Way Down* (Odum and Odum, 2001), James Howard Kunstler's *The Long Emergency* (Kunstler, 2005) and Thomas Friedman's *Hot, Flat and Crowded* (Friedman, 2008). Related documentaries include Al Gore's *An Inconvenient Truth* and Leonardo DiCaprio's *Eleventh Hour*, as well as the less well-known *What a Way to Go: Life at the End of Empire*, *The End of Suburbia*, *Escape from Suburbia*, *A Crude Awakening: The Oil Crash* and documentaries such as the 2009 UK-based Channel 4 production *Life after People*.

Good accounts of 'first wave' green political theory include J. Porritt's *Seeing Green: The Politics of Ecology Explained* (1984), D. Pepper's, *The Roots of Modern Environmentalism* (1984), C. Spretnak and F. Capra's *Green Politics:*

The Global Promise (1985), J. Dryzek's *Rational Ecology* (1987), A. Dobson's *Green Political Thought* (2007), R. Eckersley's *Environmentalism and Political Theory: Toward an Ecocentric Approach* (1992), R. Paehlke's *Environmentalism and the Future of Progressive Politics* (1989), T. Hayward's *Ecological Thought: An Introduction* (1995), L. Martell's *Nature and Society: An Introduction* (1994), R. Goodin's *Green Political Theory* (1992), J. Kassiola's *The Death of Industrial Civilization* (1990), P. Dickens's *Society and Nature* (1992), T. Benton's *Natural Relations: Ecology, Animal Rights and Social Justice* (1993), K. Lee's *Social Philosophy and Ecological Scarcity* (1989) and A. Dobson and P. Lucardie's *The Politics of Nature* (1993).

'Second wave' green politics includes works such as J. Barry's *Rethinking Green Politics* (1999), J. O'Neill's *Ecology, Policy and Politics: Human Well-Being and the Natural World* (1993), M. Mellor's *Towards a Feminist, Green Socialism* (1997), A. Salleh's *Ecofeminism as Politics: Nature, Marx and the Postmodern* (1999), T. Luke's *Capitalism, Democracy, and Ecology* (1999) and *Ecocritique* (1997), M. Wissenburg's *Green Liberalism* (1998), A. de-Shalit's *Why Posterity Matters* (1995), B. Doherty and M. de Geus's *Democracy and Green Political Thought* (1996), S. Sakar's *Eco-Socialism or Eco-Capitalism?* (1999), W. Lafferty and J. Meadowcroft's *Democracy and the Environment* (1996), B. Baxter's *Ecologism: An Introduction* (1999), J. Radcliffe's *Green Politics: Dictatorship or Democracy?* (2000) and A. Carter's *A Radical Green Political Theory* (1999).

Examples of 'third wave' green political thinking include J. Barry's *The Politics of Actually Existing Unsustainability* (2012), A. Dobson's *Citizenship and the Environment* (2003), A. Dobson's *Green Political Thought*, 4th edition (2007), M. Humphrey's *Ecological Politics and Democratic Theory* (2008), M. Woodin and C. Lucas's *Green Alternatives to Globalisation: A Manifesto* (2004), J. Barry and R. Eckersley's *The Nation-State and the Global Ecological Crisis* (2005), G. Smith's *Deliberative Democracy and the Environment* (2003), R. Eckerlsey's *The Green State* (2004), S. Hailwood's *How to Be a Green Liberal* (2004), T. Hayward's *Constitutional Environmental Rights* (2005), D. Schlosberg's *Defining Environmental Justice* (2009) and P. Cannavò's *The Working Landscape* (2007).

The turn in green political theory to critics of capitalism and orthodox economics and the development of a distinct account of green political economy can be found in the following: M. Scott-Cato's *Green Economics* (2008) and *The Bioregional Economy: Land, Liberty and the Pursuit of Happiness* (2012), T. Jackson's *Prosperity without Growth* (2009), D. Boyle and A. Simms's *The New Economics* (2009), J. Schor's *Plenitude: The New Economics of True Wealth* (2010) and B. McKibben's *Deep Economy* (2007).

Note

1   An interesting policy application of this thinking is 'choice editing' (Levett, 2003), that is, the deliberate removal of and reduction of choice in an area motivated by

a desire to remove socially or environmentally 'bad' options, but which also removes the stress most people feel when faced with a bewildering range of choices in a single area or product. As Levett puts it, *'Contrary to current rhetoric, an important job of government is to restrict choice.* The state stops us assaulting, robbing or cheating each other, with the great benefit that we can live in peace and security and do deals with strangers of unknown morals' (Levett, 2008: 11; emphasis added).

References

Barry, J. (1999), *Rethinking Green Politics: Nature, Virtue, Progress*, London: Sage.

—— (2001), 'Green Political Theory', in Barry, J. and Frankland, E. G. (eds) (2001), *International Encyclopedia of Environmental Politics*, London: Routledge.

—— (2002), 'Environmentalism', in Axtmann, R. (ed.), *Understanding Democratic Politics: Concepts, Institutions, Movements*, London: Sage.

—— (2007), *Environment and Social Theory*, 2nd edition, London: Routledge.

—— (2012), *The Politics of Actually Existing Unsustainability: Human Flourishing in a Climate-Changed, Carbon-Constrained World*, Oxford: Oxford University Press.

Barry, J. and Dobson, A. (2003), 'Green Political Theory: A Report', in Kukathas, C. and Gaus, G. (eds) (2003), *Handbook of Political Theory*, London: Sage.

Barry, J. and Eckersley, R. (2005), *The State and the Global Ecological Crisis*, Boston: MIT Press.

Barry, J. and Ellis, G. (2010), 'Beyond Consensus? Agonism, Republicanism and a Low Carbon Future', in P. Devine-Wright (ed.), *Renewable Energy and the Public: From NIMBY to Participation*, London: Earthscan, pp. 9–42.

Barry, J., Mol, A. and Zito, A. (2013), 'Climate Change Ethics, Rights and Policies', *Environmental Politics*, 22 (3): 361–76.

Baxter, B. (1999), *Ecologism: An Introduction*, Edinburgh: Edinburgh University Press.

Benton, T. (1993), *Natural Relations: Ecology, Animal Rights and Social Justice*, London: Verso.

Blühdorn, I. (2000), *Post-Ecologist Politics: Social Theory and the Abdication of the Ecologist Paradigm*, London: Routledge.

Blühdorn, I. and Welsh, I. (eds) (2008), *The Politics of Unsustainability: Eco-Politics in the Post-Ecologist Era*, London: Routledge.

Boyle, D. and Simms, A. (2009), *The New Economics: A Bigger Picture*, Cheltenham: Edward Elgar.

Cannavò, P. (2007), *The Working Landscape: Founding, Preservation and the Politics of Place*, Boston: MIT Press.

Carson, R. (1962), *Silent Spring*, New York: Houghton Mifflin.

Carter, A. (1999), *A Radical Green Political Theory*, London: Routledge.

Cudworth, E. (2003), *Environment and Society*, London: Routledge.

De-Shalit, A. (1995), *Why Posterity Matters: Environmental Policies and Future Generations*, London: Routledge.

—— (1996), 'Is Liberalism Environment Friendly?', *Social Theory and Practice*, 21: 287–315.

Diamond, J. (2005), *Collapse: How Societies Choose to Succeed or Fail*, New York: Penguin.

Dickens, P. (1992), *Society and Nature: Towards a Green Social Theory*, Hemel Hempstead: Harvester-Wheatsheaf.

Dobson, A. (1990), *Green Political Thought*, London: Unwin Hyman.

—— (2003), *Citizenship and the Environment*, Oxford: Oxford University Press.

—— (2007), *Green Political Thought*, 4th edition, London: Routledge.

Dobson, A. and Lucardie, P. (eds) (1993), *The Politics of Nature: Explorations in Green Political Theory*, London: Routledge.

Doherty, B. and de Geus, M. (eds) (1996), *Democracy and Green Political Thought: Sustainability, Rights and Citizenship*, London: Routledge.

Doran, P. (2006), 'Street Wise Provocations: The 'Global Justice' Movement's Take on Sustainable Development', *International Journal of Green Economics*, 1 (1/2): 151–68.

Dryzek, J. (1987), *Rational Ecology: Environment and Political Economy*, Oxford: Blackwell.

Eckersley, R. (1992), *Environmentalism and Political Theory: Toward an Ecocentric Approach*, London: University College London Press.

—— (2004), *The Green State: Rethinking Democracy and Sovereignty*, Boston: MIT Press.

Freeman, C. (1973), 'Malthus with a Computer', in Cole, H., Freeman, C., Jahoda, M. and Pavitt, K. (eds), *Thinking about the Future*, London: Chatto and Windus, pp. 5–13.

Friedman, T. (2008), *Hot, Flat and Crowded: Why We Need a Green Revolution – And How It Can Renew America*, New York: Farrar, Straus and Giroux.

Garner, R. (1995), *Environmental Politics*, Hemel Hempstead: Harvester Wheatsheaf.

Goodin, R. (1992), *Green Political Theory*, Cambridge: Polity.

Gray, J. (2006), 'Review of The Revenge of Gaia', *The Independent*. Available online at www.independent.co.uk/arts-entertainment/books/reviews/the-revenge-ofgaia-by-james-lovelock-524635.html (accessed October 2009).

—— (2009), 'The Earth Exhales', *Literary Review*. Available online at www.literaryreview.co.uk/gray_02_09.html (accessed February 2009).

Green New Deal Group (2008), A *Green New Deal: Joined-up Policies to Solve the Triple Crunch of the Credit Crisis, Climate Change and High Oil Prices*, London: New Economics Foundation.

Griffiths, P. (2009), 'Gaia Scientist Says Life Doomed by Climate Woes'. Available online at http://uk.reuters.com/article/2009/02/25/us-climate-britain-lovelock-sb-id UKTRE51O5EU20090225 (accessed March 2011).

Hailwood, S. (2004), *How to Be a Green Liberal: Nature, Value and Liberal Philosophy*, London: Acumen.

Hayward, T. (1995), *Ecological Thought: An Introduction*, Cambridge: Polity.

—— (2005), *Constitutional Environmental Rights*, Oxford: Oxford University Press.

Hine, D. and Kingsnorth, P. (eds) (2010), *Dark Mountain: Issue 1*, Bodmin: The Dark Mountain Project.

Homer-Dixon, T. (2006), *The Upside of Down: Catastrophe, Creativity and the Renewal of Civilization*, Toronto: Alfred A. Knopf.

—— (2010), 'Disaster at the Top of the World', *New York Times*, 22 September 2010.

Hopkins, R. (2008), *The Transition Handbook*, Totnes: Green Books.

Humphrey, M. (2008), *Ecological Politics and Democratic Theory: The Challenge to the Deliberative Ideal*, London: Routledge.

Illich, I. (1973), *Tools for Conviviality*, London: Marion Boyers.

Inglehart, R. (1977), *The Silent Revolution: Changing Values and Political Styles among Western Publics*, Princeton: Princeton University Press.

Jackson, T. (2009), *Prosperity without Growth: Economics for a Finite Planet*, London: Earthscan.

Jensen, D. (2002), *The Culture of Make-Believe*, New York: Context Books.

Kassiola, J. (1990), *The Death of Industrial Civilization: The Limits of Economic Growth and the Repoliticization of Advanced Industrial Society*, Albany, New York: State University of New York Press.

Korowicz, D. (2010), *Tipping Point: Near Term Systemic Implications of a Peak in Global Oil Production: An Outline Review*, Dublin: FEASTA.

Kunstler, J. H. (2005), *The Long Emergency: Surviving the Converging Catastrophes of the Twenty-First Century*, New York: Atlantic Monthly Press.

Lafferty, W. and Meadowcroft, J. (eds) (1996), *Democracy and the Environment: Problems and Prospects*, Cheltenham: Edward Elgar.

Lee, K. (1989), *Social Philosophy and Ecological Scarcity*, London: Routledge.

Levett, R. (2003), *A Better Choice of Choice*, London: Fabian Society.

—— (2008), 'Choice: Less Can Be More', *Food Ethics: The Magazine of the Food Ethics Council*, 3 (3): 11. Available online at www.foodethicscouncil.org/system/ files/ food-ethics-autumn-08(web).pdf (accessed March 2011).

Lovelock, J. (2005), *The Revenge of Gaia*, London: Allen Lane.

—— (2009), *The Vanishing Face of Gaia: A Final Warning*, New York: Basic Books.

Luke, T. (1997), *Ecocritique: Contesting the Politics of Nature, Economy, and Culture*, Minneapolis: University of Minnesota Press.

—— (1999), *Capitalism, Democracy, and Ecology: Departing from Marx*, Illinois: University of Illinois Press.

McIntosh, A. (2008), *Hell and High Water: Climate Change, Hope and the Human Condition*, Edinburgh: Berlinn.

McKibben, B. (2007), *Deep Economy: The Wealth of Communities and the Durable Future*, New York: Times Books.

Marcuse, H. (1964), *One-Dimensional Man: Studies in the Ideology of Advanced Industrial Society*, London: Routledge and Kegan Paul.

Martell, L. (1994), *Nature and Society: An Introduction*, Cambridge: Polity.

Martinez-Alier, J. (2001), *The Environmentalism of the Poor: A Study of Ecological Conflicts and Valuation*, Cheltenham: Edward Elgar.

Meadows, D., Meadows, D. and Randers, J. (1972), *The Limits to Growth: A Report for the Club of Rome's Project on the Predicament of Mankind*, New York: Universe.

Mellor, M. (1992), *Breaking the Boundaries: Towards a Feminist, Green Socialism*, London: Virago Press.

—— (1995), 'Materialist Communal Politics: Getting from There to Here', in Lovenduski, J. and Stanyer, J. (eds), *Contemporary Political Studies*, volume 3, Belfast: Political Studies Association, pp. 1–14.

—— (1997), *Feminism and Ecology*, Cambridge: Polity Press.

Meyer, J. and Maniates, M. (2010), *The Environmental Politics of Sacrifice*, Boston, MA: MIT Press.

Mishan, E. (1968), *The Costs of Economic Growth*, London: Praeger.

Monbiot, G. (2003), 'The Bottom of the Barrel'. Available online at www.monbiot. com/2003/12/02/the-bottom-of-the-barrel/ (accessed November 2011).

Odum, H. and Odum, E. (2001), *A Prosperous Way Down: Principles and Policies*, Boulder, CO: University of Colorado Press.

O'Neill, J. (1993), *Ecology, Policy and Politics: Human Well-Being and the Natural World*, London: Routledge.

O'Riordan, T. and Jordan, A. (1995), 'The Precautionary Principle in Contemporary Environmental Politics', *Environmental Values*, 4 (3): 191–212.

Orlov, D. (2011), *Reinventing Collapse: The Soviet Experience and American Prospects*, Gabriola Island, BC: New Society Publishers.

Paehlke, R. (1989), *Environmentalism and the Future of Progressive Politics*, New Haven, CT: Yale University Press.

Pepper, D. (1984), *The Roots of Modern Environmentalism*, London: Croom Helm.

Porritt, J. (1984), *Seeing Green: The Politics of Ecology Explained*, Oxford: Basil Blackwell.

Radcliffe, J. (2000), *Green Politics: Dictatorship or Democracy?*, Basingstoke: Macmillan.

Rawls, J. (1971), *A Theory of Justice*, Cambridge, MA: Harvard University Press.

Rosen, S. M. (2002), 'Full Employment in the United States: History and Prospects', in Carlson, E. and Mitchell, W. (eds), *The Urgency of Full Employment*, Sydney: University of New South Wales Press, pp. 24–45.

Sachs, J. (2007), 'Busting at the Seams', Lecture 1, BBC Reith Lectures. Available online at www.bbc.co.uk/print/radio4/reith2007/lecture1.shtml?print (accessed February 2011).

Sahlins, M. (1972), *Stone-Age Economics*, New York: Aldine de Gruyter.

Sakar, S. (1999), *Eco-Socialism or Eco-Capitalism? A Critical Analysis of Humanity's Fundamental Choices*, London: Zed Books.

Sale, K. (1980), *Human Scale*, New York: Coward, McCann and Geoghegan.

Salleh, A. (1999), *Ecofeminism as Politics: Nature, Marx and the Postmodern*, London: Zed Press.

Schellenberger, M. and Nordhaus, T. (2006), *The Death of Environmentalism: Global Warming Politics in a Post-Environmental World*. Available online at www.thebreakthrough.org/PDF/Death_of_Environmentalism.pdf (accessed February 2007).

Schlosberg, D. (2009), *Defining Environmental Justice: Theories, Movements, and Nature*, Oxford: Oxford University Press.

Schor, J. (2010), *Plenitude: The New Economics of True Wealth*, New York: Penguin.

Schumacher, E. F. (1973), *Small Is Beautiful: Economics as if People Mattered*, London: Harper Perennial.

Scott-Cato, M. (2008), *Green Economics: An Introduction to Theory, Policy and Practice*, London: Earthscan.

—— (2012), *The Bioregional Economy: Land, Liberty and the Pursuit of Happiness*, London: Routledge.

Shiva, V. (1988), *Staying Alive: Women, Ecology and Development*, London: Zed Books.

Shklar, J. (1990), *The Faces of Injustice*, New Haven, CT: Yale University Press.

Simms, A. (2008), 'The Final Countdown', *The Guardian*. Available online at www.theguardian.com/environment/2008/aug/01/climatechange.carbonemissions (accessed 12 January 2013).

Simon, T. (1995), *Democracy and Injustice: Law, Politics and Philosophy*, Boston, MA: Rowman and Littlefield.

Smith, G. (2003), *Deliberative Democracy and the Environment*, London: Routledge.

Spretnak, C. and Capra, F. (1985), *Green Politics: The Global Promise*, San Francisco: Bear and Co.

Wilkinson, R. and Pickett, K. (2009), *The Spirit Level: Why More Equal Societies Almost Always Do Better*, London: Allen Lane.

Wissenburg, M. (1998), *Green Liberalism: The Free and the Green Society*, London: University College London Press.

Wolgast, M. (1987), *The Grammar of Justice*, New York: Cornell University Press.

Woodin, M. and Lucas, C. (2004), *Green Alternatives to Globalisation: A Manifesto*, London: Pluto Press.

Young, S. (1992), *The Politics of the Environment*, Manchester: Baseline Books.

Feminism

Rick Wilford

Introduction

The task of establishing an agreed definition of feminism has become increasingly difficult because, as we shall see, of the sheer diversity that exists within the contemporary women's movement. Such diversity is not, though, a new phenomenon. Although it is customary to ascribe unity to earlier generations of feminists, notably in pursuit of women's suffrage, the motives of those who shared that goal were by no means universally agreed upon. Indeed, it would be misleading to attribute unanimity to the women's movement at any phase of its evolution; rather, it is more rewarding to regard the movement and feminism itself as a loose coalition of activists and ideas, embracing a wide and even conflicting range of values.

One symptom of this diversity was the emergence in 2011 of the 'slut walk' phenomenon, a spontaneous reaction by some feminists to the ill-judged remarks of a Canadian police officer. Tasked to lead a crime prevention and safety forum at Toronto's York University, the officer remarked that 'women should avoid dressing like sluts in order not to be victimized', a comment that enraged many of those present. This anger was prompted, justifiably, because it implied that victims of rape had only themselves to blame if they chose to wear what might be deemed by some as provocative clothing. That is, it focused attention on, and affixed responsibility to, women themselves rather than the perpetrators of crime: in effect, the officer's remark was interpreted as an exercise in blaming the victims.

In response many women organized marches, first in Canada and subsequently across the globe, proclaiming that women of all ages are rape victims – irrespective of their clothing – and, equally profoundly, that women must be free to wear what they choose where and when they choose, without fear of sexual assault and/or of being labelled as the authors of their own misfortune. The marches also represented the attempt to re-appropriate the word 'slut' itself – for which there is no obvious male equivalent – as an expression of 'sex-positive feminism', in some ways echoing the success of gay and lesbian activists in reclaiming the term 'queer'.

Yet, whilst 'slut-walkers' viewed their protest as an assertion both of their autonomy and of their liberation from the fear of rape, other women, including self-defining feminists, decried the campaign as 'lionizing promiscuity'. Further, the critics argued that the effort to rehabilitate the word was itself misguided since 'slut' carries only negative connotations. This was, though, to miss the point. The term was adopted in an ironic sense in order to focus attention on the vulnerability of women to sexual assault, whether they dressed soberly (as many 'slut-walkers' did) or imaginatively. What is especially pertinent about this episode for our present purpose is that it fostered not just debate but division among feminists. Such contrary reactions remind us of the kaleidoscopic character of contemporary feminism: its exponents can and do cleave to a variety of views that challenge any attempt to attribute uniformity to feminist ideas, causes and movements. This lack of uniformity means that one has to tread cautiously in trying to capture the meaning of feminism, a point made by Randall: 'It is hardly possible to specify a core of beliefs that would not be contested by some of those who call themselves feminists' (Randall 1991).

Such hesitancy is understandable. Differences between and among feminist theorists over key principles and disagreements among activists over both their preferred tactics and the wider strategies of the women's movement are testament to the complexity of feminism. This is not, however, to imply that feminism is in disarray, but it does alert us to its problematic nature. In that sense, feminism is no different from other doctrines. As the contributors to this book demonstrate, one can draw distinctions within all doctrines, including between libertarian and organic conservatives and between the exponents of lighter and darker Green politics.

The significance of this point is underscored by the outcome of the UK's 2010 general election and the subsequent formation of the Conservative–Liberal Democrat coalition: the decision to forge a governing partnership required accommodation by both parties, indicating the suppleness of their underlying values. This suggests that ideologies, in this case conservatism and liberalism, are fluid rather than solid bodies of thought which can be pragmatically interpreted, especially in pursuit of office! Such fluidity is no less true of feminism. While the diversity of feminist thought may seem baffling, even contradictory, it can instead be understood as a sign both of its growing maturity and of the increased confidence of its varied adherents.

One symptom of this maturity is that whereas in the 1970s and 1980s it was conventional to assert the existence of a universal sisterhood, such an unreflective claim to unity has been displaced by not just the awareness of differences among women, but their celebration. Instead of assuming the existence of a shared understanding of what it is to be a feminist and a woman, the *politics of identities* has become a defining feature of contemporary feminist discourse. Feminists have gravitated away from a singular preoccupation with similarities and differences *between* women and men, and towards the recognition of differences *among* women. This shift towards the politics of recognition signifies that many feminists are resolved to interrogate their own assumptions, including the unexamined belief that women enjoy a transcendent identity irrespective of ethnicity, race, religion, class, culture, marital status, sexuality and (dis)ability.

This growing variety of feminist thinking does, however, prompt cynical observers to portray feminism as a house divided, one riven with disputes over the diagnoses of women's oppression, and associated arguments over remedies. Such critics contend that its very foundations have collapsed in disarray, resembling little more than a rubble of ideas that lack any agreed form or meaning. Such a dismissive verdict is misplaced. A more persuasive approach is to understand feminism as a house within which there are many mansions, whose occupants are engaged in a series of dialogues over the causes of women's inequality and the means of resolving them.

This is not to dodge the issue of what feminism is, but it does nudge one towards what Delmar terms a 'base-line' understanding of what it means to be a feminist:

> At the very least a feminist is someone who holds that women suffer discrimination because of their sex, that they have specific needs which remain negated and unsatisfied, and that the satisfaction of these needs would require a radical change in the social, economic and political order.
>
> (Delmar 1986)

This seems a modest characterization, yet it represents a profound agenda for action. It locates the cause of discrimination in the biological identity of women, insists that the needs that arise from their role in the reproductive process are not just unmet but invalidated, and contends that they can only be satisfied by a fundamental reconstruction of wider social values and practices.

Delmar's diagnosis and her prescriptions do not, however, command consensus. Indeed, the feminist analyses and remedies on offer have multiplied to the point where one may be excused a sense of bewilderment. Yet such bafflement can be ameliorated by reformulating a key question. Instead of courting doubt in asking oneself, 'Am I a feminist?' one might instead pose the question, 'What kind of feminist am I?' In effect, this is no different from asking 'What kind of conservative is David Cameron?' or 'What kind of socialist is Ed Miliband?' or 'what kind of liberal is Nick Clegg?' Posing the question in like terms is not to evade the issue of what feminism is, but is an invitation to explore the array of feminist ideas and, in the process, to perhaps identify with a particular school of feminist thought.

A clamour of voices

One cannot, then, sidestep the matter of feminism's diversity, hence the emergence of a new orthodoxy: namely, the adoption of the plural *feminisms*, expressly intended to convey the range of views expressed by self-defining feminists. Even within what may have been popularly (mis)understood to be unified positions, diversity is the norm, including in relation to radical feminism (Crow 2000). Moreover, the emergence of postmodernism adds immeasurably to the proliferation of voices within feminism.

The insistence by postmodernists on the need to peel away the layers of thought bequeathed by the past, to subvert received 'truths' and 'objectivities' and, instead, to relish doubts and subjectivities, has profound consequences for feminists. Postmodern thinkers argue that we should disdain belief in grand doctrinal designs and instead celebrate difference, variety, uncertainty and complexity. This includes a disregard for bodies of thought that purport to reveal the 'truth' about women – indeed, the very concept 'woman' (and, indeed, 'truth') is itself contested (Gamble 1999; Zalewski 2000). What it means to be 'a woman' is not, insist postmodernists, revealed by recourse to any single doctrine, but must be apprehended by exploring one's own subjectivity.

While this perspective may seem puzzling because of its implication of dizzying relativism, it chimes with the growth of interest in identity politics among feminists which itself supplies a healthy corrective to earlier, unexamined assumptions about the existence of a universal sisterhood. Today, the identities of women are understood to be structured by a host of interacting factors, including age, sexuality, (dis)ability, ethnicity and class, which complicate the achievement of an integrated women's movement. This complexity does not, however, prevent the formation of strategic, shifting coalitions of feminists that campaign for the removal of obstacles hindering the exercise of women's autonomy. Indeed, the 'herstories' of the women's movement supply a narrative of strategic coalitions, mobilized in pursuit of a bundle of rights and freedoms but which are yet to be realized on a global basis.

Post-feminism?

Given its growing complexity, it seems sensible to adopt a minimal definition of feminism. Yet for some even this is a redundant exercise. 'Post-feminists' assert that, however defined, feminism has outlived its usefulness. Women, the argument runs, 'now have it all'. Indeed, the term 'post-feminism' (Gamble 1999: 43–54) was coined to express the idea that women are now the full co-equals of men, able to exercise unfettered autonomy in making choices about their lives, both public and private. This proposition incensed many, including Germaine Greer, who was moved to write a sequel to her seminal *The Female Eunuch* (1970) by the appearance of a 'post-feminist' literature:

> [I]t was not until feminists of my own generation began to assert with apparent seriousness that feminism had gone too far that the fire flared up in my belly. When the lifestyle feminists chimed in that feminism had gone just far enough in giving them the right to 'have it all', ie money, sex and fashion, it would have been inexcusable to remain silent . . . It's time to get angry again.
>
> (Greer 1999: 1, 3)

For Greer, the 'rhetoric of equality' had supplanted what she regards as the true task of feminism, namely the liberation of women. She identifies a host of disabling disadvantages that continue to confront women both at work and, especially, at home and ridicules the idea that an egalitarian, post-feminist world has been achieved in which women 'have it all'. Moreover – recalling those who articulated the existence of a global sisterhood in the 1970s – she insists that 'to be feminist is to understand that before you are of any race, nationality, religion, party or family, you are a woman' (Greer 1999: 7). This sense of an overarching (or perhaps submerged) sense of womanhood or 'woman-ness' does not, however, chime with identity politics and the concern with difference and diversity. Yet, undeterred, Greer also asserts the idea of female essentialism, thereby endorsing a basic difference between women and men. As she puts it: 'Liberation struggles are not about assimilation but about asserting difference [between the sexes], endowing that difference with dignity and prestige and insisting on it as a condition of self-definition and self-determination' (ibid.: 1). As we shall see, this issue of sameness versus difference between the sexes has been, and remains, a source of profound debate among feminists.

Wave-ing – or drowning?

It should now be evident that to discuss feminism is to encounter a dynamic body of thought that has evolved into a self-critical rather than a settled doctrine. One symptom of its vibrancy is the sheer volume of contemporary feminist literature, a body of work swelled by the advent of a 'third wave' of feminism, some of whom seek to distance themselves from their predecessors. Their standpoints are summarized by Barbara Arneil:

> Third wave feminism(s) are characterized by a commitment to beginning one's analysis from women's own perspective; that is, a recognition of 'differences' in perspective, both between women and men and *among women*.
>
> (1999: 9; emphasis added)

To identify a third wave, the terms of which are returned to below, implies a first and a second wave of feminism. The 'wave' metaphor is indeed helpful in suggesting that at certain periods a tide of feminist ideas surges forward to reshape the political landscape, while at others it appears to ebb into the distance.

Predominantly 'Western' accounts of the evolution of feminist ideas do conventionally distinguish between two waves: the first, from the later nineteenth century to the 1920s, set within a predominantly equal rights tradition, which crested around the campaign for women's suffrage. This tradition stressed the sameness of treatment for both sexes, although this was not based upon an entirely uniform position, as we will see. The second wave gathered momentum in the shape of the women's liberation movement in the 1960s, which was preoccupied with differences between women and men. By contrast, the third wave eddies around differences among and between women, reflecting a more developed concern with subjectivities and identity politics and, more controversially, sex-positive feminism (for a brief summary of identity politics, see Alcott 2000: 263–4).

The focus on identity politics has, though, attracted criticism because it risks frustrating the growth of a strategic, even majority, coalition among women precisely because of its emphasis upon differences. However self-defined, the critique contends that women risk either drowning in a sea of discordant voices or being channelled into self-regarding backwaters where, cut off from the main-stream, their collective political strength evaporates. Postmodernists voice a different, related, criticism of identity politics, arguing that the notion of *an* identity is itself flawed, based as it is on a legacy of assumptions that impart a settled, closed meaning to the concept. For them identities are contingent, even protean. As Alcott puts it, the task is to 'liberate one *from* identity, rather than reifying those identities' (2000: 264).

The rejection of a uniform identity has particular relevance for the relation-ship between feminism and nationalist movements and politics. Nationalism can be narrow and exclusive, or broad and inclusive (see chapter 5, on nationalism, and chapter 6, on fascism). However, as both an ideology and a political move-ment, nationalism is invariably gendered, while nations are commonly 'sexed': one thinks of 'Mother Ireland' or 'Mother Russia', or phrases such as 'mother tongue' and 'motherland'.

Yet, the female sexing of nations is no guarantee that women will be treated as equal citizens: indeed, the obverse may be the case. So, while images of women may be adopted as the symbolic forms of a nation – for example, Britannia (Britain) and Marianne (France) – men invariably emerge as the beneficiaries when nations attain statehood, whereas women are left holding the short end of the citizenship stick. This broader distrust of nationalism and of nationalist movements felt by some feminists is based on the perception that, whether the process of nation-state formation takes the form of a peaceful and orderly transi-tion from an old to a new regime or, conversely, whether there is a sharp and violent break with the past, nation- and state-building projects tend to advantage men (See Wilford and Miller 1998; Yuval-Davis 1997; Pettman 1996).

Such distrust is not just a matter of perception: for many it is founded upon the lived experiences of women who have been marginalized by nationalist movements, whether in the past or the present. But it is also informed by contemporary feminism's concern with identity politics. For those suspicious of the idea of a *national identity* – which may venerate women as symbols of the nation while simultaneously hobbling their rights as citizens – the celebration of *identities of nationality* offers a promising alternative. It allows for plurality and difference, and enables women to be (notionally) free from male-crafted notions of their 'proper' place in the national design.

An interesting example of this expression of identity politics was the (now defunct) Northern Ireland Women's Coalition (NIWC). Formed in 1996, two of its candidates were elected to the devolved Assembly in 1998, making it the first women's party in the UK (or Ireland) to achieve electoral success. It did so by refusing to identify with either of the competing national traditions in Northern Ireland, that is, unionism and nationalism, neither of which has been especially receptive to women. When the Coalition's two elected representatives signed the Assembly members' register as required by the terms of the Belfast Agreement, they chose to style themselves as 'Inclusive Other', rather than as either 'Nationalist' or 'Unionist'. This act signified their rejection of these mutually exclusive and seemingly homogeneous national identities and instead registered a preference for 'otherness' and difference.

The NIWC's modest electoral success was, however, short-lived, epitomizing the difficulty women's political parties encounter in mobilizing support. Gender and sex, despite, or perhaps because of, their ubiquity, cannot compete effectively with parties that organize around, say, class, region, ethnicity or religion. Joining established parties, rather than creating women's parties, seems to offer a more promising means of entering the public realm of politics in order to campaign for the needs and interests of women. And yet, although more than a century has passed since women secured the right to vote, with one exception (Rwanda) they have yet to secure equal representation in national parliaments. Moreover, universal female suffrage has been much more slowly implemented in some states than others. In New Zealand it was achieved in 1893, in Finland in 1906 and in Norway in 1913, whereas Swiss women had to wait until 1971, black women in South Africa until 1994 and Kuwaiti women until 2005. Such an uneven pattern of enfranchisement cautions us against assuming that suffrage was uniformly achieved or that it turned on an Anglo-American axis.

Suffrage: a brittle unity

Until the vote was won, albeit at different dates in different countries, movement or group politics were the only organized alternatives available to women, irrespective of the school of feminism to which they subscribed – if indeed they were self-defined feminists at all. But the legacy of the suffrage campaigns in Britain and the USA, secured by women of all races and religions, the young and the old, the rich and the poor, imparted an apparent unity to feminism. Here, it seemed, was an object lesson in the ability of women to act collectively for a common purpose. Yet, while suffrage movements brought together many women (and men) in a shared pursuit, it also contained underlying tensions, not least between equal rights and welfare/evangelical feminists.

What differentiated them was precisely the question of whether women should be treated the same as, or differently from, men in matters of law and public policy. Inspired by the doctrine of natural rights, equal rights feminists insisted that women be treated as human, not sexual, beings, since they are equally as capable as men of governing themselves through the exercise of reason. Mary Wollstonecraft's (1759–97) *A Vindication of the Rights of Woman* (1792) was the first systematic attempt to promote this idea. Inspired by Enlightenment principles, Wollstonecraft based her plea for women to be treated as free, independent individuals on the basis that 'the mind has no sex'. Here lay the seeds of the 'sameness' argument that informed many early proponents of female enfranchisement and which continues to reverberate within feminist debate.

The equal rights tradition of feminism advocated the removal of legal obstacles to the fulfilment of women's autonomy, thereby ending their dependence upon, and subjugation by, men. It took as its measure the rights accorded to men: in effect, the male citizen became the template upon which the rights of women were inscribed. While like-for-like treatment of women and men was the dominant motif of equal rights feminism, socially conservative evangelical/welfare feminists emphasized differences between the sexes, and campaigned for different treatment for women. In particular, they championed protective legislation intended to shield women from physically demanding occupations on the ground that they were, or would become, wives and mothers. Though an ostensibly lofty motive, the net effect was to legitimize the sexual division of labour both within and between the home and the workplace.

Besides championing protective legislation, welfare feminists saw themselves as paragons of what they believed were essentially womanly virtues, derived from their roles as prospective or actual wives and mothers. They perceived women as cooperative rather than competitive, like men: pacific as opposed to aggressive; selfless rather than selfish; and, perhaps most distinctively, morally superior to men. The assertion of such *essential* differences justified the extension of the vote to women not on the ground of equal rights but in the belief that women's *natural* qualities would enhance the public realm of politics by applying a moral brake to the equally natural excesses of men. This perception of difference was rooted in a belief in biological essentialism: that is, that ultimately, one's virtues and behaviour are governed by one's sex. By contrast, Wollstonecraft's insistence that the mind is devoid of sex led her, and succeeding generations of equal rights feminists, to understand that the roles performed by women and men are socially constructed. Though she did not employ the term, this was, in effect, the recognition by Wollstonecraft of the significance of gender – the cultural ascription of feminine and masculine roles – in shaping the life-chances of women and men.

The co-existence of the conflicting views held by equal rights and evangelical feminists did not, however, prevent them from combining to press for female suffrage. Yet, in the immediate aftermath of women's enfranchisement in both the USA and Britain, the tension between these variants of feminism came to a head.

In America the campaign for the Equal Rights Amendment (ERA), begun in 1923 and spearheaded by the National Women's Party, split the strategic coalition that had coalesced in pursuit of suffrage. The ERA sought, by constitutional amendment, to eliminate all legal inequalities between women and men. Yet, having fought for protective legislation designed to prevent the exploitation of women (and children), evangelical feminists rushed to defend, and extend, those gains: they opposed the campaign, instead reasserting the special needs of women, which, to their minds, revolved around marriage and motherhood.

The ERA campaign, which continued for six decades, ultimately failed, not least because of the divisions it had excited among women over whether they should be treated equally to, or differently from, men (Berry 1988).

An echo of these divisions occurred in Britain during the 1920s over the campaign led by self-styled 'new' or 'welfare feminists' for a state-funded family allowance scheme. Their advocacy of a state allowance payable to wives rather than their husbands offended equal rights feminists (some of whom styled themselves as 'old feminists') because of its assumption that women's wifely and maternal role anchored them to the home. Whereas equal rights feminists sought to challenge conventional beliefs about the sexual division of labour within the family, many of those who supported the scheme endorsed both marriage and maternity as means of fulfilment for women. This latter view prevailed and was embedded in Britain after 1945, when the male breadwinner model became a key organizing principle of the welfare state.

Indeed, the Beveridge Report (1942), the cornerstone of the UK's welfare state, was peppered with patriarchal assumptions about women's, especially married women's, rightful place in post-war Britain: they were to enter this brave new world as dependants of their husbands, while single women were regarded as the dependants of their male heads of household. There was, in effect, no formal equality in public policy concerning male and female concepts of welfare citizenship, which offended exponents of equal rights/'old' feminism, as had the advocacy of the earlier family allowance scheme by 'new' feminists. As a self-defined 'old' feminist reflecting on the latter scheme observed: 'The "New Feminism" emphasizes the importance of the "women's point of view", the "Old Feminism" believes in the primary importance of the human being' (Humm 1992: 43). That distinction – between 'sameness', the essential humanness of women, and 'difference', the assertion of women's distinctive needs – which had been accommodated in pursuit of female suffrage ruptured its fragile 'unity'.

Historical diversity

Understanding the evolution of feminist ideas is an uncertain process because it is impossible to identify a seminal text or a decisive moment that sparked its beginnings. One history of feminist theory identifies Christine de Pisan (1364–1430) as 'the first woman to write about the rights and duties of her sex' (Bryson 1992: 11), and another identifies Mary Astell (1666–1731) as 'the first English feminist' (Hill 1986). But though a tricky undertaking, tracing the roots of feminist thinking is important, not least because it contributes to writing women *into* history (Scott 1996), or, in this case, the history of ideas. But trying to pin down precisely *when* feminism as an organized body of theory appeared is a challenging task.

What may be stated confidently is that writing which can be placed within the feminist canon has a lengthy ancestry. For instance, the roots of the modern women's movement may be traced to the creation of women's clubs during the French Revolution, or the activities of women involved in the movements to abolish slavery and to promote temperance. In the case of abolition, the cause led to the meeting at Seneca Falls, New York State, in July 1848 and the publication of the 'Declaration of Resolutions and Sentiments'. Its opening line extended simply, but cleverly, the inclusiveness of the Declaration of Independence: 'We hold these truths to be self-evident: that all men *and women* are created equal'. This Declaration *may* be understood as a catalyst for the emergence of the suffrage movement, which dominated the agenda of first-wave feminists on both sides of the Atlantic. The point here is not, however, to insist that any one individual, event or text has a prior claim on another as the source of the first wave. Rather, it is to suggest that the trajectory of feminist ideas and activity has been uneven rather than linear – just like the motion of a wave!

The emergence of the second wave is even more difficult to identify, because much of its early activity took place in informal settings where women engaged in 'consciousness-raising' sessions, sharing their 'herstories' in relatively unstructured ways (Tanner 1971: 231–54). Indeed, the lack of structure was for some an explicit choice, one designed to signify a style of discourse unlike that practised in patriarchal and hence hierarchical institutions. This preference for privatized, women-only settings epitomized the concern with differences between women and men that was the hallmark of the second wave. The improvised and non-hierarchical nature of these sessions, dubbed by Jo Freeman (1972: 20) the 'tyranny of structurelessness', itself contributed to the diversity that has always characterized the feminist project. While it would be misleading to claim that their predecessors were concerned only with the vote, later feminists have widened immeasurably the agenda of discussion. In particular, the priority given to differences between the sexes and, latterly, among women, has expanded the feminist chorus.

Siting feminisms and subverting orthodoxy

Given that diversity is a characteristic of feminism, and that it is impossible to pinpoint a decisive moment or text as its defining source, how can we place it in the evolution of political thought? One way to offer a convenient guide is to site feminism within the context of other ideologies. This may seem a patronizing approach because it suggests that as a body of ideas it does not enjoy a life of its own, but exists only in relation to other bodies of thought. Such relationism is, however, characteristic of all doctrines, in the sense that their exponents seek to distinguish their ideas from those of their competitors; but what is implied here is that feminism evolved within the context of existing (liberalism) or emerging (socialism, Marxism) ideologies. This had two pronounced effects. First, as exponents of fresh thinking, feminists had to negotiate space for their ideas within each of these doctrines. Second, in the process of negotiation, they became aligned with the core principles of existing 'isms'.

Thus, it makes sense to discuss the evolution of a distinctively liberal, socialist or Marxist feminism.

Feminist ideas are not, however, merely derivative. Early feminists sought not only to negotiate with existing ideologies, but to interrogate them. In doing so they challenged a number of key assumptions which have underpinned the development of Western political thought since the time of Plato and Aristotle, including its 'pervasive dualism' (Coole 1993).

Feminists interested in the development of political ideas have observed that the history of political thought is invested with a series of 'binary opposites', each pole of which is accorded either a positive or negative value. Key pairings included culture–nature, reason–emotion, public–private and, crucially, male–female. The first of each pairing were arranged together, such that maleness was associated with cultural activity and rationality, each enacted in the public sphere. By contrast, femaleness was equated with nature, that is, reproduction, and passion, which belonged in the private sphere of home and family. Moreover, such associations were presented in hierarchical terms: that is, male characteristics were deemed superior, female inferior, thus men and women were not only different, but also unequal. Indeed, much of the energy of the feminist project has been directed towards undermining these dualities, thereby lending it a distinctively subversive character.

Such subversion has, though, taken different forms. Some feminists have adopted an androcentric (male-centred) strategy, encouraging women to adopt the characteristics traditionally ascribed to men, and/or to have existing male rights extended to them. Others have sought not to emulate men, but rather to prescribe an androgynous (male *and* female) solution, whereby the qualities ascribed to women and men are integrated in a common and non-hierarchical human identity. Some have sought to reverse the polarities by adopting a gynocentric (female-centred) strategy which places a positive value on the attributes conventionally ascribed to women, while yet others insist that, although women and men are biologically different, they are, nevertheless, equal in their humanity and that their biological differences should be neither denied nor merged but celebrated.

These differing strategies are influenced by the significance attached by feminists to either *sex* or *gender* as a means of explaining inequalities between women and men. Some insist upon the primacy of biological identity, that is, the distinction between the female and male sexes, as the explanation for the oppression of women, whereby inequality is understood to arise from their different reproductive roles. That is, women's child-bearing and nurturing role is used to produce and reproduce inequality between the sexes, and unless and until these roles are transformed women will continue to be subordinate to men. This perspective, as we shall see, has been characteristic of those generally described as 'radical feminists', who have been concerned largely, though not exclusively, with the politics of sexuality and reproduction, a stance abbreviated as 'body politics'.

Other feminists focus not on biological identity but rather on the ways in which societies construct gendered, that is feminine and masculine, roles to explain differences in the life-chances of women and men. Here the focus is on the cultural meanings attached to the roles learned by children and which particular societies consider appropriate for women and men. Such roles, which vary across time and space, are then social constructions rather than being biologically determined: they are neither fixed nor universal and, just as they are socially constructed, so too they can be deconstructed and reconstructed.

The significance attached to either sex or gender informs much of the feminist debate. Those emphasizing the former as the key to understanding insist that woman's social identity is determined by her sex – biology as destiny – whereas those focusing on culturally created differences emphasize the gendered and hence mutable character of woman's identity. The relative weight attached to either sex or gender critically influences this question of whether women should be regarded as being essentially the same as or fundamentally different from men.

Patriarchy: the 'man problem'

What one might term 'the man problem' became increasingly prominent within the second wave of feminism. There were, and are, feminists who cast men as the unremitting enemies of women and therefore prescribe a separatist route to the fulfilment of their needs: from this more radical perspective, men become wholly redundant in women's lives. Conversely, liberal and socialist feminists regard men as their allies in the struggle for gender equality and justice. For them, the active support of men not only is sought for pragmatic reasons, because men currently enjoy a virtual monopoly of political power, but is understood to be essential for the achievement of a genuinely just society. This perspective, unlike the former, also allows that men can lay claim to a feminist identity.

While by no means an entirely novel issue, the portrayal of men as either the allies or foes of women remains a matter of intense debate among feminists. Indeed, the salience of the 'man question' was assured by the emergence of radical feminists who rejuvenated the concept of *patriarchy* to explain the subordination of women.

In its undiluted form, patriarchy is understood in ahistoric and universal terms: that is, men always have been, and always will be, motivated to dominate women. This depiction of power relations between men and women, which describes a relationship of dominance and subordination, is not restricted to the 'public' arena but is understood to extend into the 'private' sphere of home and family. This representation of patriarchy's limitless reach led to the coining of the phrase 'the personal is political' to convey its pervasiveness and led to a renewed assault on the family, now portrayed as a private site of women's oppression rather than a haven from the depredations of the public realm. It also generated campaigns against patriarchy's manifold forms, including demands for strict controls over, if not the prohibition of, pornography; changes in the law on rape and domestic violence; the creation of refuges for battered women and children; and the liberalization of abortion laws. The renaissance of patriarchy as an explanation for women's oppression re-opened the home front earlier assaulted by utopian socialists and Marxists, in what now came to be dubbed the 'sex war' and consolidated a preoccupation with differences between women and men.

The unqualified interpretation of patriarchy – men as the enemies of women – has not, though, escaped criticism from other feminists (Bryson 1992: 28–30). One focus of criticism is that it presents all women as enduring victims of male oppression and offers only political and sexual separatism as a solution. But, such critics argue, stressing women's status as victims is more likely to disempower than to empower them; shunning men leads to an impoverished political (and sexual) life; many women succeed on their own terms; and there are many caring men – and many uncaring women. Critics further argue that the assertion of patriarchy's universalism obscures other forms of oppression experienced by women, such as that based on race, ethnicity and class, and/or their interaction. As such, it is criticized for ignoring differences among women: in short, of being race, ethnicity and class 'blind'. This criticism contributed in particular to the sparking of interest in the politics of identities, spearheaded by 'black' women in the developed world and women in less developed countries who felt ignored, patronized and marginalized by the ethnocentrism of mainstream Western second-wave feminism.

The revitalization of patriarchy undoubtedly enlivened feminist debate and thereby contributed to its diversity. But the issue of sameness/difference between women and men that it addresses has reverberated throughout the history of feminist thinking.

Early liberal feminism

As noted earlier, it is difficult to identify *when* feminism as a discrete set of ideas emerged. Yet the appearance of Mary Wollstonecraft's *Vindication* in 1792 provides a convenient starting point.

Wollstonecraft insisted upon women's capacity to engage in rational thought, and voiced the demand for equal educational opportunities as the means by which they could realize their potential. Having benefited from the same education, girls and boys would, Wollstonecraft argued, develop into rational individuals and be better fitted to enter marriage, where they could fulfil their complementary roles within the context of a companionate relationship. Such a union would displace the common pattern of (middle-class) marriage, wherein 'emotional' women, their intellects stunted by being trained for domestic docility, sought material security and hence a slavish dependence upon 'rational' men.

Here, Wollstonecraft anticipates an understanding of the gendered character of women's and men's roles. She rejected the idea of 'femininity' as a natural attribute and in so doing aimed her sights at, among others, her near contemporary, Jean-Jacques Rousseau (1712–78). His educational tract *Emile* (1762) asserted innate differences between the sexes which led him to consign women to dependence upon men: he represented women as naturally emotional, weak and obedient, and therefore lacking the attributes required for citizenship – reason, strength, autonomy – traits that he contended were naturally male. These ascribed differences led Rousseau to prescribe wholly different educational philosophies for children: boys were to be educated to become rational, moral and self-governing individuals, whereas girls were to be trained for domestic submission and equipped with the skills required to please their future husbands.

Wollstonecraft disdained this 'natural' distinction drawn by Rousseau, and while rejecting the proposition that women were possessed of any singular qualities determined by their sex, she did acknowledge that the 'peculiar destination' for most women was marriage and motherhood. But she envisaged women as enacting the independence gained from a common education within the domestic sphere, where they would perform the tasks of household management rationally and efficiently: 'Make women rational creatures and free citizens, and they will quickly become good wives and mothers' (Wollstonecraft 1974: 197). The astute Wollstonecraft was not shy of encouraging men to act in their own enlightened self-interest!

She did not, however, entertain the idea that the sexual division of labour within the family should be transformed, nor did she consider the family necessarily as the site of female oppression, a view subsequently adopted by socialist and Marxist feminists and later reinvigorated by radical feminists. Moreover, Wollstonecraft restricted her understanding of working women to those who chose not to marry: the dual burden of household labour and paid employment was not contemplated by her, because she addressed herself to an audience that could rely on servants to undertake domestic work.

Stressing equal rights, early liberal feminism was wedded to the achievement of formal legal equality for women and, in the work of Harriet Taylor (1807–58) and her second husband, John Stuart Mill (1806–73), was to encompass suffrage and the expansion of employment opportunities. A utilitarian liberal, rather than an exponent of natural rights like Wollstonecraft, Mill's advocacy was framed largely in terms of the benefits that would accrue to society from the implementation of equal rights. A wider array of talents would be available and moral progress more swiftly advanced if relations between men and women were placed upon an equal footing: in consequence, the sum total of human happiness would be increased.

Though entertaining the possibility that married women might enter paid employment, Mill considered this the province only of 'exceptional' women.

For him, it was more important that women were educated to the point where they could, rather than should, seek work beyond the private realm. Like Wollstonecraft, he envisaged married women as choosing to assume the roles of wife and mother. Taylor, however, held markedly different views. She actively encouraged women, single and married, to seek employment, as a means of assuring both financial and psychological independence. Paid employment would, she argued, buttress self-respect and facilitate an equal partnership between wives and husbands.

Though Taylor's ideas on this matter were more progressive than Mill's, she too harboured conventional assumptions about the sexual division of labour. Neither she nor her husband proposed an equitable distribution of domestic tasks: like Wollstonecraft, they assumed that (middle-class) wives would supervise the running of the home and employ working-class women and girls to wash, scrub, cook and polish.

This was a less than inclusive vision of emancipated womanhood. Moreover, neither acknowledged that there might be structural causes of women's oppression rooted in the economic bases of early and developing capitalism. A more robust critique, not only of capitalism but also of the family, emerged from the utopian socialists of the late eighteenth and early nineteenth centuries.

Utopian socialist feminism

While the early liberals encouraged men to perceive the injustice and unhappiness caused by excluding women from the enjoyment of equal rights, the utopian socialists focused more upon the material inequalities intrinsic to a class-based society and their differential effects on men and women.

Historically, utopian socialism emerged between the natural rights philosophy of Wollstonecraft and the utilitarianism of Mill. However, while the early liberal feminists saw no contradiction between women achieving civil and political rights and their remaining within the private sphere, utopian socialists – including William Thompson (1775–1833), Anna Wheeler, alias 'Concordia' (1785–?), and Robert Owen (1771–1858) in Ireland and Britain, and Charles Fourier (1772–1837) and Henri St Simon (1760–1825) in France – understood women to be doubly oppressed: within both the public sphere *and* the family. Here lay an early anticipation of patriarchy's reach: the perception that women were subject to exploitation by men in both the public and the private realms. Further, while liberal feminists sought to extinguish difference by adopting an androcentric perspective, some utopian socialists emphasized what they believed were the distinctive qualities of women.

In general, utopian socialists understood marriage as practised in capitalist society as stunting the moral, cultural and psychological development of both women and men. The solution lay in open, honest relationships founded upon cooperation, itself nourished by the disposition towards sympathy and benevolence they believed to be intrinsic to human nature. For Thompson and Wheeler, the achievement of civil and political equality for women was insufficient: the economic dependence of women upon men also had to be ended. This entailed the abolition of private property, the communal provision of tasks normally provided in the home and an economy that redistributed resources on the basis of equality.

The implications of this project for men and, particularly, for women were profound. Freed from the economic motive for marriage, liberated from the toil of running a household and enabled to engage in fulfilling and creative labour, both men and women would reap the benefits of mutual support within a society where collective ownership meant none was advantaged by material possessions.

The utopian socialists differed from the early liberals in two important respects. First, they stressed the economic dimensions of inequality, and second, they drew a distinction between women's and men's natures. Here is a clear prefiguring of the sameness/difference polarity that was to be renewed in the wake of suffrage. A belief in the moral superiority of women underlay much of their writing, as did the conviction that the feminine virtues of caring, patience and fortitude endowed women with a capacity to promote benevolence and sympathy within the context of mutually supportive communities.

Besides seeking to establish the affinity between such virtues and communal socialism, utopian socialists also expressed uninhibited views about the joys of sexual fulfilment. For them in general, it was harmony between physical and emotional needs and rationality that led to individual happiness and cooperative endeavour. Indeed, their advocacy of free sexual expression offered a marked alternative to the companionate relationships favoured by Wollstonecraft and Mill. The eradication of the sexual division of labour and the disavowal of marriage, coupled with the collective provision of childcare and housework by both sexes, demonstrated that the utopian socialists understood the rights of women to be integral to the realization of a genuinely egalitarian society.

Marxist feminism

The issue of the place of utopian socialism in the development of feminism is an important though neglected one, not least because Karl Marx (1818–83) and Friedrich Engels (1820–95) dismissed both its exponents and their prescriptions as 'unscientific'. Wedded to a theory of history founded upon class conflict and a revolutionary transition to a socialist and ultimately communist society, they subordinated feminist ideas to the primacy of class struggle. This relegation of gender relations was to prompt non-Marxist feminists to accuse Marx and others of 'sex-blindness' and later led some on the left to observe, rather wryly, that the relationship between Marxism and feminism was akin to 'an unhappy marriage'.

Such criticisms rest in part upon the near absence from Marx's own works of what socialists styled the 'woman question'. Marx paid scant attention to relations between women and men, believing that female emancipation would be a by-product of revolutionary transformation. In short, the position of women was taken for granted: the transition to communism would provide the context and the means for sexual equality to prevail.

While Marx understood, as did liberals and the utopians, that human nature was shaped by the social environment, he rejected the idea that it could be realized fully within capitalism or in the communal margins of cooperative association perched at the fringes of capitalist society. He insisted that free, self-determined human nature would flourish and sexual egalitarianism thrive only with the transformation of capitalism, which required revolution by class-conscious workers. All else was a mere distraction: hence women and men must engage in class politics, effectively setting aside 'the woman question' until capitalism was overthrown.

Marx's glib inattention to relations between the sexes was, however, redressed in some measure by both his collaborator Friedrich Engels and the German Social Democrat August Bebel (1840–1913). Both exhorted women to throw in their lot with men in the common struggle to achieve a classless society in which private property and the materialist motive for marriage would disappear. None was opposed to marriage per se, but each contended that only in a socialist society would this relationship be freed from male domination.

Marxists, then, viewed the subordination of women as an endemic feature of capitalist society which would disappear under socialism. The 1917 Bolshevik revolution seemed to create the opportunity for the achievement of this goal, which Lenin (1870–1924) termed 'the real emancipation of women'. He believed the path to emancipation lay in their full participation in economic and political life, and considerable effort was directed by the Bolsheviks into making public provision for tasks formerly undertaken by women in the home: hence, nurseries, kindergartens and public dining rooms were established as means of enabling women to play a full part in the economic and political mission to build socialism. Additionally, divorce was made easy, as was access to abortion facilities. Such policies, coupled with the mass entry of women into the workforce, were seen as essential to ending domestic slavery.

The promise of revolutionary socialism was beguiling, but it was broken. After an initial flurry of activity and reform in the 1920s designed to secure an 'equality of life' as well as equality of rights, the 'woman question' was neglected and the earlier reforms reversed with the accession to power of Stalin (1879–1953). By 1930, just thirteen years after the Revolution, he had declared the woman question 'solved'. It was only with the demise of the Soviet Union in 1989 that the full extent of women's subordination under communism became apparent. Despite the entry of women into the public sphere, notably into paid employment, far from having withered away, patriarchy was revealed as having been deeply entrenched in Soviet society. Women suffered occupational segregation, just as in capitalist societies, were subject to successive pro-natalist campaigns and, like their Western counterparts, were expected to shoulder the double burden of unpaid domestic labour and low-paid employment.

For later Marxist feminists, the legacy of the Soviet Union has been discomfiting. While arguing that women were subject to material oppression within capitalism, Marxists neglected the possibility that women were also vulnerable to patriarchal oppression in socialist societies. The premium that Marxism placed upon class solidarity glossed over relations between men and women: the portrayal of them as class allies could not allow that patriarchy would endure once capitalism had been superseded.

This attempt to associate patriarchy with a particular economic system did not, however, persuade other feminists. Convinced of its universal character, radical feminists in particular were to accuse Marxism of sex-blindness. This charge, as we shall see, left socialist feminists in the second wave struggling to reconcile the sex- *and* class-based systems of women's oppression.

The 'other' woman

The progressive, though protracted, achievement of female suffrage represents a milestone in the evolution of feminist ideas. Yet, by the 1920s, there were alternative approaches to the means of consolidating that fundamental equality. As we have noted, in both Britain and the United States debate was joined between the exponents of the 'old' equal rights tradition of feminism and the 'new' welfare feminists, revolving around the issue of sameness and difference between women and men.

The idea of women's difference is in part explained by the association of women with nature. Traceable to the origins of Western political thought, this association also characterized the emergence of modern science. As Coole (1993: 269–70) points out, Francis Bacon (1561–1626) employed explicit sexual imagery to portray the character of scientific enquiry: knowledge (male) was used to comprehend and control nature (female), thereby conveying an image of male domination over passive women. Man was the active, enquiring, rational subject, woman the object of study: pliant and submissive. Embedded in such a view was the perception of man as 'self' and of woman as 'other', that is, understood only in her relation to man.

The 'otherness' of women was explored in detail by the French philosopher Simone de Beauvoir (1908–86), whose *The Second Sex* appeared in 1949 (and was first translated into English in 1953), bridging the apparent lull between feminism's first and second waves. It is a complex work – informed by Marxism, psychoanalytic theories and existentialism's preoccupation with the ability of individuals to realize themselves – and she posed a fundamental question: 'What is a woman?' thereby anticipating the later concern with identity politics.

While recognizing the economic subordination of women, as well as the constraints imposed upon them by both the biological function of reproduction and the denial of equal civil and political rights, de Beauvoir was not entirely satisfied by structural or biological explanations of women's inferior status. Nor was she wholly convinced that Marxist or liberal projects were sufficient to secure women's liberation. Instead, she argued that the project for woman was woman herself. Here was the influence of existentialism, a philosophy that insists upon the unique capacity that human beings enjoy for self-awareness and the ability they possess to make self-conscious choices to realize themselves fully.

De Beauvoir argued that women needed to understand not just that their 'otherness' had been imposed upon them by men, but that they had internalized this condition. This signifies the psychoanalytic aspect of her ideas. She contested Freudian theory, which explained the female psyche in terms of penis envy – that women regard themselves as incomplete and, hence, imperfect men – and resolutely rejected the proposition that women's anatomy defined their destiny. Women, she insisted, were not fated to become submissive 'others' whose existence was given meaning only in relation to, and by, men. Rather, they must assert their own capacity for self-awareness, make their own choices and celebrate their own needs.

This vision of women shedding their internalized sense of inferiority and overcoming their subordination did not mean that differences between the sexes would disappear. While biological distinctions would persist, the availability of contraception and abortion meant that women would be able to take control over their bodies rather than be enslaved by them: anatomy offered opportunity, not a destiny cast in stone.

In observing the social construction of womanhood – 'One is not born but rather becomes a woman' (1972: 297) – de Beauvoir was to appeal to a subsequent generation of liberal feminists, concerned to debunk gendered rationalizations of the inequalities confronting women. Equally, she was to strike a chord among later Marxist feminists because of her insistence that the material inequalities confronting women would only be resolved in a socialist society. Moreover, her exhortation to women to take control of their bodies prefigured radical feminism's later concern with the politics of sexuality and reproduction, while her injunction that women should embark on an interior exploration of their selfhood was to commend itself to postmodern feminists more overtly concerned with the psychoanalytic aspects of women's identities. Hers was a prophetic vision and her legacy to feminism both rich and rewarding.

The second wave

The period between the first and second waves was not marked by feminist inactivity, although there was a certain ebbing of feminism's tide. Following the Second World War, and within the context of the emergence, in Europe at least, of the welfare state, provision of publicly funded support for wives and mothers reflected the fact that women were being re-privatized within the home setting. In that respect, the agenda of self-styled 'new' feminists had prevailed: 'state feminism', if it can be described as such, wore a domestic apron, certainly in the UK.

Far from generating a sense of fulfilment, the experience of being decanted back into home and family following their mobilization during the war – into the armed forces, fields and factories – created a sense of loss among many, if not most, women. That sense of forfeiture was captured by the American feminist Betty Friedan (1921–) in *The Feminine Mystique* (1963), a work regarded widely as a key text of second-wave feminism.

Friedan's approach was rooted in the liberal tradition of equal rights feminism. Set within a cultural climate that prized women's domestic role, it exposed the image of the happy, contented housewife as a disabling myth. Hemmed in by fashionable theories of 'maternal deprivation', sociological works that endorsed a traditional division of sexual labour, and a popular culture which, in Friedan's words, portrayed married women as 'brainless, fluffy kittens' (and single women as dedicated to catching a husband), women, she argued, had become trapped in a lifestyle that allowed them neither an independent identity nor a sense of achievement. She exhorted women to achieve educational qualifications and to re-enter employment as the means of escape from the snare of domestic life.

In so doing, Friedan issued an unequivocal riposte to a raft of anti-feminist sentiment that enveloped post-war America and Britain during the 1950s, which embraced baby and child-care manuals, magazines, TV shows, the cinema and the field of psychology. The appearance of *Modern Woman: The Lost Sex* (1947) by Ferdinand Lundberg and Marynia Farnham epitomized a dominant theme of popular psychology, namely that feminism was 'a deep illness', spawning the working woman, whose existence, they contended, threatened the fabric of society. The book voiced a diatribe against high levels of educational attainment by women: 'the more educated a woman is, the greater chance of sexual disorder' (see Eramo n.d.). The message was clear: working women, more especially married women, were bad mothers and wives, and impliedly responsible for a host of social ills: their proper place, one that guaranteed healthy womanhood and a stable society, was in the home having and raising children and ministering to their husbands. It was against such stultifying expectations that Friedan railed.

In 1966, frustrated by the timidity of the US government in implementing the newly won equal rights for women enshrined in the 1964 Civil Rights Act, Friedan co-founded the 'National Organization for Women' (NOW). Its remit was 'To take action to bring women into full participation in the mainstream of American society now, exercising all the privileges and responsibilities thereof in truly equal partnership with men'. Within a year, NOW had published a bill of rights for women which endorsed the ill-fated Equal Rights Amendment; urged the full enforcement of laws against sex discrimination; and demanded equal educational opportunities for women, child-care centres and, most controversially, the right of women 'to control their reproductive lives' (NOW 1968).

With the exception of the latter, which endorsed women's freedom to choose, NOW's agenda was fully consistent with mainstream American thought. It was no more, or less, than a set of liberal demands which argued for the removal of all legislative and economic barriers impeding women from participating in the full range of social, political and economic activities. It assumed no structural inequalities within society, unlike Marxist and socialist feminism, and appealed in large measure to well-educated, middle-class, white, heterosexual women. Moreover, while challenging the prevailing gendered image of woman as the dutiful wife preoccupied with pleasing her man and children, it assumed that women would pursue a career, supported by their sweetly reasonable husbands, who readily shared domestic tasks.

Friedan's set of prescriptions echoed the ideas of early liberals, although in encouraging women to enter the labour market it owed more to Harriet Taylor than either Wollstonecraft or Mill. But it was, nevertheless, reformist, believing that legislative and policy change, coupled with enhanced educational opportunities, would facilitate the entry of women into the public realm. Moreover, it accepted the family as a basic social institution, insisting that marriage could become an alliance of rational, co-equal individuals.

Friedan's renewal of liberal feminism was of course at odds with the socialist tradition of feminism, which stressed the material basis of women's oppression. However, an emerging radical feminism rejected liberal and socialist feminism alike.

Radical critiques

In the United States, radical feminism grew out of the campaign for black civil rights and the 'New Left' in the 1960s. While ostensibly egalitarian, these groups were discovered by women to be no less sexist than mainstream, or as they became styled, 'malestream', organizations: 'we [men] make the policy, you make the coffee' was a common attitude confronting women (see Bouchier 1983: 52–3; Crow 2000: 1–9).

This experience confirmed a growing belief among a number of women on the left in the necessity of developing new radical groups from which men would be excluded. Marginalized on the left, and unattracted to the liberal reformism of NOW, radical feminism began to crystallize around the issue of male power and privilege and generated a host of groups motivated to foment the liberation of women from patriarchy, including on the left. An early statement of the centrality of patriarchy to radical feminism's platform appeared in the 1969 *Manifesto* issued by the New York group 'Redstockings':

> Women are an oppressed class. Our oppression is total. . . . We identify the agents of our oppression as men. Male supremacy is the most basic form of domination. . . . All men receive economic, sexual and psychological benefits from male supremacy. All men have oppressed women. . . . we will

always take the side of women against their oppressors. We will not ask what is 'revolutionary' or 'reformist', only what is good for women.

(See Crow 2000: 223–35)

The representation of women as a universal 'sex-class' was developed by one of the authors of the *Manifesto*, Shulamith Firestone (1945–), in *The Dialectic of Sex* (1970). Both the title of the book and the phrase 'sex-class' suggest something of an intellectual debt to Marxism. But, in place of the centrality of struggle between economic classes, Firestone depicted the driving force of history as the struggle between the biological classes. What was required to secure the liberation of women was, therefore, a biological rather than an economic revolution, with women seizing control of the *means of reproduction* rather than *the means of production*.

Firestone, who dedicated her book to de Beauvoir, envisaged that new and developing technologies would liberate women by enabling fertilization to take place without intercourse, embryos to come to term outside the womb and children to be raised outside the context of the nuclear family. In effect, the family as a reproductive and economic unit would disappear and a society freed from sexually assigned roles would flourish. In its stead, she, like her contemporary Kate Millett (1934–), proffered a vision of an androgynous society wherein the virtues of men and women would be fused in a common identity.

Millett's *Sexual Politics* (1970) was the first second-wave text to elaborate at length upon the concept of patriarchy. For her, the family was the basis of patriarchal relations, functioning to indoctrinate women to accept the power of men in both the public and the private worlds. By representing male power as intrinsic to domestic as well as public life, she reinforced the idea of the personal as political. Unlike Firestone, however, Millett understood the oppression of women to be based upon the gendered construction of femininity rather than determined by biological difference. As such, she insisted upon the necessity of a sexual revolution rather than the hi-tech solution favoured by Firestone. This entailed an end to monogamy and the ideology of motherhood and the supplanting of the family by collectively provided child-care. But it was her endorsement of the free expression of sexual practices, whether heterosexual, bisexual, homosexual or lesbian, that distinguished her prescriptions. Only through such a transformation in consciousness and sexual activity would male supremacy be ended and both men and women evolve towards an androgynous future in which their positive qualities would be fused in a common humanity.

This vision of a society of androgynes did not appeal to radical lesbian feminists in the United States. Accepting fully the pervasiveness of undiluted patriarchy, they understood heterosexual relationships to be essentially about power: women in such relationships were accused of collaborating in their own oppression, of, in effect, sleeping with the enemy. The most explicit expression of sexual politics was captured in the slogan 'Feminism is the theory, lesbianism the practice'. Lesbianism was regarded not as a matter of sexual preference but as a political choice, one that signified the rejection of men as both sexual and political partners.

The response of Marxist and socialist feminism

The debate about lesbianism as a sexual practice, and the feasibility of separatism as a political strategy, was not confined to the United States. In Britain the 'separatist' issue dominated the feminist debates in the later 1970s and was to be the cause of a major split between a vocal minority of radical lesbian feminists and liberal and socialist feminists loosely joined under the umbrella of the 'Women's Liberation Movement' (Coote and Campbell 1987; Rowbotham 1990). While endorsing lesbianism as a freely chosen expression of sexuality, liberal and socialist feminists argued that political separatism offered nothing by way of engagement with the overwhelming majority of women who chose heterosexuality. Moreover, socialist feminists objected to the separatist strategy because it isolated women from their potential male allies, to whom they were ideologically wedded. However, the centrality of patriarchy to the renewal of feminist debate forced socialist feminists to respond to the charge that their ideological tradition rendered them sex-blind.

One response was the 'Wages for Housework' campaign. It, and the accompanying 'domestic labour debate' of the early 1970s, stressed the material contribution made by women to the economy through their unpaid work within the home. The provision of state-funded domestic labour would, its proponents argued, raise the political consciousness of women (and men), and drive home the lesson that without women's unpaid work in the home, capitalist society would collapse. It was, however, a debate that took a largely theoretical and somewhat abstract form among socialists, rather than engaging the attention of other feminists, less still women in general. Moreover, many socialist and non-socialist feminists objected to the idea of paying women for domestic work on the ground that it legitimized rather than confronted the prevailing division of labour within the family. A different response among socialists was to develop 'dual-systems' theory, one version of which is associated with Heidi Hartmann. She argued that it was in the material interests of men, of whatever class, to perpetuate the sexual division of labour within both the public and the private realms (Hartmann 1986: 1–41).

From this perspective, men are seen to gain material advantages both from the unequal division of domestic labour and from occupational segregation within the economy: horizontal segregation that divides jobs into lower-paid women's and higher-paid men's work; and vertical segregation whereby women occupy only the lower status positions within an occupation, now abbreviated as the 'glass ceiling' phenomenon. The combined effect, the argument ran, was to produce a mutually reinforcing system of exploitation that was termed 'patriarchal capitalism'. Thus, it was not enough to focus on the subordination of women within the economy: battle also had to be joined on the domestic front. Unless women struggled to make their partners aware of the double burden to which they were subjected, patriarchy would survive the transition to socialism.

An alternative dual-systems theory sought to fuse the Marxist analysis of women's subordination with the insights offered by psychoanalysis. Juliet Mitchell (1940–), for example, argued that women's oppression could not be explained solely in material terms; it also had to be understood in psychological and cultural terms (Mitchell 1974). To this end, she focused on the family's role in transmitting to individuals their respective social identities as members of either the male or the female sex. In essence, Mitchell was seeking to accommodate patriarchal analysis by underlining the ways in which the family engendered women's and men's roles and, in the process, placed a higher value on the latter. Thus, while understanding the appeal of patriarchy as a means of explaining the subordination of women, Mitchell rejected its determinism. She presented patriarchy as a socially constructed value system, not as a fixed and universal condition based upon biological identity. From this perspective, patriarchy could be successfully challenged and defeated.

This analysis, like Hartmann's, marked a departure from orthodox Marxism. Rather than accepting that women were only materially oppressed in the home and the economy, Mitchell contended that they were also psychologically oppressed. The site of that oppression was the family. Visualizing it as an agency that reproduced patriarchy by conditioning women to accept their subordination, she prescribed an ideological struggle within its confines. This meant that women should realize how they were subordinated in three 'structures of oppression': reproduction, the socialization of children and the expression of sexuality. Unless these structures were transformed, patriarchy would survive the demise of capitalism; thus, a psycho-cultural revolution, led by women, was crucial to the elimination of patriarchy.

Hartmann (1986) and Mitchell (1974), in responding to the critique that Marxism was sex-blind, veered from its mono-causal, class-based explanation of women's oppression. Both allowed patriarchy an independent existence, but dismissed the separatist solution preferred by some radical feminists as well as the reformist strategies of liberal feminists, which, even if successful, would leave intact the structural inequalities endemic to capitalism.

The primacy of sexual politics in radical feminist analyses of women's oppression has had a profound effect upon feminist discourse. Liberal and socialist feminists had to integrate patriarchy into their ideas and acknowledge its importance in explaining the continuing inequalities that beset women. However, rather than interpreting patriarchy in terms of biological essentialism, liberals in particular have sought to stress its gendered character by emphasizing the cultural and psychological construction of women's roles. In the case of socialist feminists, the experience has been rather more exacting, involving some intellectually athletic attempts to reconcile patriarchy with the enduring attachment to materialist explanations of women's oppression.

Pro-family, eco- and pro-woman feminism

The significance attached to sexual politics by radicals has not been accepted by all feminists, notably those who have perceived motherhood as a means of empowerment and fulfilment for women and have generated a literature of pro-family feminism that has been characterized (dismissively) as 'maternal revivalism' (Segal 1987: 145). What has united the proponents of this view is the idea that motherhood is compatible with feminism: in effect, each has sought to rehabilitate maternity (see Elshtain 1981; Friedan 1983; Greer 1984; Ruddick 1990).

Perhaps the most explicit exercise in rehabilitation was Jean Bethke Elshtain's (1941–2013) *Public Man, Private Woman* (1981). She assaulted the politicization of personal life promoted by radical feminists, defended the privacy of a child-centred family life and celebrated mothering as 'a complicated, rich, ambivalent, vexing, joyous activity which is biological, natural, social, symbolic and emotional' (Elshtain 1981: 243).

A similar perspective animates 'pro-woman' feminism, including eco-feminism. While it too embraces a variety of perspectives, it addresses the relationship between women and nature, but in terms that are entirely positive, unlike the dominant tradition in Western political thought referred to earlier. Its exponents emphasize the connectedness of human and non-human nature, and insist upon the integrity of all living things. Its exponents equate the threat posed by the untrammelled exploitation of the earth's resources and its peoples by large corporations with the development of the arms industry by politico-military elites, and insist that both are feminist concerns. The threats each pose are seen to flow from an assumed masculine psyche, motivated to dominate and subject nature and 'others', including women: that is, just as patriarchy oppresses women, so too it oppresses nature. The alternative is an ethic of connectedness and the creation of a sustainable, global economy, the realization of which will reconstruct gender relations and transform the relationship between humans and nature: 'Nature has been feminised and women naturalised, so that understanding these connections is necessary to understanding their respective oppressions' (Plumwood 2003).

Here we witness another challenge to the 'sameness' strategy adopted by mainstream liberal feminism. Instead of seeking to extend the concept of equal rights, as defined by a male model, the model is itself subverted because it is predicated upon a dualism – man = reason, woman = nature – that is hierarchical and oppressive: reason (male) deployed to subject nature (female).

Thus, pro-womanism stresses difference between women and men on an essentialist basis. Its gynocentric approach elevates women's qualities above those of men, thereby rejecting both androcentrism and androgyny. Women's attributes are seen to derive from their innate closeness to nature, to their bodies and to nurture. Hand in hand with these claims comes a rejection of rationality and instrumentality, which are portrayed as characteristically male attributes. Pro-womanism thereby asserts a biologically based, universal and established female character that transcends race, ethnicity and class.

Such essentialism is most fervently expressed by eco-feminists who equate men's rape and exploitation of the earth with their treatment of women, insisting that the future of both can only be assured through the diffusion and acceptance of womanly virtues. A more radical expression of pro-womanism is found in the work of cultural feminists, including Mary Daly (1928–2010). She advocated withdrawal into a woman-only culture untainted by patriarchal constructions of femininity. Only in such a segregated context can 'wild' and 'lusty' women express their natural and unrequited passions (Daly 1984). At this end of the feminist spectrum one may also encounter notions of women's spiritual communion with nature, invariably caricatured by critics as the literature of 'the earth mother'.

The celebration of motherhood and essentialism has also provoked criticisms from other feminists. In particular, pro-family feminists are regarded as having fallen headlong into a patriarchal snare by internalizing a value system that has been insinuated by men into Western political thought. As such, they are accused of providing ammunition to anti-feminists who perceive women's natural place to be the home. Similarly, the advocates of cultural/lesbian separatism, retailing beliefs founded upon the essential superiority of women, have been criticized on the ground that patriarchy can only be undermined if it is confronted, not avoided by a retreat into a women-only cul-de-sac.

Differences and subjectivities

The legacy of second-wave feminism was, and is, a critical discourse about patriarchy, underpinned by the insistence of radical feminists upon difference between women and men and a corresponding assertion that women share in a potential and universal sisterhood (Morgan 1970). However, the demarcation of differences between the sexes, coupled with the assertion of an overarching unity among all women, entailed the neglect of the needs and agendas of ethnic-minority women in the first world and of women in general in the less developed world. Western feminism, including radical feminism, thereby came to be regarded by non-white women as ethnocentric: focused upon the conditions of disadvantage affecting white women as if they had universal applicability. Mainstream feminism was, from this perspective, culpable of cultural and ideological imperialism. So disaffected were some 'black feminists' that they chose to style themselves as 'womanists' as an expression of their rejection of their feminist 'sisters'. Moreover, the assault by radical feminists on the family, which they perceived as a bastion of patriarchy, also served to alienate many American black feminists, for whom the family had indeed been the only safe haven, especially during the era of slavery.

bell hooks (1952–) is an eloquent critic of the colour blindness of mainstream feminism in the United States and its complicity in perpetuating racial oppression. As she puts it:

> despite all the rhetoric about sisterhood and bonding, white women were not sincerely committed to bonding with black and other groups of women to fight sexism. They were primarily interested in drawing attention to their lot as white upper and middle class women.
>
> (hooks 1981: 142)

She also articulates the dilemma black women face in tackling both patriarchy within their own communities and white racism within the wider society: by challenging black male sexism they exposed themselves to the charge that they would impede the wider struggle against racism. This disempowering accusation also consolidated black patriarchy: 'the equation of black liberation with black manhood promotes and condones black male sexism' (hooks 1996: 65). As a black feminist/womanist, hooks expresses the double-front in which she and others (Giddings 1984) have been and are engaged: fighting against both the sexism of black males and America's endemic racism, which, among other things, has infused its mainstream feminist discourse.

Such alienation fostered the growth of separate black feminist groups in, for example, the USA and the UK, seeking to explore their own 'herstories' and identities, thereby further extending the facets of feminism by generating a literature that essays black feminist thought (Mirza 1997; Collins 1991). The proliferation of ethnically distinct feminist groups not only challenges the presumption of universal sisterhood, but also deconstructs the concept of a unified 'black womanhood'. It was the emergence of such groups that stimulated interest in identity politics and helped to initiate a third feminist wave.

A third wave

The first and second waves of the feminist movement do have a generational character, although it is impossible to invest them with other than approximate dates. The same is true of a developing third wave, which has become a feature of feminism in the new millennium, although we can say that its genesis lies somewhere towards the latter part of the twentieth century. One interpretation of its emergence is that it represents a challenge issued by younger feminists to the legacy bequeathed by 'second-wavers': in that sense it has been likened to rebellion by 'daughters' against their 'mothers'. This mother/daughter analogy is, though, a gross oversimplification, not least because the stream of concern with identities and subjectivities inherited from the recent past continues unabated. Notwithstanding this continuity, one distinctive aspect of the third wave has provoked intense controversy, namely that dubbed 'sex-positive' feminism. In an abbreviated and simplified form, it celebrates what Jane

Spencer (2004) terms 'girlie things', including a concern with style, fashion, make-up and sexual pleasure.

In part, sex-positive feminism was prompted by the anti-pornography campaigns of the 1980s and 1990s spearheaded by, among others, Catherine McKinnon (1946–) and Andrea Dworkin (1946–2005). For them the pornography industry represented a fundamental debasement, exploitation and commercialization of women. Sex-positive feminists, however, defended the right of women to participate in and consume the products of the industry, leading to the accusation that they were colluding with a profound form of patriarchal female exploitation. This debate, dubbed the 'feminist sex wars', further accentuated divisions within the women's movement and among other things prompted the emergence of 'lipstick feminism', whose exponents appear concerned solely with individual fulfilment – economically, culturally, sexually – and who express disdain for collective action: whose credo, in short, is that beauty *is* power and that one can have both, even if beauty is bought, whether at the cosmetics counter or at the hands of cosmetic surgeons. This developing debate further swells the chorus of feminist voices and has added a somewhat discordant note to its orchestration.

Conclusion

The diversity of feminist thinking sketched out in this chapter may seem self-defeating, not least because it threatens to incur a political cost. If this body of thought is so plural, can feminists – however defined – combine to press for change in the conditions of women? The preoccupation with identity politics and the politics of subjectivities seems designed to create barriers among women. Consider, for instance, the controversy surrounding the wearing of hijab (modest dress) by Muslim women, now banned in France. Does the donning of the veil represent the subjection of Muslim women by their menfolk, fidelity to their religion, a form of negotiation with patriarchy, or some combination of these and other interpretations? While hijab may present an obstacle to understanding and communication, such cultural differences do not necessarily prevent contemporary feminists, just like their predecessors, from pursuing their needs, rights and interests through a succession of strategic, if temporary, coalitions. Such coalitions need not be fully inclusive of all feminisms or feminists. Some, including liberal feminists, press for legislative and policy change and operate in the mainstream of politics, while others, including cultural feminists, prefer to operate in the margins of political discourse, creating their own, separate responses to the wrongs they perceive to afflict women. But this division of labour is functional: some help to set the political agenda, while others see it through to legislative enactment and policy implementation.

Feminists of whatever persuasion do, however, share the status of social critic, employing women's experiences in various social and political contexts as raw materials that are drawn upon to analyze and explain conditions of women's inequality, whatever form it may take. It would, however, be misleading to suggest that one can reconcile the views of those who emphasize sameness with those who stress difference, whether between women and men or among women themselves. But this is not to assert that feminism has exhausted itself or lost its way: as Stacy Gillis *et al.* (2004: 3) state, 'feminisms can be multiple and polyphonous without drawing behind lines of engagement'. Hence the need to reformulate the question: not 'Am I a feminist?' but 'What kind of feminist might I be?'

Further reading

Overviews of the evolution of feminist thought and the treatment of women within Western political thought abound. Among those which I found of particular use and interest were Diana Coole's *Women in Political Theory* (1993), Valerie Bryson's *Feminist Debates* (2003) and Rosemarie Tong's *Feminist Thought* (2013). Valerie Bryson's *Feminist Debates* (1999) supplies a balanced assessment of theoretical and practical questions confronting feminists. Also recommended are Judith Squires's *Gender in Political Theory* (2000), Chris Beasley's *What Is Feminism?* (2000) and Chris Corrin's *Feminist Perspectives on Politics* (1999), another happy blend of theoretical debates and practical politics.

Choosing among the texts that survey the evolution of feminism is a challenging undertaking. One 'short-cut' is to explore the collections included in a number of readers. Among the more eclectic collections are those edited by Mary Evans (*The Woman Question*, 1994), Sandra Kemp and Judith Squires (*Feminisms*, 1997) and Maggie Humm (*Feminisms: A Reader*, 1992). More focused collections include Barbara Crow's *Radical Feminism: A Documentary Reader* (2000) and Heidi Safia Mirza's *British Black Feminism: A Reader* (1997). See also Miriam Schneir's *The Vintage Book of Feminism* (1995). Margaret Walters's *Feminism: A Very Short Introduction* (2005) offers a succinct overview of the history of the evolution of feminism.

Histories of the women's movement are plentiful, as are treatments of specific campaigns, including suffrage. Texts that address both suffrage and other campaigns in Britain and America include Christine Bolt's *The Women's Movement in the United States and Britain from the 1790s to the 1920s* (1993) and David Bouchier's *The Feminist Challenge* (1992). On suffrage see Martin Pugh's *The March of the Women* (2000 and 2008), Ray Strachey's *The Cause* (1978), Jill Liddington and Jill Norris's *One Hand Tied Behind Us* (1978) and Sylvia Pankhurst's *The Suffrage Movement* (1977). Other readable texts which survey the evolution of the women's movement include the five-volume Belknap series *A History of Women in the West* (see, e.g., Fraisse and Perrot, 1996; Thebaud, 1996) and the two-volume study *A History of Their Own* by Bonnie Andersen and Judith Zinsser (1990). Another two-volume series focused on feminist theory is *Feminism* (1994), edited by Susan Miller Okin and Jane Mansbridge. Dale Spender's *Women of Ideas and What Men Have Done to Them* (1990) is a successful attempt to place women within the history of ideas.

Debates concerning the development of feminist political thought in Britain also abound. Recommended is Juliet Mitchell and Ann Oakley's edited volume *What Is Feminism?* (1986), a 'sequel' to their earlier edited publication *The Rights and Wrongs of Women* (1979), which is equally rewarding. Terry Lovell's *British Feminist Thought* (1990) is a rich collection of writings by prominent second-wave feminists. On earlier first- and second-wave debates, see Leslie Tanner's *Voices from Women's Liberation* (1971), a compilation of extracts by American women covering both the first and second waves of feminism. A comparable British focus on the early phase of second-wave feminism is provided by Micheline Wandor's *The Body Politic* (1972).

Classic primary sources include Mary Wollstonecraft's *The Rights of Woman* (1974) and John Stuart Mill's *The Subjection of Women*, available in one volume with an introduction by Pamela Frankau (1974); August Bebel's *Woman Under Socialism* (1971); Friedrich Engels's *The Origin of the Family, Private Property and the State* (1972); William Thompson's *Appeal of One Half of the Human Race* (1983); Simone de Beauvoir's *The Second Sex* (1972); Betty Friedan's *The Feminine Mystique* (1965); and Shulamith Firestone's *The Dialectic of Sex* (1971).

On third-wave and postmodern feminism, see Marysia Zalewski's *Feminism after Postmodernism* (2000), Sarah Gamble's *The Icon Critical Dictionary of Feminism and Postfeminism* (1999), *Third Wave Feminism* by Stacy Gillis *et al.* (2004), Leslie Heywood and Jennifer Drake's edited volume *Third Wave Agenda* (1997) and Linda M. Scott's *Fresh Lipstick* (2005). A trenchant critique of lipstick and sex-positive feminism is provided by Natasha Walter's *Living Dolls* (2010). On 'third world women' and feminist critiques of nationalism and nationalist movements, see *Third World Women and the Politics of Feminism* by Chandra Talpade Mohanty *et al.* (1991), Lois West's edited volume *Feminist Nationalism* (1997), Rick Wilford and Robert Miller's edited volume *Women, Ethnicity and Nationalism* (1998) and Nira Yuval-Davis's *Gender and Nation* (1997). On interpretations of hijab, Islam and feminism, see Haideh Moghissi's *Feminism and Islamic Fundamentalism* (1999) and Fadwa El Guindi's *Veil: Modesty, Privacy and Resistance* (1999).

References

Alcott, Linda Martin (2000) Entry in Code, Lorraine (ed.) *Encyclopedia of Feminist Theories*, London: Routledge, 263–4.

Andersen, Bonnie and Zinsser, Judith (1990) *A History of Their Own*, London: Penguin.

Arneil, Barbara (1999) *Politics and Feminism*, Oxford: Blackwell.

Banks, Olive (1981) *Faces of Feminism*, Oxford: Martin Robertson.

Beasley, Chris (2000) *What Is Feminism? An Introduction to Feminist Theory*, London: Sage.

Bebel, August (1971) *Woman under Socialism*, New York: Schocken.

Berry, Mary Frances (1988) *Why ERA Failed*, Bloomington, IN: Indiana University Press.

Bolt, Christine (1993) *The Women's Movement in the United States and Britain from the 1790s to the 1920s*, Hemel Hempstead: Harvester Wheatsheaf.

Bouchier, David (1983) *The Feminist Challenge: The Movement for Women's Liberation in Britain and the USA*, London: Macmillan.

Bryson, Valerie (1992) *Feminist Political Theory: An Introduction*, Basingstoke: Macmillan.

—— (1999) *Feminist Debates: Issues of Theory and Political Practice*, Basingstoke: Macmillan.

Butler, Judith and Scott, Joan W. (eds) (1992) *Feminists Theorize the Political*, London: Routledge.

Code, Lorraine (ed.) (2000) *Encyclopedia of Feminist Theories*, London: Routledge.

Collins, Patricia Hill (1991) *Black Feminist Thought: Knowledge, Consciousness and the Politics of Empowerment*, London: Routledge.

Coole, Diana (1993) *Women in Political Theory: From Ancient Misogyny to Contemporary Feminism*, 2nd edn, Hemel Hempstead: Harvester Wheatsheaf.

Coote, Anna and Campbell, Bea (1987) *Sweet Freedom*, Oxford: Blackwell.

Corrin, Chris (1999) *Feminist Perspectives on Politics*, London: Longman.

Crow, Barbara (ed.) (2000) *Radical Feminism: A Documentary Reader*, New York: New York University Press.

Daly, Mary (1984) *Pure Lust: Elemental Feminist Philosophy*, Boston, MA: Beacon Press.

De Beauvoir, Simone (1972) *The Second Sex*, Harmondsworth: Penguin.

Delmar, Rosalind (1986) 'What is feminism?', in Mitchell, Juliet and Oakley, Ann (eds) *What Is Feminism?*, Oxford: Basil Blackwell, 8–33.

El Guindi, Fadwa (1999) *Veil: Modesty, Privacy and Resistance*, Oxford: Berg.

Elshtain, Jean Bethke (1981) *Public Man, Private Woman: Woman in Social and Political Thought*, Princeton, NJ: Princeton University Press.

Engels, Friedrich (1972) *The Origin of the Family, Private Property and the State*, New York: Pathfinder Press.

Eramo, Alessia (n.d.) 'Interesting excerpts'. Available online at webpage.pace.edu/ nreagin/tempmotherhood/fall2003/4/quotations.html.

Evans, Mary (1994) *The Woman Question*, 2nd edn, London: Sage.

Firestone, Shulamith (1970) *The Dialectic of Sex*, New York: Bantam Books.

Fraisse, Genevieve and Perrot, Michelle (eds) (1996) *A History of Women in the West IV: Emerging Feminism: From Revolution to World War*, London: Belknap Press.

Freeman, Jo (1972) 'The tyranny of structurelessness', *Second Wave*, 2 (1).

Friedan, Betty (1963) *The Feminine Mystique*, Harmondsworth: Penguin.

—— (1983) *The Second Stage*, London: Abacus.

Gamble, Sarah (ed.) (1999) *The Icon Critical Dictionary of Feminism and Postfeminism*, Cambridge: Icon Books.

Giddings, Paula (1984) *When and Where I Enter: The Impact of Black Women on Race and Sex in America*, New York: Morrow.

Gillis, Stacy, Howie, Gillian and Munford, Rebecca (eds) (2004) *Third Wave Feminism: A Critical Exploration*, Houndmills: Palgrave Macmillan.

Greer, Germaine (1984) *Sex and Destiny: The Politics of Human Fertility*, London: Secker and Warburg.

—— (1999) *The Whole Woman*, London: Doubleday.

Hartmann, Heidi (1986) 'The unhappy marriage of Marxism and feminism: towards a more progressive union', in Sargent, Lydia (ed.) *The Unhappy Marriage of Marxism and Feminism: A Debate on Class and Patriarchy*, London: Pluto.

Heywood, Leslie and Drake, Jennifer (eds) (1997) *Third Wave Agenda*, Minneapolis, University of Minnesota Press.

Hill, Bridget (1986) *The First English Feminist: Reflections upon Marriage, and Other Writings by Mary Astell*, Aldershot: Gower.

hooks, bell (1981) *Ain't I a Woman? Black Women and Feminism*, Boston, MA: South End Press.

—— (1996) *Killing Rage: Ending Racism*, Harmondsworth: Penguin.

Humm, Maggie (ed.) (1992) *Feminisms: A Reader*, Hemel Hempstead: Harvester Wheatsheaf.

Kemp, Sandra and Squires, Judith (eds) (1997) *Feminisms*, Oxford: Oxford University Press.

Liddington, Jill and Norris, Jill (1978) *One Hand Tied Behind Us*, London: Virago.

Lovell, Terry (1990) *British Feminist Thought: A Reader*, Oxford: Blackwell.

Mill, John Stuart (1974) *The Subjection of Women*, London: Dent.

Mirza, Heidi Safia (ed.) (1997) *British Black Feminism: A Reader*, London: Routledge.

Mitchell, Juliet (1974) *Psychoanalysis and Feminism*, Harmondsworth: Penguin.

Mitchell, Juliet and Oakley, Ann (eds) (1979) *The Rights and Wrongs of Women*, Harmondsworth: Penguin.

—— (1986) *What Is Feminism?*, Oxford: Blackwell.

Moghissi, Haideh (1999) *Feminism and Islamic Fundamentalism*, London: Zed Books.

Mohanty, Chandra Talpade, Russo, Ann and Torres, Lourdes (eds) (1991) *Third World Women and the Politics of Feminism*, Bloomington, IN: Indiana University Press.

Morgan, Robin (ed.) (1970) *Sisterhood Is Powerful: An Anthology of Writing from the Women's Liberation Movement*, New York: Vintage Books.

NOW (1968) *Bill of Rights*, Washington, DC. Available online at http://coursesa.matrix.msu.edu.

Okin, Susan Miller and Mansbridge, Jane (eds) (1994) *Feminism*, Aldershot: Edward Elgar.

Pankhurst, Sylvia (1977) *The Suffrage Movement*, London: Virago.

Parmar, Prathibha (1978) 'Other kinds of dreams', *Feminist Review*, 31: 55–66.

Pettman, Jan Jindy (1996) *Worlding Women: A Feminist International Politics*, London: Routledge.

Plumwood, Val (2003) *Feminism and the Mastery of Nature*, Taylor and Francis e-library.

Pugh, Martin (1992) *Women and the Women's Movement in Britain, 1914–1999*, London: Macmillan.

—— (2000) *The March of the Women: A Revisionist Analysis of the Campaign for Women's Suffrage, 1866–1914*, Oxford: Oxford University Press.

Randall, Vicky (1991) 'Feminism and political analysis', *Political Studies*, 34 (3): 516.

Rowbotham, Sheila (1990) *The Past Is Before Us*, Harmondsworth: Penguin.

Ruddick, Sara (1990) *Maternal Thinking: Towards a Politics of Peace*, London: Women's Press.

Schneir, Miriam (ed.) (1995) *The Vintage Book of Feminism*, London: Vintage Books.

Scott, Joan Wallach (ed.) (1996) *Feminism and History*, Oxford: Oxford University Press.

Scott, Linda M. (2005) *Fresh Lipstick*, Houndmills: Palgrave Macmillan.

Sebestyen, Amanda (ed.) (1988) *'68, '78, '88: From Women's Liberation to Feminism*, Bridport: Prism.

Segal, Lynne (1987) *Is the Future Female? Troubled Thoughts on Contemporary Feminism*, London: Virago.

Spencer, Jane (2004) 'Genealogies', in Gillis, Stacy, Howie, Gillian and Munford, Rebecca (eds) *Third Wave Feminism: A Critical Exploration*, Houndmills: Palgrave Macmillan, 9–12.

Spender, Dale (1990) *Women of Ideas and What Men Have Done to Them*, London: Pandora.

Squires, Judith (2000) *Gender in Political Theory*, Cambridge: Polity Press.

Strachey, Ray (1978) *The Cause*, London: Virago.

Tanner, Leslie (ed.) (1971) *Voices from Women's Liberation*, New York: Signet.

Thebaud, Françoise (ed.) (1996) *A History of Women in the West V: Toward a Cultural Identity in the Twentieth Century*, London: Belknap Press.

Thompson, William (1983) *Appeal of One-Half of the Human Race, Women*, London: Virago.

Tong, Rosemarie (1998) *Feminist Thought: A More Comprehensive Introduction*, 2nd edn, Sydney: Allen and Unwin (fourth edition, 2013).

United Nations (2000) *The World's Women: Trends and Statistics*, New York: United Nations.

Vincent, Andrew (1995) *Modern Political Ideologies*, Oxford: Blackwell.

Walter, Natasha (2010) *Living Dolls*, London: Virago.

Walters, Margaret (2005) *Feminism: A Very Short Introduction*, Oxford: Oxford University Press.

Wandor, Micheline (1972) *The Body Politic: Writings from the Women's Liberation Movement in Britain, 1969–1970*, London: Stage 1.

West, Lois (ed.) (1997) *Feminist Nationalism*, London: Routledge.

Wilford, Rick and Miller, Robert (eds) (1998) *Women, Ethnicity and Nationalism: The Politics of Transition*, London: Routledge.

Wollstonecraft, Mary (1974 [1792]) *The Rights of Woman*, repr., London: Dent.

Yuval-Davis, Nira (1997) *Gender and Nation*, London: Sage.

Zalewski, Marysia (2000) *Feminism after Postmodernism: Theorising through Practice*, London: Routledge.

Chapter 9

Anarchism

Laurence Davis

A resurgent but widely misunderstood ideology

Anarchism is one of the most vital impulses of contemporary radical politics. A heterodox way of seeing and being in the world that provides an ideological framework for understanding and acting upon some of the most pressing problems of our times, it is currently thriving in the decentralised networks of the global Occupy and European *Indignado* movements; world-wide anti-austerity and anti-capitalist mobilisations; interconnected alter-globalisation struggles from Latin America to Asia and Africa and the Middle East; deep green ecological and climate justice campaigns led by small farmers and indigenous peoples in the global South; student struggles from Chile to Quebec and the United Kingdom; and countless experiments in cooperative production and distribution, alternative media and art, and collective living. Fired by the conviction that it is possible to create another world far better than the one we currently inhabit, those now inspired by anarchist ideas have refused to acquiesce to the prevailing consensus that there is no alternative to a way of life based on domination and hierarchy.

Yet for all this resurgent political energy, anarchism remains the most widely misunderstood modern political ideology. Intelligent and well-informed accounts are a rarity in the mainstream academic literature, and inquiry into the subject, as one contemporary philosopher of anarchism has accurately observed, is typically greeted by colleagues 'with prejudicial incredulity, condescension, and even hostility – beyond the normal ignorance of the over-specialized' (McLaughlin, 2007: 14).

Such intellectually impoverished responses are perhaps not surprising when one considers the very different historical origins and development of academia and anarchism. While the former is deeply elitist and hierarchical (Boren, 2001), the latter has grown organically out of grassroots popular social formations. As Murray Bookchin, amongst others, has pointed out, anarchism constitutes a 'folk or people's social philosophy and practice in the richest sense of the term' (Bookchin, 1980). While the Hellenic origins of the term *anarche* ('without a ruler') might lead one to believe that it is at root an academic ideology, historically, Bookchin notes, anarchism has found expression in forms of humanity that institutionally involved people in face-to-face relations based on direct democracy, self-management, active citizenship and personal participation. Anarchist ideas, in turn, have tended to emerge from, and give ideological coherence to, popular social forms: from Winstanley's agrarian anarchism and the yeoman communities in seventeenth-century England; to Varlat's urban neighbourhood anarchism and the revolutionary sections and Enragés movement of Paris in 1793; to Proudhon's artisan anarchism and the craft communities of pre-industrial France; to Bakunin's anarcho-collectivism and the peasant villages of Russia and Spain; to Pelloutier's anarcho-syndicalism and the industrial proletariat and emerging factory system of the nineteenth century; to Kropotkin's anarcho-communism and the decentralised, ecological, self-governing organic associations arguably characteristic of counter-cultural left libertarian activism in the contemporary era (Bookchin, 1980). It is thus hardly surprising, as one political philosopher has recently observed, that 'most of the seminal and interesting work on anarchism has come from outside universities and standard intellectual circles' (Sylvan, 2007: 257).

Only very recently has this pattern perhaps begun to change. While anarchist studies is still unquestionably a marginal pursuit in the academy, from the late 1990s to the present interest in the field has increased significantly, especially among younger scholars. In the Anglo-American world, for example, various groups of scholars affiliated with a wide range of academic disciplines have collaborated to create the journal *Anarchist Studies*; have set up the UK Anarchist Studies Network, and later the North American Anarchist Studies Network, to 'build on the renewed interest in anarchist and anarchistic thought' and 'to provide a platform for the promotion of anarchism as a vital and viable analytical, conceptual, and pedagogical paradigm for the twenty-first century' (http://anarchist-studies-network.org.uk/HomePage); and have organised academic conferences and published a range of anthologies (see, for example, Kinna, 2012; Jun and Wahl, 2009; Amster *et al.*, 2009; Shukaitis and Graeber, 2007; Purkis and Bowen, 2004). The period has also seen the establishment of the first peer-reviewed English-language book series in anarchist studies by a major international academic publisher, namely the Contemporary Anarchist Studies series published by Continuum/Bloomsbury Press, intended to showcase 'cutting edge, socially engaged scholarship from around the world – bridging theory and practice, academic rigour and the insights of contemporary activism' (www.bloomsbury.com/uk/series/contemporary-anarchist-studies/?pg=1).

It is as yet unclear what implications, if any, these recent developments will have for the evolution of anarchism as a political ideology. On the one hand, the upsurge of creative interest in anarchism in the academy suggests that while the university may well be, as one commentator has provocatively remarked, 'the only Western institution other than the Catholic Church and British monarchy that has survived in much the same form from the Middle Ages' (Graeber, 2004: 7), it is not a monolithic institution and is vulnerable to subversion from within. To the extent this is so, we may well be witnessing the emergence of an academic anarchism that will coincide with, draw sustenance from and feed into a new chapter in the global history of student resistance.

On the other hand, the academic mainstreaming of anarchism signals the very real danger of its domestication, insofar as anarchism is transformed from a revolutionary social movement rooted in popular democratic social formations to an object of study by intellectual elites whose career prospects (and hence livelihood and social status) are largely determined by their ability to please and appease the powers that be in a rigidly hierarchical institution. Still in its early stages, the process of academic domestication of anarchism has already provoked a furious backlash from movement activists, some of whom have responded to it by dismissing the value of academic accounts of anarchism altogether. This, in turn, has deepened already existing divisions between those inside and outside the academy, and raises important but as yet under-explored (see Barker and Cox, 2002 for a notable exception) questions about the consequences of such divisions for the production of movement-relevant knowledge.

Consistent with the general anarchist opposition to both 'obedience to ideas abstracted from life *and* to action uninformed by thought' (Wieck, n.d.: 5), the following introduction to anarchism as a political ideology will attempt to steer a course between the Scylla of domesticated academic anarchism and the Charybdis of unreflective anarchist activism, illuminating an anarchism that is both scholarly and popular in the best senses of those terms. The plan for the chapter is as follows: first, we consider anarchism's ambivalent and interrogative relationship to ideological thinking; second, we identify the ideological core of anarchism; third, we ask whether anarchism is utopian; and fourth, we trace the largely hidden history of anarchy in action. The chapter's primary argument is that anarchism is a multifaceted and open-ended political ideology the core of which is the practice-grounded belief that society can and should be organised without hierarchy and domination.

Anarchism and the radical critique of ideology

Moya Lloyd opens her concluding chapter ('The End of Ideology?') to the third edition of this edited volume with the observation that all of its other contributors have not only plotted the genesis and evolution of different political ideologies, but also assumed their continuing relevance. By contrast, Lloyd suggests that our relation to the study of ideology should be interrogative. More specifically, she argues that we should ask questions not only about the contours of specific ideologies or the nature of ideology as such, but about the continuing relevance of ideological thinking. This she proceeds to do by means of an analysis of the work of Daniel Bell, Francis Fukuyama, Michel Foucault, and Ernesto Laclau and Chantal Mouffe – all of whom, she remarks, were 'in one way or another, responding to the challenges posed by the putative failure of Marxism' (Lloyd, 2003: 220).

Absent from this otherwise useful analysis is any consideration of the contributions to ideology critique made by anarchists at a time when Marxism was still in its infancy, and subsequently developed in new and original and highly challenging ways that remain acutely relevant today. As evidence for this proposition, let us consider in turn two very different examples of anarchist ideology critique that between them span the period of time from the mid-nineteenth century to the present day: Max Stirner's *Der Einzige und sein Eigentum* (1844, generally translated into English as *The Ego and Its Own*) and Uri Gordon's *Anarchy Alive!* (2008).

Dismissed by Marx and Engels in their book *The German Ideology* as an irredeemably idealist work, Stirner's *Der Einzige* has found a more receptive audience in the anarchist tradition, in the context of which it is generally regarded as a foundational individualist anarchist text, even if a deeply controversial one. In a recent sympathetic treatment of *The Ego and Its Own*, Saul Newman argues that Stirner was one of the first political thinkers to develop a radical critique of ideology, which paradoxically may now provide it with a new lease of life at an historical moment when so many are proclaiming its demise (Newman, 2001: 309–10).

The primary object of Stirner's critique is what he refers to as 'fixed ideas', that is, ideas that master the individual rather than serve him or her, insofar as they have become fixed ends rather than open questions. Stirner compares such ideas to a 'spirit-realm' which haunts us by beckoning with ideals incapable of realisation (Stirner, 1995: 42–3). He also describes the process by which such 'spooks' abase the corporeal individual, elevating an abstract conception of humanity over real flesh-and-blood human beings. For example, ideologies such as liberalism and socialism impoverish the individual personality, he claims, the former by reifying the state as 'the true person' before whom the individual personality vanishes, and the latter by fetishising the notion of society (Stirner, 1995: 91, 106–7).

What is perhaps most interesting from a contemporary philosophical perspective in Stirner's critique of ideology, Newman suggests, is the recognition that the 'subject', while constituted by ideology, is never fully determined by it. What Stirner terms the 'un-man', or a person who does not correspond to the abstract concept of man, is the point at which ideology breaks down and the contingent nature of its operation is exposed. According to Newman, this insight enables us to go beyond essentialist and structuralist (and indeed post-structuralist) theories of ideology, which he contends have hitherto limited our understanding of the concept and 'led to its premature demise in our contemporary political imaginary' (Newman, 2001: 309; see Clark, 1976 for a more critical perspective on Stirner's text and Feiten, 2013: 128–9 for a critique of Newman's argument).

Interesting as it is from an academic philosophical perspective, Stirner's critique of ideology is unlikely ever to exert significant political influence given his individualist anarchist detachment from and scepticism towards practices of organised collective resistance. More interesting in this regard is the extensive, but generally unrecognised or unacknowledged, corpus of original, challenging and exceptionally politically engaged anarchist ideology critique developed by leading movement thinkers such as Proudhon, Bakunin, Kropotkin, Malatesta, Goldman and Landauer, including their criticisms of religion and academic learning as mechanisms of indoctrination, bourgeois morality, scientism, biological essentialism, representation and abstraction, and ideological mystification. To focus on but one example, Bakunin persistently defended the values of freedom and spontaneous life against all those who fetishised theories and systems, declaring that 'natural and social life must always come before theory, which is only one of its manifestations but never its creator' (Bakunin, quoted in Knight, 2013: 181). Even more pointedly, he maintained that 'No theory, no ready-made system, no book that has ever been written will save the world. I cleave to no system. I am a true seeker' (Bakunin, quoted in Jun, 2012: 149).

More recently, a particularly interesting example of anarchist ideology critique is Uri Gordon's book *Anarchy Alive! Anti-Authoritarian Politics from Practice to Theory*. Intended as a faithful representation of, and sympathetically critical engagement with, emerging trends in the contemporary anarchist movement, *Anarchy Alive!* analyses anarchism not only as a collection of ideas, but also as a social movement and a political culture. A firmly practice-grounded work, it takes as its starting point the recognition that anarchist ideas can only be understood against the background of the movements and cultures in and by which they are expressed. The role of the political theorist, on this understanding of the relationship between theory and practice, is to 'partake in and facilitate the reflexive process of theorising among activists, functioning as a clarifier, organiser and articulator of ideas'. More specifically, her or his goal is to:

> address, in theoretical form, the issues that activists face in their everyday organising, to assemble ideas so that they can be discussed carefully, to lay open hidden assumptions and contradictory statements, and in general to advance activists' thinking by harvesting ideas from brief and informal debates and giving them more structured and fine-grained attention.
>
> (Gordon, 2008: 7–8).

This by no means implies that the political theorist ought to serve as an uncritical cheerleader of movement activity and ideas. Rather, the important point is that even the most critical theoretical analysis is thus generated as part of a dialogical process which ensures that theory speaks not from above but from within.

As a result of this distinctive methodology, *Anarchy Alive!* succeeds in its aim of separating anarchism from any expectation of a fixed dogma or precise ideology. In contrast to those contemporary anarchist writers – most notable among them Michael Schmidt and Lucien van der Walt – who offer heavily prescriptive and purportedly authoritative accounts of who is and is not an anarchist, or a revolutionary, or a member of the 'broad anarchist tradition' (narrowly defined by Schmidt and van der Walt as a particular form of class-struggle anarchism rooted in the work of Bakunin and the mid- to late nineteenth-century International Alliance of Socialist Democracy; 2009: 71), Gordon explicitly distances himself from those who 'affix anarchism with a given meaning and deny the genuineness of other variations' (2008: 27). Instead, he takes seriously the idea that anarchism is a 'necessarily heterogeneous and heterodox phenomenon-in-process' (ibid.) and applies this un-dogmatic method of analysis in scholarly interventions into a wide range of frequently emotively charged and ideologically polarised debates within the movement. In so doing he helps to break down rigid ideological barriers between the major trends in anarchism, and thus facilitates the development of political solidarity and cooperative movement practice.

In sum, anarchists have contributed innovative, if neglected, auto-critiques of political ideology that promise to breathe new life into the concept. To be sure, some anarchists reject the ascription *ideology* altogether, based on the supposition that ideologies are by definition static and dogmatic con-stellations of ideas. Iain McKay, for example, claims that ideologies are 'the nemesis of critical thinking and consequently of freedom, providing a book of rules and "answers" which relieve us of the "burden" of thinking for ourselves' (2008: 18). Hence his insistence that anarchism is 'a socio-economic and political theory, but not an ideology' (ibid.). However, other anarchists embrace the more nuanced position that anarchism is a political ideology of a particular kind: namely, one that resolutely refuses dead dogmas in favour of imagination, inclusion and diversity, intelligent self-criticism, endless experimentation, and open-ended social and political change. Moreover, regardless of their views (if any) about the concept of ideology, all consistent anarchists oppose the sub-ordination of human beings to or by fixed ideas, just as they more generally oppose domination in all its various and shifting guises. And this point, in turn, takes us to the core of anarchism.

The core of anarchism

The core of anarchism is the belief that society can and should be organised without hierarchy (understood as rule-guided, pyramidically ranked systems of command and obedience) and domination. While anarchist ideas may be traced back thousands of years to the Taoists in ancient China, anarchism first emerged as a coherent political ideology in the late eighteenth century. It developed primarily in opposition to centralised states and industrial capitalism, and by the end of the nineteenth century was a mass revolutionary movement attracting millions of adherents worldwide.

From a philosophical point of view, anarchism may be characterised helpfully in contrast to what it rejects: namely, 'archy', or centralised coercive forms. As Richard Sylvan (2007: 261) has perceptively observed, there are two interacting foci in the anarchist critique of such forms: first, a top or centre; and second, control or dominance flowing from this top, by what are deemed unacceptable – in particular, authoritarian or coercive – means. Thus a prime minister of a modern European state both stands at the top of a power hierarchy and exercises coercive control from that point. By contrast, an-archy entails structure or organisation without unacceptable top-down or centralised means.

Many analysts muddle matters with false, simplistic or misleading claims about anarchism. Three in particular merit careful scrutiny: first, the claim that anarchists are opposed to organisation; second, the suggestion that they are opposed to all authority; and third, the assertion that anti-statism is the defining feature of anarchist ideology.

The first of these three claims, that anarchists are opposed to organisation, is a myth. Its persistence in the popular mind derives in part from unreflective repetition, and in part as well from an understandable confusion of terms. As the historian of anarchism George Woodcock points out, the original Greek word *anarche* means merely 'without a ruler', and thus the English term 'anarchy' can clearly be used in a general context to mean either the negative condition of unruliness or the positive condition of being unruled because rule is unnecessary for the preservation of order (Woodcock, 1962: 10). It is with this latter sense of the term that anarchists identify, ever since the French political thinker Pierre-Joseph Proudhon proudly adopted the insignia in 1840. Organisation is thus entirely compatible with anarchism, so long as it is not hierarchical and/or coercive. As we shall see, there are a rich variety of possible forms of anarchist organisation.

The second claim, that anarchists are opposed to all authority, is simplistic and misleading. Anarchists recognise that there are many types of authority relations, not all of which are closed and coercive in character and thus morally objectionable. Sylvan (2007: 263), for instance, cites the example of the relation of a student to an authority in some field of knowledge, in which case the authority in question can support expert judgements by appeal to a range of assessable evidence (anarchists frequently refer to this form of authority as 'the authority of competence'). The example is a salient one because anyone with time and some skill can proceed past the authority to assess the claims made. By contrast, closed authorities simply stand on their position or station, or appeal to a conventional rule or procedure, thus precluding the exercise of individual autonomy. Moreover, because such authorities needn't justify themselves, they almost invariably back up their power with coercion and violence, which anarchists oppose 'for the same reason they oppose opaque authority more generally: because it violates the "self-respect and independence" of the individual' (Jun, 2012: 114).

The third claim, that anti-statism is the defining feature of anarchist ideology, is reductive and hence also misleading. The state is indeed a primary target of anarchist criticism, insofar as it is the paradigmatic 'archist' institution, distinguished above all by its claim of a monopoly of the legitimate use of force in a given territory. However, anarchists have traditionally struggled against a wide range of regimes of domination, from (to cite but a few examples) capitalism, patriarchy, heterosexism, the war system and the domination of nature to colonialism, slavery, fascism, white supremacy and certain forms of organised religion. Moreover, there is no reason to believe that a future stateless world would necessarily be one entirely free of all forms of domination. To the contrary, the evidence of history suggests that every victory in the never-ending struggle against oppression and injustice creates a new situation with its own new and unpredictable ethical problems and demands. In the words of Rudolph Rocker, 'Each generation must face its own problems, which cannot be forestalled or provided for in advance' (quoted in Jun, 2012: 131). It follows that while anti-statism has been, and for the foreseeable future will in all likelihood continue to be, a core feature of anarchist ideology, it is not (as some have claimed) its 'defining' feature. Indeed, as John Clark reminds us, it would be a mistake to define anarchism in terms of its relation to *any* one social institution, no matter how important it may be (1984: 122).

What, then, lies at the core of anarchist ideology, if not anti-statism and opposition to all forms of organisation and authority? The answer to this question, I have already suggested, consists in the anarchist belief that society can and should be organised without hierarchy and domination. As is the case with other complex and multifaceted political ideologies shaped by the experience of the French Revolution, this belief is informed in part by the anarchist commitment to a range of flexible, empirically grounded and non-hierarchical ethical values which are neither ranked by some impersonal criteria of moral worth nor derive from common ultimate principles. Foremost among these are the values of liberty, equality and solidarity.

In common with liberalism, anarchism places a very high value on individual liberty in the 'negative' sense of the term elucidated by the liberal thinker John Stuart Mill when he set out in his classic essay 'On Liberty' to define 'the nature and limits of the power which can be legitimately exercised by society over the individual' (1989 [1859]: 5), and discussed by Benjamin Constant when he compared favourably the liberty of the moderns (which consisted of 'the enjoyment of security in private pleasures') with that of the ancients (which consisted of 'active and constant participation in collective power') (Constant, 1988 [1819]: 316–17). Negative liberty, on this understanding, is a property of individuals and consists in the absence of constraint or interference by others, including (especially) government. From a liberal point of view, government threatens freedom by imposing laws and directives backed up by the threat of force, even as it secures freedom by protecting each person from the interference of others (Miller, 1991: 3). Anarchists, by contrast, agree with Thoreau's maxim: 'That government is best which governs not at all' (Thoreau, 1960 [1849]: 222, quoted in Rocker, n.d.).

In common with socialism, anarchism places a very high value on both social and economic equality, and community or solidarity. Most anarchists would agree with the socialist writer R. H. Tawney when he declared in his classic work *Equality* that 'it is the mark of a civilised society to aim at eliminating such inequalities as have their source, not in individual differences, but in its own organisation' and that 'individual differences, which are a source of social energy, are more likely to ripen and find expression if social inequalities are, as far as practical, diminished' (Tawney, 1935, quoted in Crick, 1987: 72). Many, if not most, would also share the sentiment animating the words of the medieval peasant leader John Ball, as imagined by the socialist polymath William Morris in his late nineteenth-century prose fiction *A Dream of John Ball*: 'fellowship is life, and lack of fellowship is death' (1986 [1886]: 51). For social anarchists such as Bakunin, individual liberty can thrive only in the soil of equality and social solidarity. The extreme individualism which is the antithesis of these social values 'considers all members of society . . . to be mutually unconcerned rivals and competitors, natural enemies with whom each individual is forced to live but who block each other's way'. It thus impels the individual to 'gain and erect his own well-being, prosperity, and good fortune to the disadvantage of everyone else, despite them and on their backs' (Bakunin, quoted in Jun, 2012: 121–2). Against this extreme individualist position, Bakunin argues the proposition that equality and solidarity properly understood are not obstacles to individual freedom but their conditions of possibility: 'The freedom of individuals is by no means an individual matter. It is a collective matter, a collective product. No individual can be free outside of human society or without its cooperation . . . But this freedom is possible only through equality.' And again: 'I am truly free only when all human beings, men and women, are equally free. The freedom of other men, far from negating or limiting my freedom, is, on the contrary, its necessary premise and confirmation' (Bakunin, quoted in Jun, 2012: 123–4). Unlike so many non-anarchist socialists, social anarchists such as Bakunin and Kropotkin do not assume that social and economic equality are sufficient conditions for the realisation of individual freedom. Rather, they advocate an ethics and a politics of equal-liberty, in which the two values are 'mutually dependent' (Suissa, 2010: 9) or 'symbiotic' (Jun, 2012: 125), though never fully reconcilable.

Elsewhere in this volume Vincent Geoghegan observes that the socialist critique of capitalism is a far from seamless whole, as important differences exist among socialists (see chapter 4). The same may be said of anarchists. Perhaps the most notable of such differences derive from the historical tendency of different groups of anarchists to place more emphasis on one rather than the other side of the equality–liberty dyad (Suissa, 2010: 9). Specifically, it is common to find a distinction (not altogether valid, insofar as many individualist anarchists see themselves as socialists) between anarchists of more 'individualist' leanings, who have more in common ideologically with liberals than they do with socialists, insofar as they focus primarily on the harms associated with coercion, and 'social anarchists', who have more in common ideologically with socialists than liberals, insofar as they focus primarily on the dangers associated with hierarchy and social inequality (see Davis, 2010 on the related distinction between 'social anarchism' and 'lifestyle anarchism'). As in the case of both the liberal and the socialist tradition, these differing emphases give rise to a good deal of the diversity in the anarchist movement.

Remarkably, however, only rarely have these different emphases spawned the bitter sectarian conflict that has so marred and disfigured the Marxian socialist tradition (the most notable exceptions being disputes involving anarchists most heavily influenced by more sectarian forms of Marxism). Commenting on precisely this point, the anarchist anthropologist David Graeber notes that whereas different schools of Marxism tend to be named after Great Thinkers (e.g., Leninists, Maoists, Trotskyites, Gramscians and Althusserians), anarchists like to distinguish themselves by what they do, and how they organise themselves to go about doing it. This does not mean, he hastens to add, that anarchists are or have to be against theory. Rather, the point is that while anarchism clearly has need of the tools of intellectual analysis and understanding, it does not need what he calls 'High Theory', that is, theory intended to determine the correct historical analysis of the world situation, so as to lead the masses along in the one true revolutionary direction. Anarchist-inspired groups, in contrast to their more sectarian Marxist counterparts, generally tend to embrace a form of 'Low Theory', characterised by Graeber as a non-vanguardist means of grappling with real, immediate questions that emerge from a transformative or revolutionary project. Importantly, this distinctive variety of practice-grounded anarchist theorising presumes and indeed values a diversity of sometimes incommensurable perspectives (Graeber, 2004: 4–9).

While there is an element of caricature in Graeber's analysis, which he acknowledges, and there is a great deal of potential complementarity between anarchism and Marxism (see, on this subject, Prichard *et al.*, 2012), his brief discussion of some of the distinguishing features of anarchist and Marxist theory usefully highlights yet another core feature of anarchist ideology that is frequently overlooked or misunderstood by its more critical expositors. Anarchists believe that there should be an ethically consistent relationship between the means of social change and its ends. They subscribe, in other words, to an ethics and a politics of 'prefiguration'. Whereas many Marxists would maintain that it is acceptable that 'tactics contradict principles', because the ends justify the means, anarchists insist that means must match ends because they help shape them (van der Walt, 2011, quoting Tony Cliff), and are in fact ends in the making. Hence the traditional anarchist opposition to organisational forms such as the political party, whether of a liberal democratic or Leninist revolutionary variety (see Franks, 2006: 212–18 on anarchist opposition to the Leninist political party). Hence also the anarchist preference for 'direct action', defined by Gordon as:

> action without intermediaries, whereby an individual or a group uses their own power and resources to change reality in a desired direction, intervening directly in a situation rather than appealing to an external agent (typically the state) for its rectification.
>
> (Gordon, 2009: 269)

In short, the principle of prefiguration plays a major role in anarchist ideology, nowhere more so perhaps than in its distinctive understanding of the concepts of utopia and revolution, two subjects to which we now turn in the remainder of our analysis.

Anarchism and utopianism

Over time anarchists have generated a rich variety of visions of social life structured according to principles other than hierarchy and domination. While these visions range from the predominantly individualistic to the predominantly communitarian, features common to virtually all include an emphasis on self-management and self-regulatory methods of organisation, voluntary association, decentralised federation, and direct democracy. In short, anarchists desire a decentralised society, based on the principle of free association, in which people will manage and govern themselves. Such a society, anarchists contend, is the one best suited to maximising the values of liberty, equality and solidarity.

Consider, by way of illustration, the following three quotations. The first comes from Peter Kropotkin:

> Anarchism . . ., the name given to a principle or theory of life and conduct under which society is conceived without government – harmony in such a society being obtained, not by submission to law, or by obedience to any authority, but by free agreements concluded between the various groups, territorial and professional, freely constituted for the sake of production and consumption, as also for the satisfaction of the infinite variety of needs and aspirations of a civilized being.
>
> (Kropotkin, 1910)

The second comes from Emma Goldman:

> Anarchism, then, really stands for the liberation of the human mind from the dominion of religion; the liberation of the human body from the dominion of property; liberation from the shackles and restraint of government. Anarchism stands for a social order based on the free grouping of individuals for the purpose of producing real social wealth; an order that will guarantee to every human being free access to the earth and full enjoyment of the necessities of life, according to individual desires, tastes, and inclinations.
>
> (Goldman, 1927)

The author of the third is Rudolf Rocker:

> Anarchism is a definite intellectual current of social thought, whose adherents advocate the abolition of economic monopolies and of all political and social coercive institutions within society. In place of the capitalist economic order, Anarchists would have a free association of all productive forces based upon cooperative labour, which would have for its sole purpose the satisfying of the necessary requirements of every member of society. In place of the present national states with their lifeless machinery of political and bureaucratic institutions, Anarchists desire a federation of free communities which shall be bound to one another by their common economic and social interests and arrange their affairs by mutual agreement and free contract.
>
> (Rocker, n.d.)

One important feature of all of these quotations that immediately stands out in our contemporary era 'of compromises, of half-measures, of the lesser evil' (Berneri, 1982 [1950]: 1) is the boldness and sweep of their visions of a world qualitatively different from and better than our own. Some might call them 'utopian'. Interestingly, however, at least two of the three writers quoted explicitly rejected such a label. In the same *Encyclopaedia Britannica* piece quoted above, Kropotkin declares that:

> the anarchist writers consider, moreover, that their conception is not a utopia, constructed on the *a priori* method, after a few desiderata have been taken as postulates. It is derived, they maintain, from an *analysis of tendencies* that are at work already.
>
> (Kropotkin, 1910; for a much more sympathetic and nuanced account of utopianism by Kropotkin, see his February 1914 preface to Pataud and Pouget's *How We Shall Bring About the Revolution*, 1990).

Likewise, Rocker emphasises the point that:

> anarchism is no patent solution for all human problems, no Utopia of a perfect social order (as it has so often been called), since, on principle, it rejects all absolute schemes and concepts. It does not believe in any . . . definite final goals for human development.
>
> (Rocker, n.d.)

By contrast, Goldman endeavours to vindicate the term in a pre-World War I lecture highly critical of both electoral socialism and the Marxist ideological distinction between scientific and utopian socialism that was then being used to legitimate it: 'Every daring attempt to make a great change in existing conditions, every lofty vision of new possibilities for the human race, has been labelled utopian' (Goldman, 1972 [1912]).

Stepping back from particular quotations to consider the anarchist tradition as a whole, it is fair to say that most anarchists have been ambivalent about the concept of utopia. On the one hand, they wish to avoid being tarred with the negative connotations of the term associated with influential liberal and Marxist anti-utopian criticisms of utopia, in particular the suggestion that utopian imagination necessarily represents a form of apolitical and anti-historical abstraction from existing reality. Hence the frequent emphasis in anarchist writing on its grounding in existing libertarian tendencies in society, and its anti-perfectionist commitment to endless experimentation and open-ended social and political change. On the other hand, anarchists clearly recognise that while some things are indeed impossible, others are 'impossible' only because humanly created institutions make them so. Hence the need for anarchist utopian thought experiments and experiments in living that expose the partiality of currently dominant perceptions of reality, and thus facilitate free choice from among a fuller range of practical social alternatives (Davis and Kinna, 2009: 2).

Insofar as all political ideologies have a utopian dimension – thus the utopian liberalism of the eighteenth century became the dominant ideology of nineteenth-century bourgeois society, leading not only to the utopian movements of socialism and anarchism but also to the 'counter-utopia' of radical conservatism – it makes little sense to dismiss outright the claim that anarchism is a utopia. Rather, it is far preferable from an analytical point of view simply to acknowledge the utopian aspect of anarchism, while simultaneously observing that it is a utopia of a particular kind. More specifically, the anarchist utopia is an example of what I have elsewhere termed a 'grounded' utopia (Davis, 2012: 136–7), or one that emerges organically out of, and contributes to the further development of, historical movements for grassroots social change. Emphatically not fantasised visions of perfection to be imposed upon an imperfect world, such utopias are an integral feature of that world, representing the hopes and dreams of those consigned to its margins. Part and parcel of dynamic and open-ended processes of struggle, and grounded in immediate everyday needs, grounded utopias challenge dominant conceptions of reality not by measuring them against the transcendent ethical standard of a fixed vision of an ideal society, but by opening a utopian space for thinking, feeling, debating and cultivating the possibility of historically rooted (and thus historically contingent) alternative social relations.

The grounded utopianism of anarchism is evident today in an almost endless variety of social practices, from unorthodox lifestyles and experiments in alternative education to the General Assemblies of the global Occupy movement and grassroots movements of farmers and landless people (such as the Zapatista in Mexico, the Landless Workers Movement in Brazil and the *Mukti Sangarsh* in India) seeking to reclaim their right to use common land to meet their subsistence needs. What all such instances of grounded utopianism have in common is their creation of utopian spaces in concrete individual or collective practices intended to cultivate the possibility of alternative social relations.

In their fictional guise, anarchist utopias have proven to be a particularly fruitful source of imaginative reflection about the possibilities and limits of anarchy. In works such as Joseph Déjacque's *L'Humanisphère, Utopie anarchique* (1858), Aldous Huxley's *Island* (1962), Ursula K. Le Guin's *The Dispossessed: An Ambiguous Utopia* (1974) and *Always Coming Home* (1985), Robert Nichols' four-volume *Daily Lives in Nghsi-Altai* (1977–79) and Starhawk's *The Fifth Sacred Thing* (1993), fiction writers have brought their formidable artistic talents to bear on the creative challenge of depicting a functioning anarchist society (for fuller bibliographies see www.acratie.eu/ and Killjoy, 2009: 214–16). What makes these works particularly interesting from the perspective of students of political ideologies are the ways in which they engage the reader in a complex dialogue about what is, what might be, and the relationship between the two. They are thus neither purely escapist fantasies nor narrowly didactic constructions meant to secure the reader's unquestioning assent to a particular socio-political agenda. Rather, in their most artistically sophisticated forms, they are thought experiments that invite the reader to participate in a time-sensitive journey of the utopian imagination complete with fundamental moral conflict, meaningful choice and continuing change, by the end of which she or he may return to the non-fictional present with a broader perspective on its latent emancipatory possibilities (Davis, 2012: 137).

To focus on but one especially notable example, in her science-fiction novel *The Dispossessed*, Ursula K. Le Guin manages the remarkable feat of detailing the texture of everyday life in an anarchist utopian society. Moreover, as the subtitle of the book ('An Ambiguous Utopia') suggests, she does so in a way that both, on the one hand, foregrounds the dynamic and value-pluralistic relationship between this ambiguously utopian world and a fictional analogue of our own and, on the other, critically interrogates the anarchist ideology that so deeply inspires and informs the narrative. The result is an exceptionally thoughtful and powerfully imagined work of art which dramatises one of the most distinctive and important, if frequently neglected, features of anarchist ideology: its capacity for reflective self-correction and perpetual re-creation (more in-depth discussion of these points may be found in Davis and Stillman, 2005; Brennan and Downs, 1979; Freedman, 2000: 111–29; and Ferns, 1999: ch. 7).

Another important but frequently neglected or misunderstood feature of anarchist ideology highlighted in *The Dispossessed* is its distinctive treatment of time. Much current scholarship focused on exploring the relationship between anarchism and utopianism rightly emphasises the present-tense orientation of contemporary anarchist utopian aspirations (see, for example, the chapters by Newman and Gordon in Davis and Kinna, 2009). From this perspective, anarchist utopianism is not a rigidly fixed rational projection of a perfected society of the future to be realised once and for all 'after the revolution', but a present-day process and a potential dimension of everyday life. Anarchist utopianism is, in short, profoundly shaped by the principle of prefiguration, which inspires anarchists to try to create a new world in the shell of the old by inhabiting, to the greatest extent possible, social relations that approximate their ideals for society as a whole.

True so far as it goes, this line of analysis tends to overlook the *temporally extended* nature of the present moment towards which anarchist aspirations are oriented. As the life and work of the temporal physicist Shevek in Le Guin's *The Dispossessed* demonstrates so dramatically, time may be understood as a correlation of future, past and present in which past and future *coexist* with the present *conjointly*. From this perspective, past and future are always found intertwined with the present, and actions undertaken in the present are necessarily entrained in a temporal trajectory that extends into the past and future (Davis, 2005: 3–36). It follows that anarchism is as much about the re-enactment of the possibilities of the past as it is an ideology focused on the present, or indeed the future. In the final section of this chapter we turn, therefore, from the future to the past in order to spotlight traces of the largely hidden history of anarchy in action.

Anarchy in action

So accustomed have most people now become to living in a world divided into nation states that they forget that for most of human history human beings lived without states. Indeed, the human species has lived in varied stateless societies for some forty or fifty thousand years. The state form did not emerge until roughly 5,500 years ago in Egypt, and long after its appearance most of the world's population continued to live in clans or tribes. Modern anthropology confirms, moreover, that in many of these stateless societies there is at most only the occasional *ad hoc* concentration of force, scarcely any political specialisation, and if authority exists at all it is delegated rather than imposed. Importantly, there is no vesting of the power to employ violence into the hands of a restricted group of commanders; power and force are instead widely diffused or dispersed (Marshall, 1993: 12–13, 17; Taylor, 1982: 33; Barclay, 1996: 29).

The state is thus an historical anomaly, one moreover which has always and everywhere established, extended and defended its hegemony by means of considerable violence. This violence, in turn, has engendered popular resistance, in which anarchist aspirations – and, from the nineteenth century to the present day, self-consciously revolutionary anarchists organised in popular social movements – have played a prominent part. The history of anarchism is thus not merely the history of an idea, but the history of a social movement extending, to focus on Europe alone for a moment, from the slave revolts of the ancient world, to the peasant risings of medieval Europe, to the English Revolution of the 1640s, to the revolutions in France in 1789 and 1848 and the Paris Commune of 1871 (Ward, 2004: 8). A truly global phenomenon, anarchism has both indigenous roots and distinctive grassroots movement offshoots on every inhabited continent in the world, from Asia to Africa and the Americas. In the twentieth century, it has played a key role in, for instance, the Mexican and Chinese Revolutions of 1911; the Russian Revolution in 1917; the Korean independence movement in the 1920s; the Indian independence movement and the *Sarvodaya* movement for a non-violent, land-based revolution; labour struggles in Argentina, Brazil, Chile, Cuba, France, Italy, Mexico, the Netherlands, Peru, Portugal and Uruguay; mass peasant movements in Bulgaria, Manchuria, Mexico, Spain and the Ukraine (Schmidt and van der Walt, 2009: 290–1); the global revolts of 1968; and of course the Spanish Revolution of 1936 and the continuing struggle against resurgent fascist groups.

In a recent study of anti-colonial activity in the Philippines, the historian of nationalism Benedict Anderson observes that anarchism was once the 'dominant element in the self-consciously internationalist radical Left' and 'the main vehicle of global opposition to industrial capitalism, autocracy, latifundism, and imperialism' (2005: 2, 54). Rarely, however, are these points acknowledged in mainstream or even radical history texts. The history of anarchism as a social movement is thus largely a hidden history of collective activity by ordinary people whose struggles have been written out of the 'official' historical record. Much as women were once written out of history (see on this subject Rowbotham, 1992), so too are anarchists, and for many of the same reasons. Indeed, as Judy Greenway has perceptively observed, the lively debates on feminist historiography that have flourished since the resurgence of the feminist movement in the 1970s have much to offer anarchists, 'not only on questions of gender, but – also of relevance to anarchists – for thinking about processes of marginalisation and misrepresentation' (2010: 8).

Those who are prepared to look beyond the mainstream histories will discover a rich, if widely dispersed, corpus of frequently outstanding scholarship documenting and critically analysing the achievements of anarchism in action. Collectively, this scholarship suggests that, far from being a utopia in the common-sense understanding of the term as an unachievable ideal of impossible perfection, anarchism is an eminently practical ideology that has already 'lifted a huge load of human misery' (Ward, 2004: 10). In Spain in the 1930s, for example, anarchists not only resisted the rise of fascism in the form of a military coup and insurrection by General Francisco Franco, they also undertook a social revolution that transformed the lives of millions. Over the course of three years (1936–39), in the midst of a civil war and despite the opposition of all the Spanish political parties and foreign powers including Nazi Germany, Mussolini's Italy and Stalinist Russia, rank-and-file anarchists among the workers and peasants spearheaded an unprecedented, large-scale social experiment in agricultural and industrial collectivisation. Assisted by the anarcho-syndicalist trade union the CNT (National Confederation of Labour) and the anarchist organisation the FAI (Anarchist Federation of Iberia), millions of workers and peasants took control of the land and the factories and began to work them without bosses, capitalist managers, landlords or the authority of the state. By the end of 1936 some three million men, women and children were living in rural and urban collectives based on the principle of self-management.

Many of these collectives abolished money and instituted economic equality in accordance with the communist principle 'From each according to his or her ability and to each according to his or her needs'. They built schools and hospitals, and made significant advances in eradicating illiteracy and providing essential medical services. They coordinated their activity through free association in regional federations, and actually increased production and communal wealth despite the shortage of labour created by the war effort. In place of formal representative democracy, they implemented a grassroots form of participatory democracy in which every member of the community proposed, discussed, planned and implemented major initiatives which affected their lives. In some of the rural collectives women who had previously been oppressed by illiteracy, poverty, male dominance and organised religion took on positions of responsibility and led the struggle to challenge the destructive roles of church and state in intimate life. A number of women organised an autonomous revolutionary women's group within the anarchist ranks, the 30,000-strong *Mujeres Libres* (Free Women), and campaigned for full gender equality, free sexual unions and the free availability of information about sexuality and birth control (see on the Spanish Revolution and/or the social and political background to it, Ackelsberg, 2004 [1991]; Brenan, 1950; Mintz, 1982; Leval, 1975; Peirats, 1990; Richards, 1983; Bookchin, 1998; Dolgoff, 1974).

Commenting on some of these momentous social changes in his eyewitness account *Homage to Catalonia*, George Orwell recalls arriving in Barcelona in late December 1936 to discover something 'startling and overwhelming'. It was the first time, he records, that he had ever been in a town where 'the working class was in the saddle': every shop and café had an inscription saying that it had been collectivised (even the bootblacks had been collectivised and their boxes painted in the red and black colours of the anarchists); waiters and shop-walkers looked him in the face and treated him as an equal; servile and ceremonial forms of speech had temporarily disappeared; there was no unemployment and were practically no beggars; and everywhere human beings were 'trying to behave as human beings and not as cogs in the capitalist machine'. Above all, Orwell recounts, there was 'a belief in the revolution and the future, a feeling of having suddenly emerged into an era of equality and freedom' (2001 [1938]: 32–3). Yet the achievements of the Spanish revolution were barely acknowledged at the time in the news media of Western Europe outside the journals of anarchism and the non-Soviet communist far Left (Ward, 2004: 24). Even today, many decades later, the history of anarchism in the Spanish Revolution is a largely forgotten history, including in Spain itself.

Also generally forgotten are the many smaller-scale or less dramatic victories that anarchism has won as part of a long-term process of 'hollowing out' systems of domination by building a new world within the shell of the old. Consider, as a case in point, the gender and sexual politics of anarchism and, more specifically, anarchist advocacy of 'free love' in place of traditional marriage arrangements sanctioned by church and state. Difficult to define precisely because of its different meanings in different social contexts, in Britain and the United States in the 1880s and 1890s many anarchists – women especially – saw free love as the basis of a wider social struggle around issues of gender and sexuality central to a critique of unfree and unequal societies. The term was used in this context in various ways, encompassing 'monogamous but dissoluble partnerships, non-exclusive "sexual varietism" and even – occasionally – passionate but non-sexual relationships' – all generally situated within a feminist framework of understanding linking free love to struggles around such issues as freedom of sexual expression, sex education, contraception, childcare and women's economic and social independence (Greenway, 2009: 158–9). Initially a subject of conversation in small circles of anarchist sex radicals, by the end of the 1890s free love had become a 'regular, if controversial topic of debate' in novels, plays and stories, newspaper articles and public meetings. It was the inspiration for some very public anarchist experiments in communal living, and a chief focus of public lectures by prominent anarchist women such as Emma Goldman, Lillian Harman and Voltairine de Cleyre (Greenway, 2009: 161–3).

Because the principle of free love implied the defence of any and all consensual relationships regardless of the gender of the individuals involved, the anarchist-feminist critique of marriage also opened up an ideological space within which same-sex eroticism could be legitimated. And this is precisely what happened in the aftermath of the 1895 trial and imprisonment of Oscar Wilde, which for many anarchists epitomised unjust state interference with the free expression of erotic desire, and thus spurred them to speak out on behalf of the right of people to choose their own partners free from state interference or social condemnation (Kissack, 2008: ch. 2). As the historian of sexuality Terence Kissack has documented, from the mid-1890s through the 1920s, key figures in the English-speaking anarchist movement debated and publicly defended the place of same-sex passion in the social order. Moreover, in the United States at least, they were alone in doing so. At a time when there were few public venues where the topic of homosexuality was openly discussed, let alone in a transformative political context, anarchist sex radicals 'developed and sustained a far-reaching and complex critique of "normal" social and sexual values, which circulated across a relatively broad public' (Kissack 2008: 4). They drew on the resources of a mass anarchist movement to convey their ideas to a wider public, succeeded in making homosexuality a topic of political discourse and debate, and thus 'helped to shift the sexual, cultural, and political landscape of the United States' (2008: 4).

Conclusion

Anarchism today is a very different political ideology and social movement than it was in the late nineteenth and early twentieth centuries, or indeed in the 1930s at the time of the Spanish Revolution. Two world wars, the establishment of the Soviet state, the spread of fascism and virulent nationalisms, the globalisation of monopoly capitalism, and severe political repression all took their toll on the global anarchist movement – to such an extent that by the mid-twentieth century some of anarchism's most distinguished scholars were proclaiming its demise as an organised mass movement and living body of ideas. It is now evident that such claims were premature. Anarchism is again thriving at the dawn of the twenty-first century, albeit in a form different in important respects from its pre-World War II incarnations. Perhaps most notably, the ideology is – for the time being at least – no longer sustained by a mass working-class base.

In an interesting and thought-provoking genealogical analysis of contemporary anarchist politics, Gordon argues that the chief roots of today's anarchist networks and ideas may be found in processes of intersection and fusion among non-explicitly anarchist radical social movements since the 1960s, including the radical, direct-action end of the ecological, anti-nuclear and anti-war movements, and of movements for women's, black, indigenous, LGBT and non-human animal liberation. In Gordon's historical narrative, accelerating networking and cross-fertilisation among these movements led to a convergence of political cultures and ideas, thus creating the necessary conditions for a full-blown anarchist revival around the turn of the millennium. Among the most prominent ideological features of the new anarchist formulation that emerged from this hybrid genealogy, Gordon contends, are the generalisation of the target of anarchist resistance from the state and capitalism to all forms of domination in society; a stronger emphasis on constructive direct action and prefigurative politics; and the rise of diversity to the status of a core anarchist value, resulting in an endorsement of pluralism and heterogeneity in anarchist approaches to liberation. Cumulatively, he suggests, these various qualitative changes add up to something of a 'paradigm shift' in anarchism (Gordon, 2008: 5–6, 29–30, 34–5, 40).

Persuasive up to a point, Gordon's characterisation of the roots of the 'new anarchism' overlooks the less visible grounded utopian roots linking contemporary anarchism to the unfulfilled promises of its revolutionary, radically democratic, predominantly working-class and libertarian socialist past. There is indeed a significant degree of discontinuity between anarchisms present and past, but there are also profound continuities obscured by the assumption of a paradigm shift or fundamental break in the anarchist tradition. And recognition of these continuities in turn raises important questions about contemporary anarchist ideology and its possible historical trajectories.

One such question concerns the respective roles in anarchist political theory and practice of tradition and innovation, a topic broached at the start of this chapter in the context of an analysis of current debates between anarchists inside and outside the academy. Specifically, we considered the possibility that the academic mainstreaming of anarchism, which has generated exciting new possibilities, may also signal the very real danger of the ideology's domestication, insofar as anarchism is transformed from a revolutionary social movement rooted in popular democratic social formations to an object of study by intellectual elites.

Another related but much broader question concerns the capacity of anarchism to continue to negotiate, without irreconcilable sectarian conflict, the deep ideological differences that will inevitably arise from these and other ongoing processes of change. One of the hallmarks of anarchist ideology has always been its enduring ability to embrace seemingly contradictory extremes. In the words of one recent commentator, anarchism is a cohesive school of thought 'that is comfortable with its own ambiguity and that revels in the productive possibilities of its inherent tensions' (Amster, 2012: 22). A protean and practice-grounded political ideology, anarchism is both traditional and innovative, scholarly and popular, reflective and action-oriented, libertarian and egalitarian, individualistic and communitarian, critical and constructive, confrontational and compassionate, destructive and creative, organised and spontaneous, rational and romantic, sensual and spiritual, natural and social, personal and political, feminine and masculine, rooted and cosmopolitan, evolutionary and revolutionary, pragmatic and utopian. Whether anarchism will be able to maintain this remarkable unity in diversity in a period of its profound ideological transformation is an open question, as is the future of anarchism itself.

Further reading

The best contemporary short introductions to anarchism are Colin Ward's *Anarchism: A Very Short Introduction* (2004), Uri Gordon's *Anarchy Alive! Anti-Authoritarian Politics from Practice to Theory* (2008) and David Graeber's *Fragments of an Anarchist Anthropology* (2004). The most comprehensive and reliable current history is Peter Marshall's *Demanding the Impossible* (2010).

There are a number of good books that explore the relationship between anarchism and other ideologies. On the relationship between anarchism and the liberal and socialist traditions, see Marshall's *Demanding the Impossible: A History of Anarchism* (2010), John Clark's *The Impossible Community: Realizing Communitarian Anarchism* (2013), Nathan Jun's *Anarchism and Political Modernity* (2012), Judith Suissa's *Anarchism and Education* (2010), Michael Taylor's *Community, Anarchy and Liberty* (1982) and April Carter's *The Political Theory of Anarchism* (1971). *Libertarian Socialism: Politics in Black and Red* (2012), edited by Alex Prichard *et al.*, focuses specifically on the fraught relationship between anarchism and Marxism. The stand-out work on the relationship between anarchism and ecologism, by the pioneer of social ecology, is Murray Bookchin's *The Ecology of Freedom: The Emergence and Dissolution of Hierarchy* (2005). See Andrew Light's edited volume *Social Ecology after Bookchin* (1998) for critical appraisals of Bookchin's work; Arne Naess's *Ecology, Community and Lifestyle* (1989) for an influential alternative 'deep' ecological perspective; John Zerzan's *Future Primitive Revisited* (2012) for an impassioned defence of anarcho-primitivism; Peter Ryley's *Making Another World Possible: Anarchism, Anti-Capitalism and Ecology in Late 19th and Early 20th Century Britain* (2013) for a less partisan but nonetheless lively scholarly history; Gary Snyder's *The Practice of the Wild* (1990) for a thoughtful Buddhist anarchist meditation; and Chaia Heller's *Ecology of Everyday Life: Rethinking the Desire for Nature* (1999) and Starhawk's *Truth or Dare: Encounters with Power, Authority, and Mystery* (1987) for provocative explorations of the interfaces between ecologism, feminism and spirituality. For specifically anarcha-feminist writing, the Dark Star Collective's *Quiet Rumours: An Anarcha-Feminist Reader* (2012) is a good first port of call. See also Martha Ackelsberg's ground-breaking *Free Women of Spain: Anarchism and the Struggle for the Emancipation of Women* (2004), and the feminist-friendly essays collected in Jamie Heckert and Richard Cleminson's edited volume *Anarchism and Sexuality: Ethics, Relationships and Power* (2011). The study of the topic of anarchism and nationalism is well served by Rudolf Rocker's classic *Nationalism and Culture* (1998 [1937]), as well as by Michael Forman's more recent scholarly survey *Nationalism and the International Labor Movement: The Idea of the Nation in Socialist and Anarchist Theory* (1998). Useful case studies in extra-European contexts include Benedict Anderson's *Under Three Flags: Anarchism and the Anti-Colonial Imagination* (2005), Maia Ramnath's *Decolonizing Anarchism: An Antiauthoritarian History of India's Liberation Struggle* (2011), Arif Dirlik's *Anarchism in the Chinese Revolution* (1991) and Ilham Khuri-Makdisi's *The Eastern Mediterranean and the Making of Global Radicalism, 1860–1914* (2010). See also the very helpful nation-specific anarchism entries in the eight-volume *The International Encyclopedia of Revolution and Protest: 1500 to the Present* (2009), ably edited by Immanuel Ness.

The best current guide to further research on anarchism may be found in the final part of Ruth Kinna's edited volume *The Continuum Companion to Anarchism* (2012), which includes a glossary of key terms, a list of resources, and country-specific bibliographies and reference materials. Helpful online resources include Dana Ward's Anarchy Archives (http://dwardmac.pitzer. edu/Anarchist_archives/), providing easy access to a range of transcribed and scanned documents by leading thinkers in the history of anarchism; the Research on Anarchism Forum (www.raforum.info/), a multi-lingual, up-to-date archive and database; and the Anarchist Studies Network (www.anarchist-studies-network.org.uk/), a UK-based resource which provides information about conferences and publishing opportunities, as well as subject-specific research material. The leading English-language specialist journal in the field is *Anarchist Studies* (www.lwbooks.co.uk/journals/anarchiststudies/contents. html). For original scholarly manuscripts, see the AK Press catalogue (www. akpress.org/) and the peer-reviewed *Contemporary Anarchist Studies* book series published by Continuum/Bloomsbury Press (www.bloomsbury.com/uk/series/contemporary-anarchist-studies/?pg=1).

More critical accounts of aspects of anarchist political thinking somewhat reductively and misleadingly grouped together under the label 'classical anarchism' may be found in a range of recent academic works influenced by postmodern and post-structuralist theory, including Saul Newman's *The Politics of Postanarchism* (2010), Todd May's *The Political Philosophy of Poststructuralist Anarchism* (1994) and Richard Day's *Gramsci is Dead: Anarchist Currents in the Newest Social Movements* (2005). David Miller's *Anarchism* (1984) is an older critical analysis of anarchist political ideology from a market socialist perspective. Far and away the most incisive critique of anarchist thought and practice ever undertaken, by an author committed to many of its principles, is Ursula K. Le Guin's outstanding ambiguously utopian novel *The Dispossessed* (1999 [1974]).

References

Ackelsberg, Martha (2004 [1991]) *Free Women of Spain: Anarchism and the Struggle for the Emancipation of Women*, Edinburgh and Oakland, CA: AK Press.

Amster, Randall (2012) *Anarchism Today*, Santa Barbara, CA: Praeger.

Amster, Randall, DeLeon, Abraham, Fernandez, Luis A., Nocella II, Anthony J. and Shannon, Deric (eds) (2009) *Contemporary Anarchist Studies: An Introductory Anthology of Anarchy in the Academy*, Abingdon and New York: Routledge.

Anderson, Benedict (2005) *Under Three Flags: Anarchism and the Anti-Colonial Imagination*, London and New York: Verso.

Barclay, Harold (1996 [1982]) *People without Government: An Anthropology of Anarchy*, London: Kahn and Averill.

Barker, Colin and Cox, Laurence (2002) 'What Have the Romans Ever Done for Us? Academic and Activist Forms of Movement Theorizing', in C. Barker and M. Tyldesley (eds) *Proceedings of the Eighth International Conference on 'Alternative Futures and Popular Protest'*, Manchester: Manchester Metropolitan University. Available online at http://eprints.nuim.ie/428/1/AFPPVIII.pdf.

Berneri, Marie Louise (1982 [1950]) *Journey through Utopia*, London: Freedom Press.

Bookchin, Murray (1980) 'Anarchism: Past and Present', *Comment: New Perspectives in Libertarian Thought*, 1.6. Available online at dwardmac.pitzer.edu/anarchist_archives/bookchin/pastandpresent.html.

—— (1998) *The Spanish Anarchists: The Heroic Years 1868–1936*, Oakland and Edinburgh: AK Press.

—— (2005) *The Ecology of Freedom: The Emergence and Dissolution of Hierarchy*, Oakland and Edinburgh: AK Press.

Boren, Mark (2001) *Student Resistance: A History of the Unruly Subject*, New York and London: Routledge.

Brenan, Gerald (1950) *The Spanish Labyrinth: An Account of the Social and Political Background of the Civil War*, 2nd ed., Cambridge: Cambridge University Press.

Brennan, John and Downs, Michael (1979) 'Anarchism and Utopian Tradition in *The Dispossessed*', in J. D. Olander and M. H. Greenberg (eds) *Ursula K. Le Guin*, New York: Taplinger.

Carter, April (1971) *The Political Theory of Anarchism*, London: Routledge and Kegan Paul.

Clark, John (1976) *Max Stirner's Egoism*, London: Freedom Press.

—— (1984) *The Anarchist Moment: Reflections on Culture, Nature and Power*, Montreal and Buffalo: Black Rose.

—— (2013) *The Impossible Community: Realizing Communitarian Anarchism*, London: Bloomsbury.

Constant, Benjamin (1988 [1819]) *The Liberty of the Ancients Compared with That of the Moderns*, in B. Fontana (ed.) *Political Writings*, Cambridge: Cambridge University Press.

Crick, Bernard (1987) *Socialism*, Minneapolis: University of Minnesota Press.

Dark Star Collective (2012) *Quiet Rumours: An Anarcha-Feminist Reader*, 3rd ed., Oakland and Edinburgh: AK Press.

Davis, Laurence (2005) 'The Dynamic and Revolutionary Utopia of Ursula K. Le Guin', in L. Davis and P. Stillman (eds) *The New Utopian Politics of Ursula K. Le Guin's The Dispossessed*, Lanham, MD: Lexington Books.

—— (2010) 'Social Anarchism and Lifestyle Anarchism: An Unhelpful Dichotomy', *Anarchist Studies*, 18.1, pp. 62–82.

—— (2012) 'History, Politics, and Utopia: Toward a Synthesis of Social Theory and Practice', in P. Vieira and M. Marder (eds) *Existential Utopia: New Perspectives on Utopian Thought*, New York and London: Continuum.

Davis, Laurence, and Kinna, Ruth (eds) (2009) *Anarchism and Utopianism*, Manchester: Manchester University Press.

Davis, Laurence, and Stillman, Peter (eds) (2005) *The New Utopian Politics of Ursula K. Le Guin's The Dispossessed*, Lanham, MD: Lexington Books.

Day, Richard (2005) *Gramsci Is Dead: Anarchist Currents in the Newest Social Movements*, London and Ann Arbor, MI: Pluto Press.

Dirlik, Arif (1991) *Anarchism in the Chinese Revolution*, Berkeley: University of California Press.

Dolgoff, Sam (ed.) (1974) *The Anarchist Collectives: Workers' Self-Management in the Spanish Revolution 1936–1939*, Montreal: Black Rose Books.

Feiten, Elmo (2013) 'Would the Real Max Stirner Please Stand Up?', *Anarchist Developments in Cultural Studies*, 2013.1, pp. 117–37.

Ferns, Chris (1999) *Narrating Utopia: Ideology, Gender, Form in Utopian Literature*, Liverpool: Liverpool University Press.

Forman, Michael (1998) *Nationalism and the International Labor Movement: The Idea of the Nation in Socialist and Anarchist Theory*, University Park, PA: Pennsylvania State University Press.

Franks, Benjamin (2006) *Rebel Alliances: The Means and Ends of Contemporary British Anarchisms*, Oakland and Edinburgh: AK Press and Dark Star.

Freedman, Carl (2000) *Critical Theory and Science Fiction*, Hanover and London: Wesleyan University Press.

Goldman, Emma (1927) 'Anarchism: What It Really Stands For', in *Anarchism and Other Essays*, 3rd revised ed., New York: Mother Earth Publishing Association. Available online at http://sunsite.berkeley.edu/goldman/Writings/Anarchism/anarchism.html.

—— (1972 [1912]) 'Socialism: Caught in the Political Trap', in A. K. Shulman (ed.) *Red Emma Speaks: Selected Writings and Speeches*, New York: Vintage. Available online at http://dwardmac.pitzer.edu/Anarchist_Archives/goldman/socialism.html.

Gordon, Uri (2008) *Anarchy Alive! Anti-Authoritarian Politics from Practice to Theory*, London and Ann Arbor, MI: Pluto.

—— (2009) 'Utopia in Contemporary Anarchism', in L. Davis and R. Kinna (eds) *Anarchism and Utopianism*, Manchester: Manchester University Press.

Graeber, David (2004) *Fragments of an Anarchist Anthropology*, Chicago: Prickly Paradigm.

Greenway, Judy (2009) 'Speaking Desire: Anarchism and Free Love as Utopian Performance in Fin de Siècle Britain', in L. Davis and R. Kinna (eds) *Anarchism and Utopianism*, Manchester: Manchester University Press.

—— (2010) 'The Gender Politics of Anarchist History: Re/Membering Women, Re/Minding Men', unpublished paper presented at the 2010 annual meeting of the Political Studies Association of the United Kingdom, Edinburgh. Available online at www.judygreenway.org.uk/anarchfem.html.

Heckert, Jamie and Cleminson, Richard (eds) (2011) *Anarchism and Sexuality: Ethics, Relationships and Power*, Abingdon and New York: Routledge.

Heller, Chaia (1999) *Ecology of Everyday Life: Rethinking the Desire for Nature*, Montreal: Black Rose Books.

Jun, Nathan (2012) *Anarchism and Political Modernity*, New York and London: Continuum.

Jun, Nathan and Wahl, Shane (eds) (2009) *New Perspectives on Anarchism*, Lanham, MD: Lexington Books.

Khuri-Makdisi, Ilham (2010) *The Eastern Mediterranean and the Making of Global Radicalism, 1860–1914*, Berkeley: University of California Press.

Killjoy, Margaret (2009) *Mythmakers and Lawbreakers: Anarchist Writers on Fiction*, Oakland and Edinburgh: AK Press.

Kinna, Ruth [ed.] (2012) *The Continuum Companion to Anarchism*, London and New York: Continuum.

Kissack, Terence (2008) *Free Comrades: Anarchism and Homosexuality in the United States, 1895–1917*, Oakland and Edinburgh: AK Press.

Knight, Ryan (2013) 'Mikhail Bakunin's Post-Ideological Impulse: The Continuity Between Classical and New Anarchism', *Anarchist Developments in Cultural Studies*, 2013.1, pp. 171–88.

Kropotkin, Peter (1910) 'Anarchism', in *The Encyclopaedia Britannica*, 11th ed. Available online at http://dwardmac.pitzer.edu/Anarchist_Archives/kropotkin/britanniaanarchy.html.

—— (1990 [1914]) 'Preface', in Emile Pataud and Emile Pouget, *How We Shall Bring About the Revolution: Syndicalism and the Cooperative Commonwealth*, London: Pluto.

Le Guin, Ursula K. (1999 [1974]) *The Dispossessed: An Ambiguous Utopia*, London: Millennium.

Leval, Gaston (1975) *Collectives in the Spanish Revolution*, London: Freedom Press.

Light, Andrew (ed.) (1998) *Social Ecology after Bookchin*, New York: The Guilford Press.

Lloyd, Moya (2003) 'The End of Ideology?', in R. Eccleshall, A. Finlayson, V. Geoghegan, M. Kenny, M. Lloyd, I. MacKenzie and R. Wilford (eds) *Political Ideologies: An Introduction*, 3rd ed., London and New York: Routledge.

McKay, Iain (2008) *An Anarchist FAQ*, vol. 1, Oakland and Edinburgh: AK Press.

McLaughlin, Paul (2007) *Anarchism and Authority: A Philosophical Introduction to Classical Anarchism*, Aldershot: Ashgate.

Marshall, Peter (1993) *Demanding the Impossible: A History of Anarchism*, London: Fontana.

—— (2010) *Demanding the Impossible: A History of Anarchism*, Oakland, CA: PM Press.

May, Todd (1994) *The Political Philosophy of Poststructuralist Anarchism*, University Park, PA: Pennsylvania State University Press.

Mill, John Stuart (1989 [1859]) *On Liberty*, in S. Collini (ed.) *On Liberty and Other Writings*, Cambridge: Cambridge University Press.

Miller, David (1984) *Anarchism*, London: Dent.

—— (ed.) (1991) *Liberty*, Oxford: Oxford University Press.

Mintz, Jerome (1982) *The Anarchists of Casas Viejas*, Chicago and London: University of Chicago Press.

Morris, William (1986 [1886]) *A Dream of John Ball*, in A. L. Morton (ed.) *Three Works by William Morris*, London: Lawrence and Wishart.

Naess, Arne (1989) *Ecology, Community and Lifestyle*, Cambridge: Cambridge University Press.

Ness, Immanuel (ed.) (2009) *The International Encyclopedia of Revolution and Protest: 1500 to the Present*, Oxford: Blackwell.

Newman, Saul (2001) 'Spectres of Stirner: A Contemporary Critique of Ideology', *Journal of Political Ideologies*, 6.3, pp. 309–30.

—— (2010) *The Politics of Postanarchism*, Edinburgh: Edinburgh University Press.

Orwell, George (2001) *Orwell in Spain*, London: Penguin Books.

Peirats, José (1990) *Anarchists in the Spanish Revolution*, London: Freedom Press.

Prichard, Alex, Kinna, Ruth, Pinta, Saku and Berry, David (eds) (2012) *Libertarian Socialism: Politics in Black and Red*, Houndmills: Palgrave.

Purkis, Jonathan and Bowen, James (eds) (2004) *Changing Anarchism: Anarchist Theory and Practice in a Global Age*, Manchester: Manchester University Press.

Ramnath, Maia (2011) *Decolonizing Anarchism: An Antiauthoritarian History of India's Liberation Struggle*, Oakland and Edinburgh: AK Press.

Richards, Vernon (1983) *Lessons from the Spanish Revolution (1936–1939)*, London: Freedom Press.

Rocker, Rudolf (1998) *Nationalism and Culture*, Montreal: Black Rose Books.

—— (n.d.) *Anarchism and Anarcho-Syndicalism*, London: Phoenix.

Rowbotham, Sheila (1992) *Hidden from History: 300 Years of Women's Oppression and the Fight Against it*, London: Pluto.

Ryley, Peter (2013) *Making Another World Possible: Anarchism, Anti-Capitalism and Ecology in Late 19th and Early 20th Century Britain*, London: Bloomsbury.

Schmidt, Michael and van der Walt, Lucien (2009) *Black Flame: The Revolutionary Class Politics of Anarchism and Syndicalism*, Oakland and Edinburgh: AK Press.

Shukaitis, Stevphen and Graeber, David [eds.] (2007) *Constituent Imagination: Militant Investigations, Collective Theorization*, Oakland and Edinburgh: AK Press.

Snyder, Gary (1990) *The Practice of the Wild*, Berkeley: Counterpoint.

Starhawk (1987) *Truth or Dare: Encounters with Power, Authority, and Mystery*, New York: HarperCollins.

Stirner, Max (1995 [1844]) *The Ego and Its Own*, ed. David Leopold, Cambridge: Cambridge University Press.

Suissa, Judith (2010) *Anarchism and Education: A Philosophical Perspective*, Oakland, CA: PM Press.

Sylvan, Richard (2007) 'Anarchism', in R. E. Goodin and P. Pettit (eds) *A Companion to Contemporary Political Philosophy*, 2nd ed., Oxford: Blackwell.

Taylor, Michael (1982) *Community, Anarchy and Liberty*, Cambridge: Cambridge University Press.

Thoreau, Henry David (1960 [1849]) *On the Duty of Civil Disobedience*, in *Walden and 'Civil Disobedience'*, New York and Scarborough, Ontario: NAL Penguin.

Van der Walt, Lucien (2011) 'Counterpower, Participatory Democracy, Revolutionary Defence: Debating Black Flame, Revolutionary Anarchism and Historical Marxism', *International Socialism: A Quarterly Journal of Socialist Theory*, 130. Available online at www.isj.org.uk/?id=729.

Ward, Colin (2004) *Anarchism: A Very Short Introduction*, Oxford: Oxford University Press.

Wieck, David (n.d.) 'The Negativity of Anarchism', *Interrogations: International Review of Anarchist Research*. Available online at http://quadrant4.org/anarchism.html.

Woodcock, George (1962) *Anarchism: A History of Libertarian Ideas and Movements*, New York: Meridian.

Zerzan, John (2012) *Future Primitive Revisited*, Port Townsend, WA: Feral House.

Multiculturalism

Caroline Walsh

How should the state treat ethnic minorities (whether immigrant communities, national minorities or indigenous peoples) within its jurisdiction? Should it support special legislation and policies, such as group representation and rights, to recognise and accommodate the cultural diversity of these groups (i.e. their distinct identities, languages and practices)? Or should the state instead insist that minority cultures are assimilated into the mainstream culture, whether fully or substantially (Parekh, 2000: 6)?

The development of multiculturalism over the last four decades in Western liberal democratic states (and their former colonies), including Australia, Belgium, Canada, Spain, the Netherlands, Sweden and the UK, brought these questions to the heart of political debate. This is because multiculturalism focuses on relations between majority and minority cultural groups in the public sphere, defending the political and legal accommodation of cultural differences to ensure equality between and among these groups. The emergence of the ideology in the West can be traced to the political mobilisation from the 1960s onwards by ethnic minorities within these states, resisting assimilation into the mainstream culture, and asserting their claims for institutional recognition of their particular identities, languages, practices, needs and interests.

Multiculturalists support the accommodation of cultural diversity for different reasons, which reflect the range of competing theoretical perspectives that influence them, including communitarianism, liberalism and feminism. Under this influence, different versions of multiculturalism have developed.[1] To understand multiculturalism as ideology is therefore to first understand the nature of its relationships to other ideologies.

Multiculturalism is not a neatly definable ideology, in the sense that it does not represent a uniform philosophical outlook or political doctrine (Parekh, 2000: 1). In calling for cultural accommodation, multiculturalist projects make various assumptions about culture and cultural diversity. Notably, these include assumptions about the nature of culture; the significance of culture to individuals' identities, including their political identities; the distinctness of the boundaries between cultural groups and the importance of publicly protecting these boundaries; and the cultural roots of political disagreement, social conflict and injustice. Where multiculturalists disagree among themselves – and with (non-multiculturalist) others – is in relation to debate about the normative and political implications of holding different versions of these assumptions. Debate over these assumptions includes whether multiculturalist approaches to political life rely on mistaken views of culture; whether they offer adequate protections for members of less powerful groups within cultural minorities; whether they fully grasp the relationship between the cultural and economic dimensions of justice (shorthanded as recognition and redistribution); and, whether they properly set the limits of toleration for cultural diversity (see Laden and Owen, 2007).

This chapter discusses these substantive issues in the context of looking first at the emergence of multiculturalism in Western liberal democracies under the influence of communitarianism, and then at how multiculturalism can be characterised as resistance to cultural homogeneity. After that, we consider the relationship between multiculturalism and two other ideologies: liberalism and feminism. The chapter then concludes with an examination of the claim that multiculturalism is on the wane.

Emergence of multiculturalism in theory and practice

Explicit support for multiculturalist ideas in the political decision-making of Western liberal democracies emerged in Canada in 1971, followed by Australia a few years later. Both countries officially designated themselves multicultural. In both cases, the question of accommodation for Aboriginal peoples was a central issue, complemented in the Canadian case by accommodation of a particular national minority: the Québécois. Both cases have also involved issues around the rights and status of immigrant communities. Within Europe, measures to accommodate cultural diversity in respect of national minorities, indigenous peoples and immigrant communities surfaced in the 1980s, and extended into the 1990s. Interest in cultural diversity also steadily increased within political theory and philosophy during the same period, with the result that, by the late 1980s, multiculturalist ideas were a major source of debate in the literature.

In the main, the adoption of multiculturalist measures by liberal democratic states has tended to take the form of a 'patchwork of policies', as opposed to any kind of coherent, coordinated approach across all areas of the public sphere (Vertovec and Wessendorf, 2010: 2). Furthermore, a given state may adopt contrasting multiculturalist positions for different kinds of ethnic minorities within its jurisdiction. For instance, although Sweden has resisted land claims and self-government rights for the indigenous Sami, it has been notably receptive to multiculturalism for immigrants; and although Switzerland has been a 'model' for accommodation of national minorities in respect of language rights and regional autonomy, it is 'perhaps the most exclusionary country in Europe' in respect of multiculturalism for immigrants (Kymlicka, 2007a: 79).

Of course, the question of how the state should respond to diversity was of interest to Western political philosophy in the centuries before its emergence as multiculturalism, not least in relation to the toleration of religious pluralism (Laden and Owen, 2007: 2ff.). In this section, however, we get some sense of what it was that triggered the renewed interest in the question of diversity from the 1970s onwards, and what has since sustained that interest in theory and practice. We consider how the emergence of multiculturalism may be viewed as a response to perceived limitations within liberalism, in both theory and practice. Liberalism itself also impacted upon the subsequent development of multiculturalism, and that is examined later.

Response to the limitations of liberalism

Multiculturalists have different relationships to liberalism depending on the particular brand of liberalism in question, and so the distance between the two ideologies is not fixed. Multiculturalism has been called the 'child of liberal egalitarianism', and it is important to understand why in order to more fully explain its emergence (Modood, 2007: 8). Liberalism is covered in depth in chapter 2, so it is not necessary to rehearse its central tenets. It will suffice to sketch the kind of liberalism to which theorists who first emerged as multiculturalist strongly objected: namely, abstract, 'difference-blind', profoundly individualist liberalism.

In over-simplified terms, liberalism is an individualist doctrine because it designates the individual the ultimate unit of moral concern (Pogge, 1994: 89), and consequently seeks to protect the needs and interests of all individuals equally by treating all persons similarly. Liberals contend that in order to judge individuals' claims in equal consideration, public institutions must act with neutrality or impartiality (i.e. without moral arbitrariness). Institutions act impartially by abstracting from (or ignoring) supposedly morally irrelevant differences between people, such as gender, religion and ethnicity. By abstracting from these contextual differences to work out the requirements of justice, 'difference-blind' liberal moral reasoning is said to rely on a 'pre-social' conception of the person (the 'disembedded' self). This idea of impartially protecting the freedom and equality of all citizens informs the liberal notion of universal or unitary citizenship. Liberals originally defended the notion of unitary citizenship partly on the basis that it protected a certain kind of diversity, that is, religious pluralism. As we shall later see, some liberals today also invoke the supposed virtue of unitary citizenship when arguing that liberalism is intrinsically capable of handling cultural diversity without taking a multiculturalist turn (Yack, 2002: 108; see Barry, 2001).

Multiculturalist arguments against the homogenising policies of Western liberal democratic states have directly challenged 'difference-blind', abstract liberalism by seeking to demonstrate how treating individuals equally in the public sphere does in fact require decision-makers to take account of cultural group membership as a morally relevant difference among people. So, for example, in Britain in the 1970s, in a cultural exception to motoring law, Sikh motorcyclists were granted permission to wear turbans instead of motorcycle helmets. This followed Sikhs' refusal to wear helmets after their mandatory introduction in 1972, and a subsequent campaign for the cultural exception on grounds of freedom of religion.

Influence of communitarianism

In formulating its challenges to liberalism in the 1970s and 1980s, multicultural-ism was initially informed by the attack on philosophical liberalism from communitarianism. Communitarians draw attention to the fundamental significance of community membership for moral reasoning. For them, moral enquiry should take seriously the social embeddedness of persons by appealing to the historical values, social practices and relationships that uniquely constitute shared ways of life. In other words, communitarian reasoning is antithetical to the notion of the disembedded self found in abstract liberalism.

The early communitarian critique of philosophical liberalism is famously captured by Michael Walzer. He objected to John Rawls's use of the 'original position' (a device of abstraction) to work out principles of justice for modern constitutional democracies (Walzer, 1981). Within Rawls's model, ideal (i.e. imagined) representatives of persons deliberate without knowledge of the differences between them in order to select appropriate principles from the standpoint of everyone. Differences between people are judged by him to be morally contingent or random information, that is, information that should not be taken into moral consideration. Walzer complains that hypothetical reasoning threatens political and cultural pluralism by causing citizens to forfeit democratic control over their own lives (Walzer, 1981: 395). To him, principles of justice should not cohere with abstracted truths, but with the social meanings embedded in ordinary, everyday political life, and consequently should be the product of actual democratic deliberation among actual citizens.

Under the influence of communitarianism, multiculturalism emerged as ideas that declared the failure of abstract, 'difference-blind' liberalism to do justice to, and secure equality for, all in Western multi-ethnic societies. The substance of this claim was that difference-blind principles, institutions and policies fail to protect the needs and interests of some individuals (members of minority cultures) as well as they protect the needs and interests of other individuals (members of majority cultures). The former include those constituting ethnic immigrant communities, national minorities and so-called first nations or indigenous peoples. For multiculturalists, this failure was apparent in the continuing existence within liberal democratic states in the 1960s and thereafter of deep structural inequalities derived from historical ethnic and racial hierarchies (Kymlicka, 2008: 278). These inequalities were such that minority cultures in Western liberal democracies could still face marginalisation and exclusion (whether social, political or economic), despite seminal developments in so-called 'rights culture' associated with both the post-World War II human rights revolution and the 1960s civil rights movements (Kymlicka, 2008).

Political mobilisation

Under the influence of these developments in rights culture and social protest, cultural minorities in Western states, like the Québécois in Canada,

Catholics in Northern Ireland, Caribbean immigrants to the UK and the Basques and Catalans in Spain, were inspired by ideas about freedom and equality (Kymlicka, 2007a: 90). In consequence, they became more rights-conscious and began to politically mobilise, demanding equality between groups as an entitlement and refusing to assimilate into the mainstream culture (Kymlicka, 2007a: 91). For instance, in Britain, the entry of multiculturalism into political debate can be traced in part to the refusal of South Asian and Afro-Caribbean immigrant communities in the 1960s to assimilate; while, in Germany, it can be traced in part to the refusal of large numbers of immigrant 'guest workers' from Turkey and elsewhere to assimilate (Parekh, 2000: 5).

Broadly, multiculturalist equality is about non-domination, which promotes self-determination for minorities by limiting the possibility for domination by majority cultural groups. Newly mobilised minorities in Western liberal democratic states from the 1960s onwards looked beyond the common civil and political rights of individual citizenship in order to redefine democratic inclusion in their own terms. Under this redefinition, genuine democratic inclusion meant public recognition and assistance for minorities' distinct identities, languages and practices (Kymlicka, 2007a: 16). In this sense, multiculturalism is said to emerge in, and be a response to, 'real world politics', that is, actual struggles by minorities for justice, equality and freedom (Levey, 2009: 85).

So the multiculturalist critique adopts the values traditionally associated with liberalism (such as equality and autonomy) and reinterprets them by giving them new meanings in support of political claim-making by cultural minorities in liberal democracies. It is for this reason that multiculturalism has been called the 'child of liberal egalitarianism', but not necessarily a 'faithful' child (Modood, 2007: 8). From this perspective, the emergence of multiculturalism depends upon certain preconditions to do with liberalisation, democratisation and human rights (Kymlicka, 2007a). It is also suggested that where dominant cultural groups do not fear for their geo-political or individual security, they are more likely to accept the claims of minorities for public recognition, so security is cited as another precondition (Kymlicka, 2007a: 133). The limited availability of these preconditions outside of the Western liberal democratic states is said to explain the relative concentration of multiculturalism there. Of course, the social problem of conflicting group claims that multiculturalism addresses is not confined to such states. The important differential rests with how groups in liberal democratic states have politically mobilised against this problem and also with how their governments have responded to that mobilisation.

There was, however, no consistency in how governments in liberal democracies responded to the political mobilisation of cultural minorities within their borders: some were more receptive to multicultural accommodation than others. For example, notable cases where governments responded positively to multiculturalism in respect of national minorities include the Spanish, Belgian and Canadian cases. In each case, a form of territorial, federal autonomy was granted: to the Basques and Catalans, the Flemish, and the Québécois, respectively. Notable cases where governments have been particularly unreceptive to multiculturalism for immigrant communities include the Swedish and Swiss cases. As we shall later see, with the so-called 'retreat from multiculturalism', there has been a general disengagement with multiculturalism across Western liberal democracies in recent decades.

Multiculturalism as resistance to cultural homogeneity

So far it has been suggested that multiculturalism emerged in political theory as ideas that declared the inability of difference-blind, abstract liberalism to do justice *to all* in multicultural societies. In this section, we explore how the multiculturalist critique explains this inability by drawing attention to the relationship between culture and power within state institutions, which we can abbreviate as cultural homogeneity or dominance.

Multiculturalists resist cultural homogeneity (Taylor, 1994: 43; Parekh, 2000: 1) on the basis that it jeopardises the well-being of members of cultural minorities. Cultural homogeneity, which encompasses power inequalities, occurs when the norms, habits and symbols underlying the public institutions of a given state reflect the perspective of that state's majority culture and exclude the perspective(s) of its minority culture(s). Power inequalities arise insofar as the majority culture is placed in a privileged position and minority cultural groups are consequently subordinated. Where the particular identities, values, needs and interests of minorities are not institutionally recognised, they can face injustices marked by different kinds of marginalisation (economic, political, and so on). Cultural homogeneity or dominance is therefore so named because it entails the homogenisation of difference in public institutions, whereby one cultural group is publicly dominant while others are excluded.

Cultural homogenisation in the state occurs through forces and processes that promote linguistic and institutional integration for all citizens: uniform language laws, education laws, citizenship laws, and so on (Kymlicka, 2001: 1ff.). So, for example, the state might oppose minority claims for bilingual education and bilingual media. Or, as was the case with the headscarf controversies in France and Germany, the state might insist on dress codes in public schools and not permit cultural exceptions to that code.

The French case, which became known as 'l'affaire du foulard' (the scarf affair), originated with the exclusion of three scarf-wearing Muslim pupils from their school in Creil in 1989, and grew over subsequent years with other exclusions from other schools. Following court action, the controversy was eventually legislatively addressed by the French Parliament in 2004, when it banned the wearing of any 'ostentatious signs of religious belonging in the public sphere', including a ban on the wearing of the scarf in public schools (Benhabib, 2010: 457). Parliamentarians who passed the law interpreted the wearing of the scarf as 'part of a growing political threat of Islam to the values of *laïcité*' (Benhabib, 2010: 457), which denotes the French state's commitment to secular values and a public sphere that is consequently neutral toward religions (Benhabib, 2010).

In the German case, a school in the state of Baden-Württemberg refused to employ Fereshta Ludin, a Muslim teacher of Afghani origin and a German citizen, because she insisted on teaching with her head covered. A court case ensued in which Ms Ludin argued that the refusal violated her religious freedom. Following lower court rulings, in 2003 the Federal Constitutional Court in effect 'passed the buck' to regional democratic legislatures to legislatively settle the matter by clarifying their positions (Phillips, 2007: 115). Since then, several regional states in Germany have passed legislation banning the wearing of headscarves by teachers in public schools.

In each case, the importance of allowing cultural exceptions to dress codes was articulated as an identity issue and a rights issue (i.e. freedom of religion and conscience). But this importance was ultimately overshadowed by state responses that turned the headscarf from a religious item of clothing, denoting a subjective choice, into a political symbol requiring public regulation (Benhabib, 2010: 465).

Multiculturalism, cultural homogeneity and nation-building

Culturally homogenising measures are best understood as part of the nation-building programmes that characterise the modern state project (Kymlicka, 2001: 2; Parekh, 2000: 179–85). Nation-building is intended to generate and consolidate distinct identities for citizens attached to particular territorial areas and, as such, homogenising measures institutionalise the notion of unitary citizenship. As we have seen, liberals traditionally defend this notion because they believe that instituting difference-blindness allows the state to deal with pluralism without bias. The multiculturalist critique retorts that if the state is already embedded in the values of its majority culture, then the liberal notion of public sphere impartiality is an 'illusory' ideal (Young, 1987: 68) and the concept of difference-blindness is spurious (Taylor, 1994: 43). In short, according to this critique, if the state is already culturally embedded or immersed in the majority's perspective, then clearly it cannot handle cultural pluralism without bias.

Although they resist cultural assimilation within the state, multiculturalists still acknowledge the need to cultivate a common sense of belonging (Parekh, 2000: 12) and a common focus within multicultural societies (Taylor, 2001: 123), for the sake of political stability and social cohesion and to facilitate the kind of common debate required by democratic political decision-making. So they are not opposed to nation-building efforts *per se*, but only to any deleterious impact that these efforts would have on cultural minorities. Hence multiculturalists argue that in order to prevent injustices against minorities, nation-building efforts must be constrained by special rights for minority cultures against the larger community, whether a national minority comprising indigenous people or an immigrant minority (Kymlicka, 2001).

Minority rights provide public recognition and assistance for cultural difference (embodied in distinct identities, languages and practices). For instance, this might include land claim and treaty rights for Aboriginal peoples, or, as in the case of the Canadian multiculturalist model, it might involve the granting of minority language rights and provincial autonomy. EU policy also protects and promotes minority and regional languages, such as Irish in Northern Ireland and Catalan in Spain. This language protection is provided for, in part, by Article 22 of the European Charter of Fundamental Rights, which affirms the EU's respect for 'cultural, religious and linguistic diversity'.

In resisting the cultural assimilation that the nation-state imposes on migrants and minorities (Modood, 2008a: 549), multiculturalism addresses the question of how to genuinely institutionalise relations of equality between majority and minority cultural groups, whereby minorities would receive both just recognition and a just share of economic and political power (Parekh, 2000: 343). It is argued that the norms governing these relations cannot originate in one culture, but must be the product of cross-group (intercultural) democratic dialogue (Parekh, 2000: 13). For this to happen, minorities must be actively listened to in the public sphere through deliberative democratic opportunities, so as to articulate their own distinct perspectives, needs and interests. To assist this political mobilisation of minorities, multiculturalists promote diverse measures such as state funding of ethnocultural associations and minority language media (Kymlicka, 2007a: 66ff.).

Different types of minorities can make different types of claims for justice against/within their states. While the shared goal of every kind of minority political claim-making is the realisation of meaningful equality, national minorities' claims, such as those of the Québécois in Canada and the Catalans and Basques in Spain, are also often bound up with the notion of political independence.

In practice, treating individuals equally by requiring public institutions to take account of cultural identity can mean promoting a range of group-differentiated measures. As noted, it could mean supporting minority rights. Alternatively, it could instead mean sponsoring formal systems of group representation aimed specifically at increasing the number of persons from minorities in legislatures, governing bodies, and so on. In

Northern Ireland, for example, the accommodation of diversity articulated in the Belfast Agreement includes a number of guarantees in terms of group representation.

In acknowledging the need to cultivate a common sense of public belonging in liberal democratic states, multiculturalists stress the importance of deliberative democracy both as a way of handling cultural and economic disputes between groups and as a way of achieving cross-group alliances and agreement on all kinds of public issues beyond the strictly cultural (Young, 2001b: 121). Moreover, they argue that if we restrict ourselves to theorising issues of social conflict over cultural group differences, then we lose sight of social conflicts that arise from differentials in structural power and the division of labour (Young, 2007: 88). From this perspective, public dialogue must cut across all kinds of group differences to genuinely maximise conditions of democratic inclusion and citizenship within multicultural societies. Only then can equal voice and equal influence be effectively extended to the most vulnerable and marginalised (Young, 2001b: 121).

So, the multiculturalist critique advocates rethinking the relationship between power and culture in the public domain of liberal democratic states with a view to treating minorities' claims in equal standing. In effect, they advocate that states should take a multiculturalist turn. State resistance to taking such a turn is exemplified by West Germany's treatment of its guest workers in the 1980s. Throughout the 1960s and 1970s guest workers arrived in West Germany in considerable numbers, most of whom came from Turkey. The state considered these immigrants temporary residents, but by the mid-1980s it was clear that West Germany was 'home to a permanent and "foreign" underclass' (Lenard, 2012: 188). The state's response was to adopt an integration policy, which critics observe was essentially an assimilationist policy, since it brought stricter conditions for granting and renewing residence permits, which resulted in an expanded basis for the deportation of these guest workers (Lenard, 2012).

So far we have seen how multiculturalism emerged as a reaction to the apparent failure of liberalism to do justice to minority cultures; in the next section we examine how the ideology subsequently developed in part as an attempt to rehabilitate liberalism.

Development of multiculturalism: rehabilitating liberalism

Multiculturalists have different relationships to liberalism depending on how optimistically they view the possibility of rehabilitating liberalism in order to make it more meaningfully responsive to cultural diversity. And liberals have different relationships to multiculturalism depending on how much, if indeed at all, they believe in the need for such rehabilitation.

Optimism about the possibility of rehabilitating liberalism in order to make it appropriately responsive to cultural diversity falls under the rubric of 'liberal multiculturalism'. This theoretical perspective interprets multiculturalism as 'a concept that is both guided and constrained by a foundational commitment to principles of individual freedom and equality' (Kymlicka, 2007a: 7). Accordingly, liberal multiculturalists attempt to accommodate multiculturalist arguments within liberal frameworks by allowing minority rights, but with the added proviso that liberal equality and autonomy should both support *and* check cultural and identity claims (Levey, 2009: 92).

Liberal multiculturalism views the recognition of cultural group membership as essential for individual well-being. The link between recognition and well-being was notably articulated by Charles Taylor (1994). He observed that the language and historical narratives of cultural groups constitute the lens through which the world is interpreted and experienced. Experience of cultural meaning provides the preconditions of identity formation. Withholding due respect from others in social relations can therefore distort self-identity, leading to 'a false ... reduced mode of being' (Taylor, 1994: 25). Recognition, on this view, thus constitutes a 'vital human need' (Taylor, 1994: 26).

The development of liberal multiculturalism has prompted sharply contrasting reactions from other liberals. Some hold that cultural rights are unnecessary because the liberal concepts of toleration, freedom and equality can adequately accommodate the needs and interests of minority groups. Others assert that if our reasons for supporting group-differentiated treatment have to do with increasing social integration and eliminating unfair inequalities, then we need only support temporary multi-culturalist measures, which cease when the unjust inequality ceases (Loobuyck, 2005). The obvious counterclaim to this liberal position is that if the faults of liberalism that make it inadequately responsive to cultural diversity are permanent, then we need permanent group-differentiated treatment measures to correct those faults: that is, minority rights (Eisenberg, 2005).

The more general point is that the group-differentiated treatment of individuals can worry liberals because it challenges the principle of equal treatment under law. So, for instance, the nature and extent of additional rights and resources that Australia and Canada have given to their cultural minorities to help them flourish have concerned some liberals in these countries (Parekh, 2000: 262).

The next two sections focus on key claims in the liberal critique of multiculturalism, by exploring, first, whether multiculturalist approaches to justice and political life necessarily rely on essentialist views of culture and, second, whether they sufficiently protect members of less powerful groups within cultural minorities.

Avoiding cultural essentialism

In this section, we consider what it means to essentialise culture and whether multiculturalist projects necessarily presuppose essentialist views.

By seeking to accommodate cultural differences, multiculturalists suppose that it is readily possible to discern these differences in the first place, that is, to discern what it is that distinguishes (membership of) one cultural group from (membership of) another. For example, in arguments for multicultural accommodation for first peoples in the Australian and Canadian cases, assumptions have been made about what constitutes Aboriginal cultural belonging; in arguments for accommodation of national minorities in the Spanish case, presuppositions have been made about the nature of Catalan and Basque culture; and in arguments for cultural accommodation in 'host' countries across Europe, assumptions have been made about the nature of different kinds of immigrant group-belonging.

In making these assumptions, many multiculturalists rely on 'a logic of identity' (Young, 2001b). On this logic, a cultural group is depicted as 'a unified entity defined by a set of [essential] attributes all its members share' and, since groups are enclosed, cultural difference entails 'exclusive otherness' (Young, 2001b: 118). Take, for example, Kymlicka, whose project supposes two basic categories of cultural groups in multicultural societies, whose members share basic attributes: ethnic immigrant minorities and non-immigrant national minorities (Kymlicka, 2001). His project requires these groups to be readily discernible and distinct.

It has been suggested that the essentialisation of culture tends to involve three basic assumptions (Mason, 2007). It is assumed that certain people – whether, say, national minorities such as the Flemish in Belgium, first peoples such as the Australian Aboriginals or immigrant communities in host countries like Germany and France – share certain characteristics exclusively. It is further assumed that cultures are neatly packaged, separated from one another and internally homogeneous, for instance, as in the Spanish case: Catalan culture versus Basque culture. Finally, it is assumed that we can identify a group's 'authentic' culture and so determine when a group develops in a false or 'inauthentic' way (Mason, 2007: 223–5). Because essentialism makes it more difficult for us to see what it is that people from different cultural groups may have in common (in terms of shared values and interests), we can end up viewing peoples as more innately different than they actually are (Phillips, 2007: 25). In effect, the essentialisation of culture ignores both divisions within and similarities across cultural groups.

Reliance on these essentialist assumptions makes it difficult for us to accurately discern the demands of justice in culturally diverse contexts, for at least three reasons. First, by underplaying internal diversity, cultural essentialism ignores the values and needs of groups *within* minorities. In large part, this is because if we interpret multiculturalism as protecting 'authentic' practices, then we risk privileging the perspective of conservative elites intent on preserving the *status quo*, since we make it possible for cultural spokespersons to denounce internal group claims as 'inauthentic'.

Second, the essentialisation of culture can misrepresent the nature of political disagreement by exaggerating how far culture determines people's political behaviour, thereby distorting what is at stake in democratic deliberation over minority claims. Political disagreement is complex and multi-layered. Because in their associational life people actually come together in many ways over different value issues, even when they might disagree on others, modern life is marked by overlapping values between people from different cultural groups (Young, 1995). On this view, contemporary social life is regulated far less by cultural affiliation than theorists who rely on essentialist conceptions of culture would have us believe.

Third, the essentialisation of culture takes little account of the effect of globalisation on identity. The accelerated interaction across cultural borders involving people, ideas and influences brought about by the forces and processes of globalisation adds to the complexity of people's lives. Even though cultural allegiances certainly remain important in an increasingly globalised world, these shifting patterns of association and interaction make it even less tenable to essentialise cultural differences by presenting cultures as internally homogeneous and closed-off from one another.

Multiculturalism has been variously censured for relying on all of the basic assumptions that characterise essentialist views of culture (Young, 2001b: 118–19; see also Yack, 2002). Yet there is plenty of evidence of multiculturalist support for non-essentialist conceptions of culture. For instance, James Tully notably railed against the characterisation of culture as impermeable 'social billiard balls' (Tully, 2002: 104). So multiculturalist support for cultural accommodation does not necessarily imply a fixed view of cultural differences.

To conceptualise cultural accommodation without essentialism is to take account of in-group diversity and intercultural similarities precisely by permitting all kinds of group members to have a say in the definition of their group's identity, needs and interests. Multiculturalists who have turned to deliberative democracy to frame their calls for political recognition commend it as a mechanism that best facilitates the expression of group heterogeneity. Arguably, those liberal democracies, like Australia and Canada, which have been especially committed to multiculturalism offer more space for this heterogeneity to be expressed and to flourish. Australia's 2011 policy on multiculturalism, 'People of Australia – Australia's Multicultural Policy', emphasises its commitment to providing such space by 'recognis[ing] the amazing breadth and diversity of Australian society, and reaffirm[ing] the government's unwavering support for a culturally diverse and socially cohesive nation' (Australian Government, 2011).

Multiculturalism and feminism

We turn now to the question of the fate of internal groups under multiculturalism, by looking briefly at the debate between feminism and multiculturalism.

Broadly speaking, feminist engagement with multiculturalism centres on the question of whether, given the realities of in-group power relations, the granting of cultural rights can be reconciled with the promotion of gender equality (see Deveaux, 2006; Shachar, 2000 and 2001). Or, put differently, does multiculturalist policy put women's well-being, needs and interests at risk?

According to feminist critique, 'culture, religion [and] tradition' are often invoked by in-group patriarchal power bases to rationalise violations of women's rights (Moller Okin, 1998a: 39) and multiculturalism is 'bad for women' (Moller Okin, 1999) insofar as it reinforces culture, religion and tradition in ways that may help sustain patriarchy. More precisely, multiculturalism is considered 'bad for women' on this view because it reinforces cultural and national identities, which are often reproduced by in-group patriarchal hierarchies seeking normative control over women's bodies and reproductive function (Steans, 2007: 24). By giving self-regulatory powers to minorities through cultural self-determination, in effect we risk strengthening patriarchal in-group hierarchical structures and perpetuating gender injustice, by accommodating family law traditions for controlling the marital status, sexuality and reproductive activity of women (Shachar, 2000: 76).

In short, multiculturalist measures aimed at equality *between* groups may in fact deepen inequalities *within* groups, and this is the 'paradox' of multicultural accommodation (Shachar, 2000: 65). For example, feminist critique has objected to the Israeli case of multiculturalist accommodation in respect of *halakhic* Jewish family law traditions on marriage and divorce (Shachar, 2000). Under *halakhic* law, unless both parties seek divorce, the ultimate capacity to dissolve the marriage remains with the husband. Feminist critique has concluded that this case of multiculturalist accommodation gives religious communities 'a carte blanche licence to subordinate . . . women, in the name of cultural preservation' (Shachar, 2000: 78).

Some feminists are more optimistic than others about the prospect of reconciling multiculturalist and feminist ambitions. The source of some of this optimism is theorising that seeks to reconcile both within a liberal framework. Liberal feminism seeks to depoliticise group-based identities when advocating equal rights for women; women are consequently treated fundamentally as rights bearers, not culture bearers (Shachar, 2007). On one feminist view, there is no intrinsic incompatibility between cultural self-determination and gender equality, so long as support for group rights is subject to respect for individual rights and freedoms (including gender equality rights) (Deveaux, 2000). On another, liberal and culture-specific legal paradigms could potentially be synthesised to protect the well-being of internal groups.

Given the realities of existing internal hierarchies, public discussions over multiculturalist measures cannot be delimited to the discussion of equality for groups within larger society; it must necessarily also include discussion of equality for groups within groups. So, for example, in Canada in the 1990s, Aboriginal (native) women activists challenged their community's male leaders, by seeking to have constitutional protections for sexual equality included in self-government arrangements for their communities (Deveaux, 2000). Their fear was that, under native self-government, where customary values and customary ways of social and political organisation are reinforced, gender equality could potentially be jeopardised if it was not con-stitutionally guaranteed (Deveaux, 2000). The recent experience of women in Afghanistan exemplifies this danger, where constitutional provision for women's rights has been eclipsed by patriarchal cultural 'traditions', norms and mores.

Another source of optimism about the prospect of reconciling multiculturalist and feminist ambitions involves cultural interpretation. Supporters of cultural interpretation rely on a conception of culture as flexible and open to change, which emphasises both how traditions are potentially open to external influences though intercultural dialogue, since cultural borders are not closed, and how traditions are potentially open to internally generated change when their members are involved in deliberative processes that contest and reinterpret dominant norms. The hope is that intragroup discourse and intercultural dialogue may permit dominant norms to be contested and reinterpreted in ways that generate greater respect for gender equality (An-Na'im, 1992; Othman, 1999). A culturally interpretive theory of justice thus relies on a mix of social criticism (external and internal) to ease the tension between cultural rights and gender equality norms.

Clearly for cultural reinterpretation to work, the 'voices' of less powerful members of groups (the marginalised and vulnerable) must be heard and actively listened to in the public sphere when states adjudicate group claims. This would entail opportunities for the less powerful to speak for themselves by articulating their own particular perspectives, needs and interests. Should this not happen, and should states instead rely principally on official spokespersons' perspectives to define groups' needs and interests, then states risk granting group rights on the basis of incomplete or falsified views of cultural groups. When minority spokespersons falsify traditions, they claim protections for practices that do not enjoy widespread support within their groups and are not as such actual customs (Phillips and Saharso, 2008: 295). Falsified accounts can lend support to conservative definitions of group needs and interests that cohere with patriarchal perspectives around, for example, marriage and access to education for girls and women. When cultural rights are granted in these circumstances, they shore up patriarchal power bases. So-called 'honour' killings represent a case in point.

Some feminist groups have, with some degree of success, relied on cultural reinterpretation to challenge practices that are harmful to women. Where feminist activism results in such reinterpretation, women in effect get involved in reclaiming culture and defining its terms for themselves, rather than allowing it to be defined for them by others, who might perpetuate discriminatory dominant discourses and norms (Bunch and Fried, 1996: 203). A good example of this dynamic at work is the activity of the 'Sisters in Islam', a Malaysian non-governmental organisation. This group has been able to effectively challenge interpretations of Islam that justify gender discrimination by providing competing interpretations that illustrate the injustice of such discrimination (Othman, 1999: 186).

Feminist critique highlights the need to take seriously women's agency when addressing the tension between cultural rights and gender equality. Liberal feminism draws attention to the notion of 'learnt/adaptive preferences' in this debate, according to which women are said to develop an acceptance or desire for their culturally determined second-class status. Under conditions of learnt/adaptive preferences, women as agents develop mistaken self-definitions (Nussbaum, 2005). Liberals such as Kukathas (1992a) place a lot of importance on women having the right to exit their cultural groups where their groups act illiberally. Of course, exiting minority patriarchy might not be an option for such women, since, for example, they may lack the preconditions required to make a meaningful choice, in terms of education, literacy, and so on (Kymlicka, 1992: 143; Shachar, 2000: 79–80). On this view, the right of exit is no effective solution to conditions of in-group maltreatment reinforced by multicultural accommodation (Shachar, 2000: 79).

Feminists who resist the denial of women's agency in this debate stress an altogether different point. Their specific concern is that women in unjust circumstances may not want to leave their cultures and by overemphasising the notion of learnt/adaptive preferences, we risk ignoring women's agency and choices by seeing them as 'brainwashed victims of culture' (Saharso, 2003: 210). The logic here is that, even in contexts of oppressive socialisation, women do not lose all potential for agency and choice and, consequently, the line between what is and is not consensual practice within a given cultural group may be difficult to draw (Phillips, 2007: 40–1). The result is a tension between the need to respect women's agency and the need to subject agents' claims to criticism. For example, feminist critique suggests that respect for female autonomy can require accepting the controversial decision by young women from Turkish and Moroccan immigrant communities in the Netherlands to seek hymen reconstruction, which is linked to a cultural norm that women remain virgins until marriage (Saharso, 2003).

Explicit efforts to take seriously women's agency and cultural preferences in this debate are more closely associated with 'multicultural feminism', which aims to treat women 'as *both* culture-bearers *and* rights-bearers' (Shachar, 2007: 126), and which, to that end, expressly resists the cultural stereotyping imputed to liberal feminism. On this view, the tension between gender equality norms and cultural rights is best addressed by discussing issues of recognition and equality for women *as women, as citizens, and as minority-group members* (Shachar, 2007: 129). Such thinking underscores the importance of women reclaiming their own cultural traditions and renegotiating their relationships to them in their own terms as 'agents of [cultural] renewal' (Shachar, 2007: 147).

In sum, the relationship between multiculturalism and feminism is not straightforward and continues to evolve. In the next section we examine the most recent phase in the evolution of multiculturalism by considering the contested claim that multiculturalism is in retreat.

'Retreat' of multiculturalism?

Across Europe and beyond, the post-1989, post-communist era brought about a further rise in political claim-making from minority cultural groups, including national minorities and immigrant communities (Kelly, 2002a: 3). Within political theory, as a result, there was renewed interest in the question of minority rights and the accommodation of cultural differences. As previously noted, by this stage many liberal democracies had already embraced multiculturalist measures in some shape or form, given their apparent usefulness at helping to defuse ethnic politics (Kymlicka, 2007a: 23). Consequently, by the mid-1990s, the notion of multiculturalism as both ideology and public policy had currency in various states.

In recent years, however, the term 'multiculturalism' has become 'politically damaged' (Modood, 2008a: 552). Against a background of rising immigration to the West, there has been a distinct loss of enthusiasm for multiculturalist ideas, and, subsequently, multiculturalist measures have, to varying degrees, fallen out of favour. This shift in support for cultural accommodation has generated debate in the literature and in societies at large, around questions such as 'Is multiculturalism dead?' (Modood, 2008b) and 'What is living and what is dead in multiculturalism?' (Levey, 2009). Some commentators have controversially claimed that the shift heralds the 'retreat of multiculturalism' (Joppke, 2004), and, in this section, we explore why there is disagreement about the current status of multiculturalism and about its future.

Anti-multiculturalist sentiment increased in the aftermath of 9/11 and the Madrid and London bombings. Much of this sentiment was directed at immigrant minorities, as opposed to the other kind of cultural minority with which multiculturalism is also concerned: non-immigrant, indigenous minorities. Multiculturalism was charged with obstructing the economic and social integration of immigrants into 'host' societies, in particular, Muslim immigrants (Phillips and Saharso, 2008: 292). Cultural accommodation was blamed for thwarting the kind of social cohesion and citizen commonalties judged necessary to safeguard political stability. Also fuelling this anti-Muslim, anti-multiculturalist trend was the generation and circulation of a suspicion in Western media that multiculturalism could provide cover for illiberal practices within immigrant communities as well as succour for militant international political movements (Kymlicka, 2007b: 55).

It was within this growing culture of blame that political decision-makers in Western liberal democracies became increasingly dismissive of multi-culturalist ideas. States, such as the Netherlands and Britain, which had previously been supportive of multiculturalism began to distance themselves from it and even openly reject it. In the Netherlands, following the 2004 murder of a prominent Dutch film director by an Islamic extremist, a public debate was sparked about 'whether Muslim immigrants can be good citizens at all' (van den Brink, 2007: 351). In Britain, public sphere criticism of multiculturalism grew considerably following urban riots in 2001 (Meer and Modood, 2009: 474). Trevor Phillips, the head of the Commission for Racial Equality, famously censured multiculturalism on the basis that it 'suggests separateness' and has outlived its time, since 'we are in a different world from the 70s' (quoted in Anthony, 2004). More recently, the UK Prime Minister David Cameron characterised multiculturalism as a 'barrier' that divided British society (quoted in Meer and Modood, 2009: 475).

The result, in both Britain and the Netherlands, has been the introduction of new assimilation measures for immigrants as well as stricter immigration controls. These measures represent attempts within each state to reinforce among immigrant groups a stronger sense of shared citizenship and national identity. So, for example, Britain has introduced the swearing of an oath of allegiance at naturalisation ceremonies preceded by citizenship tests, and in the Dutch case since 1998 immigrants from outside the EU have been required to attend courses in language and civic integration. Elsewhere in Europe, public sphere critiques of multiculturalism have been no less severe. In Germany, for example, an attack on cultural accommodation from Chancellor Angela Merkel declared the death of multiculturalism. She argued that multiculturalism had 'utterly failed' because Germans and foreign workers could not, as the ideology had promised, live happily 'side by side' (quoted in Weaver, 2010).

The extent and significance of this shift in support for cultural accommodation is, however, contested. Multiculturalist theorists have generally tended to be more optimistic than pessimistic about its future in light of this shift. Addressing the British experience, Meer and Modood challenge the idea of a wholesale retreat of multiculturalism (Meer and Modood, 2009). The pair assert that what has actually occurred in Britain is best described as a 're-balancing' of multiculturalism rather than its demise, involving a 'productive critique' around the relationship of multiculturalism and citizenship. On this view, the current critique of multiculturalism is no bad thing, since this re-balancing explores the degree to which recognition of diversity should be 'offset with [the need for] civic incorporation' (Meer and Modood, 2009: 490). Kymlicka also rejects the suggestion of an across-the-board retreat, emphasising that the shift is largely contained to issues concerning Western immigration, particularly Muslim immigration, that is, cases where large numbers of Muslim immigrants are unskilled, illegal and perceived as economic burdens (Kymlicka, 2007b: 50–1).

Since its emergence in Western liberal democracies, multiculturalism has reinvigorated debate in the public sphere and in the literature by challenging existing ideas on the meaning of concepts such as justice, citizenship, equality, freedom, representation and rights. It has done so precisely by elaborating on what is at stake in the everyday lives of individuals within minority cultural groups when their particular identities, needs and interests are not adequately publicly recognised. Clearly, for as long as some individuals continue to suffer from misrecognition under cultural dominance, multiculturalist challenges and ideas will remain relevant to public sphere debate, regardless of whether the political contexts in which they circulate are receptive to them.

But if multiculturalists want to further strengthen the relevance of their claims and sharpen their arguments, then they will increasingly need to widen the focus of their social critique beyond the cultural by paying due attention to the different forms of groups that suffer injustice in the public sphere as a result of intergroup relations. Because all kinds of structures (differentiated by factors such as class, age, gender and ability) are implicated in social injustice, structural domination takes pluralist and hybrid forms (Young, 2000). As noted above, some theorists already attempt to widen the scope of multiculturalist critique in this direction: for example, multiculturalist feminists address issues of recognition and equality for women *as women, as citizens and as minority-group members* – excepting that in numerical terms they constitute a majority (Shachar, 2007: 129). By extending their focus in this way, multiculturalists take more seriously the hybridised nature of marginalisation and exclusion in multicultural societies, and become better placed to take account of injustices that involve hierarchies *within* cultural groups, as opposed to fixing on hierarchies *between* and among them.

Further reading

Recent literature on multiculturalism is extensive. The following edited collection of essays provides a useful overview of many of the main issues that characterise current debate on this topic: *Multiculturalism and Political Theory* (2007), edited by Anthony Laden and David Owen.

Significant contributions from leading multiculturalists include the following four texts: Will Kymlicka's *Politics in the Vernacular: Nationalism, Multiculturalism, and Citizenship* (2001); also by Kymlicka, *Multicultural Odysseys: Navigating the New International Politics of Diversity* (2007a) (this text is unusual in that it considers multiculturalism in the international context); Bhikhu Parekh's *Rethinking Multiculturalism: Cultural Diversity and Political Theory* (2000); and Tariq Modood's *Multiculturalism: A Civic Idea* (2007). For an instructive review of Barry's, Kymlicka's and Parekh's work, see Bernard Yack's 'Multiculturalism and the political theorists' (2002).

On the liberal critique of multiculturalism see Brian Barry's important polemic *Culture and Equality: An Egalitarian Critique of Multiculturalism* (2001). For liberal and multiculturalist retorts to Barry's attack, the following edited collection is particularly valuable: Paul Kelly's *Multiculturalism Reconsidered: Culture and Equality and Its Critics* (2002b). See especially James Tully's 'The illiberal liberal: Brian Barry's polemical attack on multiculturalism' (2002). To get a handle on the substance of earlier debate between liberal multiculturalists and their non-multiculturalist liberal critics, see Chandras Kukathas's 'Are there any cultural rights?' (1992a) and 'Cultural rights again: a rejoinder to Kymlicka' (1992b); and Will Kymlicka's 'The rights of minority cultures: reply to Kukathas' (1992) and *Multicultural Citizenship* (1995). Another important earlier multiculturalist reference is Charles Taylor's 'The politics of recognition' (1994).

For insightful overviews of the relationship between feminism and multiculturalism, see Anne Phillips and Sawitri Saharso's 'Guest editorial: the rights of women and the crisis of multiculturalism' (2008) and Ayelet Shachar's essay 'Feminism and multiculturalism: mapping the terrain' (2007). On the tension between multicultural accommodation and gender equality, see Ayelet Shachar's *Multicultural Jurisdictions: Cultural Differences and Women's Rights* (2001) and Monique Deveaux's *Gender and Justice in Multicultural Liberal States* (2006). Earlier influential commentaries on the relationship between feminism and multiculturalism from a liberal-feminist perspective include two by Susan Moller Okin: 'Is multiculturalism bad for women?' (1999) and 'Feminism and multiculturalism: some tensions' (1998b).

On the shift in support for multiculturalism, see Nasar Meer and Tariq Modood's 'The multicultural state we're in: Muslims, "multiculture" and the "civic re-balancing" of British multiculturalism' (2009); Tariq Modood's 'Is multiculturalism dead?' (2008b); Christian Joppke's 'The retreat of multiculturalism in the liberal state: theory and policy' (2004); and Will Kymlicka's 'The new debate on minority rights (and postscript)' (2007b: 51ff.).

Note

1   For a discussion of the different forms of multiculturalism, see Kymlicka (2007a: 99ff.).

References

An-Na'im, A. (1992) 'Introduction' and 'Conclusion', in A. An-Na'im (ed.) *Human Rights in Cross-Cultural Perspectives: A Quest for Consensus*, Philadelphia: University of Pennsylvania Press.

Anthony, A. (2004) 'Multiculturalism is dead. Hurrah?', *Guardian*, 8 April. Available online at www.guardian.co.uk/world/2004/apr/08/religion.race (accessed 15 November 2010).

Australian Government (2011) Department of Immigration and Citizenship, *The People of Australia – Australia's Multicultural Policy*. Available online at www.immi.gov.au/living-in-australia/a-multicultural-australia/multicultural-policy/.

Barry, B. (2001) *Culture and Equality: An Egalitarian Critique of Multiculturalism*, Cambridge: Harvard University Press.

—— (2002) 'Second thoughts – and some first thoughts revived', in P. Kelly (ed.) *Multiculturalism Reconsidered: Culture and Equality and Its Critics*, Cambridge: Polity Press.

Benhabib, S. (2010) 'The return of political theology: The scarf affair in comparative constitutional perspective in France, Germany and Turkey', *Philosophy and Social Criticism*, 36(3–4), pp. 451–71.

Bunch, C. and Fried, S. (1996) 'Beijing '95: moving women's human rights from margin to centre', *Signs*, 22(1), pp. 200–204.

Carens, J. (2004) 'A contextual approach to political theory', *Ethical Theory and Moral Practice*, 7, pp. 117–32.

Deveaux, M. (2000) 'Conflicting inequalities? Cultural group rights and sexual equality', *Political Studies*, 48, pp. 522–39.

—— (2006) *Gender and Justice in Multicultural Liberal States*, Oxford: Oxford University Press.

Eisenberg, A. (2005) 'The limited resources of liberal multiculturalism: a response to Patrick Loobuyck', *Ethnicities*, 5(1), pp. 123–7.

Joppke, C. (2004) 'The retreat of multiculturalism in the liberal state: theory and policy', *British Journal of Sociology*, 55(2), pp. 237–57.

Kelly, P. (2002a) 'Introduction: between culture and equality', in P. Kelly (ed.) *Multiculturalism Reconsidered: Culture and Equality and Its Critics*, Cambridge: Polity Press.

—— (ed.) (2002b) *Multiculturalism Reconsidered: Culture and Equality and Its Critics*, Cambridge: Polity Press.

Kukathas, C. (1992a) 'Are there any cultural rights?', *Political Theory*, 20(1), pp. 105–39.

—— (1992b) 'Cultural rights again: a rejoinder to Kymlicka', *Political Theory*, 20(4), pp. 674–80.

—— (2003) *The Liberal Archipelago*, Oxford: Oxford University Press.

Kymlicka, W. (1992) 'The rights of minority cultures: reply to Kukathas', *Political Theory*, 20(1), pp. 140–46.

—— (1995) *Multicultural Citizenship*, Oxford: Clarendon Press.

—— (2001) *Politics in the Vernacular: Nationalism, Multiculturalism, and Citizenship*, Oxford: Oxford University Press.

—— (2007a) *Multicultural Odysseys: Navigating the New International Politics of Diversity*, Oxford: Oxford University Press.

—— (2007b) 'The new debate on minority rights and postscript', in A. Laden and D. Owen (eds) *Multiculturalism and Political Theory*, Cambridge: Cambridge University Press.

—— (2008) 'Review symposium: reply', *Ethnicities*, 8(2), pp. 277–83.

Laden, A. and Owen, D. (eds) (2007) *Multiculturalism and Political Theory*, Cambridge: Cambridge University Press.

Lenard, P. T. (2012) 'The reports of multiculturalism's death are greatly exaggerated', *Politics*, 32(3), 186–96.

Levey, G. B. (2009) 'Review article: what is living and what is dead in multiculturalism?', *Ethnicities*, 9(1), pp. 75–93.

Loobuyck, P. (2005) 'Liberal multiculturalism: a defence of liberal multicultural measures without minority rights', *Ethnicities*, 5(1), pp. 108–35.

Mason, A. (2007) 'Multiculturalism and the critique of essentialism', in A. Laden and D. Owen (eds) *Multiculturalism and Political Theory*, Cambridge: Cambridge University Press.

Meer, N. and Modood, T. (2009) 'The multicultural state we're in: Muslims, "multi-culture" and the "civic re-balancing" of British multiculturalism', *Political Studies*, 57, pp. 473–97.

Modood, T. (2007) *Multiculturalism: A Civic Idea*, Cambridge: Polity Press.

—— (2008a) 'Multiculturalism and groups', *Social and Legal Studies*, 17(4), pp. 549–53.

—— (2008b) 'Is multiculturalism dead?', *Public Policy Research*, 15, pp. 84–8.

Moller Okin, S. (1998a) 'Feminism, women's human rights, and cultural differences', *Hypatia*, 13(2), pp. 32–52.

—— (1998b) 'Feminism and multiculturalism: some tensions', *Ethics*, 108, pp. 661–84.

—— (1999) 'Is multiculturalism bad for women?', in J. Cohen, M. Howard and M. Nussbaum (eds) *Is Multiculturalism Bad for Women?*, Princeton: Princeton University Press.

Narayan, U. (1997) *Dislocating Cultures: Identities, Traditions, and Third World Feminism*, New York: Routledge.

—— (1998) 'Essence of culture and a sense of history: a feminist critique of cultural essentialism', *Hypatia*, 13(2), pp. 86–106.

Nussbaum, M. (2005) 'Women's bodies: violence, security, capabilities', *Journal of Human Development*, 6(2), pp. 167–83.

Othman, N. (1999) 'Grounding human rights arguments in non-western culture: Shari'a and the citizenship rights of women in a modern Islamic state', in J. Bauer and D. Bell (eds) *The East Asian Challenge for Human Rights*, Cambridge: Cambridge University Press.

Owen, D. and Tully, J. (2007) 'Recognition and redistribution: two approaches', in A. Laden and D. Owen (eds) *Multiculturalism and Political Theory*, Cambridge: Cambridge University Press.

Parekh, B. (2000) *Rethinking Multiculturalism: Cultural Diversity and Political Theory*, London: Macmillan.

Phillips, A. (2007) *Multiculturalism without Culture*, Princeton: Princeton University Press.

Phillips, A. and Saharso, S. (2008) 'Guest editorial: the rights of women and the crisis of multiculturalism', *Ethnicities*, 8(3), pp. 291–301.

Pogge, T. (1994) 'Cosmopolitanism and sovereignty', in C. Brown (ed.) *Political Restructuring in Europe: Ethical Perspectives*, London: Routledge.

Rawls, J. (1993) *Political Liberalism*, New York: Columbia University Press.

Saharso, S. (2003) 'Feminist ethics, autonomy and the politics of multiculturalism', *Feminist Theory*, 4(2), pp. 199–215.

Shachar, A. (2000) 'Multicultural vulnerability', *Political Theory*, 28(1), pp. 64–89.

—— (2001) *Multicultural Jurisdictions: Cultural Differences and Women's Rights*, Cambridge: Cambridge University Press.

—— (2007) 'Feminism and multiculturalism: mapping the terrain', in A. Laden and D. Owen (eds) *Multiculturalism and Political Theory*, Cambridge: Cambridge University Press.

Steans, J. (2007) 'Debating women's human rights as a universal feminist project: defending women's human rights as a political tool', *Review of International Studies*, 33, pp. 1–27.

Taylor, C. (1994) 'The politics of recognition', in A. Gutmann (ed.) *Multiculturalism: Examining the Politics of Recognition*, New Jersey: Princeton University Press.

—— (2001) 'Multiculturalism and political identity', *Ethnicities*, 1, pp. 122–8.

Tully, J. (2002) 'The illiberal liberal: Brian Barry's polemical attack on multiculturalism', in P. Kelly (ed.) *Multiculturalism Reconsidered: Culture and Equality and Its Critics*, Cambridge: Polity Press.

Van den Brink, B. (2007) 'Imagining civic relations in the moment of their breakdown: a crisis of civic integrity in the Netherlands', in A. Laden and D. Owen (eds) *Multiculturalism and Political Theory*, Cambridge: Cambridge University Press.

Vertovec, S. and Wessendorf, S. (eds) (2010) *The Multicultural Backlash: European Discourses, Policies and Practices*, London: Routledge.

Walzer, M. (1981) 'Philosophy and democracy', *Political Theory*, 9(3), pp. 379–99.

—— (1990) 'A critique of philosophical conversation', in M. Kelly (ed.) *Hermeneutics and Critical Theory in Ethics and Politics*, Cambridge, MA: MIT Press.

Weaver, M. (2010) 'Angela Merkel: German multiculturalism has "utterly failed"', *Observer*, 17 October. Available online at www.guardian.co.uk/world/2010/oct/17/angela-merkel-german-multiculturalism-failed (accessed 15 November 2010).

Weissman, D. (2004) 'The human rights dilemma: rethinking the humanitarian project', *Columbia Human Rights Law Review*, 35(2), pp. 259–335.

Yack, B. (2002) 'Multiculturalism and the political theorists', *European Journal of Political Theory*, 1(1), pp. 107–19.

Young, I. M. (1987) 'Impartiality and the civic public: some implications of feminist critiques of moral and political theory', in S. Benhabib and D. Cornell (eds) *Feminism as Critique: Essays on the Politics of Gender in Late-Capitalist Societies*, Cambridge: Polity Press.

—— (1995) 'Survey article: Rawls's political liberalism', *Journal of Political Philosophy*, 3(2), pp. 181–90.

—— (2000) *Inclusion and Democracy*, Oxford: Oxford University Press.

—— (2001a) 'Equality of whom? Social groups and judgments of injustice', *Journal of Political Philosophy*, 9(1), pp. 1–18.

—— (2001b) 'Thoughts on multicultural dialogue', *Ethnicities*, 1(1), pp. 116–22.

—— (2007) 'Structural injustice and the politics of difference', in A. Laden and D. Owen (eds) *Multiculturalism and Political Theory*, Cambridge: Cambridge University Press.

Chapter 11

Political theology, ideology and secularism

Jolyon Agar

Religion is once again firmly on the political agenda. The idea that ours is a 'Godless' age has surely been reduced to a platitude when the twenty-first century itself has been defined with reference to an act of religious fanaticism. The so-called 'post-9/11' era within which we now live is of central importance to a whole range of political disciplines, from International Relations to Terrorism and Security studies to political thought itself. The carnage that came from the New York sky on that bright autumn morning in September 2001 was more than just the act of deranged individuals motivated by a twisted interpretation of Islam. To dismiss it in such terms is to ignore a message about the state of our world that desperately needs to be heard. It was also the most shocking and tragic culmination of a tense historical relationship between the religious and the secular that has been evolving in western societies for over two thousand years.

I wish to suggest that the fundamentalist political thought that made the horrors of that day possible, as well as more temperate endeavours to rethink the relationship between religion and secularity, can only be understood as the products of a long historical narrative which begins with the birth of western political philosophy itself, in Greek antiquity. Fundamentalism as a political philosophy can only be understood as an intemperate rage against the so-called crisis of modernity and secularism. And the more temperate approach (which is known as post-secularism) is born from a concern with the theoretical and practical implications of the so-called 'loss of the sacred' that the secularising process has increasingly come to involve, especially since the Enlightenment. This loss has arguably contributed, if not to the emergence of these dangerous fanatics, then certainly to the perception that their attack on our most cherished values is at least relevant to increasingly large numbers of people who place their faith at the absolute centre of their lives and who feel marginalised and even ridiculed in our modern societies.

A crucial aspect of our discussion in this chapter will be an exploration of the intellectual climate of the Enlightenment age, when religiously informed political and social ideas were increasingly marginalised from public discourses (as they continue to be). This is because, as I have said, we are living with the consequences of the approach characteristic of this age – both positive and negative – especially in the post-9/11 world. The traditional definition of secularity is derived from the Latin word *saecularis*, meaning 'of this world' or 'temporal'. Secularism generally refers, in the case of political thought, to the formation of normative political concepts that are free from any particular religious component. By the time of the Enlightenment, religion, when given political institutional embodiment, was seen as a particularly potent cause of conflict, injustice and exploitation and was often attacked as a dangerous vestige of medieval political systems. Secular ideas and political institutions, it was argued, were vital components of a new culture of equality and tolerance. Much of this discourse presumed that religion was something that had to be sidelined or quarantined from public deliberations about the good society. But this in turn often presupposed that religion was inimical to reasoned public discourse and was best left to the preserve of the private individual. As we will see, however, this portrayal of the religious and the secular as binary opposites misses some of the most glaring facts of the historical relationship between the two and in particular how some of our most cherished secular ideas were nurtured *within* a religious context. This is why some political theorists (known as post-secularists) think it is time we radically rethink what we mean by secularism. Accordingly, in this chapter we will trace the narrative of the emergence of secularism so that we can best appreciate why religion appears to be firmly back on the agenda in our contemporary age.

As I have just implied, it is useful to focus on the role given to human reason in ordering the social and political world. From where should we equip ourselves in our endeavours to realise key normative political ideals? Should we regard our capacity for rational thought as a product of divine grace? If so, should we always submit to divine guidance? Should human reason be permitted a degree of autonomy in ordering the social and political world within the wider religious framework of divine rationality, or should we dispense with the idea of divine guidance altogether? In tracing the trajectory of this complex process, our story begins with the recovery of paganistic thinking of the ancient Greek philosophers and its massive impact on western notions of the role of unaided human reason in the later medieval and early modern periods.

Reason, faith and the divine: late medieval scholasticism and natural rights discourse in the Renaissance and early modern period

As paganists, neither Plato (429–347BC) nor Aristotle (382–322BC) had a concept of 'God' as such. In the absence of the personal God of the later Abrahamic tradition, it was incumbent on human beings to take charge of their own destiny and have confidence in their own abilities to order the social and political world. The discovery of Aristotle's writings in particular and their impact on Christian scholars of the later medieval period had a profound impact on the trajectory of political theologising and would leave an indelible mark on western political thinking for centuries.

Saint Thomas Aquinas (1225–74) exemplified the intellectual ambitions of later medieval Christianity by his synthesis of Aristotelian rationalism with Christian theology in his magnum opus *Summa Theologiae* (1266–73). Indeed, he was the prime exponent of the methodical and rational system of thought known as 'scholasticism', which expressed the confidence that far from being the enemy of faith, the rationalism of non-Christian thinkers like Aristotle was of fundamental importance in coming to as much of an understanding of the nature of God as was humanly possible. There was much about God's creation that we could know by unaided reason, but for complete knowledge of the world reason had to enrich what we already know through faith. For example, Aquinas argued that Aristotle's 'prime mover' was the Abrahamic God of scripture. This is not to say that natural philosophy (the term medieval scholars used to refer to science) had a role in explaining everything. When it comes to understanding the mystery of the Holy Trinity, for example, natural philosophy was ill-equipped. It was only faith that could make sense of such intangibilities.

Aristotle helped the application of this naturalistic approach to political science by the recovery of his *Ethics* and *Politics*. This meant that politics could become *its own* discipline, where this naturalistic approach could be applied to the study of human society. Aquinas accepted the inherent validity of the study of politics because it was part of the natural order, which can be grasped *via* reason, and in this he was influenced by the Aristotelian principle of the state and society being *natural*. He therefore prefigures the fundamental principle that would animate modernist political thought, namely the role of unaided human reason as the means of framing important political concepts like justice, morality and freedom. But we must remember that this was not a straightforward appropriation of Aristotelian paganism, but rather a synthesis of Aristotelian rationalism with Christian theological ambitions.

For example, Aquinas departed from Aristotle in his view that the state – when it exists as the unity of the common good, the perfect community of the ancient Greek city-state – is not the fulfilment of human nature but only *one* of the ends, and not even the highest end. This is how Thomasian philosophy amalgamated Aristotelian reason and Christian theology in arriving at a Christian view of human nature, which has significant implications for political thought. For Aquinas, the state is not the perfect community. The latter was the exclusive preserve of man's relation with God, which indicates a clear transcendent element to Aquinas' appropriation of Aristotelian human nature theory. Thus it was not political virtues (which were key to Aristotle's perfect community) that were the final goal of man, but faith, hope and charity, the virtues that contained within them transcendent goals of unity with and enjoyment of God. The virtuous life of the citizen could not be an end in itself but merely a means. Aquinas tells us in *On Kingship to the King of Cyprus*: 'the final end of a congregated multitude, therefore, is not to live according to virtue, but through a virtuous life to arrive at the enjoyment of God' (D'Entreves 1970: 15).

An important and unintended consequence of Aquinas' epistemological revolution was the emergence of a secularising logic which would come to threaten, rather than enrich, Christian theology. This is a theme that dominates the so-called *age of reason*, which we will come to in a moment. But this logic was also prefigured in the writings of Niccolo Machiavelli (1469–1527). *The Prince* (1975) very quickly came to represent political ideas that incurred the wrath of the Catholic Church, because it promoted an unorthodox relationship between the state and religious ethics. Saint Augustine of Hippo (354–430) began the medieval period by emphasising the special role of politics in realising Christian ethical principles by constraining fallen man's sinfulness. Machiavelli ended it by preaching the virtues of political thinking freed from its subservience to theological doctrine. As such, the latter paved the way for the secularising revolution that would take hold of political thinking into the age of modernity and Enlightenment in the centuries that followed.

The fundamental purpose of *The Prince* was to provide rulers with the essential means of gaining political stability in circumstances when relations between states were volatile. Such circumstances were to be found in Renaissance Italy and in particular the dominant principalities: Naples, Venice, the Papal States, Milan and Machiavelli's home state, Florence. In addition to their own squabbles, these states were vulnerable to foreign invasion, especially from France. For Machiavelli, political stability was a virtuous end in itself and any prince who had ambitions of securing his own rule could not afford to be hamstrung by any other moral code, and especially not of a religious variety. This secularising of political ethics provided an important prefiguration of the modern state. Indeed, even though the term 'Machiavellian' is often used to describe amoral cunning and unprincipled behaviour, the fact remains that much of the motivation of *The Prince* was the very real concern with what were the necessary measures for the protection and development of statehood. For Machiavelli, while these measures were themselves morally questionable, they served a greater moral purpose, namely state security from which not just princes but all citizens would benefit. It was sometimes necessary to act in ways that seem in themselves unprincipled and even amoral in order to secure the security and stability upon which the life, liberty and property of the people depended. Such reasoning echoes the liberal theory that the principal obligation of political rulers is to provide stability, security and defence of the territory for their citizens as the pre-requisite to the realisation of liberal ideals for the individual (Femia 2004). Echoes too can be heard of the civic republican ambition to create the social and political conditions for the emergence of justice and the common good (Viroli 1998). In short, the private sphere of the individual and the public sphere of citizenry had moral expectations that the state must be free of if these values were ever to be realised.

There is a strong cynical realist thread running through *The Prince* that eschews the formulation of moral doctrine on how human beings ought to behave in favour of one based on the reality of their untrustworthy, gullible, selfish and fickle nature. Such ideas were hardly conducive to Christian doctrine. Indeed, they threatened medieval political thought's presumption that the primary function of the prince was to act as an intermediary between God and man with concern for the material well-being of the latter. Man's ultimate purpose was to attain a state of grace. Machiavelli expunged all idealised visions of humanity from his mind, whether Aristotle's teleological view of the perfect citizen devoted to the common good of the city state or Aquinas' Christian application of Aristotelian ends to involve man's enjoyment of God. Such traditional Greek and Christian virtues of kinship, benevolence, humility and civic duty as ends in themselves in accordance with transcendent natural law and justice were substituted for the historically grounded alternatives of ambition, bravery, drive, shrewdness and will-power. The Renaissance context in which Machiavelli was operating can be seen here, as these latter qualities were seen much more as distinctively Roman attributes.

It is instructive to look at this revolutionary usurpation of Greek and Christian thought in terms of the rejection of natural *laws* that guide political action in favour of natural *necessity* – an empirical calculation of the moral strictures that are needed to succeed in politics. But this does not mean that Machiavelli saw the state's embracing of religious ethics as synonymous with political weaknesses and failure. Indeed, he even went as far as to advise the prince 'to maintain the ceremonies of their religion uncorrupted' (Machiavelli 1975: xi, 74). The wholesome fear of divine retribution that pervaded medieval political thought seemed to have considerable instrumental utility for Machiavelli. But Christian sensibilities were utterly absent from his cosmology. Gone was the idea that princes should have any moral constraint placed on them, and Machiavelli even sanctions murder as a legitimate tool of political coercion. Gone too was the theistic principle of Divine Providence. Instead, the fickle mistress Fortuna reigned, to whose uncontrollable whims the political world must submit but who may nevertheless grant *virtù* to men who display the Roman qualities of courage and audacity (ibid.: xxv). Less a cosmic 'super subject' and more a metaphorical device, Fortuna usurped the Abrahamic God from the role He had held in political affairs for more than a millennium.

This sidelining of God was itself a symptom of the crisis of natural law. We have seen how Machiavelli ushers in a more secular interpretation of the dynamics of political life by his invocation of the idea of natural necessity. He is, therefore, part of a philosophical tradition that questions Aristotelian teleological theories of the idealist ends to which human nature was directed. In the years following the Machiavellian earthquakes that shattered much of the old system of thought, the effort to rethink the *raison d'être* of the state–society relationship evolved beyond a focus on natural necessity into a coherent theory of natural *rights*. But we should not think that this immediately took the form of a secularising logic in political thought. Such a revolutionary development would have to wait for the Enlightenment. Rather, the role of the divine in the early modern period was being *rethought* rather than rejected.

Thomas Hobbes (1588–1679) is a pivotal figure in this development. In his masterpiece *The Leviathan*, first published in 1651, he presents a vision of humanity that is sharply at odds with the Aristotelian tradition when he describes human beings as self-interested, anti-social and violent. He imagines a natural condition in which humans exist: the state of nature. In this asocial environment humans enjoy natural equality by virtue of Hobbes' identification of rationality in every man rather than in simply a select few. But in this world we use our rationality in the service of our selfish passions. We fight to impose our will on others. Hobbes identifies a primary passion here, namely the instinct of survival and self-preservation, and we are entitled to its unfettered pursuit even if it results in the suffering and death of others. Unlike in the Aristotelian discourse, we are not immersed in a set of natural laws that orientate us to communal and harmonious relations with others. Rather, we are naturally inclined to struggle against each other in the pursuit of our passions and whims.

Hobbes' position on religion has divided scholars. Some have presented him as a strong proponent of secularism and even atheism (Skinner 1966; Curley 1996). Much of his reputation for these portrayals results from his conviction that knowledge of any of the specific attributes of God was impossible. This rendered any attempt to base our understanding of humanity on a connection with a higher transcendent reality very problematic. The Aristotelian teleological conception of human nature is jettisoned in favour of a mechanical materialist determinism, from which Hobbes' basic contention that humans are motivated to act on the basis of an egoistic calculating rational self-interest is derived. He then deduces a decidedly irreligious conception of human nature where we are possessed, as a natural right, of an instinct for self-preservation. We are motivated, not by some destiny to be active participants in the community or to know and enjoy God, but by rational calculations of how to secure our own safety against others and impose our will on our fellow man. The basis of social living results from nothing more than the sensual experience of pain and conflict that is ever present in the state of nature that forces us to rationally reflect that the best means of ensuring our own safety is to consent to the absolute sovereign under the terms of the contract. Nor does Hobbes, on this view, have much truck with the miracles of the Bible, and he makes considerable efforts to find non-supernatural explanations for many of them. He found the new sciences of his age extremely useful in this regard.

Martinich (1992, 1996), however, presents a very different picture of Hobbes as an orthodox Calvinist. For Martinich, Hobbes' attack on Aristotelian teleologism, far from being anti-religious, was in fact entirely consistent with Reformation Christianity in general and Calvinist concepts of human nature in particular. His deterministic understanding of human nature, on this account, cannot be reduced to a mechanistic materialism but rather reflects Calvin's theory of predestination and belief in the omnipotence of God. The negative image of anti-social man is perfectly in line with Calvin's own characterisation when he says:

> [I]t is futile to seek anything good in our nature. Indeed, I grant that not all these wicked traits appear in every man; yet one cannot deny that this hydra lurks in the brest of each. For as the body, so long as it nourishes in itself the cause and matter of disease . . . will not be called healthy, so also will the soul not be considered healthy while it abounds with so many fevers of vice.
>
> (Calvin 1960: II.3.2)

Hobbes' attacks on dominant medieval political theology should therefore be seen as not anti-Christian but rather motivated by the Reformation attempt to expunge Christian doctrine of its association with the methodology of pagan Aristotelianism. Nor should the considerable influence of the new sciences on his political thought be seen as grounded in a distinctively atheistic materialism. Indeed, it could easily be argued that he tried to reconcile the new scientific discoveries with a biblical account of nature and man, and there is even evidence that he tried to defend religion against some of the challenges posed by Copernican and Galilean astronomy.

In short, in order to do justice to Hobbes' thinking, any attempt to summarise his political philosophy would have to acknowledge that a major ambition was to contribute to a new theory of Christianity that expunges Aristotelian teleologism and to render it compatible with the new scientific thinking of seventeenth-century Europe. His association with irreligious secular discourse should be seen more as an unintended consequence of this project than as a conscious effort on his part. We may think that any attempted marriage of mechanical determinism with Christian doctrine may end with rather unfortunate consequences for the latter, but this is not enough to label Hobbes himself as anti-religious. We may see in his attempts to replace Aristotelian–Thomasian political theology with a Calvinist alternative an inevitable danger of secularism and even atheism, but this does not mean we should label him with such values.

Perhaps a more successful attempt to reconcile social contract thinking with Christian purposes can be found in the writings of John Locke (1632–1704). As in Hobbes, we see evidence of an attempt to incorporate Christian morality into the scientific determinism of the age in general and contractarian conceptions of society and politics in particular. With Locke, just as with Hobbes, radical Protestant theology was used to defend the idea of natural equality between men and the attack on the medieval idea of a fixed hierarchical social structure. This formed the basis of Locke's sustained polemic against exponents of Anglican Absolutism in England, especially the paternalism of Robert Filmer (1588–1653). In his *Two Treatises of Government* (1689) one can detect distaste for aspects of Platonic-Aristotelian Christianity, as Locke railed against Filmer's argument that monarchical political authority was biblically justified and was therefore the natural state of human social existence. Rather, as in Hobbes, political authority was seen as an *unnatural* necessity to curb the worst excesses of human sin. But Locke's greater emphasis on liberal pluralism and general abhorrence of authoritarianism of any kind, whether Anglican or Hobbesian-liberal, is reflected in his more measured approach to the role of religious matters in social and political policy.

Unlike Hobbes, Locke appeared to be less hostile to some aspects of Aristotelian natural law tradition, and this helped him to hypothesise a slightly less grim state of nature. Although he rejected the idea of society as natural, he posited an objective moral law that acted to constrain the worst aspects of our sinful nature. And so we were obligated, to preserve not just ourselves (as Hobbes contended), but also others. Hobbes' immersion in Calvinism meant that it was relatively easy for him to imagine that such things as social justice were entirely artificial constructions meant to curb our wretchedness. The state of nature symbolised our utter alienation from God in the Fall. But for Locke, it was impossible to imagine how God's benevolent influence on us was not also evident in the state of nature. Rather than dispensing with natural law entirely and focusing exclusively on natural rights, as Hobbes had done, Locke thought that a sense of natural obligation to respect others was easily in keeping with social contract theory. The principles of natural law to respect others seemed to dovetail with the mutual recognition of each other as bearers of rights. But this natural law was now stamped with the inimitable mark of radical Protestantism. These rights were evidence of an individualism that had the character of a divine moral law of nature. Indeed, their basis in the divine was crucial to how we distinguish Locke's conception of rights from Hobbes' as well as how they had slightly differing views on the character of the social contract.

It is more accurate to say that Locke embraced a concept of natural *duties* to God rather than rights and thereby had a theological source for his rejection of Hobbesian absolutism. For Hobbes, absolutism is justified in the act of men surrendering their unfettered rights to the sovereign. But this was simply not possible in Lockean discourse, because our human rights are not, strictly speaking, ours to give up. Rather, they belong to God, and we discharge them in the form of our duty to realise His will. The stamp of Protestantism is clear here. Our relationship with God is something that happens at the level of the individual. The state form Locke envisaged, therefore, had to be such to allow us to thrive as individuals, which would include the incorporation of property rights and free speech. Anything short of the minimal state would be literally a blasphemous denial of God's law. In this way, Locke ingeniously turns political theology, as it had traditionally been understood, on its head.

Throughout the middle ages divine authority was often used as a defence of absolutism, but now Locke utilised it to demonstrate that such a governmental system was not only tyrannical but impossible to defend intellectually. Here we see how the origins of the traditional liberal argument for minimal government and the sanctity of individual freedoms against the state had unmistakably theological origins, albeit grounded firmly in the Reformation tradition. It is in this context that we are to grasp Locke's limited theory of toleration in *A Letter Concerning Toleration* (1689). Religious pluralism was to be protected, with the exception of Catholics and those without any faith. A part of my individual duties is my freedom to choose my own relationship with God and my own road to salvation.

The freedom of religious conscience that this demanded was the basis of the modern liberal emphasis on carving out a clear domain of existence for the individual where she or he can operate free from state interference. This stood in stark contrast to absolutism, which desecrated the private sphere, preventing the individual worshipper from discharging his or her religious duties. The ecclesiastical and secular edifices of the medieval church and state respectively were to be regarded as diabolical autocracies that violated this sacred bond of duty between the individual and God. Catholicism was not to be tolerated on two main grounds. First, it was by definition a threat to God's law, and second,

Catholics owed their allegiance to a foreign prince (i.e. the Pope). But neither was atheism to be tolerated, because Locke could not imagine how liberal freedoms could be defended without recourse to the divine authority from which they derived.

The rise of secularism: the Enlightenment

It is not until the age of Enlightenment that liberal natural rights discourse adopted a distinctively secular character. Humankind's reliance on scriptural revelation as the bedrock upon which ethics for the political world were built was only threatened with the emergence of entirely new religious traditions themselves, and so the conflict between new secular ideas and older modes of thought that had the character of political theologies was a symptom of a wider struggle which saw the three monotheistic systems themselves placed under sustained attack. In particular, the rise of deism had a profound effect on the direction of natural rights discourse away from its Hobbesian and Lockean reconciliation with established Christianity. The scientific revolution that was given its nourishment during the medieval and early modern periods by traditional theisms was by the 1700s beginning to reveal knowledge of nature that seemed to cast considerable doubt on the biblical account of creation. Deism emerged as the most profound expression of this new doubt in the Bible as a reliable form of knowledge.

This break from the secure foundations of Christianity can be seen with the intellectual development of Thomas Paine (1737–1809). His *Common Sense* (1776) was an eloquent case for the independence of the American colonies from Britain that belongs firmly within the liberal democratic tradition. But, as with Locke, it was a liberalism infused with Christian views. Paine invokes natural rights discourse in his defence of the war of independence. Americans had been engaged in legitimate self-defence against tyrannical authority. The British had declared war on human natural rights and so had violated the 'common sense' principles of legitimate government. But he was no social contract theorist. His direct experiences of the war were telling. The collapse of the rule of law had not heralded a return to a Hobbesian or even Lockean state of nature, because basic ordinary social relations between men had persisted. This convinced Paine that society was in fact natural and that it was government that was artificial. But there are echoes of Lockean political theology in his contention that government is a kind of necessary evil. He tells us in *Common Sense* that 'society is produced by our wants and government by our wickedness' (Paine 2009: 3). Government is evidence of the Fall, a necessary curse that results from our sinfulness. The presumption that scripture is an essential authority on human nature is a persistent feature of the early Paine. But by the publication of *The Age of Reason*, we see a much more radical Paine who is more eager to attack this presumption.

His rejection of Christianity was due in no small part to his experience of the Great Terror into which France had descended after the 1789 Revolution. The explanation of the betrayal of the emancipatory goals of the revolutionaries was the continuing power of religious and political tyranny. Paine identified an intrinsic authoritarianism in the Christian mindset that was utilised in defence of the atrocities of the revolutionary French state. The *Age of Reason*, completed just before his imprisonment at the hands of the Jacobin authorities, was his attempt to formulate the grounds of a new religion that was more reflective of the emancipating thrust of the Enlightenment. A Unitarian conception of God was to replace Christian Trinitarian doctrine, which Paine now dismissed as predicated on an anthropomorphic vision of the personal God of monotheism. Instead, God was to be grasped more in line with Enlightenment reason as a supreme rationalist principle. Accordingly, the path to knowledge of God was exclusively *via* the innate reason of each individual.

This strong individualism is the secularisation of his previous Reformation Christian principle of the capacity of each individual person to know God. But by dispensing with a scriptural path to knowledge of the divine, Paine was explicitly undermining traditional religious institutions and creeds, which for him were the authoritative basis of oppression. As merely human constructions, all organised religions were little more than 'human inventions set up to terrify and enslave mankind, and monopolise power and profit' (Paine 2013: 3). If the disclosure of the divine to man is a personal matter for the individual, then the authoritative basis of the second-hand revelation contained in scripture is invalid. Paine draws on the empiricism of seventeenth- and eighteenth-century science and a secularised application of Reformation individualism to undermine Christian defences of the biblical path to knowledge of the divine. For the later Paine, liberal individualism and Enlightenment empiricism rendered biblical knowledge mere hearsay and conjecture.

The influence of deistic thought on the American Enlightenment can also powerfully be seen in the writings of Paine's close friend Thomas Jefferson (1743–1826), third president of the United States and principal drafter of the US Constitution. Jefferson, however, displayed a more conciliatory mood than his friend in attempting to develop a sound ethical foundation for deism that is not easily distinguishable from conventional Christian morality. In his main religious treatise, 'Religious Liberty and Toleration' (Appleby and Ball 1999), he imagined a secular Jesus divested of his divinity and preaching a moral philosophy that was very much compatible with the rationality of Enlightenment liberalism and deism. But Jefferson was as sure as Paine that as a source of divine revelation and moral authority, the Bible was redundant. Its moral content was entirely the extent to which it could be seen as an expression of natural reason. Indeed, Jefferson shared Paine's concerns over the tyrannical implications of placing one's faith in scriptural revelation. The history of 'priestly societies' was one of oppression and slavery justified by a misplaced confidence in biblical revelation. For Jefferson, as for Paine, the success of liberalism lay in its abolition of forms of social and governmental tyranny in the form of traditional Christian churches and monarchy. In short, secularism and republicanism were the essential foundation of a just and free society. Thus, religion could have no role in the operation of politics but was a matter for the private individual, albeit one given constitutional protection as an essential aspect of the exercise of liberty in a secular society.

If Paine and Jefferson were busy turning the guns of scientific rationalism against the idea of divine scriptural revelation in order to undermine the Lockean marriage of Protestantism and liberalism, in eighteenth-century Britain those same weapons would be deployed for the purposes of an even more radical secularism. This was characterised by the work of the giant of the Scottish Enlightenment David Hume (1711–76). Like Paine and Jefferson, Hume had little time for organised religion and was keen to explore the implications for religious belief of the natural sciences, especially in his *Dialogues Concerning Natural Religion* (1947), published posthumously in 1779. What makes the *Dialogues* so interesting is less a critique of theism than its assault on the application of scientific rationalism for deistic purposes. There is almost a paradoxical secularism at work in its pages. On the one hand, Hume goes much further down the atheistic road than Paine or Jefferson by questioning the whole idea of the existence of a divine architect at all. But on the other, his attack on the secure scientific foundations of deism was interpreted by many as an inadvertent rehabilitation of the validity of traditional theistic faith.

The book is written as a dialogue between three fictional characters: theist (Demea), deist (Cleanthes) and sceptic (Philo), the last of which, for most scholars, represents Hume's position. The deistic conception of God as a rational architect constitutes for Philo (Hume) the utterly unwarranted elevation of what is, as far as we can possibly know, a merely human attribute – reason – to the status of divinity. On this issue Philo had an unlikely ally in the figure of Demea, to whom the deistic reduction of the infinitely mysterious God of monotheism to a mere rational architect was an anthropomorphic absurdity. The seemingly fatal undermining of the key intellectual basis of Paine's attack on scriptural revelation appeared to give those of traditional faith welcome relief from the bombardments of deism. But Hume's *Dialogues* was by no means meant to give succour to monotheistic sensibilities and indeed nurtured the soil of intellectual irreligion within which the seeds of radical atheism were being sown.

Atheism and religion in the nineteenth century: Hegel, Marx and Nietzsche

Hume's critique of deism was predicated on Cleanthes' anthropomorphic confusion of order and regularity in the universe with conscious purposive design. It was much more likely, Philo tells us, that that order was nothing more than the *appearance* of design and was in actual fact the product of a mindless mechanical process, 'by the blind, unguided force' (Hume 1947: 192) of matter.

This is a brilliant anticipation of the nineteenth-century Darwinian theory of evolution by natural selection. Indeed, this latter period represented in many ways the highpoint of secularism, sustained as it was by a renewed and confident atheism that left an indelible mark on several of the giants of political thought. By undertaking perhaps the most powerful critique of worldviews that posited a mind-first cosmology, Hume had opened the door for the emergence of political ideas that were deeply infused with explicitly scientific *materialistic* presuppositions. Not least among these was the socialism of Karl Marx (1818–83).

The importance of the materialism of Marx and his lifelong friend and collaborator Friedrich Engels (1820–95) can be seen in what is arguably their main contribution to political thought, namely the radical reinterpretation and critique of the political theology of G. W. F Hegel (1770–1831). This critique characterised the so-called 'Left Hegelians' in 1830s and 40s Germany. Hegel had attempted a rather curious reconciliation of Enlightenment rationalism and individualism with traditional theistic metaphysics by declaring the very concept of freedom as understood from the ancient Greeks to the Enlightenment to be identical with divine purposes. On the one hand, he was convinced by the likes of Paine, Jefferson and Hume that theism as it was traditionally conceived got itself enmeshed in some fairly serious political problems in relation to issues of human freedom. In particular, Hegel was convinced that Christianity's problem lay in its 'other-worldliness'. God is posited as a fundamentally transcendent Being distanced from a material world seen as fallen, wretched and of itself valueless. In practice, this was the essential basis of the slavish religion that all three monotheisms embraced, namely a debased humanity all too ready to submissively acquiesce to a celestial patriarch. But on the other hand, Hegel was convinced that ultimate reality was spiritual in essence and that God did indeed exist. Moreover, theism was surely correct, in Hegel's view, in that any conception of freedom was not worth the paper it was written on unless it involved a defence of God's existence. But this God was not the complete perfected deity of the Aristotelian–Thomasian tradition but rather a Being trying to reach full consciousness of Himself as entirely self-determining. The other-worldliness of this Being is overcome because the material universe is the domain in which this self-realisation is to occur; indeed, it is the very reason why God creates the universe in the first place. In fact, it is why He *must* create it. In reaching this understanding of Himself as entirely self-determining, God realises His nature as *rationality* and *freedom*. Materiality and spirituality presuppose each other, therefore, and are engaged in a historical and dialectical inter-relation in the quest for freedom as their condition of possibility of existence. Hegel defined his cosmic super subject as Spirit (*Geist*), and this was the basis for his directional and developmental view of history. He accordingly rejected traditional theism, deism and materialism as embracing unworkable and incoherent conceptions of freedom by virtue of positing unworkable and incoherent conceptions of God as either transcendent or non-existent.

It is for this reason that any engagement with Hegel's political thought will be incomplete without an understanding of his philosophy of religion. As conscious material beings, humans play a pivotal role in Spirit's self-realisation. Far from being wretched sinners lost from God until we achieve salvation in the afterlife, we are a fundamental aspect of the divine *in the here and now*. And it is one aspect of our humanity that is of particular importance in our role as the vehicle of Spirit's quest for self-realisation: our social and political struggle and conflict towards freedom that has characterised human history. But this was not the rather narrow freedom of Locke and Paine, which for Hegel was an illusory and incoherent freedom grounded entirely in the subjective desires of the isolated individual. Rather, it was a freedom predicated on the individual's cognisance of his or her place in this wider organic unity of humanity in its cosmic role as the vehicle of Spirit's realisation of itself. The state therefore becomes crucial as the manifestation of divine *Geist*. It is only through our participation as members of the community that we can be truly self-determining – that our subjective ideas of what makes us free as individuals are harmonised with our wider species freedom in the community. The realisation of this freedom *in* the community and state is the moment of God's *own* self-realisation.

Hegel's main work in political thought is his *Elements in the Philosophy of Right* (1991), first published in 1821. It is in the context of the critical engagement with this text and Hegel's political theology in general that we must understand the early Marx's materialist atheism. Hegel's system, in which the state is the embodiment of *Geist*, and especially a somewhat conservative application of the system in the defence of the existing Prussian state as the supreme embodiment of rationality, dominated German society in the 1830s and 40s. State forms at the time were strongly stamped with the mark of Lutheranism, which was Hegel's professed faith. Marx belonged in his youth to a radical group of 'Left' Hegelians, who insisted that the Hegelian system could only be realised if essentially the opposite conclusion was reached: rather than religion being the embodiment of rationality and freedom, it was in fact the principal obstacle to it.

In particular, Marx and Engels were both deeply influenced by Ludwig Feuerbach (1804–72) and his *Essence of Christianity* (2008), first published in 1841. For Feuerbach, God did not actually exist, and so rather than the struggle to realise rationality and freedom being evidence of our experience of a transcendent Being manifesting Himself to us (theism) or of divine self-realisation (Hegel), they were in fact attributes of humanity itself. We make mystifications of these rational qualities as compensation for our failure to realise them concretely in a world we take to be limited by our depiction of ourselves as irrational and in need of divine mediation and guidance. Marx adapted this attempt to arrive at a psychological explanation for the religious phenomenon to the search for possible socio-economic causes of our mystified thinking. Feuerbach was correct to see religion as irrational, but it was not the cause of irrationality but rather a symptom. In *On the Jewish Question* (written in 1844) (McLellan 2003), Marx tells us that rather than the Prussian Lutheran state of the 1840s acting as the vehicle of infinite reason and freedom, it was in fact the expression of irrationalities such as injustice, discrimination and enslavement that originated in our concrete social lives. This linkage between real human suffering and religion helps us understand Marx's famous line from the 'Introduction' to his *Critique of Hegel's Philosophy of Right* (McLellan 2003) about religion being the 'opium of the people'. This is usually taken wildly out of context as evidence of his hostility to religion. Once we place it in its proper context, we can see immediately how sensitive he was (as was Feuerbach) to the utopian content of religious thought: 'Religious suffering is, at one and the same time, the expression of real suffering and a protest against real suffering. Religion is the sigh of the oppressed creature, the heart of a heartless world, and the soul of soulless conditions. It is the opium of the people' (McLellan 2003: 64). Religion is filled with some of humanity's most sublime wish-imagery of a better world free from suffering and exploitation. Sadly, many scholars (including those who profess adherence to Marx) have missed this rather salient point that although religion may be both metaphysically wrong and an instrument of oppression, for Marx it is also a utopian treasure trove containing humanity's most cherished dreams of a better world.

But Marx criticises another fellow Left Hegelian, Bruno Bauer (1809–82), for simply taking it as given that society could never hope to be rational so long as the state was poisoned with religious prejudice. The mere secularisation that Paine and Jefferson called for would not be enough for Marx. The state is not the *vehicle* of irrationality any more than is religion, as Feuerbach had mistakenly believed. Rather, it is the *reflection* of concrete socio-economic irrationalities. Just as religion itself is the distorted expression of humanity's utopian vision of itself, so the state, even when secularised, is the distorted expression of utopian political ideals of democracy, freedom and justice. The strong parallels between religion and the political state as distorted reflections of material injustices provided the foundation of Marx and Engels' later theory of class struggle. Their socialist materialism and materialist humanism are indelibly linked.

The attempt to provide a social and psychological explanation of religion also characterised the fierce criticism we see in the writings of Friedrich Nietzsche (1844–1900). But it seems that Nietzsche has more in common with Hume than Marx in the critique of religion, in the sense that the former's sceptical erosion of the old certainties provided by theistic metaphysics found echoes, albeit not conscious ones, in Nietzschean irreligion. While in Feuerbach and Marx we see much more of an atheistic logic, Nietzsche was equally unimpressed with the Enlightenment influence on the Hegelian tradition generally, that is, the confidence of being able to identify secure rational bases for our values. To Nietzsche there were close similarities with the deistic attempt to replace the theistic God with a scientific and rationalist deity who would be the new route to securing knowledge in ways more palatable to the more 'liberal' sensibilities of the age. In *The Gay Science* (1991), first published in 1882, Nietzsche was much closer to Hume in thinking that there were no secure foundations, whether theistic, deistic or humanistic, to our knowledge that could provide us with a reliable way to orient ourselves in our values, including the domain of politics. Coupled with this was the fact that Nietzsche was much more interested in looking at the psychological impact religion in general and Judeo-Christianity in particular had on people than in looking at ontological reasons for disbelief. For this reason he was more of an 'anti-theist' than an atheist as such. In *The Anti-Christ* (2002), first published in 1895, Nietzsche tells us that in a sense, whether God exists or not is somewhat of a moot point: even if He does exist, He is not worthy of anything other than our contempt. Like Paine and Jefferson, he regarded Judeo-Christianity as having fairly serious ethical and political consequences, because it is so enslaving and dehumanising, and like Feuerbach and Marx, in their more negative appraisals, he viewed God as the mystified manifestation of our own self-contempt.

This view that God is a human creation that we divest ourselves of when we recognise Him as such lies behind Nietzsche's famous proclamation in *The Gay Science* that 'God is dead'. Humanism and socialism in particular were powerful nineteenth-century examples of how humankind had advanced a powerful atheistic alternative to both the old certainties offered by the traditional faiths and the rationalistic gods of deism and Hegelianism. But without the securities these alternatives to theism offered, there was the danger of lapsing into an unliveable nihilism where the universe becomes a cold place indifferent to the fate of humanity. To avoid this conclusion, Nietzsche thinks we need to appropriate the key positive aspects of our concept of God – creation of value and purpose *ex nihilo* – and will them to become concrete, what he calls in *The Gay Science* our 'will to life. . . . our will to power' (1991: 292).

Secularism in crisis: fundamentalism and post-secularism

Nietzsche's polemical critique of Enlightenment secularism was by no means the only one to be found in the later nineteenth and early twentieth centuries. An increasingly vocal anti-secular minority within traditional faith structures can be detected at these times, and their ideas are on the rise once again in the so-called post-9/11 era. Fundamentalism, as it is called, is a frustratingly difficult phenomenon to define because it is both emergent from and a rejection of what we might describe as *cultural modernity*. Fundamentalists are present within all of the world's major religions, and so there is no single 'movement' of which we can speak, as the sociologist of religion Bruce Lawrence has articulated. The closest we can get to a coherent definition would be to describe fundamentalism as 'a series of parallel socioreligious movements in the *modern* world that accept the instrumental benefits of modernity but not its value orientations' (Lawrence 1990: 6). While fundamentalists embrace the instrumental gains of the scientifically and technologically advanced society that modernity has given us, they simultaneously reject some of its key values. Principal among them are, of course, the values of secularism. Fundamentalists of all religious persuasions are implacably opposed to the rationalist individualism of the Enlightenment, the rationalism of Hegel, the rationalist humanism of the post-Hegelian tradition and the anti-foundationalist scepticism of Nietzsche. The very least we could say about fundamentalists is that they are dismayed by what they regard as the unwarranted elevation of autonomous human rationality to the privileged status that it enjoys in the secular age. The moment we, in our political thinking, diluted or abandoned the role of divine scriptural revelation in our political deliberations, we were set upon a road to ruin. Fundamentalists never tire in pointing out, for example, that the century from which we have just emerged, where direct scriptural guidance was least in evidence, was the century where violence, inhumanity and general social chaos were most in evidence. Those who defend secularism say it has brought us popular sovereignty, human rights and tolerance. Fundamentalists say it has brought us the hydrogen bomb, the Holocaust and the Gulag. Fundamentalism may be a fractured and disparate phenomenon that has an ambivalent and perhaps even contradictory relationship with modernity, but what unites it is the common conviction that secularism has been an unmitigated and spectacular failure.

Such ideas are articulated in the Islamist thought of Sayyid Qutb (1906–66), whom Osama Bin Laden listed among his intellectual and spiritual mentors. Qutb was a prominent figure in the Islamist Egyptian Brotherhood and was executed for his radicalism in 1966 by the secular Arab Egyptian leader Gamal Abdel Nasser. The anti-secularist tone of his polemic is captured by his insistence that the explanation for the disorder of the modern world is to be found in humanity's rebellion against its status as an inextricable part of a unified divine order of nature, life and the universe. Qutb calls this harmonious order the *tawhid*, 'the oneness of Allah in His existence, in His acts, and in His attributes such as sovereignty or total authority or knowledge' (cited in Khatab 2006a: 87). In short, the cause of humanity's failure to attain equality, justice and freedom in the modern age has been the cosmic disharmony with this divine universe. Rather than a misplaced confidence in manifestations of unaided human reason such as popular sovereignty, Qutb calls for a return to the divine sovereignty of the Qur'anic scriptures. In this he demonstrates a concern for the possible abuse of power and authority that secular reason has provided. Conversely, Islam is the means of disempowering abusive human authority and is therefore the only route to an attainable freedom, equality and social justice. As he argues in his treatise of Islamist political thought *Milestones*:

> when Islam recognises Shari'ah [Allah's laws governing human affairs] as the right of God, it liberates the people from submission to the people declaring the liberation of humankind ... A human being is not a human being unless he is liberated from the rule of another human being and is equal in this affair with all people before the Lord of all people.
>
> (Qutb n.d.)

This suspicion of what are seen as the negative social and political implications of secularism is echoed in other parts of the fundamentalist tradition, not least the Christian Right in the United States and its problematic relationship with the hallmark of secular human rights discourse in America, the Constitution. For some it is a blasphemous violation of the sacred divine harmony of the divine universe and abandonment of Christ's Law. Others are more sensitive to the Constitution as a focal point of patriotism and instead attempt to identify underlying religious sentiments and argue that its reputation as a secular document is misplaced and erroneous. This latter move seems curious and strained, because we have seen how the US founding fathers who penned the Constitution were keen to construct a secular foundation for the new-born American republic (e.g. Jefferson's declaration of a Church–State separation, which is given clear legislative expression in the Constitution). Despite attempts to question the secularist thrust of the Constitution by some adherents, most Christian fundamentalists are keenly aware of the secularist agenda of the founding fathers. Irrespective of these differences, there is the common hope of renouncing the secular orientation of the US.

William Stahl (2010) is an important scholar of Christian fundamentalism in the US. In particular he explores the close association between specifically Protestant fundamentalism and the revival of pseudo-scientific Creationism. The obsession with the latter is, in his view, a direct manifestation of the former's response to the so-called 'crisis of meaning' that has resulted from the perceived nihilism of modernity. Protestant fundamentalism is the radical attempt to re-ground science and socio-political morality in inviolate and secure epistemological foundations (Stahl 2010: 99). Paradoxically, precisely the same intellectual ambitions are behind the recent rise of the so-called 'New Atheist' movement of Richard Dawkins, Sam Harris, Christopher Hitchens and others: an intemperate attack on the epistemological and moral foundations of religion from an essentially radical Enlightenment scientism. Both traditions, Stahl tells us, are obsessed with forging an empirically robust set of first principles in which moral and socio-political thinking are nourished. For the fundamentalists, this is achieved through constructing a return to the political theology of scriptural literalism on scientific Creationist foundations, and for the New Atheists, through Enlightenment scientism.

A more temperate critical engagement with secularism can be found in the writings of prominent post-secular thinkers such as Charles Taylor, Jürgen Habermas and Ernst Bloch (1885–1977). Rather than dismissing secularism as a failure, these philosophers identify much that is worth protecting in secular discourse, in particular the values of popular sovereignty, human rights and tolerance that fundamentalists are so quick to dismiss. What they do not accept, however, is the tendency by some of the principal exponents of secular thinking to regard religious tradition as a dangerous threat to these values and something to be quarantined in the realm of the private individual. Rather than viewing religion and secularity as mutually exclusive, post-secularists combine the most progressive aspects of the secular and the religious in a way that rehabilitates religious discourse in the public sphere. Religion, rather than acting as a hindrance to the realisation of a fairer and more democratic society, can be an important contributor to it. And post-secularists think that religion can contribute to the public sphere without sacrificing important benefits secular discourse brings to political theory.

Although this endeavour may have been given additional impetus since 9/11, it would be a mistake to think of it as a phenomenon of the early twenty-first century. As I will argue in a moment, of those thinkers in the history of political thought who have contributed powerfully to the formation of our secular age, many have not wished to dispense with a sense of the sacred. It may therefore be useful to define post-secularism, as Vincent Geoghegan has done in his study of how religion was a presence in interwar British socialism, as 'the most recent manifestation of a recurring phenomenon within the rise of modern secularism' (Geoghegan 2011: 191).

A key plank of the post-secular project is the identification of religion's rationalist content, for example in scripture. Similarly, Charles Taylor's paper 'A Catholic Modernity' (1999) praises secularism as the guarantee of political accountability and defines the human rights agenda and governmental account-ability measures as the practical realisation of progressive Christian ideas. Indeed, some other scholars, including Graeme Smith (2008) and Jürgen Habermas (2004), explore the religious origins of key secular political concepts. On the one hand, secularism is to be congratulated, Taylor tells us, because it has freed Christianity from its more dogmatic morality. But on the other, he warns against a narrow secularism that can triumph if we seek to marginalise and discredit religion in its entirety.

There is an echo of this warning in Habermas, one of whose major concerns was to confront the subjectivism and anti-foundationalism of Nietzschean secularism. Habermas brings to his treatment of religion his wider deference to Enlightenment rationality against Nietzsche's deconstruction of its secure epistemological foundations. Nietzsche's own bulwarks against nihilism – the will to life and power – are inadequate for Habermas, because they rest on a flimsy subjectivism that is vulnerable to the degeneration into the gloomy and unliveable realm of despairing and relativistic nihilism. We have seen how Nietzsche regards Enlightenment reason as the mere secularisation of ideals that have a fundamentally religious basis. But rather than this observa-tion being the ground of a positive reconciliation of the religious and the secular, as we have seen, it is a reason why we should abandon both systems. This sub-jectivist assault on religious foundationalism at least partly explains, Habermas tells us, the potency of the fundamentalist backlash against the secular age, because it is an age partly nourished by a secularism that is closely associated with a despairing nihilism. Much of the fundamentalist perception of the moral decay of contemporary western society is based on these contentions. Like Taylor, Habermas makes certain key secular values inviolate but insists that a mutual enrichment between the religious and the secular can be reached by encouraging the faithful to contribute to public deliberations over social and political issues (Habermas 2006). And so, the public sphere, rather than being constructed around a narrow secularism that demands believers find non-religious reasons for their social and political opinions, should be ready to include and respect the truth content of much religious morality.

Although Taylor is in broad agreement with this agenda, his post-secularism has somewhat greater ambitions than exploring the common social and political ground the religious and the secular may share. He argues in *A Secular Age* (2007) that western secularism has been *nurtured* in western Christendom. For this reason he dismisses attempts to divest secularism of its 'earlier, confining horizons' (Taylor 2007: 22). He therefore rejects a popular explanation for the rise of secularism in the emergence of superior non-religious belief systems (such as science) that have 'disenchanted' the universe and forced religion into retreat. From this erroneous epistemological position deistic, Feuerbachian and Marxian dismissals of scriptural religion have developed. Religion has lost its status as its own explanation and so becomes a dependent variable of something else (such as an alienated expression of the human essence or compensation for socio-economic injustice). Taylor, rather, wishes to rehabilitate transcendence as a valid knowledge form and defines the secular age instead as a move from an unproblematic belief in God in pre-secular ages to the position where belief is merely one option among many others. Rather than disenchantment discrediting traditional faith structures, it has created the opportunity for the emergence of new forms of belief as well as stimulating new directions in older faiths:

> Thus my own view of 'secularisation' . . . is that there has certainly been a 'decline' of religion. Religious belief now exists in a field of choices which include various forms of demurral and rejection; Christian faith exists in a field where there is also a wide range of other spiritual options. But the interesting story is not simply one of decline, but also of a new placement of the sacred or spiritual in relation to individual and social life. This new placement is now the occasion for recompositions of spiritual life in new forms, and for new ways of existing both in and out of relation to God.
>
> (Taylor 2007: 437)

We can also see a post-secularism that is animated by a defence of trans-cendence, this time a specifically materialist variety, in the writings of Ernst Bloch (2009). Bloch wished to uncover the utopian content of the religious condition from within the socialist tradition. Drawing on Hegel's reconciliation of rationality with religion, Bloch attempts to show how it is in faith that human emancipative discourse receives perhaps its clearest utopian expression. To be sure, Bloch operates within a materialistic and atheistic Marxist viewpoint, but when he reads the Marx of *On the Jewish Question*, he does not see an implacable opponent of religion but rather the thinker we saw above who is deeply sensitive to its potential contribution to radical political discourse.

For Bloch, when Marx criticises religion for its alienating irrationalities, he was referring not so much to its content as to its theistic cosmology. Once we dispense with the transcendent supernaturalism of religion, as Feuerbach and Marx implore, then what we are left with is the rational kernel, the gold-bearing seams of the religious consciousness that are replete with the promise of a liberated and emancipated humanity. We therefore have a specifically humanist transcendence where the reality religiosity puts us in touch with is not a supernatural realm but a future state of human emancipation, one that dovetailed with communistic visions of utopia.

For prominent contemporary anti-utopian philosopher John Gray, however, recognising the common utopian content of the religious and the secular is not something that reflects particularly well on either. In *Black Mass* (2007) he argues that the Enlightenment is entrenched in a Christian utopian mindset. The dominant ideological movements in the west over the last 200 years – Marxism, Nazism and neo-conservatism (including neo-liberal economics) – are basically radical Enlightenment projects consisting of a search for meaning and purpose of human existence shorn of theistic metaphysics. These are obviously secular projects, but what is interesting about them for Gray is that they all share three core utopian characteristics which are basically Christian in origin. The first is *historicism*. This is the claim that there is a definite directionality to history towards an end state. The second is the presence of *apocalyptic beliefs* about the world. Cataclysmic events are predicted (especially wars and revolutions to destroy evil), culminating in a new age of peace, justice and happiness. The third is the notion of *human perfectibility*. According to this idea, human nature is malleable. Through social engineering and conditioning we can eliminate negative characteristics. 'Sin' (to use religious parlance) is a product of the 'fall' (capitalism, racial tolerance, Islamism or Communism). There is the absolute confidence that humankind is thus redeemable.

For Gray, these movements would not even have been possible if they had not grown out of Christian culture. The radical Enlightenment belief in a sudden break with history, after which the flaws of humanity would be eradicated, is but a by-product of Christianity. To be more precise, these ideas are all inheritances from a particular strand within Christianity – millenarianism. This is the belief that humanity is living in the End Time, in which we await the imminent return of Christ, under whose rule all injustice, suffering and death would end. The only difference is that the vehicle of the realisation of the new age of humanity has changed. For Christianity it is obviously Jesus, while for secular millenarians it is humanity itself (the workers, the racially pure or modern 'bourgeois' man and woman). This confidence in the emancipative power of human endeavour is demonstrated in the respective 'sciences' that each Enlightenment offshoot embraces. For Marxism it is historical materialism, for Nazism it is scientific racialism and for neo-conservatism it is neo-liberal economics and the convergence of the world on a single governmental model (US liberal democracy). For Gray, all are pseudo-scientific and all are equally deluded.

To ground theories of progress in science is nonsense, because such theories are myths, not scientific hypotheses (Gray 2007: 2). The parallels with Christian millenarianism are clear for Gray:

> Modern revolutionaries from the Jacobins onwards share these beliefs, but whereas the millenarians believed that only God could remake the world, modern revolutionaries imagined it could be reshaped by humanity alone. This is a notion as far-fetched as anything believed in medieval times. Perhaps for that reason it has always been presented as having the authority of science. Modern politics has been driven by the belief that humanity can be delivered from immemorial evils by the power of knowledge. In its most radical forms this belief has underpinned the experiments in revolutionary utopianism that has defined the last two centuries.
>
> (Gray 2007: 14)

They are all faith-based endeavours. Worse than that, they are dangerous. Gray points out (with some accuracy) that the attempt to re-make the world in its own image by each of the three movements has been less than encouraging. With Marxism we have the disaster of the Soviet and Chinese experiments. With Nazism we have the horrors of Nazi Germany, the Holocaust and World War II, and with neo-conservatism we have the failures of the Afghanistan and Iraq wars and the collapse of neo-liberal economics in 2008.

Although there is much to criticise in Gray's account of the relationship between millenarian Christianity and the Enlightenment (for example, I feel his attempt to label Marx as a secular millenarian is strained and misrepresentative), his argument is an attack less on religion itself than on what he sees as its potential to dovetail with utopianism. In fact, he posits the permanence of religion and regards faith divested of millenarian/utopian ambitions as largely benign. It is the attempt to transcend it and eliminate it that is immeasurably more dangerous and sustained by utopian ideas that are at least as deluded as anything found within the realms of religious faith.

Conclusion: religion and political ideology post-9/11

The main thrust of this chapter has been that the best way to understand the relationship between political and religious thinking is to frame the discussion in terms of the role of human reason in ordering the social and political world. At one end of the spectrum of thought we have those for whom there can be no possibility of any role for human reason unshackled from direct divine guidance and decree. It is in scripture alone that we are to locate all we need to know about the essential ethical foundations of our society and even our science. At the other, we have the antithetical view that such constriction has been the Trojan Horse of an enslaving and immoral worldview demanding that we embrace a debased vision of ourselves. Rational thinking can only flourish if we dispense with the irrationalities of religious dogma and superstition. The political thinkers we have examined have formulated their views on religion with a response to these questions in mind – from Aquinas' Aristotelian Christianity through to Hobbesian Calvinism; from Machiavelli's cynical realism and Locke's radical Protestant liberalism to the deistic rationalism of Paine and Jefferson; from the anti-theistic and anti-humanist polemics of Nietzsche to the anti-rationalist rage of the fundamentalists; and from the atheistic materialism of Feuerbach and Marx to the musings of the post-secularists.

What our story has taught us above all is that most political theorists of the last one thousand years of history have stopped short of taking up either extreme on this spectrum of options. Those extremes are best repre-sented today by fundamentalism and New Atheism. As we have seen, what unites these bitterly opposed traditions is a rather sterile intemperate response to the crisis of meaning of our modern age predicated, respectively, on the first principles of scriptural literalism and crude scientism. But most of the great minds in western thought have eschewed the very idea of taking humanity down such intellectual cul-de-sacs. Even the architects of the Age of Reason (Paine and Jefferson) found space in their thinking for the divine. With Ernst Bloch we have seen that it is even possible that the unlikely bedfellows of religion and materialist atheism of the Feuerbachian–Marxian fold can be allies. And even John Gray's attack on the Enlightenment is premised on its Christian-utopian origins. The renewed attempt to locate the important religious origins of some of the most cherished principles of the secular rational age characteristic of post-secularism is an acknowledgement of this message that these thinkers have imparted. To denigrate either human reason or religious tradition and dismiss their capacity to deliver on key normative ideals is to impoverish both. Perhaps what comes out of the so-called 9/11 experience and the 'clash of civilisations' we are enduring is a renewed appreciation that the religious and the secular may indeed have something important to say to each other.

Further reading

The seminal writing of Aquinas is, of course, his massive *Summa Theologiae* (1964–80). For his political theory, see J. G. Dawson's *Aquinas: Selected Political Writings* (1970). Maurizio Viroli (1998) interprets Machiavelli as defender of civic republican ideals rather than tyranny and amoralism, while Joseph Femia (2004) thinks he prefigures important liberal pluralist ideals. There has been a recent increase in debates surrounding Hobbes' religious beliefs. While Quentin Skinner (1966) and E. Curley (1996) present him as a secularist and probable atheist, A. P. Martinich (1992, 1996) detects a current of Calvinist Christianity running through his work. Thomas Paine's *Age of Reason* (2013) is the most important statement of his mature deistic position and its implications for his liberalism. John Keane's *Tom Paine: A Political Life* (2009) and A. J. Ayer's *Thomas Paine* (1990) provide insightful commentaries on Paine's wider political theory, while Edward Royal's edited volume *The Infidel Tradition: From Paine to Bradlaugh* (1976) examines the relationship between his liberalism and deism. On Jefferson, see Charles B Sanford's *The Religious Life of Thomas Jefferson* (1987) and J. Appleby and T. Ball's *Jefferson: Political Writings* (1999). Hume's most important work is his magisterial *Dialogues Concerning Natural Religion*, edited by Norman Kemp Smith (1947). Any engagement with Hegel's political thought must begin with *Elements in the Philosophy of Right* (1991). An excellent introduction to Hegel and the centrality of his concept of God to his concept of freedom is Stephen Houlgate's *Freedom, Truth and History: An Introduction to Hegel's Philosophy* (1991), although it is one that regards Hegel's thinking as consistent with Christianity. I also explore Hegel's political theology in chapter four of *Post-secularism, Realism and Utopia: Transcendence and Immanence from Hegel to Bloch* (2014). Robert Wallace's *Hegel's Philosophy of Reality, Freedom and God* (2005) is difficult but worth the effort. On Left Hegelian atheism, Ludwig Feuerbach's *The Essence of Christianity* (2008) should be the starting point of any engagement with Marx's early humanist critique of religion. I explore Feuerbach in chapter five and Marx in chapter six of *Post-secularism, Realism and Utopia*. Marx's own writings on the subject can be found in his *On the Jewish Question, Economic and Philosophical Manuscripts* and the 'Introduction' to the *Critique of Hegel's Philosophy of Right*, all of which can be found in David McLellan's *Karl Marx: Selected Writings* (2003). See Nietzsche's *The Gay Science* (1991) and *The Anti-Christ* (2002) for his critique of religion. Examinations of problems of definition in relation to fundamentalism, not least his informative exposition of Christian fundamentalism in the United States, can be seen in Bruce Lawrence's excellent (if slightly dated) *Defenders of God: The Fundamentalist Revolt against the Modern Age* (1990). Various editions (including internet sources) of Qutb's *Milestones* are available (see for example www.kalamullah. com/Books/MILESTONES.pdf). Discussion of his political thought can be found in Sayed Khatab's *The Power of Sovereignty* (2006b) and *The Political Thought of Sayyid Qutb* (2006a). On post-secularism, see Graeme Smith's *A Short History of Secularism* (2008), which includes a highly accessible discussion on the religious origins of important secular political ideals. See also Jürgen Habermas' 'Religious Tolerance: The Pacemaker for Cultural Rights' (2004), 'Faith and Knowledge' in his *The Future of Human Nature* (2003) and 'Religion in the Public Sphere' (2006). Taylor's principal works on religion are *A Catholic Modernity?*, edited by J. L. Heft (1999), and *A Secular Age* (2007). I discuss his post-secularism in chapter three of *Post-secularism, Realism and Utopia*. For Bloch's atheistic post-secularism, see his *Atheism in Christianity* (2009). A useful commentary can be found in Vincent Geoghegan's *Ernst Bloch* (1996), chapter four. I explore Bloch's ideas in chapter six of *Post-secularism, Realism and Utopia*.

References

Agar, Jolyon (2014) *Post-secularism, Realism and Utopia: Transcendence and Immanence from Hegel to Bloch*, London and New York: Routledge.

Appleby, J. and Ball, T. (1999) *Jefferson: Political Writings*, Cambridge: Cambridge University Press.

Aquinas, Thomas (1964–80) *Summa Theologiae*, 61 volumes, ed. T. Gilby *et al.*, London: Eyre and Spottiswoode.

Ayer, A. J. (1990) *Thomas Paine*, Chicago: University of Chicago.

Bloch, Ernst (2009) *Atheism in Christianity*, London: Verso.

Calvin, John (1960 [1559]) *Institutes of the Christian Religion*, ed. John T. McNeill, 2 volumes, Philadelphia: Westminster.

Curley, E. (1996) 'Calvin and Hobbes, or, Hobbes as an Orthodox Christian', *Journal of the History of Philosophy*, Vol. 34, No. 2, 275–1.

D'Entreves, A. P. (ed.) (1970) *Aquinas: Selected Political Writings*, Oxford: Basil Blackwell.

Femia, Joesph (2004) *Machiavelli Revisited*, Cardiff: University of Wales.

Feuerbach, Ludwig (2008) *The Essence of Christianity*, New York: Dover Publications.

Geoghegan, Vincent (1996) *Ernst Bloch*, London and New York: Routledge.

—— (2011) *Socialism and Religion: Roads to Common Wealth*, London and New York: Routledge.

Gray, John (2007) *Black Mass: Apocalyptic Religion and the Death of Utopia*, London: Penguin Allen Lane.

Habermas, Jürgen (2003) 'Faith and Knowledge', in Jürgen Habermas, *The Future of Human Nature*, Cambridge: Polity Press.

—— (2004) 'Religious Tolerance: The Pacemaker for Cultural Rights', *Philosophy*, Vol. 79, 5–18.

—— (2006) 'Religion in the Public Sphere', *European Journal of Philosophy*, Vol. 14, No. 1, 1–25.

Hegel, G. W. F. (1991) *Elements in the Philosophy of Right*, ed. Allen Wood, trans. H. B. Nisbet, Cambridge: Cambridge University Press.

Hobbes, Thomas (1968) *Leviathan*, ed. C. B. Macpherson, Harmondsworth: Penguin.

Houlgate, Stephen (1991) *Freedom, Truth and History: An Introduction to Hegel's Philosophy*, London: Routledge.

Keane, John (2009) *Tom Paine: A Political Life*, London: Bloomsbury.

Kemp Smith, Norman (ed.) (1947) *Dialogues Concerning Natural Religion*, London: Nelson and Sons Ltd.

Khatab, Sayed (2006a) *The Political Thought of Sayyid Qutb: The Theory of Jahiliyyah*, London: Routledge.

—— (2006b) *The Power of Sovereignty: The Political and Ideological Philosophy of Sayyid Qutb*, London: Routledge.

Lawrence, Bruce (1990) *Defenders of God: The Fundamentalist Revolt against the Modern Age*, New York: Tauris.

Machiavelli, Niccolo (1975) *The Prince*, trans. George Bull, Harmondsworth: Penguin.

McLellan, David (2003) *Karl Marx: Selected Writings*, Oxford: Oxford University Press.

Martinich, A. P. (1992) *The Two Gods of Leviathan: Thomas Hobbes on Religion and Politics*, Cambridge: Cambridge University Press.

—— (1996) 'On the Proper Interpretation of Hobbes' Philosophy', *Journal of the History of Philosophy*, Vol. 34, No. 2, 273–83.

287

Nietzsche, Friedrich (1991) *The Gay Science*, trans. Walter Kaufman, New York: Random House.
—— (2002) *The Anti-Christ*, Chestnut Hill, MA: Adamant Media Corporation.
Paine, Thomas (2009) *Common Sense*, Vancouver: TheCapitol.net.
—— (2013) *The Age of Reason*. Available online at www.deism.com/images/theageofreason1794.pdf (accessed 28 October 2013).
Qutb, Sayyid (n.d.) *Milestones*. Available online at www.kalamullah.com/Books/MILESTONES.pdf.
Royal, Edward (ed.) (1976) *The Infidel Tradition: From Paine to Bradlaugh*, London: Macmillan.
Sanford, Charles B. (1987) *The Religious Life of Thomas Jefferson*, Charlottesville VA: University of Virginia Press.
Skinner, Quentin (1966) 'The Ideological Context of Hobbes's Political Thought', *Historical Journal*, Vol. 9, 286–317.
Smith, Graeme (2008) *A Short History of Secularism*, London: I. B. Tauris.
Stahl, William A. (2010) 'One Dimensional Rage: The Social Epistemology of the New Atheism and Fundamentalism', in Amarnath Amarasingam (ed.) *Religion and the New Atheism: A Critical Appraisal*, Boston: Brill.
Taylor, Charles (1999) *A Catholic Modernity?*, ed. J. L. Heft, New York: Oxford University Press.
—— (2007) *A Secular Age*, Cambridge, Massachusetts: Harvard University Press.
Viroli, Maurizio (1998) *Machiavelli*, Oxford: Oxford University Press.
Wallace, Robert (2005) *Hegel's Philosophy of Reality, Freedom and God*, Cambridge: Cambridge University Press.

The end of ideology

Moya Lloyd

Declarations of its end have shadowed discussions of ideology since at least the nineteenth century. In 1886, in what has been credited as the first use of the idea, Friedrich Engels, Marx's collaborator, confidently proclaimed that 'there would be an *end to all ideology*' (cited in Lipset, 1985: 82). And, indeed, some thirty years later in 1929, according to Seymour Martin Lipset, Karl Mannheim claimed to observe that very thing: a 'decline of ideology', as he called it, made evident in the reduction of politics to economics, 'the expression of the natural impulses in sport' and a rise in pragmatism (Mannheim cited in Lipset, 1985: 83). Despite periodic reassertions of the claim that the age of ideology has passed, other analysts of ideology have strenuously rejected this argument, pointing instead to the continuing influence of ideological thinking on politics.

In part, this debate is a product of the fact that different writers define or understand ideology differently. Since its coinage in the eighteenth century by Antoine Destutt de Tracy to signify a science of ideas, ideology has been understood in a variety of divergent ways, including as a set of political ideas that furnish practical rules to live by; as a useful analytical tool to understand how people think about politics; as a way of referring to radical or 'totalising' political ideas; and as a synonym for brainwashing and false consciousness. Moreover, as Mostafa Rejai has noted, ideology may also be examined as a political concept ('its nature, functions, and types') or as what he calls 'ideology as ideology' (Rejai, 1971: 1, 2), by which he means something akin to the approach adopted in this book (the examination of liberalism, conservatism, and so on). How the term 'ideology' is used, therefore, has a significant bearing on what it means to argue that ideology has ended. If one understands ideology to be sets of action-guiding political beliefs (such as feminism, liberalism and conservatism), then to say ideology is in decline is to say that all such belief systems are now politically redundant. If, however, one understands ideology to be the ideas of the ruling class that enable them to dominate and exploit the working class, to hail the end of ideology is to imply something very different: the overcoming of illusory ideas and false consciousness and the attainment of truth about the world.[1]

The various end-of-ideology theses that have been espoused thus raise a series of questions about the nature and continuing relevance of ideological thinking, including: What is meant by ideology? What, if any, is its role today? Do ideologies help us to make sense of the world in which we live, or has that world changed so much that ideologies are now irrelevant? Are there different ideologies competing for people's support, or have globalisation and the expansion of capitalism, for instance, brought about a convergence between nations to the point where we all share the same views and values? If so, then does this signal the triumph of liberal capitalism in a positive sense, or are we, as Marxists have suggested, all victims of 'false consciousness', mistakenly believing that the capitalist system is the optimum system? If our values and ideals have indeed converged – though many question this – then how do we make sense of the resurgence of national, religious and ethnic conflicts that have marked recent history? Is this resurgence evidence of a revival of ideology, of the fact that ideologies never actually disappeared in the first place, or, perhaps, of a realignment of global politics along, for instance, cultural lines? Have any new ideologies emerged since the 'end' of ideology was last hailed?

This chapter will focus on two central issues. The first is the questions that have been raised about the continuing relevance of ideology today. The second is the issue of whether or not the opposition laid down by some Marxists between ideology and science can be sustained. The chapter will begin by exploring the end-of-ideology debate that took place in the 1950s and early 1960s and will focus, in particular, on the work of Daniel Bell. This will be followed by an examination of the arguments put forward by Francis Fukuyama, whose 1989 thesis concerning the 'end of history' reframed these earlier discussions of the end of ideology. The final section will look at a slightly different set of issues, relating not to whether ideology is still relevant but, more fundamentally, to the question of whether ideology is a meaningful analytical term at all.

The end of ideology: the decline of socialism in the West

From the mid-1940s onwards, academics in Western Europe and the United States began to advance the idea of 'the end of ideology'. Writing in 1946, for example, the French philosopher Albert Camus counselled the French Socialist party to renounce Marxism 'as an absolute philosophy' so as to 'exemplify the way our period marks the end of ideologies' (cited in Bell, 1988a: 133). In 1955, the American sociologist Edward Shils and the French sociologist Raymond Aron drew attention to what Shils described as 'the end of ideology' (Shils, 1955) and Aron as 'the end of the ideological age' (Aron, 1957 [1955]). For Shils this 'end' was presaged by the decline of 'comprehensive explicit system of beliefs' such as Marxism, National Socialism and Fascism (1955: 57), while for Aron it was signified by the disappearance of the social-structural conditions of ideological debate in the advanced industrialised nations of the West, made manifest in the failures of nationalism, liberalism and Marxism. In 1963, another version of the end-of-ideology thesis appeared, this one advanced by the American political sociologist Seymour Martin Lipset, in *Political Man*. Here he argued that since the 'fundamental political problems of the industrial revolution have been solved', the 'democratic class struggle' would, henceforth, be 'a fight without ideologies' (1963: 407, 408).

Perhaps the most important intervention in this particular phase of the discussion, however, was Daniel Bell's *The End of Ideology: On the Exhaustion of Political Ideas in the Fifties* (1962 [1960]). More than any other work, it is this book that is taken by commentators and critics alike to epitomise the end-of-ideology thesis. Some have alleged that Bell's version of the thesis implies a rejection of all 'ideals, ethical standards, general or comprehensive social views and policies' (Shils cited in Lipset, 1985: 98): that he is claiming, in other words, an end to political ideology as such (see also Skinner, 1985: 3–4) and, with that, 'the end of politics' (Bay, 1961) or even 'the end of society' (Freeden, 1996: 19). Some commentators have read *The End of Ideology* as being itself an ideological work espousing a liberal vision (Mills, 1968). Others have attempted to refute Bell's argument by pointing to the radicalism of the 1960s, which seemed to attest not to the decline of ideology but rather to the emergence of a new era of ideology, or possibly even an era of new ideologies (see essays in Waxman, 1968 and Rejai, 1971; see also Freeden, 2003: 37). It has also been suggested that Bell simply ignored empirical evidence that contradicted his conclusions (Mills, 1968: 126–40).

Reflecting in a 1987 lecture upon the legacy of his book, Bell notes: 'There are some books that are better known for their titles than their contents. Mine is one of them' (1988a: 126). If its title is, in some respect, misleading, then what, if not the 'end of ideology', is *The End of Ideology* about? In a new essay in the 2000 edition of the volume, Bell identifies its three main themes: a concern with 'the vicissitudes of the concept of ideology as derived from Marx and elaborated by Karl Mannheim'; the decline of Marxism as a political creed; and the decreasing usefulness of class as an analytical tool, particularly with regard to American society (2000: xi). From this description, the ideology of the book's title would seem to be Marxism.

A repeated claim of Bell's – both at the time and since – has been that ideology is to be understood as 'an historically located belief system' (2000: xi) or, more specifically, as he pointed out in the introduction to the first revised edition of the text, as 'a special complex of ideas and passions that arose in the nineteenth century'. Ideology, in this regard, is thus not synonymous with '*any* "belief-system"' (1962: 17) or 'any creed held with the will to believe . . . [such as] the ideologies of Black Power, the New Right, Feminism' (Bell 1988b: 331). In fact, it is precisely the over-extended use of the concept that Bell laments: 'In the twenty-five years since *The End of Ideology* was published', he notes, 'the concept of ideology has unravelled completely. What is not considered an ideology today? Ideas, ideals, beliefs, creeds, passions, values, *Weltanschauungen*, religions, political philosophies, moral systems, [and] linguistic discourses' (Bell, 1988b: 321).

When Bell refers in *The End of Ideology* to 'ideology' being in decline, he specifically means the ideologies of nineteenth-century Europe, most particularly the ideologies of the left, especially Marxism.[2] These ideologies he describes as being 'universalistic, humanistic and fashioned by intellectuals', driven by the desire for 'social equality and, in the largest sense, freedom' (Bell, 1962: 403). Following Mannheim, Bell classifies them as 'total' ideologies: 'all-inclusive' systems of thought (1962: 399, 400) oriented to bringing about the complete transformation of society. When he determined that ideology was no longer relevant in the West in the 1950s, it is these ideologies, likened by him to secular religions, to which he is referring. The question is why? What were the factors explaining ideological 'exhaustion' in the West?

For Bell, there were several. First, and in particular, developments in the former communist states: the alliance of the Soviets with the Nazis during the war; the show trials, purges and labour camps of the Soviet Union; and the crushing of the Hungarian uprising in 1956. These led to a widespread disillusionment with socialism and Marxism. At the same time, the West experienced a period of rapid economic expansion and modernisation, together with the growth of the welfare state. Faith in so-called simplistic and rationalistic beliefs began to wane, and a political consensus emerged amongst Western intellectuals based, Bell argued, on political pluralism, a mixed economy and an acceptance of the welfare state (for a critical response, see Freeden, 2003: 35–9).[3] By 1960, he observed, few liberals were totally opposed to state intervention in the economy, and few conservatives (in Europe, at least) doubted the value of the welfare state. As a consequence, people no longer trusted the 'old ideologies' and, just as importantly, he argues, they no longer believed in the possibility of 'blueprints' for social transformation or in 'social engineering' as a means to create a new, more egalitarian society (Bell, 1962: 403, 402). By the 1950s, ideology, once 'a road to action', Bell declared, had become a blinkered, even distorted way of looking at the world (1962: 393).

As noted earlier, Bell's analysis is especially concerned with the relevance of Marxism as a way of apprehending the world. Marxism as an ideology, he ventured, was not just tainted by what had happened in the communist states in the 1930s, 40s and 50s, a view shared with the likes of Lipset and Aron. Its predictions about future developments in the West were also inaccurate. This was made evident in the US, Bell speculated, by the fact that by the 1950s politics was no longer 'a reflex of any internal class divisions' (1962: 14). Instead of deepening economic crises and heightened class conflict, since the 1930s American society had witnessed a reduction in the size of its industrial working class. By the end of the 1950s, 'property', he averred, had also 'increasingly lost its force as a determinant of power' (1962: 398). Methodologically, therefore, a Marxist-inspired sociology (the subject that particularly concerned him; see also Bell 1988a, 1988b) was no longer an historically viable way to analyse American society, for the US had become what he later termed a 'postindustrial society' (Bell, 1974).

When Bell sounded the death-knell of ideology, he intended something quite specific. Not that ideology *per se* had ceased to matter, as some have suggested; rather he was notifying his readership that, in his view, the old 'total' ideologies of the left – socialism and Marxism – were no longer either historically viable or persuasive. This explains why he was able to describe his own analysis of American society as 'anti-ideological' (1962: 16), since it was neither universalising nor grounded in a class analysis. It also explains why, apparently paradoxically, he was able to draw attention to the emergence of the 'new ideologies' of 'industrialization, modernization, Pan-Arabism, color and nationalism' in Asia and Africa, because to him they were 'parochial' rather than universal, 'instrumental' rather than humanistic, and 'created by political leaders' rather than by intellectuals (Bell, 1962: 403).

Popular as this version of the end-of-ideology thesis initially was, by the mid to late 1960s it had lost favour. Developments such as the emergence of the new social movements in the later 1960s, the economic crises of the 1970s, and the rise of the New Right, among others, put many of its core beliefs into question, including the sense that ideological thinking could be eliminated from politics. It would, however, be wrong to assume that as a consequence, time had passed on the end-of-ideology thesis *per se*: quite the reverse, for the events of the mid to late 1980s were to usher in a new wave of 'endism' (Huntington, 1989).

The year 1989 was a tumultuous one in the political world. In the spring, Chinese students demanding democratisation occupied Tiananmen Square in Beijing. In June, watched by the world's media, the tanks of the Chinese army ruthlessly crushed this protest, killing hundreds in the process.[4] In July the trade union Solidarity, the first independent trade union in the Eastern bloc (that is, the first union *not* controlled by the Communist Party), was elected to govern Poland. Throughout the summer of 1989, thousands fled East Germany to the West, an exodus culminating ultimately in the fall of the Berlin Wall in December 1989. A series of 'velvet revolutions' followed in Eastern Europe as one regime after another overturned communist rule. Within two years, as a consequence variously of economic exhaustion, *glasnost* and *perestroika* and improving Soviet–American relations, the Soviet Union itself had collapsed and the Cold War was nearing its end. What did these developments mean? Were they confirmation that communism was now a spent force ideologically in Eastern Europe, as well as in the West?

In the summer of 1989, while many of the events above were still unfolding, an essay appeared in what was at the time a relatively new American periodical devoted to international affairs called *The National Interest*. Written by the then little-known deputy director of the State Department's planning staff, Francis Fukuyama, the essay, entitled 'The End of History?', endeavoured to provide answers to questions of this kind. It proved to be a highly controversial text.

The end of history: the triumph of liberalism

The idea that history has ended, Andrew Gamble comments, 'sounds preposterous'. Taken literally, it suggests that humanity is perpetually destined to live in the present (2000: 19) and that nothing of note is ever going to happen again, a fact seemingly belied by the countless historically significant political events that have occurred since 1989: the construction of post-apartheid South Africa; the end of pervasive terrorist violence in Northern Ireland; the breakup of the former Yugoslavia and the ethnic conflict that ensued; the Rwandan genocide; wars in the Gulf, Iraq and Afghanistan; the events of September 11, 2001; even the election in 2008 of the first African American president of the United States. So what was it about the events of 1989 that led Fukuyama to state: 'What we may be witnessing is not just the end of the Cold War, or the passing of a particular period of postwar history, but *the end of history as such*' (Fukuyama, 1989: 4, emphasis added)?

The second part of the sentence from which this quotation is extracted gives the answer. The end of history signals 'the end point of mankind's ideological evolution and the universalization of Western liberal democracy as the final form of human government'. It is thus synonymous with the end of ideology. Not, however, with the end of ideology understood as the end of social-ism, as Bell had previously characterised it, but rather with the end of ideology apprehended as the 'the victory of liberalism' over all other competing ideolo-gies (Fukuyama, 1989: 4). Fukuyama's assertion that history had ended is, in other words, another way of saying that a consensus had emerged worldwide that liberalism was the only viable ideology and liberal democracy the only via-ble system of government. In order to make sense of why Fukuyama deploys the phrase 'the end of history' rather than 'the end of ideology' to describe this process and why, in particular, he regards the putative spread of liberalism as evidence of that 'end', we need to understand more about the ideas that inform Fukuyama's argument.

The 'notion of an end of history is not an original one', Fukuyama notes (1989: 4). Popularised by Marx, the idea, as he indicates, derives initially from the work of G. W. F. Hegel. It is not directly from Hegel that Fukuyama draws, however, but rather from the very distinctive interpretation of Hegel promul-gated by Alexandre Kojève, a Russian *émigré* philosopher who gave a series of highly influential lectures on Hegel in Paris in the 1930s.[5] According to Hegel, history is an evolutionary process moving towards a final culmination. In con-trast to Marx, who focuses attention on material production and class conflict, Hegel's theory is idealist: it focuses on developments in the realm of conscious-ness or what Hegel terms *Geist*, meaning mind or Spirit. History is thus the progress of *Geist* along a logically necessary path leading to the goal of freedom. For Hegel, history culminated with the triumph of Reason. At that moment a rationally ordered society and state would emerge. The tensions or contradictions existing in previous historical moments (those between master and slave, for instance) would be transcended. Individual and collective interests would be harmonised within the rational state. Human freedom would be realised.

When Fukuyama talks about history, then, he is not using the term in its conventional sense to refer to events such as those itemised above (the collapse of the Berlin Wall or the Iraq War). Events such as these, he allows, will continue. He is using it to refer to history in a (quasi-)Hegelian sense as an evolutionary process moving towards a particular goal or 'end': what he describes in a later work as 'directional history' (Fukuyama, 1992: xiii). The 'end' of history in this sense refers both to its culmination or endpoint (the victory of Reason, for Hegel, and of liberalism, for Fukuyama) and to its underlying purpose (how developments and events play a part in the progression towards this endpoint).

Three years after 'The End of History?', Fukuyama published *The End of History and the Last Man* (1992), in which he elaborates on the two factors that lead, in his view, to the cessation of history and to the attainment of liberalism. The first is natural science and the second is the human struggle for recognition. Let us take each in turn. Modern natural science, according to Fukuyama, alone is able to explain the 'directionality and coherence of History' (1992: xiv). It is the only activity that is progressive in direction and cumulative. Moreover, it is the only social practice that has a uniform effect on all those who experience it, because science follows the laws of nature and not of human invention. 'The second law of thermodynamics', he later wrote, 'is no different in Japan or Rwanda than it is in the United States' (1995: 32). It is the connection between natural science and the development of technology that is crucial to historical evolution. This guarantees human progression towards liberal democracy. How?

First, nations possessed of technology are militarily superior to those without it: it guarantees their independence and thus their security. Second, technological advance has beneficial effects on economic development, which is a universal goal of all societies. Technology allows the continued accumulation of wealth and the satisfaction of continually expanding material desires (the so-called 'Victory of the VCR': Fukuyama, 1992: 98). What is more, this process leads to the homogenisation of societies; that is, all economically modernised societies, despite national and cultural variation, resemble one another. Despite the historical traditions, religious values, and so on that differentiate one liberal democracy from another, the logic of scientific or technological development pushes all states towards a universal consumer culture – guaranteed by the globalisation of markets (and he cites developments in Eastern Europe, the spread of liberal capitalism throughout Asia, and the increasing commercialisation of the Chinese economy in support of this). Thus it is that societies will all eventually become capitalist. The emphasis on natural science, however, explains only one part of the movement of history towards liberalism: that is, the seemingly unbreakable connection of liberalism with the emergence of capitalism. In order to account for the development of liberal democracy, Fukuyama turns his attention to the other plank of his argument – the idea of the struggle for recognition.

For Hegel, Fukuyama contends, the essence of man is the desire to be recognised as fully human by others (all other characteristics of his identity are culturally and historically determined). This involves him in confrontation with others 'in which each contestant seeks to make the other "recognize" him by risking his own life' (Fukuyama, 1992: 147). Initially, this produces relations of master and slave as one conquers and the other concedes defeat in return for his life. Since a slave is not fully human, because she or he is denied freedom by being in thrall to a master, this relation is basically unsatisfactory and contradictory: the slave cannot provide the master with the recognition the latter desires, which is the desire to be recognised (or to be valued) by another human being endowed with dignity and worth.

The contradiction inherent in the relation between lord and bondsman is overcome, according to Hegel, by the French Revolution, and according to Fukuyama also by the American Revolution. These were democratic revolutions based on the principles of equality and liberty for *all* men. Here the inegalitarian relation between master and slave is replaced by 'universal and reciprocal recognition' embodied in the rule of law and the distribution of equal rights (Fukuyama, 1992: xviii). As Fukuyama puts it, liberal society entails the 'reciprocal and equal agreement among citizens to mutually recognize each other' (1992: 200). Liberalism, for Fukuyama, represents the end of history because it is the *only* ideology with the ability to guarantee the universal recognition of humanity. *No* other existing ideologies are able to do so.

The visible spread of capitalism and of liberal democracy around the globe indicate to Fukuyama the *necessary* logic of historical development as more and more countries move towards the End of History. This spread may be uneven (some states remain in history while others are post-historical), but in the West history has ended. There are no ideologies remaining that can compete with liberalism: fascism and Nazism were defeated in the Second World War; communism in the Eastern bloc was in the course of disintegrating; and the fortunes of communist and socialist parties throughout Europe were on the wane. Moreover, the ideologies that remained (nationalism, religious fundamentalisms of different kinds, and so forth) all lacked the capacity for universalisation necessary to establish them as serious contenders to liberalism. In short, human history (in the West, at least) had reached its developmental end point.

Just as Bell's earlier book had spawned a debate, so too Fukuyama's writings generated considerable interest, and not all of it favourable. Charges of inconsistency were levelled at his argument (Ryan, 1992). Critics contended that Fukuyama was simply defending the ideological status quo (Norris, 1991). Others challenged the historical approach adopted by Fukuyama (Huntington, 1989; Burns, 1994). Some writers, in particular, contested the idea that the decline of communism could be equated with the end of socialism as such (Anderson, 1992; Hobsbawm, 1995; see also Bertram and Chitty, 1994 and Kumar, 2000), while others argued that it was fallacious both to assume that the demise of communism meant the global victory of liberalism and thus to deduce that ideology was no longer politically relevant in international relations (Huntington, 1989). Others even saw Fukuyama's own thesis as evidence of the 'pervasiveness' rather than the disappearance of Marxism (Huntington, 1989).

Two sets of criticism are of particular interest. Fukuyama, as we have seen, yokes together capitalism and liberalism in his account of historical development. There is, however, a question mark hanging over the potential for continued economic expansion across the globe, exemplified perhaps by the ongoing global financial crisis that began in 2007, which challenges Fukuyama's claim that people's material desires can be endlessly sated.

From at least the late 1980s, when Fukuyama was writing, there has been ample evidence of growing opposition to economic neo-liberalism, the activities of powerful transnational corporations, and what are perceived by critics to be unaccountable international financial institutions. Increasingly high-profile protests have been held at the meetings of the World Bank and IMF in Berlin in 1988 and Washington in 2000 and 2002, the G7 in Paris in 1989, the G8 in Genoa in 2001, and the G20 in London in 2009, as well as perhaps more famously at the meetings of the WTO in Seattle in 1999. At the time of writing (2012), the Occupy movement is protesting against social and economic inequality in numerous countries across the world. Recall that the end-of-history thesis advanced by Fukuyama rests on the idea that economic modernisation is a *universal* goal (see Fukuyama, 1995); yet the examples listed above indicated that there are those who spurn it: people, that is, who either question or, in some cases, repudiate capitalist values and practices. This suggests that commitment to modernisation is less widespread than Fukuyama asserts.

Moreover, amongst those who criticise capitalism, some have already begun to embrace an ideology, namely environmentalism or its more radical variant, ecologism, which actively reject materialism and contend that current levels of capitalist development are simply unsustainable (Anderson, 1992; see also chapter 7 in this volume). Yet Fukuyama takes little notice of environmental issues; indeed, his argument concerning the spread of liberal capitalism rests on one of the very beliefs that environmentalists and ecologists refute: that capitalist accumulation will proceed unproblematically 'in a linear fashion into the future' (Dresner, 2008: 154).

Doubt was also cast on Fukuyama's analysis from another quarter: from the pen of the American political scientist Samuel Huntington (1993, 1997). Huntington's specific focus was on world politics and, in particular, sources of conflict therein. Conflict rooted in ideology, Huntington challenged, marked what he called the 'Western phase' of international politics. This phase began with the Russian Revolution and the adverse reaction it elicited, continued through the Second World War when 'the conflict of nations yielded to the conflict of ideologies' (between communism, fascism and Nazism, and liberal democracy), and culminated in the Cold War, with its clash between communism and liberal democracy (Huntington, 1993: 23). With the end of the Cold War, according to Huntington, came the end of ideology as the basis of international conflict.

The reason for this is not, however, as Fukuyama surmised, because liberalism (or liberal democracy) had triumphed over communism; such a line of reasoning, Huntington counsels, merely perpetuates Cold War-style thinking. The reason is that international politics has moved into a new phase where the 'dominating source of conflict will be cultural' (1993: 22), expressed, as Huntington notes, through clashes over ethnicity (such as 'ethnic cleansing' in the former Yugoslavia), religion (the rise of militant Islam or the Gulf War) and other civilisational differences.

In short, therefore, for Huntington, while Fukuyama might be right to point to some kind of end of ideology, the conclusions he drew from this observation were problematic. He failed to recognise the significance of religion as 'a, or perhaps *the*, central force that motivates and mobilizes people' (Huntington, 1997: 66–7, original emphasis; see also Kumar, 2000: 64–6); that humans are moved less by a desire for equal dignity than by the 'need [for] enemies: competitors in business, rivals in achievement, opponents in politics' against whom to define themselves (Huntington, 1997, 130; see also Kurtz, 2002); and that far from it being the case that the rest of the world follows the lead of the West (the assumption behind Fukuyama's depiction of liberalism as a universal ideology), the 'clash of civilisations' that Huntington claimed to observe involves a rejection by many non-Western nations of Western values (including those of capitalism and democracy).

In the two accounts that we have considered so far the emphasis has been on the continuing relevance of ideological thinking. Both Bell and Fukuyama, that is, assume that ideology once had its place but that its time has now passed; it has become redundant, though the arguments each adduces in support of that claim are significantly different. One of the features of Bell's discussion of ideology related to its utility as a way of assessing reality, that is, explaining what was happening in a particular context. In the next section, I turn to the work of another thinker who contests the usefulness of ideology but does so, as we will see, in a matter quite distinct from Bell, and that is Michel Foucault. Like Bell's and Fukuyama's, Foucault's discussion of ideology is partly prompted by the challenges posed by the putative failure of Marxism. Before we proceed to look at Foucault's analysis, a few preliminary words are needed to situate the discussion.

Although Foucault resolutely refused to define his theoretical position (1997: 113), he is usually characterised as a post-structuralist (others so-designated include Jacques Derrida, Jean-François Lyotard and Jacques Lacan). Post-structuralism is a tricky stance to define, not least because the term is used interchangeably with the term 'postmodernism' and because those labelled post-structuralist hold very different views about numerous issues. Nevertheless, simplifying considerably, we can identify a number of broad themes: the rejection of teleological or progressive accounts of history of the kind associated with Marx and Hegel; the refusal of overarching or 'totalising' explanations; the denial of the possibility of absolute truths or values; and a particular view of subjectivity that denies the existence of a stable or unified subject who can be defined in terms of particular qualities such as rationality or a desire for pleasure. It will be useful to bear this description in mind when considering Foucault's account of ideology. For, unlike either Bell or Fukuyama, Foucault casts doubt on the very notion of ideology itself. He does so by engaging, often implicitly, with the ideas of one of the twentieth century's leading neo-Marxists, the French philosopher Louis Althusser, his former tutor.

From ideology to discourse

Althusser famously set out his account of ideology in *For Marx* (1969), originally published in French in 1965. Ideology for Althusser is a 'system (with its own logic and rigour) of representations (images, myths, ideas or concepts, depending on the case) endowed with a historical existence and role within a given society' (1969: 231). Althusser contrasts ideology with science, which is knowledge produced through theoretical practice.[6] The crux of the difference between ideology and science is the function that each performs. Ideology is 'a matter of the *lived* relation between men and their world' (Althusser, 1969: 233). It has what Althusser calls a 'practico-social' function, which enables individuals to orient themselves to the world around them, '*to be formed, transformed, and equipped to respond to the demands of their conditions of existence*' (1969: 235, original emphasis). This is in contrast to science, which has only a 'theoretical' function. It is for this reason that Althusser describes ideology as 'an organic part . . . of every social totality', a 'structure essential to the historical life of societies' (Althusser, 1969: 232): because it has an indispensable role to play in all of them, including, importantly, a future communist society.

What is more, ideology is not merely, or even mostly, conscious; it is in great part unconscious. People are often unaware that their activities and beliefs are ideological. Ideology, as he puts it in a later essay, thus consists in the 'imaginary relationship of individuals to the relations of production' (Althusser, 1971: 155), one that '*expresses a will* (conservative, conformist, reformist or revolutionary), a hope or a nostalgia' (1969: 234), but does not describe reality. Althusser regards ideology as determining the real historical conditions of people's lives, their beliefs and how they experience the world. It is a coherent and logical way of making sense of the world, and yet this making sense may itself involve misrepresenting power and class relations. I may genuinely believe, as Fukuyama suggested, that capitalism allows the expression of individual freedom, and I may understand my working day in that way, even when the reality is that I am systematically exploited by my employer and that far from being free, I am, in fact, a 'wage slave'. (For further discussion of Althusser's account of ideology see Barrett, 1991 and chapter 1 of this volume.)

It is not how Althusser understands ideology that concerns us here; it is the version of ideology critique offered by Michel Foucault. Although he touched on the topic of ideology briefly in earlier works, including *The Order of Things* (1970) and *The Archaeology of Knowledge* (1972), Foucault gives his most accessible statement of his reasons for doubting that ideology is a useful analytical tool in the interview entitled 'Truth and power' (1980), in which he comments:

> The notion of ideology appears to me to be difficult to make use of, for three reasons. The first is that, like it or not, it always stands in virtual opposition to something else which is supposed to count as truth . . . The second drawback is that the concept of ideology refers, I think necessarily,

to something of the order of a subject. Thirdly, ideology stands in a secondary position relative to something which functions as its infrastructure, as its material, economic determinant, etc. For these three reasons, I think that this is a notion that cannot be used without circumspection.

(Foucault, 1980: 118)

In brief, then, Foucault offers three reasons for questioning the usefulness of ideology: first, that ideology is seen as the opposite of truth or science; second, that it is linked in a particular way with the subject; and third, that it relies upon the base–superstructure model of Marxism. So, once again it is the Marxist understanding of ideology specifically that is under scrutiny and, in particular, the conception of ideology advanced by Althusser.

It is, of course, the first of these reasons that is most important in respect of Althusser. One of the main concerns shared by critics of Althusser, including Foucault, had to do with Althusser's attempt to distinguish ideology from science, a distinction Foucault challenged. The question is, why did he challenge this distinction? The answer lies in how he believes truth should be understood. For Foucault:

the problem does not consist in drawing the line between that in a discourse which falls under the category of scientificity or truth, and that which comes under some other category [such as ideology], *but in seeing historically how effects of truth are produced within discourses which in themselves are neither true nor false.*

(1980: 118, my emphasis)

Two points are of note here: first, Foucault rejects the idea that ideology and science are of a different order relative to truth. 'Ideology is not exclusive of scientificity', he argues, and the 'role of ideology does not diminish as rigour increases and error is dissipated' (1972: 186). Science, in other words, is no more truthful than ideology and ideological thinking no more distorted or false than scientific thinking. The two thus cannot simply be differentiated in the way that Althusser suggested. Second, and this explains why such differentiation is ultimately impossible, instead of trying to discern which is more truthful, we should examine the way in which 'effects of truth' are produced. That is, we should explore what he calls 'regimes of truth' (Foucault, 1980: 131). To do this, first we need to examine discourse.

Discourse, for Foucault, connects language and practices (Foucault, 1972). Discourses bring together groups of statements that combine to produce and delimit an area of knowledge (say, psychoanalysis). They operate by a set of internal rules and procedures. These rules and procedures are what then enable the psychoanalyst, in this case, to practise psychoanalysis. They determine what she or he does, says and thinks in relation to psychoanalytic practice. How then do these relate to regimes of truth?

By regimes of truth, Foucault means a '"general politics" of truth: that is, the types of discourses which it [society] accepts and makes function as true' (1980: 131), together with the techniques that enable us to distinguish true from false; the methods society approves of as appropriate to the acquisition of truth; and who is charged with speaking the truth. In today's society, we generally see conventional medicine as a more 'scientific' and, thus, more truthful 'discourse' than magic; the use of an MRI scan as a better way to detect certain illnesses than consulting with a soothsayer; and a medical doctor as more legitimate authority on the state of our health than a shaman. We might very well believe that it is entirely right and proper that medicine should have a more elevated status than magic, but, for Foucault, this is because our understanding of the world has been structured to see this hierarchy as necessary. Even though we differentiate between magic and medicine in this way now, it was not always the case (see Foucault, 1970: 365). What this suggests to Foucault is that (medical) science is no more intrinsically truthful or non-ideological than magic. The fact that it is perceived today as more authoritative than magic is not an effect of ideological distortion; it has to do with the operation of power.

When Foucault describes 'truth' as being 'a thing of this world' (1980: 131), he not only means that it is historically contingent, that is, that different regimes of truth (or different epistemological frameworks) operate at different historical periods. He also uses 'truth' to refer to the 'system of ordered procedures' (Foucault, 1980: 133) that produce, regulate, distribute and circulate the statements that we regard as 'true'. Systems of power produce and reinforce the truth. Clearly, in making this claim Foucault is using 'power' in a way that differs from many of its conventional uses, including within Marxism, where it is usually associated with misrepresentations of the truth (that is, hiding or distorting the truth in the interests of the powerful: producing 'false consciousness').

By contrast, Foucault regards power as productive: it creates effects, one of which is the generation of 'truth'. But 'truth' is not just an effect of power; in turn, it also produces power effects (it helps to structure the world in particular ways). Power and truth are not opposites. To say that science is not in some sense authentically true is not, however, for Foucault, to contend it is thus 'what others call by the bizarre name of "ideology"' (1970: 365). The point for him is that the very opposition between ideology and science is itself untenable. Instead, therefore, of placing ideology and science at the heart of analysis, Foucault advocates focusing on 'truth itself' (Foucault, 1980: 133), which in turn requires analysing the interconnections of truth and power (or power/ knowledge, as he puts it in his later work). This requires a focus on the discourses (and practices) that construct our sense of reality.

What, though, of Foucault's second and third reasons for questioning ideology: its relation to the subject and its secondary status? When talking about the subject in this context, Foucault is referring to the idea of a unified subject (with certain essential qualities, such as the capacity for creative labour, described by Marx as 'species-life'). This is the subject who is deceived by the workings of ideology: the labourer under capitalism who fails to recognise the truth of the fact that she or he is alienated and is deluded into believing that she or he has chosen freely to sell her or his labour power to company X. Moreover, this is the subject who once it becomes conscious of its situation will be able to liberate itself from deception and achieve emancipation.

Foucault offers a very different account of the subject. He rejects the idea that humans have any essential qualities (be they reason, labour power or other qualities). Instead, as noted earlier, Foucault sees subjects as the effects of power/knowledge. The qualities we are ascribed (sex, rationality, compassion, emotion, and so forth) are effects of particular discourses and practices. One of Foucault's famous examples is the creation of the homosexual. According to his *History of Sexuality* (1978), sexologists and psychoanalysts, including Freud, produced the category of the homosexual at the end of the nineteenth century (indeed, the terms 'homosexuality' and 'heterosexuality' were both only coined in the nineteenth century). As forms of power/knowledge, sexology and psychoanalysis thus created a new sexual identity, spawning new terms and new laws of sexual behaviour. Before this point in history, that is, no one would have been regarded as 'homosexual' or would have understood him or herself in such terms.

One might argue that something similar is at work in the production of 'racialised' subjects (see, for instance, Carter, 1997). Here discourses of immigration, scientific racism, and imperialism, together with practices such as censuses, birth records and the use of passports, converge to form a power/knowledge nexus creating different categories of racialised subjects, including those who see themselves, and are seen by governments, as belonging to a particular nation and thus as entitled to certain benefits from that nation. In opposing ideology, Foucault is also opposing its understanding of the subject and offering an alternative account in its place.

The final objection Foucault levels at ideology concerns its secondary status. He rejects the idea common to many forms of Marxism that the economic base determines the cultural and political superstructure. Nothing, for Foucault, has the determinist role of the economy. That is, there is no overall logic such as capitalist logic behind the ideas operating at any one time, the kind of subjects that exist, or the way that society as a whole is organised. Quite the contrary: discourses and practices emerge in chance and haphazard ways. Indeed, it is one of the features of Foucault's work that he stresses the importance of local 'micropractices' of power. Often it is at the margin or periphery of society, in a local asylum or at a particular hospital for instance, that new technologies of power or new discourses are produced. These technologies or discourses may be appropriated or utilised later on by different institutions or organisations for different purposes than those for which they were initially conceived.

Psychoanalysis, Foucault suggested, appropriated and modified the practice of confession common to Catholicism. Television shows such as *The Oprah Winfrey Show* and *The Jerry Springer Show* might be said to appropriate the confession for another purpose: voyeuristic television. Alternatively, a technique like ultrasound, used to monitor foetal health and to detect abnormalities, gets borrowed for other purposes: for sex determination or sex selection. Images of foetuses in the womb have also been deployed to bolster the claims of the anti-abortion movement (Zalewski, 2000). The point, for Foucault, is that there is no necessary logic linking one element with any other. His approach to understanding politics and society is thus an anti-reductionist one, in the sense that he repudiates any idea that the economic base determines all other political, social and cultural phenomena (unsurprisingly, Foucault also abandons the teleological history of Marxism).

Foucault's repudiation of ideology as a useful tool of analysis thus entails a rejection of many of the tenets of Marxism as a political ideology, a critique of the distinction between science and ideology that underpinned especially Althusser's reformulation of Marx, and the development of what was to become a highly influential alternative analytical framework for examining social, cultural and political phenomena, sometimes referred to as discourse analysis.

Foucault's alternative approach generated considerable interest, both critical and supportive. One feature critics discerned in this approach that many applauded was that it decentred questions of class and class struggle and allowed for a fuller consideration of gender, race and sexuality. In this regard, it appeared to address one of the alleged deficiencies with Marxism, which was that it tended to treat non-class aspects of identity as epiphenomenal – or second-ary – to class. Additionally, Foucault's way of thinking also seemed to answer another of the criticisms levelled at Althusserian Marxism in particular, which was that it was insufficiently attentive to history; that is, that it tended to employ the concept of ideology in an ahistorical fashion (Vighi and Feldner, 2007). Foucault's approach, by comparison, allows for an exploration of the chance ways in which particular practices develop historically and how they extend throughout the social body. Critics argued, however, that these advantages could not compensate for the deficiencies of Foucault's analytical method: it could not deal with structural inequalities – that is, with the systematic nature of power – and by representing truth as an artefact, it undercut any attempt to discriminate between true and false forms of knowledge (and, by extension, between good and bad sets of ideas). For this reason, some have proposed that Foucauldian discourse analysis does not offer a viable or satisfactory alternative to ideology critique (Žižek, 1994, 2000; Vighi and Feldner, 2007). Far from dis-course analysis displacing ideology critique, therefore, these writers argue, there is utility, politically, in retaining the idea of ideology.

Conclusion

Questions about the future of ideological thinking have punctuated the history of ideology since the late 1940s. One factor impelling this recurrent questioning of ideology has been the issue of the viability of socialism, and by extension of Marxism. When Daniel Bell declared the end of ideology in 1960 he was motivated to do so by the apparent failures and corruption of socialism. Likewise, when Francis Fukuyama confidently proclaimed not just the end of ideology but also the end of history almost thirty years later, he justified his claims by pointing to (among other things) the dissolution of the socialist regimes of Eastern Europe and events in China. But it was not only actually existing socialist regimes that prompted the raising of serious questions about the relevance of ideology; Marxism as a theoretical and analytical approach also came under scrutiny. As noted earlier, Foucault cast doubt on the distinction in Althusserian Marxism between science and ideology and opened up for debate the question of truth and its relation to power relations. He queried the assumptions underlying Marxism's conception of history and its belief in progress towards a communist end. He also initiated another highly influential way to understand the phenomena previously explored under the guise of ideology critique.

Does this mean that ideology is now redundant, both as a way to understand the world and as a critical approach? As the writers examined in this chapter suggest, the answer to this question depends on one's conception of ideology.

Further reading

General

Adam Lent's edited volume *New Political Thought* (1998) provides a succinct introduction to the concept of ideology, particularly in relation to ideas such as post-Marxism and postmodernism. Gary Browning, Abigail Halcli and Frank Webster's edited volume *Understanding Contemporary Society* (2000) is a useful supplement; this textbook surveys a number of the key debates that frame this chapter (such as post-history and post-feminism). Together, Michael Freeden's *Ideologies and Political Theory* (1996) and the more introductory volume *Ideology* (2003) offer a distinctive and very important new approach to ideology (see also the further reading suggested in chapter 1 for general texts on ideology). On the topic of post-structuralism and postmodernism, in general, see Madan Sarup's *An Introductory Guide to Poststructuralism and Postmodernism* (1993); this is a user-friendly and comprehensive textbook charting these complex ideas. *Ideology after Poststructuralism* (2002), edited by Sinisa Malesevic and Iain MacKenzie, offers an important contribution to a largely neglected area of debate: the intersection between post-structuralism and ideology. For a book that contests the idea of a post-ideological consensus, see John Schwarzmantel's *Ideology and Politics* (2008). Andrew Gamble's short and lucid text *Politics and Fate* (2000) explores 'endism' in general in political thinking.

Bell and the end of ideology

The classic text here is Daniel Bell's *The End of Ideology* (1962). For an examination of Bell's own reassessment of his ideas, see his '*The End of Ideology* revisited' parts I and II (1988a and 1988b), as well as the essay 'The resumption of history in the new century', which appears in the 2000 edition of *The End of Ideology*, in which Bell also reflects on the end-of-history thesis. This edition of the book also contains '*The End of Ideology* revisited'. To explore the debate engendered by Bell's book, see C. L. Waxman's edited collection of essays (many of them polemical) *The End of Ideology Debate* (1968), and for a more analytical and applied set of responses, see M. Rejai's edited volume *Decline of Ideology?* (1971).

Fukuyama and the end of history

The obvious starting point for an exploration of the ideas of Fukuyama is the essay that generated the initial debate, 'The end of history?' (1989). To fully appreciate the complexity of Fukuyama's account, I would recommend examining his book-length account of the same topic, *The End of History and the Last Man* (1992). Since then, Fukuyama has published two essays reflecting back on his earlier publications. The first is 'Reflections on *The End of History*, five years later' (1995). The second, published in 2006, is called 'After the "end of history"'. An early critical engagement with Fukuyama's original article was Samuel Huntington's 'No exit: the errors of endism' (1989). One of the first assessments of Fukuyama's book was Alan Ryan's review essay 'Professor Hegel goes to Washington' (1992). This has been followed by a number of other interventions. For a difficult but erudite piece exploring the end of history in general, as well as in relation to Fukuyama specifically, see Perry Anderson's lengthy essay 'The ends of history' (1992). A collection of essays that considers the implications of Fukuyama's thesis from a left-wing perspective is *Has History Ended?*, edited by Christopher Bertram and Andrew Chitty (1994). Another wide-ranging collection is Timothy Burns' edited book *After History?* (1994). A helpful overview of Fukuyama's account of the end of history, written with students in mind, is Krishnan Kumar's essay 'Post-history: living at the end' (2000). A more challenging critique of Fukuyama, drawing on ideas from postmodernism, is Chris Hughes' *Liberal Democracy as the End of History* (2011).

Althusser and Foucault

The literature both by and about these thinkers is vast. The most useful sources by Althusser to read in relation to the concerns of this chapter are his edited collection of essays *For Marx* (1969) and 'Ideology and ideological state apparatuses' (1971). Neither is easy and both require some prior knowledge of

Marxism and of Althusser's own work. A good guide to Althusser's thought is *Althusser's Marxism*, by Alex Callinicos (1976). For concise explanations of key terms in Marxism (including Althusserian terminology), *A Dictionary of Marxist Thought*, edited by Tom Bottomore (second edition, 1991), is an excellent resource. The piece where Foucault outlines, somewhat cryptically, his views on ideology and truth is 'Truth and power' (1980). It is worth the effort of reading. Michèle Barrett's comprehensive and stimulating account of the role of ideology in Marxist and post-structuralist thought, *The Politics of Truth* (1991), offers an overview of the relation between Althusser and Foucault, and considers in detail Foucault's critique of ideology and his alternative account of discourse, truth and power. Commentaries on and critical assessments of the work of Foucault abound. Alec McHoul and Wendy Grace provide a clearly written and accessible guide to Foucault in *A Foucault Primer* (1993). Lois McNay's *Foucault: A Critical Introduction* (1994) provides a more searching account of Foucault's thought that touches, albeit briefly, on the question of ideology. *Understanding Foucault* (Schirato et al., 2012) provides a useful critical introduction to Foucault's ideas that takes account of his recently published lectures. *Michel Foucault: Key Concepts* (Taylor, 2010), containing essays exploring many of Foucault's key ideas, provides useful background to his work. An example of an approach that combines Foucault's account of discourse, power and truth with ideology is Davina Cooper's essay 'Strategies of power: legislating worship and religious education' (1997).

Notes

1   Marx contended that the ruling ideas in every society served the interests of the ruling class. The working classes, however, were often unaware of this and assumed instead that capitalist values benefitted everyone. They suffered from 'false consciousness' in the sense that they were unaware of what was really happening to them: that is, that capitalism exploited and alienated them.

2   In response to critics, Bell acknowledges that he is only focused on left-wing ideologies but justifies his emphasis on the basis that 'the word *ideology* was a product of the "left"' (1962: 17).

3   In particular, Freeden suggests that ideological dispute is intrinsic to the very consensus politics that Bell presented as characteristic of the decline of ideology (Freeden, 2003).

4   Events in China tended to receive minimal, if any, international television coverage at this time. The arrival of Gorbachev in Beijing brought news crews from around the world, many of which were still present and able to broadcast as events unfolded in Tiananmen Square (Mosstig, 2009).

5   There is not the space here to go into a detailed discussion of Kojève's reading of Hegel, except to say that it involves a reworking of Hegel's idea of universal history that gives greater prominence to the 'end of history' and to the struggle for recognition (or master–slave dialectic). The question of whether Fukuyama is faithful in the development of his own argument to Hegel, or indeed to Kojève for that matter, is also a topic for debate elsewhere.

6   Specifically, knowledge was a system of production involving ideas (the raw materials) and a set of questions, concepts and methods labelled the problematic (the means of production). Through a 'symptomatic reading' – that is, focusing on the gaps and silences in a text – it was possible to discern the true questions and concerns behind the text. This was 'science'. (See Althusser, 1969: 161–218.)

References

Althusser, L. (1969) [1965] *For Marx*, London: Verso.

—— (1971) [1970] 'Ideology and ideological state apparatuses', in *Lenin and Philosophy and Other Essays*, London: New Left Books.

Anderson, P. (1992) 'The ends of history', in *A Zone of Engagement*, London: Verso.

Aron, R. (1957) [1955] *The Opiate of the Intellectuals*, London: Secker and Warburg.

Barker, C. (2000) *Cultural Studies: Theory and Practice*, London: Sage.

Barrett, M. (1991) *The Politics of Truth: From Marx to Foucault*, Cambridge: Polity Press.

Bay, C. (1961) 'The end of politics? A review', *Journal of Conflict Resolution*, 5(3): 326–35.

Bell, D. (1962) [1960] *The End of Ideology: On the Exhaustion of Political Ideas in the Fifties*, revised edition, New York: Free Press.

—— (1974) *The Coming of Post-industrial Society: A Venture in Social Forecasting*, London: Heinemann.

—— (1988a) '*The End of Ideology* revisited', I, *Government and Opposition*, 23: 127–50.

—— (1988b) '*The End of Ideology* revisited', II, *Government and Opposition*, 23: 321–31.

—— (2000) 'The resumption of history in the new century', in D. Bell, *The End of Ideology: On the Exhaustion of Political Ideas in the Fifties*, Cambridge, Mass.: Harvard University Press, pp. xi–xxviii.

Bertram, C. and Chitty, A. (eds) (1994) *Has History Ended? Fukuyama, Marx and Modernity*, Aldershot: Ashgate.

Bottomore, T. (ed.) (1991) *A Dictionary of Marxist Thought*, 2nd edn, Oxford: Blackwell.

Browning, G., Halcli, A. and Webster, F. (eds) (2000) *Understanding Contemporary Society: Theories of the Present*, London: Sage.

Burns, T. (ed.) (1994) *After History? Francis Fukuyama and His Critics*, New York: Rowman and Littlefield.

Callinicos, A. (1976) *Althusser's Marxism*, London: Pluto Press.

Carter, B. (1997) 'Rejecting truthful identities: Foucault, "race" and politics', in M. Lloyd and A. Thacker (eds) *The Impact of Michel Foucault on the Social Sciences and Humanities*, Basingstoke: Macmillan.

Cooper, D. (1997) 'Strategies of power: legislating worship and religious education', in M. Lloyd and A. Thacker (eds) *The Impact of Michel Foucault on the Social Sciences and Humanities*, Basingstoke: Macmillan.

Dresner, S. (2008) *The Principles of Sustainability*, 2nd edn, London: Routledge.

Foucault, M. (1970) [1966] *The Order of Things: The Archaeology of the Human Sciences*, London: Routledge.

—— (1972) [1969] *The Archaeology of Knowledge*, London: Routledge.

—— (1978) [1976] *The History of Sexuality, Volume I: An Introduction*, Harmondsworth: Penguin.

—— (1980) 'Truth and power', in C. Gordon (ed.) *Michel Foucault: Power/Knowledge. Selected Interviews and Other Writings 1972–1977*, London: Harvester Press.

—— (1997) [1984] 'Polemics, politics, and problematizations: an interview with Michel Foucault', in P. Rabinow (ed.) *Michel Foucault. Ethics: Subjectivity and Truth. The Essential Works of Michel Foucault 1954–1984*, volume I, London: Allen Lane.

Freeden, M. (1996) *Ideologies and Political Theory: A Conceptual Approach*, Oxford: Oxford University Press.

—— (2003) *Ideology: A Very Short Introduction*, Oxford: Oxford University Press.

Fukuyama, F. (1989) 'The end of history?', *National Interest*, 16: 3–18.

—— (1992) *The End of History and the Last Man*, Harmondsworth: Penguin.

—— (1995) 'Reflections on *The End of History*, five years later', *History and Theory*, 34(2): 27–43.

—— (2006) 'After the "end of history"'. Available online at www.opendemocracy.net/democracy-fukuyama/revisited_3496.jsp.

Gamble, A. (2000) *Politics and Fate*, Cambridge: Polity.

Hobsbawm, E. (1995) *Age of Extremes: The Short Twentieth Century, 1914–1991*, London: Abacus.

Hughes, C. (2011) *Liberal Democracy as the End of History: Fukuyama and Postmodern Challenges*, London, Routledge.

Huntington, S. (1989) 'No exit: the errors of endism', *National Interest*, 17: 3–11.

—— (1993) 'The clash of civilizations?', *Foreign Affairs*, 72: 22–49.

—— (1997) *The Clash of Civilizations and the Remaking of the World Order*, New York: Touchstone.

Kumar, K. (2000) 'Post-history: living at the end', in G. Browning, A. Halcli and F. Webster (eds) *Understanding Contemporary Society: Theories of the Present*, London: Sage.

Kurtz, S. (2002) 'The future of "history"', *Policy Review*, 113: 43–58.

Lent, A. (ed.) (1998) *New Political Thought: An Introduction*, London: Lawrence and Wishart.

Lipset, S. M. (1963) *Political Man*, London: Heinemann.

—— (1985) 'A concept and its history: the end of ideology', in S. M. Lipset, *Political Sociology*, New Brunswick, NJ: Transaction Publishers, pp. 81–109.

McHoul, A. and Grace, W. (1993) *A Foucault Primer: Discourse, Power and the Subject*, London: UCL Press.

McNay, L. (1994) *Foucault: A Critical Introduction*, Cambridge: Polity Press.

Malesevic, S. and MacKenzie, I. (eds) (2002) *Ideology after Poststructuralism*, London: Pluto Press.

Mills, C. Wright (1968) [1960] 'Letter to the New Left', in C. L. Waxman (ed.) *The End of Ideology Debate*, New York: Funk and Wagnalls.

Mosstig, M. (2009) 'Reporter's notebook: how Tiananmen Square expanded global coverage'. Available online at www.pbs.org/newshour/updates/asia/jan-june09/tiananmenrep_05–29.html (accessed 3 September 2012).

Norris, C. (1991) '*The End of Ideology* revisited: the Gulf War, postmodernism and *Realpolitik*', *Philosophy and Social Criticism*, 17: 1–40.

Rejai, M. (ed.) (1971) *Decline of Ideology?*, Chicago: Aldine Atherton.

Ryan, A. (1992) 'Professor Hegel goes to Washington', *New York Review of Books*, 26 March.

Sarup, M. (1993) *An Introductory Guide to Poststructuralism and Postmodernism*, 2nd edn, London: Harvester Wheatsheaf.

Schirato, T., Danaher, G. and Webb, J. (2012) *Understanding Foucault: A Critical Introduction*, 2nd edn, London: Sage.

Schwarzmantel, J. (2008) *Ideology and Politics*, London: Sage.

Shils, E. (1955) 'The end of ideology?', *Encounter*, 5: 52–8.

Skinner, Q. (ed.) (1985) *The Return of Grand Theory in the Human Sciences*, Cambridge: Cambridge University Press.

Taylor, D. (ed.) (2010) *Michel Foucault: Key Concepts*, London: Acumen.

Vighi, F. and Feldner, H. (2007) 'Ideology Critique or Discourse Analysis?', *European Journal of Political Theory*, 6(2): 141–59.

Waxman, C. L. (ed.) (1968) *The End of Ideology Debate*, New York: Funk and Wagnalls.

Zalewski, M. (2000) *Feminism after Postmodernism: Theorising through Practice*, London: Routledge.

Žižek, S. (1994) 'The spectre of ideology', in S. Žižek (ed.) *Mapping Ideology*, London: Verso, pp. 1–33.

—— (2000) *The Ticklish Subject*, London: Verso.

Index

Please note that page numbers relating to Notes will have the letter 'n' following the page number.